Born in London to Jamaican parents in 1961, Geoff Small studied racial and ethnic relations at Lancaster and Bristol universities before joining the BBC's *Ebony* programme as a researcher. In 1988, he went undercover (with Tim Marshall) to expose hidden racial discrimination in Bristol for the BBC's controversial 'Black and White' documentary series. He has produced and directed numerous programmes for the BBC, Channel 4 and BSB, and directed black drama and comedy films. Married with three children, he lives in London where he works as a freelance television producer/director, journalist and writer.

Ruthless

The Global Rise of the Yardies

GEOFF SMALL

WARNER BOOKS

A *Warner* Book

First published in Great Britain
by Warner Books in 1995

Copyright © Geoff Small 1995

The moral right of the author has been asserted.

A CIP catalogue record for this book
is available from the British Library.

ISBN 0 7515 1123 4

Typeset by Palimpsest Book Production Limited,
Polmont, Stirlingshire
Printed and bound in Great Britain by
Clays Ltd, St Ives plc

Warner Books
A Division of
Little, Brown and Company (UK)
Brettenham House
Lancaster Place
London WC2E 7EN

For my wife, Akungwa Nwagbara

Contents

	Acknowledgements	ix
CHAPTER ONE	The Life and Times of Jim Brown	1
CHAPTER TWO	The Rude Boys, Politics and Crime	22
CHAPTER THREE	The Rude Boys and Jamaica's Cold War	52
CHAPTER FOUR	Frankenstein's Monsters	99
CHAPTER FIVE	The History of Violence	143
CHAPTER SIX	A Culture of Violence	169
CHAPTER SEVEN	Confessions of a Spanglers Posse Gangster	217
CHAPTER EIGHT	Exodus – Movement of the Posses	248
CHAPTER NINE	The Posses: A Problem Identified	261
CHAPTER TEN	The DC Experience	313
CHAPTER ELEVEN	Canada – The View from Across the Border	338
CHAPTER TWELVE	The Rude Boys, Britain and the Yardie Myth	363
CHAPTER THIRTEEN	Impressions on a Criminal Landscape	397
	Index	454

Acknowledgements

A lot of people played active and supportive roles in getting this book off the conceptual starting block. I should like to thank as many of them as I can.

On a general level, I have to start by thanking Miss Vee, my mother and the fount of endless love and support for me. Similarly, I am always reassured to know that my sisters, Carmen, Karenne, and Sheree, and my extended family are there for me.

The list of friends who have encouraged me in this venture is too numerous to mention; I thank them all. However, I'd like to send a 'big shout' out to, in alphabetical order, Cecil Black and family, Krishna Govender, the Johnsons – both families, Tony Mason, Maraizu and Uzoma Nwagbara, Brian Puig, Rory, the Sauvages, Niall Sookoo, 'Ulysses' and 'The Wolfman'.

In terms of the book itself, John Laughton deserves thanks for pointing me in the right direction, when all I had was an idea. I am also particularly grateful to Anne McDermid, my first agent, for her endless enthusiasm and blinkered determination to get this project off the ground. Alice Wood, my unfazeable editor, merits praise for her tremendous patience and endless efforts to keep me on the right track; thanks to Rebecca Holford at Little, Brown, too. It was also a pleasure to deal with Linda Silverman, who carried out the arduous and time-consuming task of tracking down photographs for the book. I thank Alexandra Marzec, for her cheery disposition and legal advice, and Jonathon Geller at Curtis Brown for his support.

Finally, I should like to thank Paul Blake for his patience, encouragement and understanding throughout the planning, research and writing of this volume. Most of all, I have to express my gratitude to my good friend, Heenan Bhatti, for making the production of this book a lot less painful than it was shaping up to be.

CHAPTER ONE

The Life and Times of Jim Brown

The hall of Tivoli Gardens Community Centre had been specially decorated for the occasion – a funeral service. But as the lavish preparations suggest, this was no ordinary send-off. The deceased was so highly regarded that an estimated 20,000 mourners turned up to pay their last respects. Marshalled by a phalanx of orderly security guards, the crowd had descended on west Kingston from all over Jamaica to accompany the dead man on his final journey. Had he been a rock star who had died unexpectedly in his prime, the whole affair would not have looked out of place. But a rock star he was not, although in life he had enjoyed all the trappings of stardom associated with that type of existence.

The deceased was Lester Lloyd Coke. That he had been an accomplished man was apparent in a number of ways aside from the turnout at his funeral. To begin with, Coke's death was reported by the international press. For example, the *Independent* an influential British broadsheet, ran two pieces on the circumstances and events surrounding his mysterious death. And the international news magazine *Newsweek* published an article which, amongst other things, likened Coke to a modern-day 'Robin Hood'.

However, no more fitting an ovation for the deceased's

considerable standing was given than that of the catalogue of Jamaican dignitaries who attended his final
public appearance. One side of the community hall
was reserved for some of Jamaica's most influential
politicians. The list included the Rt. Hon. Edward Seaga
MP, the Opposition Jamaica Labour Party (JLP) leader
and erstwhile Jamaican Prime Minister. Seaga, a longtime
associate of Coke, had been the Member of Parliament for
the dead man's Western Kingston constituency for some
thirty years.

Seaga was joined by party colleague Senator Olivia
'Babsy' Grange, reputedly a friend of Coke's since
childhood. In fact, they had attended the same school.
JLP chairman, Bruce Golding, and other notable front
benchers including Mike Henry and Ryan Peralto also put
in an appearance. Tom Tavares-Finson, Coke's and one of
Jamaica's sharpest lawyers was another noteworthy guest.
(A society lawyer and JLP stalwart, Tavares-Finson is
married to former Miss World, Cindy Brakespeare. She,
in turn, is the mother of one of late reggae superstar Bob
Marley's sons, Damian.)

Jamaica's political household names were assembled
on one side of Lester Coke's coffin. The deceased's
grieving relatives congregated on the other. The bereaved
included his common-law wife, Beverly Burgess, the
mother of three of his children. Coke's daughter, Camille,
was inconsolable; she wept uncontrollably as she cradled
her little baby. It was as if she had been told that after
that day she could never shed another tear.

Camille's grief – and that of the family as a whole
– was doubly understandable coming, as it had, exactly
three weeks after the premature death of her brother, Mark
Anthony Coke. It probably did not help that Mark had lost
his life in violent circumstances. He had been tragically
gunned down on Maxfield Avenue, one of the Jamaican
capital city's notorious killing zones.

The cruel hand of Fate had snatched away the elder Coke's chance to attend the younger's funeral. And Death had selfishly intervened to deprive him of an opportunity to grieve beside his progeny's final resting place. Indeed, by a strange coincidence, Coke senior's life was ended in a freak fire a matter of hours after Mark's burial ceremony on Sunday, 23 February 1992. Best known by his chosen *nom de guerre*, Jim Brown, Lester Lloyd Coke was only forty-four years old when he died.

It is customary at Jamaican funerals for the deceased's family and friends to inspect the body before the funeral service gets underway. Remarkably, when the lid was removed from Brown's casket there were no signs of the second-degree burns that had distorted his face and body during his final moments. Rather, he was a picture of tranquility, his torso bedecked with sprays of red roses. The roses also provided a nice foil to Brown's attire: a grey and black suit with matching black shirt and velvet cap. His burial outfit was topped off with a pair of mirror sunglasses.

When the funeral service finally got underway the 'dearly departed' was showered with tributes and eulogies. Appropriately enough, the celebration of the life of Jim Brown was led by Edward Seaga, or 'Mr Eddie' as he is affectionately known to many in his constituency. The former two-term Prime Minister, who had only recently led Mark Coke's funeral cortège, started the proceedings by reading the first lesson.

In the midst of his wife and daughter's audible grief, a procession of guests praised Brown for his family values, strong disciplinary codes and positive convictions. Clearly a man of immense influence, the congregation heard that Brown had single-handedly accomplished what the massed ranks of the security forces could never do. According to Desmond McKenzie, the JLP councillor for troubled Tivoli Gardens, he had 'ensured

and maintained the peace'. The sermon was read by
Bishop Samuel Dreckett, who had earlier helped to
identify Brown's body. A former JLP councillor himself,
Dreckett assured the mourners that Brown had 'fought a
good fight, finished the race and kept the faith'.

Finally, after the tributes had been exhausted, Brown's
remains were ferried in style to May Pen Cemetery.
The Tivoli Gardens Marching Band provided a musical accompaniment for the funeral cortège. Brown was
interred beside Mark, whose body had earlier been
exhumed from its original resting place. A fitting climax
then, as father and son were united in the eternal peace
of death.

Jim Brown enjoyed a peaceful, statesman-like send-off.
There was certainly no repetition of the spasms of gun
violence that left a dozen or so dead after his son's
assassination; and led to the security forces laying siege
on west Kingston. But certain members of Jim Brown's
funeral party certainly were made to endure a violent,
albeit verbal, media attack.

Most of the flak was aimed at Mr Seaga. Without
exception, the question everybody wanted an answer
to was 'what was he doing there?'. In fact, it was
abundantly clear from the venomous line of questioning
directed towards Seaga that there were those who believed
that someone of his stature should not have been seen
associating with a man with Jim Brown's 'background',
even after his death.

A man not known for having a diplomatic disposition,
the JLP supremo was typically unrepentant. Seaga shrugged
off the insinuations and hit back at his critics with a
stinging rejoinder. Manifestly aware of the 'background'
his detractors were alluding to, the ex-Prime Minister
gave the Jamaican media some rhetorical advice. 'Ask
the lawyer if he looks at background, ask the clergyman
who takes a confession if he looks at . . . background?' he

demanded. 'Of course not!' came the rhetorical rejoinder. The crucial factor, Seaga maintained, was to 'Look at the man in terms of how the community respects and treats him as a protector from their community.'

'He'll tell you that . . . Lester Lloyd Coke was seen as a protector of the Tivoli Gardens community from the [governing] PNP [People's National Party], police brutality, [and] from party political partisan policemen,' says Lloyd Williams of Seaga's explanation for attending Brown's funeral. An immensely respected investigative journalist and specialist on Jamaican criminal gangs, Williams runs the News Independent Caribbean Agency (NICA) from an office in New Kingston. He strongly endorses the prevalent view that Seaga *et al* sent out the 'wrong signal' by attending Jim Brown's funeral.

Moreover, Williams's qualifying statement puts an altogether different construction on Jim Brown and his lifetime 'achievements'. 'Going to Jim Brown's funeral,' he maintains, 'is saying to the youth who may have known [Lester Lloyd] Coke as a drug dealer . . . [that] Jim Brown is accepted by a former Prime Minister, so what he's doing is probably right.'

'A drug dealer?' Surely not! Williams must have made an unforgiveable error. Surely a man who openly harbours ambitions of returning to the premiership would not have jeopardised his public standing by attending, not to mention playing a leading role in, the funeral of a common drug dealer. No more than British Labour Party leader, Tony Blair, would have attended the funeral of Ronnie Kray; or Prime Minister, John Major, would lobby for the immediate release of Ronnie's twin brother and partner in crime, Reggie. In short, that kind of public gesture would be tantamount to committing political suicide.

The problem, though, is that if Williams was mistaken, then so was Dawn Ritch. Ritch is an often irreverent columnist for the *Daily Gleaner*, Jamaica's leading and purportedly pro-JLP broadsheet. She dedicated one of her contributions exclusively to Edward Seaga's attendances at the funerals of the two Cokes; men she denounced as 'terrorists', murderers and drug dons.

Ritch's article, appropriately entitled 'Is Seaga a victim of moral relativity?', is worth quoting extensively; it offers an extremely eloquent insight into the relationship between politics, politicians, crime and the present state of Jamaica from a Jamaican perspective.

Written after Jim Brown's death but before his interment, the columnist commented on the unthinkable implications of Seaga's presence at Mark 'Jah T' Coke's send-off on what she pronounced the 'de-culturation of Jamaica'. 'Jah T's funeral,' she stated, 'shows quite clearly that the culture of the underworld is now the dominant one, and if anybody missed the point Seaga was there to tell us that it has a morality that the rest of the island lacks.'

Whatever his reasons for going, the *Gleaner* columnist considered Edward Seaga to be a Janus-like figure. Seaga was, she argued, a politician whose unconscionable behaviour differed according to the particular constituency he was addressing. It was one rule for the ghettoites of his Western Kingston constituency, and another for the remainder of the Jamaican people. 'Thus,' she continued, 'when Jim Brown returns a gold chain by threatening to shoot the boy who stole it in his foot, Jim Brown is a beacon of hope for his community.' By now in top gear, she continued: 'This is not a Robin Hood, this is just a brigand elevated by Seaga and his like-minded supporters to a kind of territorial sainthood.' Ritch even suggested that the Rt. Hon. gentleman might bestow the Order of Jamaica posthumously on Brown if he ever reassumed power.

There was no let up from Dawn Ritch when she came to consider Seaga's political standing, either. 'A politician cannot claim to have any moral authority whatsoever,' she surmised, 'when he openly associates with and gives praise to organised crime leaders. The only thing he can claim is a lack of hypocrisy, to which Mr Seaga obviously feels himself entitled.'

Short of uncovering some sinister media conspiracy to defame Edward Seaga then, it would seem that there really was a whole lot more to Jim Brown than met the eye. But even the oxymoronic revelation that Brown was a widely-respected community 'protector', drug dealer and murderer, throws up more questions than it answers. Why, for example, would tens of thousands of people travel so far to see him off? Are we to suppose that they were all drug dealers or junkies? And why would so many Jamaica Labour Party household political names turn out at Brown's funeral? It is one thing to show solidarity with one's leader, but quite another to do so at the possible expense of one's political career. Unless, of course, it is socially acceptable for the cream of Jamaica's political élite to fraternise with criminals, living or dead.

The only way to explain these apparent contradictions is by unfathoming the complex relationships that clearly exist in Jamaica between politics, politicians, the criminal underworld and the ordinary, law-abiding citizenry. For only by unlocking these secrets can we begin to understand why gangsters like Jim Brown – and Jamaica's violent gangs as a whole – have developed into powerful criminal bogeys of national and international notoriety.

These complex and often bizarre relationships will be examined in greater detail throughout the following chapters. But suffice to say at this stage, Jamaica has a long history of such associations. To paraphrase Ritch and others, over the past three decades they have resulted in the gradual social, economic and political ascendancy of the island's powerful crimino-political gangs to global importance.

*   *   *

Perhaps more than any other Jamaican – dead or alive – Jim Brown's various activities epitomised why Jamaica's Rude Boy gangs or posses, as they are known in the United States, have developed in the way that they have. In many ways, Brown's life was a metaphor for the numerous qualities that have gone into making Jamaica's sophisticated narcotics gangs and ruthless Rude Boy gangsters what they are today.

So who was Jim Brown, and what exactly did he do to command so much national and international attention?

Whatever else can be said of Jim Brown, there was never any scope for indifference about him. A man whose life was filled with raging contradictions, one either loved or loathed, respected or despised, worshipped or denounced him. To those who benefited from his political activism and questionable business dealings, Jim Brown was a modern-day Messiah. To those who suffered as a result of them, a Lucifer. Religiously involved in Jamaica Labour Party politics, Brown was a hero to fellow Labourites, and the living arch-demon of every PNP supporter or sympathiser. Over the years, Brown was implicated in a host of serious criminal offences in Jamaica and abroad. Yet, at the time of his death, he had never been convicted of any offence. Defining who Jim Brown was then, greatly depends on where one stands in relation to his beliefs and activities.

Yet there are certain aspects about Jim Brown and his life that are beyond dispute. For example, in life, he was endowed with a commanding physical presence. A man mountain, he stood five feet ten inches tall, and weighed in at a hulking 240 pounds. Not surprisingly, perhaps, his considerable bulk had made him susceptible to bouts of hypertension. But in all other aspects, it seems, Jim Brown was a healthy family man with a vibrant personality.

Brown was born and raised in Back-o-Wall, the most poverty-stricken area of the overflowing west Kingston

ghetto. A ramshackle squatter camp, it was controversially transformed into Tivoli Gardens after urban
developers bulldozed the settlement in the 1960s. Brown
spent most of his life in Tivoli Gardens, an impoverished, sprawling, government-constructed, low-income,
concrete ghetto wedged between the Kingston shoreline
and the Spanish Town Road.

As a boy Brown had attended neighbouring Denham
Town Primary School, where he was a friend of later
JLP politician and recording artist management company
owner, 'Babsy' Grange. However, he was not cut out for
school work, and dropped out of school at an early age.

For all his academic under-achievement, though, Brown
was allegedly descended from good stock. It is said, for
instance, that he was closely related to B.B. Coke, a
one-time PNP Speaker in the Jamaican Parliament. Jim
Brown was successful, too. He worked for a Tivoli-based
company owned by one of his relatives; a construction
company. While he kept up a humble home base in the
Tivoli ghetto, he had done well enough for himself to
be able to afford to live in a plush residence in one of
Kingston's leafier suburbs.

Much of the rest of Jim Brown's personal story
is shrouded in mystery and controversy. There can
be no doubt, however, that he was a narco-political
gangland boss par excellence. In fact, Brown had not
even entered his teens before he became steeped in
the gang subculture that emerged in the burgeoning
slums of west Kingston during the late 1950s and early
1960s.

Jim Brown's name is synonymous with the Shower
Posse of the 1980s and 1990s. Under his (co-) leadership,
the posse went on to become the biggest and most
infamous of Jamaica's foreign-based drug gangs. Indeed,
it was in the Tivoli Gang from the mid-1960s onwards
that Brown began to cement his reputation for being a

fearless protector of, and ruthless enforcer in, the Tivoli Gardens community.

The Tivoli Gang was one of a handful formed by the legions of disaffected, unemployed and inevitably unemployable youth in impoverished west Kingston. Known as Rude Boys or rudies, they were rabidly anti-authoritarian, violent and fearless to boot. Initially, the rudies lumped together for much the same reasons as teenagers do the world over. They were looking for a sense of kinship, purpose and common identity which they could not find in their own ramshackle homes and blighted communities.

However, raised in abject poverty with little realistic prospect of escaping it outside of a coffin, the Rude Boys turned to their own devices for solutions. In the adverse economic climate that was – and is – ghetto Kingston during the mid-1960s, the gangs embarked on a life of frequently violent crime. Outfits like the Tivoli Gang helped to propel the city's hitherto modest crime rates into hyperspace. Moreover, they terrorised the communities in which they resided, and caused the capital's police untold problems.

Initially, the Tivoli Gang enjoyed harmonious relations with its local peer groups. However, the nature of those liaisons was to change dramatically in the mid-1960s, a few years after Jamaica won its independence from Britain. The change was brought about by the politicisation of Kingston's youth gangs; a process whose origins have been widely attributed to Edward Seaga within the confines of his Western Kingston constituency.

Wherever it started, and whoever was responsible for starting it, the criminal Tivoli cohort was recruited into active political service. At a time of heightened political tension and violent inter-party 'tribalism', the gang was enlisted to help preserve the identity of Seaga's political stronghold. In what became known as 'garrison constituencies', the gangsters were given small arms (or 'vote-getters' as some not-so-jokingly referred to them) and a high degree of political protection by the ruling JLP to keep areas like Tivoli Gardens politically 'pure'.

In brief, this arduous task was split into three parts: ensuring the electoral support of local voters; protecting local residents from armed enemy insurgents; and enforcing the will of the party hierarchy. In this sense, ostensibly criminal gangs like the Tivoli crew were transformed overnight into 'respectable' private political armies.

The quid pro quo for the dubious services of gang members came in the form of political patronage. During a time when resources and benefits were extremely scarce, loyal Tivoli gunslingers were remunerated with rewards such as cash, government construction, road-repairing and other lucrative contracts, and one-offs like short-term Christmas jobs. Access to public housing was another highly-treasured commodity. In fact, Tivoli Gardens, the first purpose-built government housing complex of its kind, was – and is still – populated to a person by the JLP party faithful.

As the holder of political patronage leading henchmen or dons like Jim Brown were able to provide paid employment for their gunslingers and 'loyal' members of the surrounding community. They were also able to act as providers for the sick and the needy. Both functions endeared them to the people of their respective political tribes, and helped to enhance their power, popularity and prestige into the bargain.

Over the years, the Tivoli Gang's duties saw them party to frequent cross-border clashes with PNP-sponsored elements like the equally infamous Garrison Gang. Indeed, a measure of the longevity of these political-criminal associations came as early as March 1975. When

Winston 'Burry Boy' Blake, the Garrison Gang leader, was shot dead during 'frontline' political duty, his funeral was attended by none other than the then Prime Minister, Michael Manley, and a high-powered party delegation. A leading PNP combatant in the tribal political war, Blake's coffin was draped with the party's flag.

It was in this intriguing world of organised crime and political warfare that Jim Brown carved out his reputation. That said, he spent a great deal of time abroad during the PNP's eight-year reign in the 1970s. Even so, he was widely tipped to be the heir apparent to Claudius 'Claudie' Massop. A gambler and 'businessman', Massop was also credited with being the first leader of the Shower Posse, and when he died Brown was certainly the local population's choice to succeed him.

Like so much of its activities, even the origins of the gang's name is the subject of some dispute. Popular wisdom states that it came from the ruthless predilection of gang members to 'shower' their opponents with bullets. Another lobby maintains that 'shower' was to Tivoli-ites what 'howdy' is to Texans, a simple, everyday greeting.

Also steeped in controversy is the issue of whether or not Brown actually succeeded Massop as the Shower Posse don. Massop was gunned down by the Jamaican police in a 'shoot-out' on 4 February 1979. It is said that Jim Brown was overlooked in favour of a top-notch Tivoli gunman named 'Baya' Mitchell. Mitchell, a locally-despised building contractor with a ruthless disposition, later died of a cocaine overdose. However, others maintain that there was a power vacuum in Tivoli for several years after Massop's death. And just to confuse matters, Lloyd Williams is adamant that Mitchell was never top dog. 'Jim Brown definitely replaced Massop,' he argues. 'Although someone like "Baya" Mitchell was a ranking gangster, he was never the Number One.'

Wherever Jim Brown fitted into the chronology of Shower Posse donmanship, he got there on the strength of his violent derring-do and public-spirited good works.

One might have thought that the presence of lawless, criminal gunmen in one's community would be off-putting. Not so in Jamaica's volatile, politically-partisan ghettoes. Rather than being perceived as undesirable neighbours by the people of Tivoli Gardens, gunmen like Jim Brown were invariably welcomed with open arms. In a socio-economic environment where the acquisition of scarce benefits largely depended on one's political affiliations and the strength of one's relationships with politicians, the gunslingers turned out to be an area's best friends. 'They were the right-hand men of the politicians,' says Williams, 'and other people came to look upon them as their local leaders, and liaison between them and the politicians.'

Beyond that, the stark nature of the political climate in ghetto Kingston necessitated the emergence of people like Brown. They manfully stood in the breach between hostile outside forces and local residents. Hence, war-ravaged JLP communities looked upon the crimino-political gun hawks as their own home-grown protection force against rogue police officers and armed PNP guerrillas. And vice versa.

These were the people who were prepared to lay down their lives for the political cause – or at least the benefits emanating from it. 'In a violent situation,' argues Williams, 'without people like Jim Brown, one side couldn't keep political meetings. The other side would overwhelm it.' For 'overwhelm' read massacre the rival party supporters.

Another important role Jim Brown held was the part he played as an enforcer. Without putting too fine a point on it, 'community leaders' of Brown's ilk wrote and administered the local law. They arbitrated in local

disputes. They policed their communities. They exacted
punishments on those deemed to be offenders, including
sentencing some to short terms in impromptu ghetto
prisons and violent death.

So, for example, whatever their political persuasions,
political dons took a particularly dim view of petty thieves
and other undesirables who preyed on their communities.
Jim Brown featured prominently in a legendary case of
this order. 'There was a woman who lived in Denham
Town and operated a business there,' recalls Williams.
'They [thieves] held her up, robbed her of her money
and jewellery. Anyway, she went and complained to Jim
Brown. He set up an enquiry, and within a couple of
hours she had got back her pocket book, her money and
her jewellery.' Such was the power and influence of Jim
Brown. (Incidentally, the perpetrators received a severe
beating for their sins.)

Acts or threats of violence had a major bearing on
Brown's dual career as political and gangland don. He
was alleged to have been shot on several occasions –
his life being saved on some by a bullet-proof vest. He
was involved in occasional punch-ups like the one he had
with a disrespectful petrol pump attendant. But most of the
acts of violence he perpetrated – or, rather, was accused
of perpetrating – were far more serious.

Although he was never convicted of any criminal
offence, Jim Brown was arrested and charged with
offences ranging from rape to shooting, robbery to
murder. According to a confidential US federal report
on the posses, the Shower 'don dadda' 'was responsible
for 68 homicides and the shooting of 13 police officers
in Jamaica in during the fist six months of 1990'. This
has proved impossible to corroborate, although it is
definitely not beyond the realm of possibilities. What
is certain, though, is that 'Bomber', as he was sometimes

known, was charged with fourteen separate murders in Jamaica, alone.

In January 1984, three of those (alleged) victims were eliminated on Salt Lane in downtown Kingston. A prime suspect, Brown was said to have been one of seven M-16-toting gunmen to carry out the attack. The killings – as so many are – were thought to be in reprisal for the earlier gun slaying of a friend of Brown's called 'Massa'. Accordingly, like Wild West lawmen, Brown and his posse rounded up some of the burghers of Salt Lane for 'questioning'. Apparently, the three who perished were trying to break ranks when they were gunned down. Brown was arrested on suspicion of murder, but was subsequently released from police custody after a gaggle of JLP supporters surrounded the station where he was being held and demanded he be released.

In May of the same year, Jim Brown was alleged to have led anywhere up to seventy armed men on a mission into Rema. A JLP enclave similar to Tivoli Gardens but in a PNP constituency, the purpose of the raid was to punish what Brown's mob considered to be the duplicity of their fellow party supporters. The word was that the Rema Labourites were defecting to the enemy PNP; they had to be disciplined. Accordingly, over a two-day period, Brown and his combatants slaughtered eight people including a fifteen-year-old male. In a typical episode of west Kingston life, heavily-armed joint police-military patrols were dispatched to the Rema battlefield to quell the internecine violence.

In the aftermath of the killings the police arrested and charged seven suspects. The men, who were freed on bail, did not include Brown. In fact, he left the island for the United States at the end of the year and was not charged with the murders until his return in 1987.

Interestingly, the trial and its immediate aftermath provided a vivid illustration of Jim Brown's power and prestige. By now one of only four men answering murder charges, the prosecution's case collapsed at the first hurdle. The main prosecution witness, a twenty-year-old woman from Trench Town, dramatically withdrew her statement leaving the court with no alternative but to acquit Brown and his co-defendants. As the men left the court in downtown Kingston, they were greeted by a large following of Brown's fan club. In a wild expression of their jubilation on his release, members of the group fired a volley of gunshots into the air. It caused pandemonium on the busy shopping streets, sending police officers and civilians rushing for cover. The next day a *Gleaner* editorial mourned the anarchy that was sweeping the country.

In the summer of 1988, Jim Brown was supposed to have committed another murder. Like the earlier alleged attack on the gas station attendant, this one had a personal motive to it. Brown was said to have beaten and shot a bus driver who had 'bad driven' him; cut him up on the road. Once again, the Tivoli hardman was arrested and charged with murder. And, once again, the main witness against him failed to testify in court. On this occasion, however, the witness failed to show up in court and he had supposedly 'gone missing'. As a result, Jim Brown was released on bail to appear when the elusive witness finally showed up. (The witness never showed up, and was more than likely not in a condition to do so.)

The next occasion on which Jim Brown was arrested was in July 1990; the same month that the US federal report cited above alleged that 'Brown and about 60 of his posse members were involved in a shoot-out with [the] police.' Thirty of his posse members and four police officers were said to have been shot, one of the officers fatally. Surprisingly, though, Brown's arrest did not stem from this incident. Neither did it have anything to do with personal or political violence.

Rather, Brown's encounter with the Jamaican police stemmed from his activities during his lengthy sabbaticals in the United States. In short, his arrest, as he was driving along Duke Street, was at the behest of the American authorities. It related to a string of serious criminal offences committed in the United States that they wanted him and a cohort, Richard 'Storyteller' Morrison, to stand trial for.

In fact, it was during Brown's voluntary exile in the United States that he was formally identified by federal law enforcement agencies as a co-leader of the Shower Posse. The network of the Shower's international operations was a fitting tribute to Brown's organisational talents and leadership abilities. By the time of his arrest the Shower Posse had also been identified in Kingston, Jamaica and Toronto and Montreal in Canada.

The Shower Posse had also been positively identified in London. In fact, by March 1988, Brown had made (at least) two flying visits to the British capital. On both occasions, he had been tailed to Heathrow Airport by undercover intelligence officers of the Jamaican Defence Force (JDF), the island's military establishment. He used a typical Rude Boy ploy to enter Britain on both occasions: bogus travel documents.

Meanwhile, the Shower Posse was also known to have branches in at least sixteen major American cities. The list included Anchorage, Atlanta, Denver, Houston, Los Angeles, Miami, New York, Pittsburgh, and Washington DC. In addition, Shower Posse 'mules' or drug couriers had been arrested in countries including Australia, Italy and Japan. The Shower Posse was a mammoth, organised criminal enterprise by any standards.

Two days after the arrest – which Brown courteously acceded to – the Americans made a formal request for his extradition to South Florida. Even though the Americans never detained him, the protracted extradition process marked the beginning of the end for Jim Brown. The indictment against him included charges of racketeering, conspiracy to distribute cocaine and ganja, firearms trafficking, money-laundering, murder, attempted murder, and conspiracy to commit murder.

The Jamaican courts finally ordered Brown's extradition on 18 February 1991. Naturally, he and 'Storyteller' Morrison vigorously contested the proceedings, although they were remanded into custody at Kingston's General Penitentiary while they did so. Both men sought leave to appeal against their extradition orders to the Judicial Committee of the Privy Council in the United Kingdom, the final arbiter of Jamaican legal matters.

Unfortunately for Morrison, while a decision on his appeal was still pending, an administrative cock-up in Jamaica led to his premature – many claimed illegal – extradition to the United States in June. And, once they had got him, there was no way the American authorities were going to let him go. The Americans' refusal to return Morrison culminated in a heated diplomatic row with their Jamaican counterparts. In fact, the Jamaican authorities threatened to review the entire basis of the bilateral extradition agreement between the two countries.

In the meantime, Morrison was made to stand trial on a charge of possession with intent to distribute 330 pounds of cocaine. Another alleged leader of the Shower Posse, the Tivoli-ite was convicted by the Middle District Court in Fort Myers, Florida. In May 1992, he was sentenced to twenty-four years and six months imprisonment, without parole. At the time of writing he still faced a string of state charges. If convicted of those, 'Storyteller' will probably spend the rest of his natural life behind bars.

Back in Jamaica, Jim Brown's application to the Privy Council was finally turned down late in February 1992.

As 'Free Jim Brown' graffiti was scrawled on walls throughout JLP strongholds, the man himself was about to play his last card in a bid to avoid extradition. His lawyer, Tom Tavares-Finson, had prepared a writ of habeas corpus to be heard in the Jamaican Supreme Court on 24 February. It was most unlikely to have succeeded, but, in the event, the hearing never took place.

The reason Jim Brown was unable to attend his son's funeral was because he was in jail. In fact, Brown spent the last twelve months and six days of his life behind bars.

In life, Jim Brown had been a controversial figure to say the least. His death – or the circumstances surrounding it – carried on that tradition. A post-mortem on Brown concluded that he had died as the result of smoke inhalation and carbon monoxide poisoning. His death was caused by a mysterious prison fire.

However, the timing of this fire (hours after his son's funeral and on the eve of his most important court hearing to date) and the circumstances surrounding it – it broke out in his cell and killed only one other inmate – aroused lingering suspicions among Brown's supporters and impartial observers alike. 'I suspect that he didn't [die accidentally],' says Williams, 'there was something far more sinister than that.' Brown's lawyer was far more forthright. 'If you believe Jim Brown just burned to death, by accident, in his cell,' *Newsweek* quoted Tavares-Finson as saying, 'you'll believe in the tooth fairy.'

The suspicions of Tavares-Finson and others were further fuelled by a number of inexplicable occurrences on either side of the fire. Why had a prison officer visited Brown's cell minutes before it broke out? Why did prison officers take at least fifteen minutes to respond to the alarm sounded by other inmates? Why, when evidence suggests that he was still alive half an hour after he was released from his cell, did it take an eternity to get Brown transported to the Kingston Public Hospital, a matter of minutes away? And why had evidence been removed from his cell before an investigator, who was flown in specially from Canada, could look into the cause of the blaze?

For all the questions, in the end and to the great amazement of those concerned, a coroner's court jury handed down an open verdict.

While these questions and others are likely to go unanswered, a number of theories were mooted in an attempt to solve the riddle of Brown's untimely death. One of the most popular concerns an escape bid that went tragically wrong. Escapes are nothing new in the history of Jamaica's prisons. Indeed, many are known to have been facilitated by poorly-paid prison staff in return for backhanders. In this case, the fire was literally supposed to provide a smokescreen. Supporters of this theory point to the mysterious cell visit by a prison warder, and suggest that he got cold feet at the eleventh hour. The speculation is compounded by the fact that Brown's widow, Beverly Burgess, was seen in her husband's Mercedes Benz at a roadblock near the prison when he was eventually ferried to hospital.

Another more brutal, but equally straightforward, theory is that Brown was 'silenced' because he knew too much. This relates equally to the Shower Posse's criminal operations and the JLP's subversive funding of political violence. Ironically, the name of one leading Labour Party member features prominently as the architect of plans to get rid of Brown in either case.

Yet another hypothesis concerns Brown's murder by prison officials. It suggests that he was actually tortured, and states that the fire was an attempt to cover the killers' tracks.

So Jim Brown, the don of Jamaica's narco-political dons, is dead. Dead, but not forgotten. As dubious as his lifetime's achievements were, he left a legacy that many a budding 'Yardie' (Jamaican) gangster aspires to replicate: fearless 'garrison' protector; ruthless JLP enforcer; cold-blooded murderer; hardcore disciplinarian; selfless community provider; loving husband and father; and, to cap it all, the *capo di tutti capi* of the Shower Posse, a truly world-class narcotics organisation.

Still, times have changed quickly since Jim Brown's demise. 'If he were alive today,' suggests Lloyd Williams, 'his influence would be on the wane.' The reason – or part of it – is that today's gangster has turned his back on the tribal political warfare. The raging gun battles that left hundreds dead in the ghettoes of west Kingston during the 1970s and 1980s, in particular, are a thing of the past. Politics does not pay the rent, not in the way that dealing drugs does, anyway.

Nowadays, the 'coup' is all about making money; big, fast, easy money. And, whether Jim Brown's pretenders set up base in Toronto, London, Kingston, Washington DC, or Hartford, Connecticut, is irrelevant. The success or failure of this ambition is invariably secured through a recipe of unlikely guile, gun-toting ruthlessness and crack cocaine.

CHAPTER TWO

The Rude Boys, Politics and Crime

'We [the Jamaica Labour Party and People's National Party] are supposed to be concerned with the nation's business but we operate like two military camps. What I am dealing with within my party is military tactics and strategy . . . we take the people's business and we manipulate it in a way analogous to the Serbs and their opponents in Bosnia.'

Bruce Golding, Chairman,
Jamaica Labour Party, 1993

If Bruce Golding was trying to be lyrical, then he failed abysmally. Besides that, he had good cause to be slightly more circumspect in his choice of analogy. He had once come close to becoming a statistic of this bloody inter-party factionalism. The heir-apparent to Edward Seaga's leadership crown, Golding was nominated for assassination by a gun-toting political gang during Jamaica's apocalyptic 1980 General Election campaign.

However tongue-in-cheek, the fact is Golding's conflict-laden allusions belie a deep-seated affliction that runs like a scar across Jamaican politics: the links between the two major political parties and armed criminal gangs. In turn, this frightening relationship has given rise to a deadly, undemocratic phenomenon known as political tribalism. A central feature of Jamaican political life for the past fifty years, political tribalism refers to violent inter-party warfare.

In spite of repeated denials by top politicians, political tribalism is an open secret in Jamaican society. Every Jamaican knows that their political élite is somehow hand in glove with the island's most vicious gangsters. Why else, they ask, would 'respectable' politicians openly commune with 'known criminals' and gunmen? Why would they arrange bail for such undesirables, and ensure that criminal charges against them were dismissed or reduced to misdemeanours? And what other reason could there be for their political leaders to pay their last respects to Rude Boy gangsters like Jim Brown?

One of the more curious anomalies of Jamaican democracy relates to the fact that Jamaica's press has been free to pass judgement on politically-sponsored violence without fear of life-threatening recriminations. Accordingly, Jamaican scribes tend to tell it like it is. And if the following examples are anything to go by then *it* is extremely worrisome.

Clifton Segree, a veteran *Gleaner* reporter, freely admitted to having known self-confessed JLP and PNP gunmen in the 1970s; gunmen, moreover, whose mercenary activities he firmly believed were sanctioned by rival party bosses. With this in mind, in October 1992 Segree urged his readers to 'not tolerate any longer a political system that nicely accommodates the killing of people in the quest for power'.

Joan Williams went one step further. To her it was not a matter of conjecture that Jamaica's politicians were solely responsible for masterminding tribal inter-party violence. 'It has long been known,' she wrote in the *Jamaica Observer* in July 1993, 'that it was the [two major political] parties which spawned the "yardies" and

the "posses" who not only drive terror into Jamaicans but
other citizens in far away lands.' What Ms Williams could
not understand, though, was why the nation's political
élite was doing nothing to stop those who had 'substituted
the concept of democracy with the politics of murder and
wanton violence'.

Tony Johnson provided a possible answer to Williams's
perplexing question as well as another dimension to
this vexed issue. Writing in the *Sunday Gleaner* a few
months later, he pointed to 'clear instances where the
use of violence in the electoral process has ensured
success at the polls for candidates'. Ergo, if actions have
consequences, that candidate must be indebted to a violent
gang. Furthermore, Johnson reasoned, that politician must
also 'be beholden to that method of electioneering – pure,
barbaric violence'.

And therein lies what Shakespeare called the 'core of
the wound'. Namely, that Jamaica's political duopoly
has been compromised and corrupted by decades of
patronising their so-called supporters based on the latters'
willingness to perpetrate acts of terroristic violence in the
name of party loyalty, in the hope of electoral victory or
simply for financial gain.

In one way or another, political patronage has been a
'democratic' reality in Jamaica since the mid-1940s. Its
roots are coeval with Jamaica's fifty-year-old black-led
democracy. The practice has been emasculated during the
1990s, but that it is a permanent fixture of the Jamaican
democratic process is unquestionable.

Political patronage has been used to encourage political
tribalism. Over the decades, the promise of receiving
rewards for taking up arms against rival party supporters
has been sufficient to raise armies of criminal ghetto
gunmen; Rude Boys who are prepared to do whatever it
takes to be on the winning side. In this sense, sponsored
political violence has become a 'legitimate' electioneering

tool; the Jamaican equivalent of door-to-door canvassing in countries like Britain.

Since their unwelcome arrival, this toxic combination has poisoned the Jamaican body politic; basically splitting the electorate into two mutually venomous factions. For the stricken, ideological and policy differences pale into insignificance in their midst (although much less so in recent years). The bottom line is that Jamaican politics are about 'us' and 'them'. There is no middle ground; no safe one, anyway.

The tremors of patronage and tribalism have not only registered on the social scale. Significantly, they have also greatly assisted Jamaica's present-day rudie criminal gangs (and their forerunners) in becoming the formidable criminal entities they are today.

The establishment and maintenance of so-called garrison constituencies is a case in point. These ghetto-based battle zones, reminiscent of the Falls and Shankhill roads in west Belfast, started out as party strongholds 'policed' by political mobsters. In effect, they comprised reservoirs of guaranteed voters for prospective parliamentarians to exploit come election time, no matter which 'tribe' was in power or got elected.

Over the years, though, the garrisons have taken on another, equally sinister role, simultaneously doubling as almost feudal fiefdoms for today's powerful narcotics gangs. In fact, the 1990s has seen the pendulum of overall authority swing firmly in their favour; the gangsters now run the ghettoes under their own banners, and not the politicians'.

The reasons for this transformation are manifold. Political patronage and tribal violence are key. But they also touch on Jamaica's living culture of violence. The macroeconomic plight of the nation, and the micro-economics of ghetto existence are also relevant. Importantly, they embrace the overall failings of the island's political and

criminal justice system, which are intractable from the
origins and development of the country's illegal drug
industry.

Significantly, though, the rise of the gangs or posses
began long before they made their ignominious entry
into the demonology of Jamaican crime. Their origins
are inseparable from the ancient tradition of ruthless
violence that is Jamaican history. But of immediate import
is the question of when, why and how Jamaica's élite
criminals and politicians joined together in their sordid
relationship.

An infectious air of great expectancy hung over Jamaica
on the evening of 5 August 1962. Excited crowds congregated in parish capitals to witness a series of symbolic
ceremonies, events the impoverished majority especially
hoped would begin a revolution in their tortured lives.

As clocks throughout the island beat out the mechanical
chimes that signalled midnight, the simultaneous lowering
of Union Jacks and their replacement with a new black,
green and gold motif on the island's flagpoles suggested
6 August would not be just another day in the life of this
struggling tropical paradise. Those midnight bells rang in
the start of a new era in Jamaican history. Jamaica had
finally won its independence from Britain.

The Jamaican population treated independence as anyone would – they partied. Young and old, rich and poor,
men, women and children immediately fell into an orgy
of unrestrained celebration, which was to last for several
days. A procession of boisterous and colourful street
parties and noisy, drunken dances were held in every
corner of the island. And for a while all petty jealousies,
unbridgeable differences and creeping uncertainty about
the future were put to one side as the country wallowed in
the splendour of its new freedom.

Earlier on 5 August, the Queen's representative, Her

Royal Highness Princess Margaret, had performed the penultimate rite on the road to transforming the relationship between Britain and Jamaica. At an official ceremony held in the parliament building, the Princess had presented the constitutional documents that confirmed Jamaica's graduation to political and economic self-determination to its first elected Prime Minister, the charismatic Sir William Alexander Bustamante.

Bustamante, an egotistical middle-class money-lender, had been patiently awaiting this unique distinction since he led the JLP to victory in the general election of April 1962. But the limelight actually fell on to 'The Chief's' cousin, the vanquished Opposition party leader Norman Washington Manley. And, in the end, it was the PNP supremo and gifted lawyer who stole the show.

The Opposition leader's speech was incredibly poignant. In one of his most brilliant deliveries, Norman 'Moses' Manley passionately articulated the meaning of independence to Jamaica and its citizens. A man not known for his commanding stage presence, he spoke of the tremendous responsibilities now facing the people to whom that baton of freedom had been passed.

Jamaica's leaders were ready, he declared. More than that they were also united in the single hope 'that we may make our small country a safe and happy place for all our people'. Through Jamaica's new 'great motto' – 'Out of many one people' – he continued, 'we can become a worthwhile and shining example of the sort of world men sometimes dream to live in'.

Unfortunately, somewhere along the line several of Jamaica's key political players forgot to read the script. Manley's optimistic view of his country's future did not last any longer than it took to enunciate. It made great copy, but in truth it never was and was (probably) never to be, the direction of the country's political fate having been sealed almost twenty years earlier. The 'safe and happy'

country Manley dreamt of would never progress beyond
his imagination.

The fact is that even before Jamaica won its independence, its black, future leadership had already embarked on
a disastrous political course; one that would shatter any
future illusions about unity and common purpose. Back in
the 1940s, it seems the promise of (unrestrained) political
power was the guiding light followed by its home-grown
politicos.

In his *Poetics*, Aristotle observed that 'man is by nature
a political animal'. If so, every Jamaican politician was a
power-hungry predator who lived to dominate the ghetto
jungle, even if it meant annihilating all other meat-eaters.
The founding fathers of modern Jamaica were political
megalomaniacs; intelligent and educated people intent on
doing almost anything to get their hands on the mace of
government.

The political patronage system was the first tactic they
exploited to secure their ambitions. In practice, it is little
more than a corrupt version of the 'I'll-scratch-your-
back-if-you-scratch-mine' principle. Over the years, a
shower of non-partisan observers have produced forceful arguments to attribute the origins of the patronage
syndrome to the JLP. They are probably correct. Still,
blaming the Labourites is tantamount to holding Britain's
Conservative Party solely responsible for the effects of
global warming. The idea being that the Tories were
in power when it was discovered, and earlier Labour
Party policies had nothing to do with it. In the final
analysis what matters most is that political patronage
has been applied with equal vigour by both of Jamaica's
'establishment' parties.

But what started out as a corrupt economic means to
a political end has backfired on Jamaica's politicians.
Like power-crazed junkies, successive Jamaican political
pretenders have manipulated the system in the hope of

buying the votes they need to attain the ultimate 'high' of unfettered governmental control. The problem is that the longer this compromising practice went on, the more it became habit-forming. And, as every drug addict will attest, the more one indulges one's habit, the more difficult it becomes to break.

So as the decades progressed, political patronage became a bane to the power-mad politicos and the country's democratic structure. This cycle of abuse finally peaked in 1980 when the gun-wielding dealers went on a deadly rampage slaughtering around a thousand Jamaicans. Then, fearing a total loss of self-control to the vicious dealers, the political druggies decided to drastically reduce their intake of sponsored bloodshed; to restore some semblance of normality to their tattered political existences.

Still, the physical damage had already been done. Political patronage, and the tribal violence it finances in the quest for power, had become a self-fulfilling prophecy; Jamaica's politicians were hopelessly hooked.

It started back in 1944, a watershed year in the history of Jamaica's social and political development. More than a century after the emancipation of the island's slave population, it began the momentous era in which their adult progeny won their first taste of democracy.

This noteworthy victory came partly in the form of universal suffrage, one of a batch of hard-fought con-stitutional reforms implemented by the colonial auth-orities in Britain. Prior to this the franchise had been jealously guarded by a wealthy, predominantly white, property-owning clique; the decaying remnants of a once omnipotent plantocracy.

In theory, universal suffrage promised to give the historically repressed masses a voice of their own. In practice, it was at best a pyrrhic victory for the people, or Sufferers, as they christened themselves. In the event, their aspirations were prostituted by the political activists who had spearheaded the campaign for their rights in the first place.

The route leading to universal suffrage was as long as it had been arduous for the Jamaican masses. The final stop was the cataclysmic series of workers' riots that engulfed the island in 1938, another crucial year in the history of twentieth-century Jamaica.

By 1938, the island – and the world as a whole – had been writhing under the enormous weight of the Great Depression for nigh on a decade. That the island's colonial government had generally proved itself to be intellectually myopic and morally bankrupt only served to heighten the suffering of the dispossessed, and add to the growing potential for mass disorder.

The recession was the final straw. The position of the Sufferers had shown no signs of sustained improvement after more than a century of what they had been informed was freedom. At best, the perennially poor eked out a subsistence-style existence.

Unemployment levels were such that only one in five Jamaicans enjoyed paid work. For the fortunate few, even working was not a passport to prosperity. Incredibly, in the 1930s unskilled Jamaicans laboured for exactly the same rates of pay that their great grandparents had a century earlier. And it showed: malnutrition and preventable disease among the slum-dwellers had reached epidemic proportions; the prospect of premature death was a sad fact of life.

Things were bad for the masses, but things had always been bad. What helped to make 1938 different was the revolution that had taken place in black consciousness around that time, which included uncomfortable memories of their treatment after the First World War.

As citizens of the Commonwealth, Jamaicans had volunteered for military service in their droves. Meanwhile, on the home front, loyal Jamaicans had put their backs into the effort to feed and equip the Allies in their monumental struggle against German authoritarianism. And for what? Once the conflict was over the British treated them exactly the same as before.

The Harlem Renaissance was the major catalyst. In the 1920s and early 1930s, the black diaspora's finest poets, singers, artists, novelists, politicians and thinkers had fallen together under the umbrella of the Harlem Renaissance. Their goals: to celebrate the wealth of black expression; and to rally for black equality, liberation and justice from a black perspective.

Great black separatist leaders such as Marcus Mosiah Garvey helped to instil a sense of militant racial pride into the black diaspora. He taught them that they were descended from a glorious African heritage; that they were not – as they had been taught – second class. One of Jamaica's élite band of National Heroes, Garvey and others also showed the Sufferers that their lot was the result of centuries of pernicious white exploitation. The unprecedented support shown for his Universal Negro Improvement Association (UNIA) proves the message got through. With twenty million 'New Negro' members, UNIA remains the largest black mass movement in history.

The failure to address black grievances boiled over into six months of fever-pitch civil disorder in 1938. A volley of bitter strikes, protest demonstrations and hunger marches – and their violent suppression by the State – became everyday occurrences. A dozen Jamaicans were martyred in the vulcanic battles for black political rights.

When the dust finally settled, the British Parliament dispatched a Commission to the British West Indies to investigate this and other uprisings. (Jamaica was, in fact, almost the last of a half dozen British dependencies to mutiny.) So damning were the Commission's findings that

the British Government suppressed them until 1945, fully
six years after production of the report.

Yet the charges of neglect and ineptitude it levelled
were grave enough to push the British authorities into
implementing a new style of local government; one which
gave the increasingly nationalistic common people a
meaningful stake in the democratic process. That process
began in Jamaica with the elections of 1944.

The 1944 General Election – like all but the one boycotted
by the PNP in 1983 – was contested by the Jamaica Labour
and People's National parties. Capitalising on widespread
popular discontent, the PNP was formed during the workers' struggles of 1938. The JLP was set up five years later
when news of the forthcoming British reforms hit Jamaica.

The Jamaica Labour Party was founded by a breakaway
PNP faction led by the near-white, middle-class trade
union leader Alexander Bustamante. Even so, both parties
agreed that Jamaican self-rule was a must, although 'The
Chief's' initial reaction was to liken such a move to
slavery.

The major sticking point was where self-rule would lead.
Norman Washington Manley, the near-white, middle-class
PNP leader and the major architect of Jamaican national-
ism, considered gradual self-rule to be but the first step
along the difficult road towards black independence. By
contrast, his cousin wanted somehow to retain Jamaica's
bonds with Britain.

These seemingly innocuous early differences were to
provide the foundations for much deeper political divi-
sions, and culminate in the bloody political tribalism
of later years. The main problem was that the rival
parties were almost identical. Both promulgated similar
ideologies, were affiliated to powerful, heavily-patronised
trade unions, and drew their support from across the
classes.

At best, the JLP was right of centre, while the PNP leaned towards the left. In fact, the biggest and most telling difference between the JLP and PNP revolved around perceptions of their leaders. Even then, there was little to choose between them. Not only were Bustamante and Manley descended from the same socio-economic stock, but they were from the same family.

What separated them – and circumscribed support for their respective parties most – was the politics of the cult of the personality. Bustamante, the itinerant son of an Irish father and high-brow mother, was infinitely more charismatic than his cerebral, Oxford-educated cousin.

Importantly, what this did was to make a complete and permanent mockery of Jamaica's democratic political system. For, with the onus on leadership appeal, the burden of having to frame distinctive and appealing political policies was effectively removed from the parties. Basically, the Jamaican electorate was torn into two hostile camps on the basis of leadership style, as opposed to political content.

Bustamante's charisma (and well-organised trade union base) proved decisive in delivering his party a resounding 1944 election victory. Crucially though, the election campaign was marred by an undertow of political violence. Compared to future elections – especially 1976 and 1980 – the violence was minor and largely spontaneous; the skirmishes amounted to mutual barrages of verbal abuse punctuated by occasional bouts of stone-throwing and the odd stabbing. And, as mournful as they were, these small-scale confrontations were largely confined to fanatical political animals in the capital's growing slum areas.

Tribal violence worsened as the years progressed. Significantly, after the 1955 election it had become almost impossible for the nation's political leaders to convince the electorate that they played no part in organising it. That battle was lost altogether a decade later when the final traces of spontaneity were sucked out of violent

political confrontation. Tribalism had become organised
– and everybody knew who was pulling the strings. At
the same time, it ceased to be a sword that was only
unsheathed in the run-up to an election; tribal violence
became as common to Jamaican politicking as changing
one's clothes.

Neither party has ever denied that their supporters are
involved in tribal warfare. Somewhat predictably, though,
they blame each other for provoking it. What is clear,
however, is that the introduction of large-scale, organised
violence in the mid-1960s was of potential benefit to
everyone involved in it.

The key to understanding why is sewn up in the idea
of resource politics. In what is termed a 'developing
country', the Jamaican government has limited funds
and resources to spread around. Invariably, there are
scarcely enough to satisfy the interests of one party's
own supporters, let alone their rivals'. Inevitably, because
the winner takes all, this means that the highest premium
is placed upon forming the government.

The stakes were raised considerably during the early
1960s with the onset of independence. However, like the
Republican and Democrat parties in the United States,
there was still very little to distinguish the JLP and PNP
in terms of ideology or policy.

In the end, it was Bustamante's larger-than-life personality that prevailed in the 1962 General Election. Still, the
ballot was a perilously close encounter, with less than two
percentage points separating a popular vote of 576,000
electors.

The narrowness of their victory aside, the JLP had
other worries. Ill health meant 'The Chief', the party's
top vote-getter, was unlikely to lead the party into the
next scheduled election in 1967. So, the Labourites had
to find a way to shore up their popular support before the
next electoral showdown.

Political patronage became the key to the JLP's strategy. The practice was simple in its application. Basically, those who demonstrated their loyalty to the JLP were patronised, and those who did not were not. So, throughout the ten years of the party's reign the only people to benefit from government contracts and employment were party supporters. Worse than that, PNP supporters were actually booted out of government jobs. The brutal message then was 'it pays to vote JLP'.

The abuse of patronage was like a coup d'état. But nowhere was this strategy more obvious than in the JLP Development Minister's constituency. Down in Western Kingston, Edward Seaga's battle to win the hearts and minds of the electorate took on a sinister hue.

It started innocuously enough, though. In return for prized commodities such as sporting equipment – football kits and the like – local, apolitical gangs of workless Rude Boys signed up to JLP-affiliated youth organisations, and pledged their allegiance to the JLP. Their motives probably had more to do with kidology than political sentiment, but the results were the same.

The 'politicisation' of these rudie youths wreaked havoc. It redefined the way gangs in Seaga's constituency were perceived by non-partisan friends and foes alike, and precluded any semblance of 'normal' relations between them from thereon. So when a youth gang in Seaga's constituency battled with another from, say, a PNP enclave, the tendency was to embue the resulting fracas with a political significance it did not deserve.

By the mid-1960s that was inevitably the case. However, before describing these tribal encounters, it is worthwhile getting to grips with the dominant players and their rationale for getting involved. Equally, in explaining these latter themes it makes sense to start with an exposition of the environment which spawned these political hoodlums.

*   *   *

In the 1940s and 1950s Jamaica was revered – even
envied – in some international circles for the comparative
smoothness with which it ran its democratic machinery.
That perception changed dramatically by the mid-1960s,
the take-off point for hardcore political tribalism, after
the respective paramilitary political war machines began
to lay their hands on firearms.

The background to the advent of political gun violence
at this time embraced a raft of social and economic
changes. Jamaica, and Kingston in particular, enjoyed
something of an economic boom after the Second World
War. This rare but welcome trend continued into the independence era under the JLP's conservative, pro-Western
stewardship of the economy. In fact, the island's economic
good fortune surpassed all expectations, posting higher
growth rates than many Western nations.

It was not to last. In all honesty, the only time the
Jamaican economy had really flourished had been during
the sugar boom of the plantation slave era.

The island's economy was subjected to a major over-
haul after the war. As Jamaica's agricultural sector became
a less important earner of foreign exchange, the Jamaican
Government lost interest in it. JLP and PNP governments turned their attentions to new enterprises, especially
manufacturing, tourism and the mining of bauxite.

Bauxite was a particularly successful departure for the
Jamaican economy. From the late 1940s to the early
1970s, the so-called 'red gold' vital to the production
of aluminium, accounted for up to fifty per cent of
Jamaica's export earnings. The second half of this period
saw Jamaica enjoying the distinction of being the world's
largest bauxite producer.

But the bauxite success story was not without cost.
With American- and Canadian-owned companies pushing hordes of peasant farmers off the land to facilitate
their operations, more and more poor Jamaicans looked

towards the industrialised areas for fresh employment opportunities.

Cities like Kingston had become the centres of the new industrial generation. There were new manufacturing jobs – mainly for women – to be filled, but not nearly enough factory work to accommodate the legions of hopeful workers flocking to the urban areas. Neither did these jobs pay sufficiently well to keep their recipients (and their dependants) above the encroaching poverty line.

Disparities of wages grew out of all proportion – a gulf that would finally cost the JLP its government at the end of its second term in 1972. Meanwhile, with unemployment reaching forty per cent and more in the most depressed urban communities, the poor suffered hardship on a scale they had never experienced before.

Demographic and population shifts had seen the slums of Kingston swell to unimaginable proportions; the ghettoisation of Kingston was well underway. At 420,000, the population of the Corporate Area (Kingston and the neighbouring parish of St Andrew) almost doubled between 1943 and 1960. In 1960, the capital's 375,000 residents accounted for just over a quarter of the national population. Six years on, it was almost a third.

Predictably, in the 1960s the vast majority of Kingstonians lived in abject poverty. Basic amenities such as asphalted roads, schools, running water and electricity were outstripped by the human growth. In the notoriously lawless suburb of Trench Town, for instance, more than half the households had no electricity.

More than ever before, overcrowding and the appalling living conditions it created were becoming major issues, not least because of the serious crime wave that accompanied them. Equally, the chronically unemployable urban dispossessed grew increasingly disenchanted about living on skid row.

* * *

No group felt the privations and frustrations more than the growing ranks of young, out of work black males. Their misery, neglect and anger spawned a new breed of young Kingstonian: the (Original) Rude Boy.

The Rude Boys were James Dean-like rebels with a serious attitude problem. Authority sucked; respect for it had merely made them targets for persecution by the police, and exploitation by the 'Babylon system' as a whole. Authority could go to hell.

Rude Boy was coterminous with 'bad', with a capital 'B'. Arrogant, ambitious and streetwise, the rudies wanted it – whatever *it* was – *now*. Predictably it was the sexiest girls, the most dapper threads, their own transport, the best of good times and, of course, the single commodity that made them all possible: money. And they really did not care how they got it; they had nothing to lose. The ghettoes were nothing more than stifling, overcrowded prisons, anyway, and the 'system' had already sentenced them to Death Row.

The marginality of rudie existence gave birth to a *Weltanschauung* which emphasised the cheapness of life. Simply put, the Rude Boy philosophy was live hard, die young, and leave a healthy-looking corpse.

When the rudies exploded onto Sixties Jamaica their anti-authoritarianism lent an anti-social celebrity to their disturbing presence. This mood was vividly captured by ska, the first major indigenous music form to emerge out of Jamaica. A vulcanic, US-Jamaican rhythm and blues hybrid with jazzy overtones, ska was immediately adopted by the Rude Boys. They treasured its blood-red rawness and 'no-prisoners'-style militantism, which nicely complemented their philosophy and lifestyle.

Much of the idiom was instrumental, but such was the rudies' infamy that the odd lyric was written about them. 'Simmer Down', (Bob Marley and) The Wailers' first release in 1963 was a supplication to the rudies to turn their backs on 'badness'. However, along with 'Rude Boy', another of the group's smash hits, it became more of an anthem than a warning.

With a paucity of legal employment avenues open to them – not that they wanted to slave for the 'Babylon system' anyway – and little else to occupy their time, jobless rudies quickly fell into gangs. These outfits were the prototypes upon which today's ruthless narcotics gangs were built.

Gang members looked to the United States for inspiration. Devotees of low-brow culture, especially glamorously violent westerns and thrillers, they gave their outfits names designed to put the fear of God into anyone who heard them: the Dirty Dozen, The Roughest And The Toughest, Zulu and Skull, to name but a few.

Initially these cohorts wielded knives and machetes to fight each other for territorial superiority, and generally made their collective presence felt by intimidating their law-abiding neighbours – and the police. But financial imperatives soon got the better of them.

Armed with machetes, knives and their sociopathic profiles, the rudies set off on a violent crime spree. They held up liquor stores and organised daring bank raids. They robbed passers-by and shoppers. They looted uptown stores. They burgled ghetto hovels, and staged daring night time raids on affluent 'uptown' households. They extorted 'protection' money from neighbourhood businesses and residents. They hustled, fenced and pimped. And when the mood took them, they would get 'blocked up' on a cocktail of ganja (marijuana) and booze, and go and rape some innocent girl, just for kicks.

As a result Jamaica's crime rate shot up as rapidly as a thermometer on a typically sun-scorched Kingston afternoon. The God-fearing, law-abiding majority was understandably horrified; certain pillars of the community

openly called on the police to adopt a shoot-to-kill policy.
Little did they know that even in 1967 – when homicides
smashed through the hundred mark for the first time
– they would one day look back on the 1960s as the
halcyon days.

The emergence of the rudies during the 1960s was a
boon to Jamaica's politicos, who quickly enlisted them
into active political service. Political patronage came
in a number of forms for the loyal, chosen few, but
most were attracted by the material rewards. Patronage
boiled – and boils – down to the dispensation of food,
money, jobs, public housing, leases on government land,
public contracts, precious social and welfare services,
and favours such as financial assistance for would-be,
small-time businesspeople. Whatever was on offer, it was
only available to bona fide party members.

Money was an obvious and much sought-after induce-
ment. Apart from benefiting their recipients, cash handouts were an important tool in shoring up a Member of
Parliament's (or parish councillor's) popular support. For
example, a typical political ploy was, and still is, to fund
temporary 'Christmas work'. The 'work', which consists
of menial tasks, such as street sweeping, was doled out
by politicians in recognition of their loyalists' selfless
devotion to the 'cause'.

In 1965, the dispensation of 'Christmas work' led to
violent confrontations in west Kingston. Almost totally
excluded from consideration for such employment, PNP
leaders and sympathisers took to the streets to voice their
anger at the unjust practice. The only thing to come of the
protests was a tear-gassing from the police, presumably
under instruction from the ruling JLP hierarchy.

Decent public housing was another highly valued form
of patronage for rudie slum dwellers. The most sordid
example of this rotten practice occurred in the Rt. Hon.

Edward Seaga's constituency after his party's 1962 General Election victory.

A Harvard-educated Member of Parliament and one of the JLP's intellectual rising stars, Seaga was handed the Government's Community Development and Welfare portfolio. It was during his tenure in this office that Seaga cemented his popularity amongst his constituency's JLP supporters.

Seaga's ministerial position provided him with an ideal platform to address inner-city Kingston's appalling housing conditions. And where better to start than in his own impoverished constituency?

In fact, the community development minister decided to redevelop the Back-o-Wall squatter camp. As luck would have it, Back-o-Wall was at the time 'home' to a large contingent of militant Rastafari PNP sympathisers; voters who, if left to their own devices, might one day tip the scales of electoral misfortune in Seaga's direction.

In the event, circumstances conspired to prevent that scenario. One day in the summer of 1966, a fleet of bulldozers with a posse of 250 soldiers and police made an unannounced call on Back-o-Wall. The militia then forcibly evicted the bewildered squatters, and the bulldozers demolished and razed their ramshackle shacks. The problem was that good old 'Mr Eddie' had neither given the newly homeless prior warning of his intentions, nor made any provisions to rehouse them.

They were certainly not earmarked to occupy the purpose-built community housing estate that emerged like a Phoenix from the ashes of their misery. Funnily enough, all the dwellings at Tivoli Gardens, the new complex, were populated to a person by local JLP stalwarts – the sorts of people who mobilized support for the JLP candidate come election time.

Indeed, people like these have been instrumental in getting Seaga re-elected to parliament over more than

30 unbroken years. The JLP leader is so popular locally that, as Dawn Ritch pointed out, he has been returned on occasion 'with more votes than there are people in the constituency'.

The political contract system is a form of patronage which embraces entire communities. In essence, this corrupt system gravitates around the granting of government contracts to 'worthy' political activists. 'Worthy' not in the sense that the beneficiaries possess the necessary qualifications to complete the job. 'Worthy' instead because they have proven themselves loyal to the political struggle.

The contracts ranging from local maintenance works to lucrative building projects are awarded to dons, career criminals who control armed gangs. Like their namesakes in the Mafia, dons are invariably involved in the 'construction business'. These gangland bosses are crucial cogs in keeping the wheel of political control turning; the only link between the political paymasters and the trigger-happy rudie hoodlums.

Because of their pivotal role, the dons are given a free hand to service the contract. Naturally, they keep the lion's share of the proceeds for themselves. But, equally importantly, they employ local unemployed youth – most of whom double as their soldiers anyway – to carry out the specified work. This service also helps to maintain the emotional bonds between gangster and criminal overlord.

Still, patronage is not a political one-way street. Naturally, control of the nation's coffers is a great boon. However, the party in Opposition is able to call upon the considerable monetary resources of its affluent backers. The point is that both sets of politicians have the means to keep the tribal violence going, even when sitting on the Opposition benches.

'Democracy passes into despotism,' observed Plato,

and by 1965 Jamaica seemed to be heading that way. That was the year when the apocalyptic, so-called West Kingston Wars erupted. The ensuing tribalism, the worst Jamaica had experienced, was heightened by the début of rudie shock troopers and their politically-sponsored firearms. Gun fever was about to set in on the streets of Kingston, but the starting point and worst-affected area was Seaga's constituency.

The first major conflagrations involving gunplay were triggered by JLP insurgents' attempts to wrest control of the machinery of Kingston's local government. The PNP-controlled Kingston and St Andrew Corporation (KSAC), the capital's equivalent to London's ill-fated Greater London Council, had actually been dissolved by the JLP Government in 1964 as part of a bitter struggle to consolidate its power base there. However, the intake of its reconstituted (and considerably weakened) replacement rallied once again around the nationalist party. Inevitably, the ballot swiftly gave way to the bullet. Using 'Mr Eddie's' constituency as a springboard, gangs of pistol-wielding rudies launched violent incursions into neighbouring PNP territory with the explicit purposes of annihilating Opposition activists, 'encouraging' any survivors to switch to the JLP, and strengthening the party base.

The strategy failed, but the tactics remained intact. Over the next couple of years the Kingston ghetto battles intensified in both quantitative and qualitative terms. Gunplay – still in its infancy and by no means universal – was joined by bombing attacks. And for the beleaguered citizenship of the ghetto in west Kingston it seemed that the battle of Armageddon was underway in their streets.

After a brief post-Christmas lull in the hostilities, the political street battles began again in February 1966, and lasted fully a year until the 1967 General Election had been consigned to history. Up to 150-strong gun-wielding

gangs fought pitched street battles with their rivals for
control of ghetto borderlines. Rude Boy gangs from both
factions attacked and shot up political meetings, constituency offices, youth clubs, bars – even city bus services.
The feeble defences of rival party supporters' homes were
breached in the cloak of night, and their occupants shot and
killed. Later, as the tribal battle broadened in scope, power
lines were cut in west Kingston. And, in another sinister
departure, dances in Opposition areas were Molotoved and
shot up.

Most of the tribalism was restricted to Edward Seaga's
stronghold; Denham Town, Trench Town, Foreshore
Road and Tivoli Gardens becoming major hotspots. But as
the scourge of political tribalism worsened, the pandemic
of gun violence spread throughout the sprawling west
Kingston badlands. In the summer of 1966, for example,
the battle was joined between the infamous JLP Phoenix
Gang from Waterhouse on the western fringe of the ghetto
and Trench Town's notorious Blue Mafia based a stone's
throw away from the city centre.

Throughout the tenure of the bloody mayhem, the
3,000-strong Jamaica Constabulary Force (JCF), tried
in vain to separate the warring factions. Dusk-to-dawn
curfews were put in place, increased patrols mounted.
But instead of keeping the peace, the police literally
found themselves caught between the cross-fire. They
were seen as agents of State oppression, particularly by
JLP die-hards who believed them to be in cahoots with
the PNP.

This was not a good time to be a cop. In scenes
reminiscent of Beirut, Belfast and Soweto rudies sniped
at the police as they patrolled volatile (JLP) ghettoes in
armored vehicles. In one attack a dynamite bomb was
hurled at the Commissioner of Police. In another, eleven
officers were injured as they protected health officials
along the Spanish Town Road. Apart from returning

fire, the police used tear-gas grenades to flush out the gun bandits.

Meanwhile, the politicos made public but manifestly disingenuous attempts to bring a halt to the tribal factionalism. In August 1966, Members of Parliament and parliamentary candidates for the four affected Kingston constituencies held 'peace talks'. (The JLP had initially refused to be a party to them.) Seaga and Acting Prime Minister Donald Sangster, who was effectively running the Government owing to Bustamante's ailing health, made up the JLP delegation. PNP Vice-President and veteran Member of Parliament Wills O. Isaacs, whose supporters had clashed violently with Bustamante's in Kingston in 1949, and Senator Dudley Thompson, Seaga's bellicose opponent in Western Kingston, represented the Opposition.

Almost as soon as they had started, the 'peace talks' broke up in acrimony, Seaga refusing to sign any peace treaty. Not known for his tact or restraint, Seaga took it upon himself to make inflammatory statements about PNP subversion, including accusations about importing and dispensing guns to its supporters.

Meanwhile, the radical Thompson led the PNP in denouncing Seaga as the Minister for Devilment and Warfare. Earlier PNP chief, Norman Manley, had recalled an alleged threat made by Seaga in 1965 to let loose his 'well armed' 'private army' in the name of 'blood for blood and fire for fire'.

'Moses' Manley could also point to the JLP hardman's active involvement in rabble-rousing escapades. In mid-November 1965, for example, a red-shirted Seaga (the JLP colour) had led a provocative march through the predominantly pro-PNP Back-o-Wall enclave. Like a red rag to a bull the march degenerated into open party political warfare. As a consequence, Seaga and eight of his cronies were arrested and charged with offences including riot, causing affray and assault on a police officer.

The case came to court in March of the following year. A Superintendent who had policed the march gave evidence that he had been attacked by Seaga's red-shirted supporters. However, the court refused to credit his testimony, and Seaga was cleared on all counts. As he left the court building the jubilant, red-shirted Seaga was greeted by a posse of similarly clad party loyalists.

As the West Kingston War raged on and the toll of dead and injured climbed into the hundreds, the JLP was forced to take drastic measures to curtail the violence. At midnight on 2 October 1966, after only four years of independence, the Government imposed a State of Emergency on west Kingston. In the first major joint police-military operation in the island's history, National Reserve soldiers were drafted in to assist the JCF.

The whole operation lasted a month during which time extensive house-to-house searches were conducted in west Kingston. In all, fifty guns, 800 rounds of ammunition, sixty-six sticks of dynamite and a few Molotov cocktails were recovered. More than 400 suspects were rounded up, of whom almost 120 had criminal records.

The State of Emergency achieved a lot more than the haul suggests. It succeeded in bringing the bulk of the hostilities to an abrupt end. However, within a week of it being lifted in November, the assassination of a PNP Rude Boy enforcer outside a cinema signalled the resumption of all-out tribal warfare.

As the February 1967 General Election drew near, the rudie-fuelled tribalism escalated. And if anyone still doubted that the politicos were masterminding the troubles, compelling confirmation arrived a few weeks before the poll.

A small arsenal of weaponry was uncovered during one

of a series of police raids on various Kingston constituency offices. The raid on the JLP's Central Kingston
constituency headquarters alone netted five revolvers,
two semi-automatic pistols and a couple of hundred
rounds of ammunition, some machetes, Molotov cocktails,
home-made bombs and sundry stolen goods.

And there was more. A related raid on adjoining
premises belonging to a JLP parliamentary candidate
turned up an illegal weapon, ammunition and explosives.
In all a dozen suspects were arrested; including one
wanted on a murder charge. Undeterred, the prospective
parliamentarian went on to put his signature to a peace
declaration between the eight candidates fighting the four
Kingston seats.

Such seemingly disingenuous occurrences were not
surprising in the context of the West Kingston Wars.
It was merely an extension of a pattern that had been
established during the internecine factionalism; a pattern
in which despotic politicians openly demonstrated their
contempt for law and order. The deceit was played
out by politicos, some of whom employed Rude Boy
bodyguards, who openly condemned violent tribalism
while surreptitiously funding and directing it from the
sidelines. And when things went wrong, the same politicians would quietly organise bail for their cronies; or,
not so quietly, proceed to police stations to pressurise
officers into releasing them. And, when the political
heavies were booked to appear in court, they would
pressurise judges into dropping or reducing the charges
against their gun-wielding henchmen.

The election took place on 22 February 1967, but the
JLP's victory did not signal the immediate end of political
gang violence. That continued unabated for several more
weeks. The reason for this is not so easy to explain. The
likelihood, however, is that the rudies felt empowered.
After all, they had been armed and protected by the

nation's omnipotent political bigshots. And when the
politicos demanded the return of their guns, the Rude
Boys' refusal was not met with violent sanctions. In short,
they probably believed that they could act with impunity.
Whatever the case, the political aspect of Rude Boy gang
warfare was short-lived. After a month the rudies went
back to business as usual: organised crime.

The duplicity of Jamaica's political duopoly helped to
turn the Rude Boys into a menace to society. But the
politicians cannot be held completely responsible. The
fact is they were not the only ones to exploit the rudies'
obvious potential.

As luck would have it, the Rude Boys emerged from
Kingston's ghetto swamps at roughly the same time as the
island's embattled small farmers discovered a new, highly
lucrative export crop: ganja. Soon after, ganja became an
important export commodity and the rudies were drafted
in by its suppliers (including certain politicians) to fill
important positions in the illicit trade.

Ganja has had a strange career in Jamaica. The 'herb',
which is a by-product of hemp, the plant used in the manufacture of rope, arrived in Jamaica in the late nineteenth
century with the influx of Indian indentured labourers. The
Indians came to replace the emancipated slaves who had
fled the stigma of plantation labour.

The cultivation, sale and use of ganja was not officially
frowned upon until 1913, when the island's Legislative
Council banned its importation and cultivation. Up until
that point, in fact, British merchants had actually imported
it specifically for sale to the Indians.

But Jamaican attitudes to the 'herb' hardened in later
years. When the League of Nations prohibited the social
use of *cannabis sativa* (to give it its medical term)
in 1924, Jamaica sheepishly followed suit. All of a
sudden law-abiding ganja users were transformed into

common criminals. The anti-ganja stance calcified soon
after Jamaica was gripped by the epoch-making workers'
riots of 1938. The island's Dangerous Drugs Law was
amended, and in the early 1940s individual users could
expect to receive mandatory custodial sentences, coupled
with a heavy fine. By 1964, under the JLP, the punishment
for possession of even a spliff (a ganja cigarette) was
raised to five years imprisonment.

However, judicial deterrents did nothing to stop the
massive island-wide popularity of the wonder weed.
'Herbalists' continued to swear by its properties, and the
growing ranks of Rastafari consumed vast quantities to aid
their religious meditation. Plus, in the climate of creeping
austerity, struggling small farmers saw raising ganja crops
as a vital means to bolster their frugal incomes.

In many ways, the increasingly draconian measures
relating to ganja in the mid-1960s were prefaced by
three simultaneous changes in the trade. Firstly, the
trade had become more secretive. Secondly, small-scale
ganja farming had been supplanted by large-scale and
better organised cultivation. And, finally, two new sets of
players had come on board: influential Jamaican dealers;
and enterprising American traffickers.

By the mid-1960s the ganja trade had mushroomed into
a multi-million dollar export industry, making a substantial invisible contribution to Jamaica's robust economy.
The United States, which at its closest point is a mere 550
miles off Jamaica's north coast, had developed a booming
market for the narcotic. (Remember, during the 1960s
the children of materialistic America were into sex and
drugs and rock 'n' roll, and plenty of them.) Enterprising
American traffickers commandeered a squadron of small
planes and a flotilla of small boats to transport tons of
some of the world's most narcotic ganja back to the United
States to meet the rising demand.

As for the tremendous profits. Well, if arrest seemed

imminent traffickers would simply abandon their (gun- or) ganja-laden craft, and flee. It would not take long to recoup the losses.

Meanwhile, in Jamaica, a new breed of businessman had surfaced to service American demands and get rich in the process. Prosperous entrepreneurs who owned legitimate export businesses, such as furniture exporters, used their extensive nexus, products and resources as a cover to smuggle tons of ganja out of the country. Regrettably, corrupt politicians and high-ranking public servants (including some senior police officers) used their considerable influence to do the same.

With so much now at stake, the Jamaican end of the equation was forced to implement harsh measures to protect its investment. Clearly, it was incumbent upon the cultivators to safeguard their ganja plantations against police discovery – both legitimate and crooked – and unscrupulous rival outfits.

These urgent business concerns prompted the new wave of Jamaican drug overlords to establish personal armies. Enter the Rude Boys, ruthless and fearless gun-men *primus inter pares*. They were pressed into active service in a range of drug-related jobs. Where once the cultivators abandoned their remote plantations when the police raided them, now the rudies shot back. Where once ganja shipments were prone to appropriation by Johnny-come-latelys, now Rude Boys rode shotgun. And where once the ganja bosses compromised or bowed to others, now they had the rudies to enforce their will – no matter how violent it was.

Still, to carry out their assorted security jobs the Rude Boy gangsters needed arms. Their paymasters had no difficulty acquiring them. With hundreds of thousands of hard American dollars flooding in from the international trade in ganja, the rudies' paymasters could buy the cream of American weapons by the crateload.

Failing that, they could use the easy three-step plan to bartering their drugs for guns. One, place an order with the American connection. Two, sit back, relax and wait for the Americans to exploit lax gun laws in states like Florida to fill it. Three, proceed to a desolate, improvised airstrip in the dead of night, and exchange the weapons for a ton or two of premium ganja. What could be simpler?

With both drug dealers and politicians arming the rudies it was impossible at times to determine the motive for some of the violence. On a Saturday night in December 1966, for example, The Roughest And The Toughest gang stormed four ghetto dances, and shot them up; four revellers were killed, dozens injured. One theory is that the shootings were drug-related – even though they occurred at a time of growing pre-election violence. Another, that the gangsters in question, some of whom hailed its name as they sprayed into the crowds, merely wanted to flex their muscles and show everybody how rough and tough they were.

One certainty is that the Rude Boys' gunshooting was not always inspired by the orders of their patrons; the rudies' freelance work kept Jamaica's rapidly worsening violent crime wave alive. In the wake of the 1967 election, for instance, the JLP and PNP cold-shouldered their mercenaries. Spurred on by public fear and outrage, the governing JLP even went so far as to issue a no-nonsense directive for the police to get tough with the gun hawks.

In less than a decade then, the Rude Boys had grown from being apathetic, small-time hoods into major league gangsters and political terrorists. During the 1970s their phenomenal rise was to continue, and their bloody excesses to become more outrageous.

CHAPTER THREE

The Rude Boys and Jamaica's Cold War

'It is a fact that Cuban Communist Secret Police and Master Spies have been delegates to the PNP's annual conference in Jamaica. That's no lie!'

Edward Seaga, 6 December 1976

'They deny it to this day, but I prefer the judgements of the heads of the Jamaican security forces at the time. Police, army, and special branch concurred the CIA was actively behind the [destabilisation of Jamaica in the mid-1970s]. My common sense left me with no option but to agree.'

Michael Manley, 1982

On 19 June 1976 a grim-faced Prime Minister Michael Manley made a stunning address to the nation. 'Over the past several months,' the son of PNP party founder Norman Manley said, 'we have witnessed a type and scale of violence unique to our history.' This was not as revelatory as he made it sound; violent crime had been on the rise for over a decade in Jamaica. Still, according to Manley, there was something deeply disturbing about this nascent trend; for the first time, it embraced 'terrorist activities'.

A few days later, the embattled Prime Minister defined these nebulous acts of terrorism more sharply. Since the start of the year, he said, Jamaica had been beset by 'urban terrorism, confrontation with the Security Forces and other agents of the State, and widespread arson'.

The Jamaican Prime Minister was convinced that this violence had been stage-managed, the work of seditious forces whose sole ambition was to destabilise Jamaica and render his elected government incapable of leadership. In Manley's mind, the whole situation smacked of an attempted coup. 'We cannot and will not stand by and allow this sabotage of our country to continue,' he declared.

And with that Manley dropped the bomb-shell on his unsuspecting audience. He announced that, in accordance with the Constitution, his government had requested the Governor General tp declare an indefinite State of Emergency.

Under its wide-ranging provisions the security forces were instructed to 'arrest and detain all persons whose activities are likely to endanger the public safety'. Suspected gunmen and terrorists, of which Jamaica had no shortage, were given top priority. However, Manley was at pains to stress that his sole interests lay in preserving the safety of the Jamaican people, and safeguarding their duly elected government.

This was not the first time a Jamaican government in independence had presided over a State of Emergency. The JLP had requested one in 1966. But, and this is perhaps indicative of how seriously Jamaica's problem with violence had regressed, the JLP's lasted a mere month, while the PNP's was to run for ten months.

The Jamaican public warmly welcomed the Manley government's uncompromising initiative – another indication of how severe the mayhem had become. The

JLP, however, was suspicious of Manley's motives. To the Labourites the premier's State of Emergency was the central plank of a highly sinister hidden PNP agenda.

A couple of days after Manley's shock announcement, the Labour party leader issued a voluminous press release laying out the Opposition's fears. To begin with, he said, the new powers accorded to the security forces were only marginally different from those they enjoyed under the Suppression of Crime Act. But, according to Seaga – the JLP's new boss – that difference was extremely significant. Under Manley's measure, he complained, the Government had cunningly withdrawn the suspect's hitherto 'right to defend himself before a Court and his entitlement to face his accuser,' and opened him up to a period of indefinite detention. In this light then, the State of Emergency was a blatant attempt by the PNP to stifle mounting political opposition to its objectionable Government.

On the face of it Seaga's objections were somewhat disingenuous. As Manley's self-appointed political *bête noire*, he was never averse to scoring political points at his arch-enemy's expense. The truth is Seaga had himself made an unsuccessful call for a State of Emergency the previous year; and the nightmare of criminal and political violence had only become more frightening since then.

Viewed in the context of the PNP administration's rapidly changing politics, however, the Opposition leader was right to be suspicious about Manley's motives. At the heart of Seaga's concerns was the PNP's recent lurch leftwards into what it termed 'democratic social-ism'; a policy that looked like, as far as 'Mr Eddie' was concerned, the introduction of communism by the back door.

Anyone who doubted this had only to refer to the PNP's 1972 election manifesto. For that document made absolutely no mention of what, two years later, had become the centrepiece of the Manley government's feeble domestic policy.

But the danger of 'democratic socialism' was not the only thing on Seaga's mind. On the international front, there was Michael Manley's open and growing friendship with Fidel Castro, and his self-confessed admiration of the uniform-wearing, Kremlin-backed communist dictator's Cuban Revolution.

To Seaga and his party faithful it was more than coincidental that, under Manley's leadership, Jamaica had cajoled British Commonwealth partners, Barbados, Guyana and the Republic of Trinidad and Tobago into agreeing to establish diplomatic relations with Cuba in October 1972. By formalising Jamaican-Cuban relations, Manley had effectively stuck two fingers up at the United States, which sought to isolate communist Cuba from the rest of the Caribbean, and the world.

Anyone still prepared to give Manley the benefit of the doubt must surely have reviewed their position in 1973. A big shot in the Non-Aligned Movement (NAM), he accepted Castro's invitation to accompany him to its Algiers summit aboard his private plane. Then, in the following year, the governments of Jamaica and Cuba established direct air links.

And if that were not enough, Manley and a cadre of PNP 'comrades' trotted off on a high-profile official visit to Cuba in 1975. Whilst there the Jamaican Prime Minister was awarded, and graciously accepted, the National Order of Jose Marti by his host. Named after the distinguished nineteenth-century Cuban revolutionary, it was Castro's way of applauding Manley's courageous stand against Western imperialism, and for his support of Cuba.

And now, to cap it all, there was the patently pernicious move to suppress individual rights and freedoms at home. Only one conclusion could be drawn, and Seaga spelt it

out in his own inimitable fashion. The Manley government, he declared, was in no position to justify the State
of Emergency given its deification of 'the Government
of Cuba where there is no elected Parliament, where
no Opposition is allowed, where inhuman treatment is
practised . . .' and so on. Moreover, 'Any talk about
"free elections",' under such adverse circumstances was,
the Opposition leader asserted, 'about as meaningful as
the holding of so-called elections in Cuba.' Seaga was not
as friend of Cuba.

For Seaga the bottom line was that this whole state-of-
emergency fiasco was a government diversionary tactic;
a none too subtle ploy by the PNP's Reds-under-the-Bed
to justify the imposition of a revolutionary Cuban-style
Marxist one-party state on democratic Jamaica. Well
Seaga was having none of it. In concluding his tome,
a selfless Seaga and would-be martyr served notice that
he was 'fully prepared to suffer the same detention [as
Bustamante had during the Second World War] . . . rather
than see Jamaica become a new Cuba in our lives'.

There was never any concrete evidence that Manley
planned to transform Jamaica into a communist state;
and it is equally doubtful that Seaga genuinely believed
that this was Manley's intention. But the furore over the
State of Emergency was important in another respect.
It was symptomatic of the global Cold War politics of
the day: rampant suspicion bordering on paranoia over
the alleged influence of seditious internal and external
forces on the politics of Third World countries; forces,
moreover, which were bent on destroying the fabric of
whichever society they infiltrated.

Jamaica was a willing player in this East-West political maelstrom. Rather than influencing its outcome,
though, the island became a mere pawn in a highly-
charged chess match between the United States and Cuba.
Expressed in its crudest form, the Yankee Imperialists

were determined to rid the world of the scourge of communism, while the Soviet-backed Cuban commies were equally intent on spreading their communist 'liberation struggle' throughout the oppressed world. In terms of Jamaica, the Central Intelligence Agency (CIA) and its allies on the island fought it out with Cuba's KGB-trained intelligence arm, the General Directorate of Intelligence (DGI).

In the end, it was to prove an extremely costly game for Jamaica – especially for the thousands whose lives were sacrificed in the interests of a decisive political victory that never materialised. After almost a decade, the game would end in the frightening consolidation of political tribalism. The tribal endgame, so to speak, would be the inferno of the 1980 general election campaign, which dragged the country to the brink of all-out civil war.

There was to be no outright winner, but one group of Jamaicans benefited more than any other. This was the assortment of vicious, political-cum-drug trafficking gunmen; the Rude Boys who defended the garrison constituencies, and waged a bloody war on their enemies in the interests of their political paymasters.

Not only did they receive guns and money for their murderous services, but through their associations with the foreign players they gained invaluable insights into espionage techniques. As the rudies branched out in later years these techniques would greatly assist their gangster careers. Over the same period, the growing involvement of these gangsters in the illicit, money-spinning international ganja trade would see them become more and more independent of their political patrons. The posses were riding in.

The advent of the posses was greatly assisted by a number of other adverse factors: the continuing decline of the Jamaican economy; government inefficiency; the

uncheckable expansion of the ghetto suffering and neglect;
the growing involvement of Jamaican criminals in the
international drug trafficking trade; and, the failings of
the island's political establishment, security forces and
judiciary to stamp out violent crime.

The Jamaican economy went through a boom period in
the 1960s under the JLP government's tenure. However, as
the country entered the 1970s the economic bubble burst,
and the world was plunged into recession. In spite of adverse
overseas developments, at home people grew more and more
dissatisfied with the Government's overall performance.

The forgotten agricultural sector, once the envy of the
British Empire, was moving closer to enforced extinction.
Jamaica, a natural foodbasket, was forced to import
increasing quantities of basic foodstuffs from abroad
to feed its own people. Meanwhile, hundreds of small
farmers were being forced off the land to accommodate
foreign bauxite interests, and thousands of acres of
government land lay fallow.

Unemployment hovered around the twenty-five per
cent mark, double or more in the ghettoes and shanties. For everyone, the cost of living outstripped their
frugal resources; poverty was becoming big business.
The newly-formed Organisation of Petroleum Exporting
Countries (OPEC) massively increased petrol prices and
as a result Jamaicans saw the price double, and then treble,
at the petrol pumps.

Ordinary Jamaicans blamed their problems on the JLP's
rudimentary mismanagement of the national economy.
The 'free enterprise' culture, the masses complained, was
only making the rich richer, and them poorer. By the time
of the 1972 General Election the vast majority of the Sufferers were ripe for a radical change of political direction.

And who better to chart a new course than a revitalised
People's National Party with a new captain on the bridge?
The new skipper was the inspirational and charismatic

Michael Norman Manley, a former Second World War Royal Canadian Air Force gunner who had been elected to replace his father as PNP supremo in 1969.

Descended from a struggling, lower-middle class family, Michael Manley was (and is) an unrivalled champion of the rights of the poor and the dispossessed. In 1978, for example, he was awarded a medal by the United Nations for his forceful stand against apartheid.

A London-trained journalist and a gifted orator to boot, Manley put his communication skills to good use during the 1972 election campaign. He wooed the middle classes, and projected himself as a saviour-in-waiting of the working poor. An unlikely phenomenon, perhaps, but Manley was highly persuasive.

That said, it was with the Sufferers that he registered most success. Out on the hustings Manley sported 'regulation' Third World leaders' khaki suit fatigues, and carried a cane, his so-called Rod of Correction. A gift from Emperor Haile Selassie of Ethiopia – the living God of Rastafari – along with his Black Power-laden speeches, it helped him to enlist the support of disillusioned voters. Manley was especially successful with the Rastas and militant young dispossessed.

From thereon, like Midas, everything Manley touched turned to gold. He became a sensational hit among Jamaica's forgotten who affectionately dubbed him 'Joshua', the warrior successor of Moses who led the Jews into the battle of Jericho. Even his election campaign song, 'Better Must Come', stormed to Number One in the Jamaican reggae charts.

Finally, after ten years of independence and two terms in the political wilderness, the PNP was returned to government with a mandate in 1972. Now all Manley had to do was to honour his election pledge to deliver 'Power for the People'.

*   *   *

Under Prime Minister Michael Manley the PNP's laudable
intentions were to improve the lot of the common people,
with the emphasis firmly on the beleaguered poor. In fairness
to him, there were mixed successes. Tens of thousands of
desperately needed public jobs were created but they merely
drained the public reserves. Basic wages were raised to
keep pace with inflation. Unfortunately, though, inflation
was hovering round the twenty per cent mark at the time.

Indeed, most of Jamaica's woes were precipitated by
the arrant failure of his government's fanciful policies and
myopic mismanagement. In short, the PNP's remedies
only accentuated the nation's heartache.

Between 1972 and 1976, the PNP's reforms dealt a
severe bodyblow to the economy and the people. Not
helped by the worldwide recession, agricultural exports
slumped and industrial output was retarded. Unemployment rose, and the cost of living shot up.

Then in September 1974 the Prime Minister instigated
his disastrous and ill-conceived flirtation with 'democratic
socialism', a paradoxical, tragi-comic and unworkable
mixture of free marketeering and rabidly anti-capitalistic
Marxism. It was instant anathema to the party's middle-
class 'uptown' supporters, many of whom simply packed
their bags, emptied their foreign currency-laden bank
accounts and checked out of Jamaica.

The government's overall problems were heightened by
the island's mushrooming population. The census of 1960
estimated the national population at 1.6 million people.
Ten years later that figure had risen by 300,000 to 1.9
million. Fuelled by a birth rate of more than two per
cent, Jamaica, or Jamdown, was becoming much younger.
Inevitably, finding employment was an impossible task,
even for the able-bodied younger generation.

The demographic shift towards Kingston also continued. By the mid-1970s, the population of the Corporate
Area had swollen to about 750,000. More than anywhere

else, Kingston's columns of inner city misery, neglect and deprivation were becoming monuments to the failure of the Jamaican Government to build a meaningful social and ecomomic future for the country.

For ghetto Kingston's youthful aspirants – many of whom were runaways from the poverty-stricken rural interior – this was not good enough. After all, they had seen *The Harder They Come*, the seminal Jamaican movie in which singer-actor Jimmy Cliff made it big; the Jamaican reggae star's country boy character had made its mark on the embryonic reggae industry. The hopeful young were equally determined to make it anyhow they could – even if it meant joining the overcrowded ranks of the capital's nihilistic two-gun kids.

The expansion of all types of crime was a by-product of Jamaica's ongoing slide towards social and economic anarchy; had it been a bona fide industry, crime would have qualified for attractive government tax incentives. Violent offences – especially political and crime-related – were particularly well represented. But previously unknown acts of violence such as mob attacks and domestic incidents also emerged to take their place in the demonology of Jamaican crime.

One crime, a foiled, attempted armed hold-up, went tragically wrong for one of the villains. The bungled robbery took place in Trench Town in mid-November 1974. It started when two men – one brandishing a gun, the other a knife – burst into a building, and announced their intentions. The victims were ordered to lie down. As the robbers made the rounds collecting booty, one of the prostrate victims wrestled the gunman to the ground. While his accomplice fled, the captured man was set upon by his would-be victims. They beat him to death. Exceptional though this was, it became a metaphor for the way crime had degenerated in Jamaica – it took place

in the hallowed confines of a church. In fact, the lynch
mob was comprised of Seventh Day Adventists. Since
the 1970s fatal mob attacks of this kind have become
commonplace. As the combined forces of the State failed
to arrest the unprecedented crime wave, otherwise law-
abiding Jamaican citizens were transformed into violent
vigilantes. And vigilantism was joined by record levels
of social and domestic violence in an ever expanding
catalogue of Jamaican violent crime. Almost overnight
the simmering pressures of ghetto existence boiled over
into a wave of frenzied attacks.

Gone were the days when minor disputes were settled
by idle threats; the 1970s were about payback. Retribution
and revenge, not reconciliation. The new 'mediators'
were knives, machetes and, in middle-class households,
guns. So husbands set about their wives, and wives
their husbands. Families attacked hostile neighbours,
unwelcome strangers and even friends. And disgruntled
business associates clashed violently with one other. It
was as if brute force had supplanted reason.

Naturally, there was mounting concern amongst ordinary Jamaicans about the progress of violent crime. Yet,
it was nothing compared to that registered over the disturbing consolidation of political and criminal offences.

In the topsy-turvy world of 1970s Jamaica Rude Boys
saw violent crime as the ultimate antidote. Intrinsically
passive offences such as prostitution, gambling and petty
theft began to face stiff competition from the growth of
violent pretenders. Robbery, rape and mugging became
the latest 'in' crimes, reported incidents doubling over the
fifteen-year period ending 1990.

Violent crime reached its peak in the 1970s. In 1978,
halfway through the Manley government's second term,
cases of reported violent crime stood at 16,000, an almost
150 per cent increase since 1970. Astonishingly, the homicide tally in the 1970s surpassed even that astronomical

rate of growth. Acquiring reliable homicide statistics for Jamaica has proved extremely difficult – numerous murder victims 'go missing' – but there can be no denying the unrelenting upward spiral Jamaica suffered.

Thus, in the 'halcyon' days before guns became as common as dogs in the ghettoes, the annual murder rate oscillated between fifty-seven (1962) and seventy-seven (1964). It topped the hundred mark for the first time in 1967, and has continued its relentless ascent ever since. The statistics for the 1970s tell their own story. One hundred and thirty homicides were perpetrated in 1970; 226 in 1975; and a staggering 409 in 1977 – a fourfold increase in only a decade. Far worse was to come in the 1980s and 1990s.

Kingston, the scene today of three-quarters of the island's crimes, bore the brunt of the sharp increase in shootings and murders. In the decade after independence reported shootings increased tenfold, while there was a 450 per cent rise in the murder rate. In fact, by 1973 Kingston's gunmen were significantly outkilling their peers in New York on a per capita basis.

Most murder victims fell foul of gang-related crime or violent political tribalism. Ruthless rudie deviants were behind much of the slaughter. This knowledge, however, did not assuage the fears of the mass of ordinary, law-abiding Jamaican people, Kingstonians especially.

During the 1970s, Kingston's middle classes and the property in their well-fortified homes had become regular targets for downtown gun bandits. Petrified for their personal safety, the victims had begun to aggressively lobby the Government for protection.

Matters came to an abrupt head early in 1974 when, within the space of a week, four prominent Kingston business leaders were shot dead by robbers. The shootings all bore what was becoming the all too familiar hallmark of Kingston's rudie gunslingers: the premeditated slaughter of the victims; dead victims cannot make statements to the police.

These mindless murders led the whole of Jamaica to vigorously renew its demands for remedial government action. All over the ghettoes graffiti called for public executions – even charitable societies wanted firing squads. The long-suffering Jamaican people had had enough.

In March 1974, a beleaguered Prime Minister Manley launched an unprecedented counter-offensive to save his struggling government. He announced a unilateral war on violent crime and the gun terrorists. A Ministry of National Security, under the command of Eli Matalon, was expeditiously formed to spearhead the war effort. Matalon, who blamed the crime crisis on the mushrooming trade in ganja, guns, and cocaine, was given two new legislative weapons: the Suppression of Crime (Special Provisions) Act and the Gun Court Act.

The introduction of the new measures was warmly welcomed by the Jamaican public – initially at least. The harsh measures attracted strong cross-party support, too. Manley's government had temporarily been spared.

The Suppression Act was enacted as a 'temporary' measure to tackle the island's serious and growing crime epidemic. That it was not repealed until March 1994 provides a cogent indication of just how deeply the culture of violent crime has become engrained into the fabric of Jamaican society.

As soon as the public wised up to its repressive nature, however, the Act became a magnet for controversy. In theory, it granted extraordinary powers to the security forces – hence (Special Provisions) – to give them a much-needed edge in their losing battle against the rudie offenders. Amongst other things they were empowered to set up roadblocks and implement curfews.

But in reality, the measure empowered law enforcement agents at the expense of those whose rights they were putatively there to protect. The Suppression Act was a blatantly unconstitutional breach of the civil, legal and human rights of the individual. 'Special Provisions' was coterminous with giving police and soldiers *carte blanche* to search, arrest and detain people in the supposed search for illegal guns and ammunition; to raid private homes and seize property on spurious grounds. Both without producing a warrant.

As unpalatable as the Act turned out to be, it was innocuous in the face of the Gun Court Act, the most draconian piece of legislation ever to be entered on to independent Jamaica's Statute Books. Passed rapidly through Parliament it, too, was supposed to be a stop-gap measure. But, unlike the Suppression Act, this legislation is still in force.

Under its auspices, the Gun Court was constructed on wasteland off Camp Road in Kingston. It is a truly imposing structure, resembling the centrepiece from the set of a movie about a German concentration camp, and the effect is deliberate. The camp boasts towering look-out posts manned by heavily-armed police officers. It is fortified by ten-feet-high mesh fencing, topped off with coils of barbed razor wire four feet in diameter. When it was originally constructed the whole compound, including the wire, was painted bright red in a rather theatrical attempt at psychological warfare. Whatever its outward appearance, the Gun Court stands as a living monument to the inexorable rise of criminal gun violence in Jamaica, and the Governments' failure to reduce it to manageable levels.

The purpose of the Gun Court was, and is, to expedite the judicial process. Trials are held *in camera* before a single magistrate. The court-cum-jail deals with criminal cases in which an illegal gun has allegedly been used (even if the weapon has not been discharged) and with people found in possession of weapons and ammunition. One can even be tried for alleged possession of a spent shell casing.

Introduced by Michael Manley, an acclaimed advocate of human rights causes, the judicial process is conspicuous for the way its operation militates against the interests of those on trial. Defendants have few rights in this conveyor-belt system of justice. No bail. No appeals process.

When it was launched in 1974 Gun Court cases were intended to be dealt with within a week, but the weight of pending cases soon created a substantial backlog. At first, those convicted faced indeterminate sentences, usually at hard labour. But the Privy Council in Britain (the final arbiter of Jamaican justice issues) protested against the unconstitutional nature of the court's sentencing policy. Under severe pressure, the Manley government made a marginal volte-face. The maximum sentence for gun crimes was downgraded from limitless detention to mandatory life imprisonment.

In spite of the controversy it attracted, the Suppression Act achieved some success; many suspected felons were rounded up. But the most destructive criminals were too slick to be caught out by the Act. They merely wrapped up their guns, buried them and took time out to plan their next offences while the heat died down. There was only one failsafe method to stop the 'hard gunman', confided Thomas Surridge, the Commissioner of Corrections at the time, and that was 'to shoot him'. Everybody agreed.

Still, the Gun Court Act enjoyed by far the most success. Before it was enacted, a moratorium had been placed on the owners of illegal weapons and ammunition. Posters were plastered throughout the island urging felons to turn in their guns and ammunition at churches, with no questions asked. This progressive strategy netted a substantial armoury of illegal weaponry, which no doubt made a significant contribution to the brief, but noteworthy reduction in gun crimes over the following months. During the second quarter of 1974 – the first three months of the Gun Court – there were eight gun killings and sixty-nine shootings. By contrast, in the first quarter of 1974, twenty-nine people had been shot dead and another 180 wounded.

However, as the galloping homicide statistics demonstrate, the Gun Court's 'honeymoon' period was short-lived. Like rats that develop a tolerance to poison, rudie gunmen returned to their murderous exploits in short order. After all, the appalling social and economic conditions that characterise Jamaican ghetto life had not miraculously evaporated with Manley's legislative double-whammy. Critically, though, the island's ruthless gangsters were patently aware that their murderous deeds could end with a judge ordering that they be hanged until dead.

The death penalty has been on the Jamaican Statute Books since the Offences Against the Person Act was passed in 1864, a year before the epoch-making Morant Bay uprising. From the end of the Second World War to April 1976 Jamaica executed an average of five people a year.

Interestingly, execution was placed in abeyance from 1976 to 1980 while the Jamaican Parliament debated the issue of capital punishment. By the time the House of Representatives voted in favour of its retention, the Death Row population had jumped from thirty-six to seventy-nine – another vivid expression of the upsurge in murder. Jamaica's condemned prison population continued to expand until the 1990s, when a change in the law led to a reduction in those awaiting death.

When Michael Manley had been out on the election trail in 1972, there were those who believed that once in office, this paragon of socialist virtues would legalise the people's drug, ganja. The optimism was ill-founded. Manley's crisis-ridden government initiated an unprecedented rearguard action against the island's burgeoning international drug trafficking industry.

In some respects, Manley's offensive was symptomatic of the PNP Government's wider assault on violent crime. The fact was that competition stemming from expansion of the underworld industry had sparked a serious escalation of gun violence. The already entrenched JCF was finding that more and more of its energies were consumed in a never-ending, increasingly dangerous, uphill battle against ruthless narco-terrorists; rudies who were now routinely slinging M-16s and more powerful pistols at the law, and their drug rivals. There was untold slaughter on the streets.

A growing number of murders were of the original big-time drug dealers. Instrumental in the starting up of the trade in the 1960s, the Rude Boys deemed some original movers surplus to requirements in the 1970s. At the other end of the spectrum, public figures who vociferously opposed the trade were also being singled out for termination. In 1974, for example, an attempt was made on Matalan's life in Miami – it was put down to irate Jamaican ganja interests.

The illegal ganja trade, and the Rude Boy gangs' role in it, had grown tremendously, making the tens of millions of American dollars it accumulated during the mid- to late 1960s seem like small change.

In only ten years, Jamaica had grown to become the principal supplier of ganja to the United States. American drug enforcement operatives reckoned at least a ton of ganja (valued at US$400,000) was breaching the country's coastal defences every day. That made the industry worth approximately US$200 million a year; the *Financial Times* put annual profits as high as US$400 million. Another indication that ganja trading was where the smart money was came in the belated entry of the American Mafia, the corporate giant of organised crime.

Manley's cash-strapped security forces could not combat this bustling illegal industry on their own. Instead, in a bold and some said irresponsible move, the Jamaican Prime Minister enlisted the support of the United States. In what was to become the biggest operation of its kind mounted by the United States in a foreign country, a multi-agency government task force set about the arduous task of eradicating Jamaican ganja plantations, and cutting off supply lines for hard and soft drugs to American markets.

Codenamed Operation Buccaneer, the venture was spearheaded by America's Drug Enforcement Agency (DEA). The Americans were determined to leave no stone unturned. Undercover agents, intelligence analysts and troops were deployed. Radar, ships and planes were utilised. Helicopters were used to locate plantations in slash and burn sorties. It must have seemed as if an invasion force had taken over the heart of rural Jamaica.

Naturally, the joint American-Jamaican anti-drug effort did not accomplish its lofty ambition, but nonetheless it enjoyed unparalleled success. In five months, the task force had confiscated 325 tons of ganja and twenty pounds of cocaine, and seized about a dozen firearms and numerous boats.

The success of the first Buccaneer programme was built upon in its sequels. By 1993 Operation Buccaneer was on to its seventh installment.

Not long after after Manley turned to the Americans for assistance with his anti-ganja crusade, he was to implicate them in the destabilisation of Jamaica. And so began one of the most intriguing and bloody periods in modern Jamaican history.

The roots of this era can be traced back to the tensions between the United States and Cuba from the early 1900s onwards. From the turn of the century until 1959, the former Spanish Caribbean colony was little more than a large doormat with 'Welcome to the US territories' scrawled across it. Government, although nominally democratic, was corrupt, and took its orders from the United States. Alternatively the White House would dispatch its troops – as it did in 1906 – to make way for a compliant puppet regime.

That was the pattern up to 1 January 1956. Then Fidel Castro's 26th of July Movement inherited the government; and a new and unsavoury phase in US-Cuban relations began.

Had Castro's primary intention been to ward off the Americans he could not have been more successful. Over the next several years his reforms sent the Americans into a rage of paranoia; the biggest fear being that he intended to install a communist regime in their 'backyard'.

Castro started out by liquidating American business interests in Cuba, giving American-owned land to the peasantry, and installing an avowedly socialist, one-party government. At the same time, he began to befriend Nikita Khruschev's Soviet Union.

Alarmed, the Eisenhower Administration imposed a unilateral trade embargo on Cuba in October 1960. Even before this the President had endorsed a plan to overthrow the Castro regime. There had even been talk of an American military invasion; anti-Castro exiles had been trained in readiness, but the plan was put on hold. The plan was later approved by President John F. Kennedy; opening one of the most ignominious chapters in modern American history, the Playa Giron fiasco.

Better known as the Bay of Pigs, it involved well over a thousand CIA-armed and -trained Cuban exiles who returned to Cuba in April 1961. However, their planned takeover failed, and the Cuban dictator had the self-styled 'salvation' force rounded up on 1 May 1961, coincidentally the same day Castro declared that Cuba would become a socialist state.

Eighteen months later Kennedy was notified of hidden Soviet ballistic missiles and silos in Cuba. In retaliation, the American President imposed an immediate naval blockade of the island, and only lifted it when the missiles had been removed.

As US-Cuban relations reached their nadir, the Cuban-Soviet relationship went from strength to strength. Cuba began to receive millions of dollars in economic assistance, and billions of dollars-worth of military hardware from the Soviets. For decades to come, America's foreign policy implementation with regard to Cuba was defined by blinkered hostility and lunatic suspicion; Cuba had to be placed in international purdah, and prevented from spreading the disease of communism to other countries.

By the mid-1960s, the inherent weaknesses in this isolationist strategy were exposed. An emboldened Cuba demonstrated its utter contempt for the United States by dispatching small-scale troop contingents and weaponry to support various liberation struggles in Africa. The Cubans were going global.

Equally galling, by the early 1970s, headed by Michael Manley, Caribbean countries were extending the olive branch of friendship towards Cuba. But the Jamaican demagogue's affinity for Castro was not the Americans' sole worry; his arrant 'Anti-Americanism' was becoming a greater concern.

In May 1974, Manley had introduced a unilateral, non-negotiable 700 per cent increase in the bauxite production levy, and the spontaneous nationalisation of most of the industry. Then, in the autumn, the PNP adopted borderline-Marxist 'democratic socialism'. What could the Americans expect next? They waited an anxious eighteen months for the answer.

Beginning in the winter of 1975, Castro had posted tens of thousands of Cuban soldiers to Angola, a former Portuguese colony, to fight alongside the freedom fighters of the Popular Front for the Liberation of Angola (MPLA). Soldiers of the legitimate Marxist MPLA Government had been waging a long and losing battle against the American-backed South African army and, until the Cuban troops arrived, had been staring a crushing defeat in the face.

In the United States, Gerald Ford's administration had 'advised' Manley's increasingly wayward government to keep its nose out of the affair. Already jumpy about Manley's intentions and quickly losing patience with him, the United States wanted this latest issue resolved once and for all.

Proof came in December 1975 when Henry Kissinger, the American Secretary of State, paid an unofficial visit to Jamaica. At a luncheon with Manley, Kissinger, who was honeymooning in Jamaica, drove home the American position in a classic piece of iron-fist diplomacy. The diplomatic heavyweight all but threatened to cancel a US$100 million trade advance to Jamaica if the Prime Minister uttered his support for Cuban intervention in Angola.

Manley supported the Cubans, anyway. Needless to say, the anticipated American trade package never materialised. What there was, however, was a marked increase in the visible problems encountered by the Manley Government at home and abroad in the period leading up to the 1976 General Election.

It was against this conflict-ridden background that the destabilisation of Jamaica began in the mid-1970s. It is virtually impossible to pin a precise date on the start of the United States' anti-Jamaica campaign, – not least because the PNP was doing a good job of destabilising the country on its own. What is clear, though, is that once the plan had swung into motion it found a formidable ally in a revitalised JLP.

A major change had taken place in the JLP not long before the PNP started talking about a concerted and organised dirty tricks campaign being waged against the party. In November 1974, Edward Seaga took over as party leader. The Americans had always favoured the JLP (a vehemently anti-communist party since Bustamante's day) over their socialist-inclined rivals. It is well known, for example, that the American Ambassador to Jamaica had wanted the conservative JLP to win the 1972 election.

In Seaga, the Americans found a man who was tailor-made for the job of undermining Manley; a sleeper who, if needed, could be activated whenever they saw fit. Whispers about 'Mr Eddie' being an American stooge began immediately after he assumed command of the JLP – a year before Manley's public support of Castro's intervention in Angola.

All of a sudden throughout PNP strongholds a new line in graffiti emerged to confirm these suspicions. Seaga became *CIA*ga. It did not help that he was born and raised in the United States. It was even whispered that the Opposition boss had been recruited by the CIA while studying at Harvard in the 1950s.

Sleeper or not, Seaga was responsible for the opening shots of the destabilisation campaign. The volley came in January 1975, just two months after his promotion. It related to the JLP supremo's demand for a State of Emergency to counteract the worrying upsurge in frenzied criminal violence in the capital. Explicit in this failed demand, however, was the notion that the violent political and criminal disorder was being executed by PNP factions with the blessing of high-ranking government ministers.

colleagues went so far as to single out the notorious
Garrison Gang, a pro-PNP faction from Concrete Jungle,
the purpose-built government housing project in Arnette
Gardens.

It cannot be denied that the ruthless Garrison gangsters
kept JLP areas under a constant barrage of attacks. The
mobsters attacked and shot up JLP rallies and meetings, and terrorised, shot and killed JLP supporters. In
one infamous incident, heavily-armed Garrison guerrillas
stormed the JLP's office in neighbouring Jones Town brutally murdering a staunch JLP supporter, a seventy-nine
year-old woman.

Whatever the scale of the Garrison Gang's atrocities,
the JLP and its supporters were not totally blameless.
Manley was quick to answer his detractors by drawing
attention to the bloodthirsty excesses of violent pro-JLP
criminal gangs in Tivoli Gardens and Rema.

In the same way that the political war had begun to
intensify around the end of 1974, so too the propaganda
offensive was injected with new venom. Seaga scored the
first major victory in March 1975. The occasion revolved
around Manley's attendance at the funeral of Winston
'Burry Boy' Blake. An acclaimed PNP enforcer and
criminal who had been tried and acquitted of murder
on a least two occasions, Blake's coffin was draped with
a PNP flag, and he was sent on his way with a mighty
graveside gun salute.

In the event, the PNP dignitaries almost did not make
it to the cemetery. Eight mourners were injured when
the large procession was sniped at as it moved through
Tivoli Gardens. Seaga never denied his supporters did
the shooting, but characteristically blamed the incident on
the funeral cortège for passing so close to Tivoli Gardens,
even though they were on a public thoroughfare.

Manley's biggest problem, though, was how to explain

away his presence at a gunman's funeral. His lame attempt to pass his former chauffeur-cum-bodyguard off as a reformed character was met with howls of derision.

The events of the following months and years were to see the JLP come under increasing suspicion as the prime fomenters of subversive mayhem and sadistic violence. Similarly, as the destabilisation campaign took its toll, Michael Manley's and his government's problems were to become immense.

The beginning of 1976 marked a turning point in the Government's abysmal fortunes. At the beginning of what was to become the most violent and bloody election year in Jamaican history, the idea of a concerted effort to destabilise Jamaica was seriously considered for the first time.

The unlikely setting was the staging of a three-day International Monetary Fund (IMF) and World Bank convention in Kingston during the first week of the year. With the finance ministers and officials of 128 countries and 150 representatives of the world's media in attendance, the last thing the Manley government needed was the embarrassment of an outbreak of violence.

On the eve of the delegates' arrival, heavily-armed JLP Rude Boys swamped the PNP's Trench Town stronghold near the city centre. Fierce gun battles erupted between rival rudie factions, and carried on throughout the night. But the sporadic machine-gun fire was barely audible against the roar of the twenty-house inferno ignited by JLP firebombs.

There was no relief the following day. As the delegates assembled at the plush multi-storey Pegasus Hotel on Knutsford Boulevard, a highly-organised phalanx of the PNP supporters protested outside about the participation of a delegation from apartheid-ridden South Africa. JLP infiltrators cajoled them into moving their protest to the American Consulate around the corner on Oxford Road.

Chanting regressed into stone-throwing. Fully-fledged violence followed, and the disturbances fanned out like a fire across the city. In the course of the mayhem, shops were looted and burned to the ground. An untold number of civilians were wounded and killed. And four policemen were slaughtered, including two who were guarding the American Consulate, and their service revolvers stolen.

With the shockwaves still ringing in his ears, Manley, who had started a 'destabilisation diary', went on national television to spell out his analysis of these disgraceful incidents, and invoked the Suppression Act to impose martial law on the affected areas. The Prime Minister was convinced that what he called the 'sustained display of political violence' had been orchestrated to give the impression to the world that Jamaica was ungovernable.

Manley and others were equally unambiguous about the cause of the violent unrest. In a rare display of directness, Manley accused the JLP of hiring criminal gunmen to usurp his government's power. Keble Munn, the National Security and Justice Minister, made full use of his political privileges to charge the JLP of arming, training and bankrolling the political terrorists.

There was to be little respite for the beleaguered Manley government over the coming months as JLP Rude Boy gangs led sustained attacks on PNP positions. His ongoing – some maintained, politically suicidal – relationship with Castro also made him the focus for JLP attacks.

Some good came of this, too. One highly controversial piece of Cuban assistance was the *brigadista* training programme. Beginning in May 1975 Castro agreed to train a group of largely unemployed young men in construction techniques. The training schedule lasted a year, and, to the dismay of the Labourites, took place in Cuba. Needless to say, the JLP used the exercise to insinuate that Manley was packing off PNP thugs for political indoctrination and military training.

The overall plot was thickened by other visits paid by top-ranking Jamaican civil servants and leading politicians to Cuba. The JLP was unhappy to see senior police officers making the ninety-mile trip to Cuba for additional training, exercises party leaders claimed were a prelude to covert police spying missions on their committed activists.

Neither were the Opposition enamoured of top PNP ministers flying to Cuba for regular meetings with their counterparts in Castro's 'Politburo'. They, too, were accused by JLP stalwarts of going to Havana for covert training in how to manipulate the privileges of state office in order to keep their slimy grip on power.

Of equally grave concern was the growing spectre of Cubans on Jamaican soil. Castro had dispatched a number of construction workers and engineers to work on various humanitarian projects. The first of them was the Jose Marti School, a technical high school in Spanish Town. A present from Cuba, it was officially opened shortly before the 1976 General Election.

Castro's construction task force was joined by teachers and agronomists. Cuban nurses and doctors also helped to provide basic health care in neglected rural areas. In the main, these workers were welcomed by Jamaicans.

The same cannot be said of other Cubans who visited the island during the mid-1970s. According to the JLP's propaganda machine, this group was comprised of shadowy official figures. The JLP had it that Manley's government was being overly influenced – run even – by Cuban secret agents. Leading KGB-trained General Directorate of Intelligence subversives were said to be making regular trips to Jamaica to brief and advise the Government. It was even suggested that Castro was supplying the PNP with arms and money to ensure the success of his seditious communist empire-building project.

This intriguing situation gave a heightened intensity to the tribal gang war when it resumed with a vengeance in May 1976. It almost seemed that with the stakes so high, renewed barbarity was required to prevail in the struggle. On the same day that a policeman was fatally gunned down by a vicious gang in the course of a £30,000 bank raid, political shootings claimed another five victims. In all, sixteen people were murdered as a result of political tribalism in the week starting 3 May. The PNP was particularly hard hit. At least twenty members of its 60,000-strong left-wing Youth Organisation were killed in the month to mid-May.

The spate of gun killings was carried out in tandem with massive destruction of property. Bombings – explosive and incendiary – left gaping holes all over the decaying ghetto landscape of west Kingston, consuming shops, homes and anything else that stood in their path.

Then, on 19 May, probably the most ghastly episode in the war to that point was perpetrated. In a methodical display of ruthlessness, up to fifty armed JLP strongmen surrounded an overpopulated, ramshackle PNP tenement yard and firebombed it. As frightened residents tried frantically to escape they were forced to retreat into the fireball by shooting from the callous guerrilla forces. There were even reports of fleeing residents being manually tossed back into the blazing building – even fire crews were shot at.

By the time the situation had been brought under control three adults and eight small children had been killed in the inferno, and another 500 rendered homeless. The police killed one of the gun-toting arsonists, a thirteen-year-old boy.

The political and criminal atrocities continued in June. These included an indiscriminate JLP machine-gun attack on a PNP club which left six dead. And the murder of Fernando Rodriguez, the Peruvian Ambassador, stabbed to death at his residence. This killing actually bore all the hallmarks of a tragic, but straightforward burglary. But, for the Government, it just added further to fears about destabilisation.

By June the year's death toll had climbed to 163, including nineteen policemen. Once again, the Manley government was forced to contemplate ever more draconian measures to stem the plague of gun madness that was threatening to bring it to its knees. By all accounts, the declaration of a State of Emergency had already been mooted when a sensational development occurred which was to make one inevitable.

On 18 June, the oddly named Herb Rose resigned from the Jamaica Labour Party. A JLP Executive Member, Rose had been working closely with the deputy leader, the then Senator Pearnel Charles, on the party's pre-election campaign strategy. He had performed similar duties within the PNP in the early 1970s.

In dynamite style, Rose alleged that the Labour Party was both masterminding and fomenting the wave of criminal and political violence. At the behest of senior politicians, the JLP was 'training young men to commit violent crimes as part of its strategy to undermine confidence in the government,' he claimed. Furthermore, he alleged that the party was giving ammunition to 'half starved and maltreated youngsters and encouraging them to take up a life of crime' in a fiendish bid for electoral success.

The JLP responded to the allegations by branding Rose – a man they said they sacked – a troublemaker. Later, the timing of his allegations were said to be a PNP ploy to justify the imposition of the seditious State of Emergency which came into force on the following day.

The State of Emergency crystallised the Government's

belief that the lawlessness was being whipped up by a treacherous JLP-CIA coalition. Manley never mentioned the agency by name, but manifestly believed its operatives were arming and training the rudie guerrillas. He reminded the people that Dr Salvador Allende's democratically-elected Chilean socialist government had been overthrown by a military coup in September 1973, and screened a film on the CIA's role in it at his constituency office.

Naturally, the United States vehemently denied any CIA interference in Jamaica. Similar denials had been made as regards the CIA's role in Chile. However, the world had learned otherwise during the congressional hearings in the traumatic aftermath of the Watergate Scandal. Three years later, Manley had every reason to suspect the CIA was helping to destabilise Jamaica.

Manley's State of Emergency enjoyed a measure of success unseen since the the introduction of the Suppression and Gun Court Acts in 1974. The Jamaican security forces carried out more than 800 raids; a cache of 257 sticks of dynamite and twenty-five rolls of fuse turning up in one raid in Montego Bay.

Violent crime also underwent a significant decrease. In the month before the emergency 121 shooting incidents had been reported. That fell to sixty during the two succeeding months. An air of normality returned to the island.

This was no doubt aided by the arrests and detention of almost 600 known criminals and (principally JLP) political activists. The disproportionately high number of Labourites detained led to a prolonged assault on the Government's alleged bias from the Opposition benches. By July Seaga was even insinuating that party supporters were being tortured in detention.

One notable JLP detainee was Senator Pearnel Charles.

On Wednesday, June 22 1976, he was arrested and detained in the impromptu detention centre erected at JDF headquarters in Up Park Camp. He would not be released until April 1977, well after the General Election.

Charles was charged with numerous offences, including incitement to murder persons unknown – none of which stuck. (At one stage he went on hunger strike to draw attention to his detention.) The most damning piece of evidence raised against him surrounded the alleged discovery of tape recordings of all military and police broadcasts on the night of the Orange Street Massacre. Sophisticated electronic surveillance equipment was also allegedly unearthed in the search of his home. It was suggested that Charles intended to use the fruits of his espionage for unspecified subversive purposes.

The compromising of Charles, the JLP's election campaign organiser, was a devastating blow to the JLP. But the allegations against Charles were almost inconsequential with the furore over the discovery of certain documents in the possession of a JLP stalwart less than a week later.

At a JLP convention at the Holiday Inn in Montego Bay, a delegate was found to have in his possession two incriminating documents of a highly subversive content, in his handwriting. One referred obliquely to 'ST. ANN'S AREA'. There was a list which read: '22 Trained men; 100 ideological indoctrinated' (sic) and '300 Supporters'. Below that, under the heading 'SUPPLIES', was another list. This one recorded '200 rifles; 100 Sub machine-guns; 2 Barrels of gunpowder'; and '50,000 Anti-government pamphlets'.

The intrigue peaked with the other document which seemed to contain specific plans for the violent overthrow of the Manley government. Headed 'Anti-Communist League' – an unknown force – it mentioned a para-military exercise called 'Operation Werewolf'. (Adolf

Hitler's Fascist admirers had dubbed him Werewolf.)
The whole point of Werewolf, it seemed, was to bring
about a revolutionary change in the way Jamaica was
governed. 'Michael Manley and his Government,' it read
'are dedicated Communists, and we intend to destroy
them at all cost . . . Werewolf is now willing to take up
arms against the Communist regime and purge them from
our shores.' Interestingly, the takeover was to be directed
by a 'High Command', a body which would liaise with
sympathetic 'local or foreign' forces.

Manley informed the House of Representatives about
these two incidents on 29 June. The 'Werewolf Plot'
vindicated his earlier warnings about 'terrorism or even
the overthrow of the duly elected government', he said.
In addition, he denounced 'the standard lie of the Opposition that I am a Communist heading a Communist
government'.

But while Manley made the most of this political wind-
fall, the JLP put in some serious overtime in an attempt to
defuse the charges, passing the 'Werewolf' document off
as the draft of an unpublished anti-communist pamphlet.
It claimed the other list related to plans being hatched
by PNP subversives in the event of the JLP triumphing
at the coming election. Thus, the '22 Trained men' it
mentioned were supposed to be PNP diehards who
had recently returned from Cuba. It was all a cunning
government plot to distort the facts and make the JLP
look like revolutionary terrorists.

In September, it was the turn of the JLP's supposed
mentors to come under fire – literally and metaphori-
cally. That month Philip Agee, an ex-CIA officer with
field experience in Latin America, visited Jamaica. The
veteran's tour, at the invitiation of the Jamaica Council
for Human Rights, was part of a one-man crusade to
expose the CIA's dubious and clandestine practices
around the globe.

Agee's revelations amounted to a carbon copy of what had been happening to Jamaica. He highlighted CIA techniques such as wild domestic and international disinformation campaigns. He mentioned the use of destabilisation techniques such as inciting strikes, organising arson attacks and murders, and the funding, arming and advising of opposition groups.

More damagingly, Agee alleged that the agency was working in concert with the bauxite companies and unnamed JLP supporters to topple the Manley government. The CIA's Kingston station was 'on a war footing', he added. The whistleblower even went so far as to name eleven Kingston-based CIA agents, three of whom left on the first available flight out of Jamaica. The plot thickened.

Although there was a dramatic decline of both political and criminal violence after the State of Emergency came into force, there was not a total cessation of hostilities. In late September, for example, three women were gunned down at their home in Tivoli Gardens. The victims, none of whom had political connections, were shooting the breeze when two PNP rudie gunmen burst in and shot them.

October saw a daring PNP attack on Seaga and former prime minister Hugh Shearer during unofficial election campaigning. As their twenty-car motorcade drove through York Town, a small settlement about forty-five miles outside Kingston, the convoy was sniped at by PNP gunmen sheltering in their party's local office. A fierce gun battle erupted forcing the nationalists to abandon their position. The building was then unceremoniously torched. Seaga and Shearer escaped unharmed, but both sides sustained heavy casualties. In all, ten people were shot, six seriously including two with facial injuries.

However, it seemed the dogs of political warfare were

conserving their energies for the imminent General Election. When, at the end of November, Manley finally called it for 15 December, the tribalism gathered momentum.

By the end of the three-week campaign both parties had lost about ten supporters each in tribal encounters. The dead included two of Seaga's party faithful who were brutally murdered as they slept in a car outside their burned-out party office. PNP insurgents had casually approached the vehicle and shot the occupants in the head at point blank range.

Amid repeated calls for calm – most notably from Manley's faction – the security forces worked overtime to keep the warring gunmen apart. Army reservists were drafted in to boost the peace keeping force to 12,000 islandwide. A permanent security force presence was installed in west Kingston; steel-helmeted soldiers sporting M-16s patrolled the garrison borderlines of volatile party strongholds.

Less than a week before polling day, the Joint Military and Police Command announced that it had thwarted a sinister plot to exacerbate the rising political violence. The plot, which bore all the ghoulish hallmarks of destabilisation, involved a JLP assassin donning a false JDF uniform, and killing a JCF officer. The heads of both institutions jointly appealed for calm.

However, the security forces were powerless to prevent probably the most sensational shooting incident of the campaign. The victim was reggae ambassador, Bob Marley. Marley had been identified, quite correctly, as a PNP sympathiser, a point confirmed by his agreement to perform free of charge at a PNP-organised outdoor concert a fortnight before the election. Unfortunately, three days before the 'Smile Jamaica' event, his Hope Road mansion was stormed by around seven JLP gunmen – Marley's self-styled Echo Squad bodyguard inexplicably having 'vanished' from their posts. Marley, who was shot in the chest, was one of four victims including his wife, Rita Marley. Miraculously, all four survived, although Marley began a period of voluntary foreign exile soon after.

Tribal violence continued right up to election day, including another attempt to kill Manley on polling day. Throughout the campaign Seaga had bullishly continued to associate the Manley government with political violence and Cuban communism. However, the ballot showed his warnings had fallen on deaf ears – in fact many JLP supporters had switched to the nationalists, appreciating Castro's contributions and believing the PNP to be the more passive of the two parties. Manley won what was predicted to be a closely contested poll by a landslide; Seaga had scored a double own goal.

For all that, the Opposition leader continued his attacks, and the Americans their dirty tricks campaign. Jamaica's version of the Cold War was to continue until Manley had been completely erased from the political picture. On his return to office, one of Manley's most pressing priorities was to get the economy back on to an even keel; an economy which had suffered tremendously during his first term.

It did not happen. The 15,000 Manley had added to the mountain of unemployment during his first term grew by another 70,000 during his second. The cost of living rose by 320 per cent; wage rises were capped and taxes increased, helping to set record levels for industrial disputes between 1976 and 1979. Business confidence drained away as hundreds went to the wall, and industrial output dipped sharply. Tourism, a vital earner of foreign exchange, paid the price for Jamaica's developing reputation for violent lawlessness. Bauxite shipments plunged as vital export agriculture stagnated – by the mid-1970s Jamaican sugar cost more to produce than it sold for on the international market.

The impetus for Manley to do something to reverse this situation was apparent long before Jamaica's balance of payment deficit crossed the billion-dollar threshold. In 1977, Manley reluctantly approached the International Monetary Fund (IMF) for assistance.

The 'partnership', which he later denounced as one of the harshest ever imposed by the IMF, was to cost Jamaica dearly. The IMF's stringent 'structural adjustment' programmes caused untold hurt to Jamaica's population. Not without justification, Manley blamed the IMF (an American ally) for their suffering. The people also blamed the IMF, the only problem was that in street parlance its meaning had been changed to 'It's Manley's Fault'.

In March 1980, fourteen months after the tripling of petrol prices had precipitated widespread street demonstrations, the PNP's National Executive voted unanimously to sever its links with the IMF. As an alternative, Manley came up with the grandly-named Operation Reconstruction initiative to rescue the country. It was such a radical departure from the IMF course that the Prime Minister decided the appropriate thing to do was to call a General Election to allow the people to determine its and his government's future.

In doing so, though, Manley had inadvertently made the most catastrophic mistake of his political career. By setting the date for 30 October, eight months away, he put the rudie gun terrorists on an immediate war footing. The price of this honest oversight would become starkly apparent as the bodies piled up in unprecedented numbers along the road to the poll.

While the economy continued to deteriorate during Manley's second term, islanders joked that the illegal earnings from ganja were the only thing that kept it from collapsing altogether. It was no joke. During the late 1970s, Jamaica continued to be a world leader in ganja exports – especially to the United States – pumping tens of millions of American dollars into the ailing economy. Ganja was by far Jamaica's biggest 'agricultural' foreign money-earner, and second only to bauxite, contributing an estimated quarter of the island's total export wealth.

The adverse economic conditions lured more and more people into the drug trade and crime in general. Thousands of peasant farmers began cultivating ganja. Indeed, the fragile economies of entire villages in the hinterlands of Jamaica were shored up by such earnings. Meanwhile, across the island, growing numbers of poorly-paid public officials were finding the lure of the ganja trade irresistible.

But it was society's big fish and the gangsters who continued to profit – and lose – most from the passion for the weed. In spite of increasing competition from Columbia and Mexico, Jamaican ganja kingpins were taking the lion's share of an industry valued at anything up to US$500 million-a-year. Seaga put a US$2 billion tag on it in 1980.

As usual, though, the violence stemming from the trade was often difficult to separate from that emanating from general crime and political tribalism. The only certainty was that record numbers of murders and shootings were being carried out under the broad umbrella of crime.

There was no let up in ganja-for-guns arrangements, either. The main difference now was that the incoming weaponry was increasingly sophisticated and deadly. Such was the heavy traffic in firearms that the ghettoes were reaching saturation point. As a result, perhaps, entrepreneurial ganja dons began to diversify, getting their American contacts to load boats and planes with scarce commodities to be sold illicitly at extravagant mark-ups in Jamaica.

There was one very important change in the perception of the ganja trade, though. It had become politicised, and quickly became another victim of Jamaica's continuing Cold War.

The activities of the Ethiopian Zion Coptic Church (EZCC), a mercurial, Florida-based Rastafari chapter, threw the spotlight on to the CIA. EZCC members, who called for ganja's legalisation, led a most unRasta-like opulent lifestyle. They were Jamaica's second largest landowners, their immense wealth allegedly stemming from growing and exporting ganja, some argued with the complicity of the CIA.

This notion was given added currency towards the end of the 1980s when it was alleged that the CIA had actively supported its allies' drug trafficking escapades in Central America and South-east Asia. And, as recently as October 1994, a former Burma-based DEA agent decided to sue former CIA and State Department officials for allegedly undermining his anti-drug work in this heroin-producing giant.

The American authorities were not alone in incurring the ire of suspicious observers. Pro-JLP forces in Jamaica began to insinuate that a stockpile of lethal weaponry was being supplied by Cuba. Legend had it that the Cubans were selling weapons to anti-democratic PNP forces. The guns, ex-American weapons captured by the North Vietnamese during the Vietnam War, were said to have been purchased with the profits of ganja trafficking in the United States.

The allegation had good destabilisation propaganda value, but was most improbable. Critics rightly asked why ganja traffickers would make a dangerous detour from the United States to Cuba to buy guns when they could get them just as easily in the States? It was nonsensical.

Violent crime continued to add to Manley's fears about an active destabilisation campaign. Only now some of these atrocities were becoming barbaric enough to qualify for consideration as 'war' crimes.

Minor by comparison with those that would follow, Manley's first 'shocker' came in the first week of January 1977. It followed an attack on Lady Sarah Spencer-Churchill – the cousin of British wartime leader, Sir Winston Churchill, who was assaulted and robbed by four armed villains at her Jamaican mansion. A house guest of the friend of the British Royal Family was shot in the shoulder during the frenzied raid.

Lady Spencer-Churchill told reporters that she did not think the assault was connected to Jamaica's unstable political situation; the bandits – 'clearly out of their minds on ganja' – had simply demanded cash and guns. But, even as she vowed to stay on in her beloved Jamaica, the global press reported that many of her wealthy peers were leaving. A case of destabilisation by default.

In the following month the Manley government was rocked by tribal gunplay in Wilton Gardens, or Rema as most know it. The action unfolded in one of the capital's government-built housing projects in a JLP stronghold on the southern fringe of the PNP-held South St Andrew constituency. When the fighting between rival political supporters was over, one JLP supporter was dead, and several others injured.

The Manley government's woes continued for the next four years. On many occasions, Manley resembled an accident-prone somnambulist, clumsily sleep-walking from one crisis to another. Many of his problems unfolded against a background of claims and counter-claims about subversive Cuban and American interference in Jamaica.

One of the biggest scandals surrounded the Moonex Affair. In 1980, Moonex, a company believed to be owned by the Cuban regime, was caught trying to smuggle 200,000 rounds of ammunition into Jamaica.

The company's boss, a Cuban by the name of Ruperto Hart Smith, was arrested as he was about to board a flight from Kingston to Havana, a flight allegedly chartered by the Cuban Ambassador to Jamaica, Ulises Estrada.

Estrada had only recently been taken to task by the JLP. In September 1979, he had warned that the Cubans would fight back against JLP and *Gleaner* smears. Unfortunately for him, his fighting talk was taken literally, leading to calls for his immediate expulsion.

Meanwhile, the Moonex saga was aggravated by the fact that Dudley Thompson, the leftist firebrand in charge of national security, was a passenger on the controversial flight. The *Gleaner* insinuated that Thompson's frequent trips to Cuba were undertaken to facilitate weapons shipments. Meanwhile, the JCF called for the minister's sacking on the grounds that his alleged activities were incommensurate with his lofty position.

Manley's biggest scandal surfaced in January of the previous year. And, with it, the veneer of non-violent respectability the PNP had miraculously managed to maintain throughout its government was painfully stripped away.

Jamaican history records the event as the Green Bay Massacre. Like much of the political turmoil of the time, the precise circumstances surrounding the incident are confused. Not disputed, however, is the fact that five young JLP rudies were massacred at the Green Bay firing range. Equally, no one contests the fact that the killings were carried out by members of the Military Intelligence Unit (MIU) – a branch of the Jamaican Defence Force – during a period when their colleagues were being singled out for execution for the first time.

It was, however, the motivation for the slayings that caused considerable confusion. Was it a reflection of the army's war on violent criminals? Or was it simply a cold-blooded massacre perpetrated by renegade

soldiers in retaliation for the murders of their colleagues?

Manley opted for the former, stating that the dead
were part of Jamaica's biggest and most ruthless criminal
gang, one headquartered in his Kingston constituency.
The longer the controversy raged, however, the more the
smart money was placed on the second option. In fact, it
was rumoured that the victims were among twelve rudies
lured to their deaths on the pretext of picking up weapons
to use in murderous raids on PNP targets.

The Government's handling of the crisis went against
it. In short, it dragged its feet, steadfastly declining to
order the eight soldiers involved to stand trial. (In the
end, the Director of Public Prosecutions offered no case
against the suspects.) Then, the radical tam-wearing
Dudley Thompson sealed its fate when he rather foolishly
declared that 'no angels died at Green Bay'. After that,
the PNP was considered to have come of age as a political
warmonger.

Ironically, the damaging Green Bay Massacre was followed by some rare good news for Manley *et al*, the
announcement of a Rude Boy gang truce in west
Kingston.

The architects were the PNP's Aston 'Bucky Marshall'
Thompson and the JLP's Claudius Massop, two of the
most feared and hated rudie gang leaders in the capital. 'Marshall' controlled the Spanglers gang, while his
entrepreneurial adversary was the Shower Posse's first
commander. They held together a peace that lasted just
over a year.

The sole reason for the peace was the mutual and unacceptable realisation that the rudies and their communities
were being exploited by the politicos. However, the armistice was only the first chapter of the 'Marshall'-Massop
relationship; these were men with a serious mission.

'Marshall,' a twenty-three-year-old whose small frame bore the scars of many a political battle, and Massop, a tall thirty-year-old of débonair appearance, agreed that without revolutionary change the peace could not last. And the only people who could deliver it were the politicians who had something to gain from the violence.

And so the gangland leaders insisted upon a joint meeting with Manley and Seaga where they demanded an end to tribalism, and food, proper sanitation and decent housing for their communities. In addition, what few government jobs there were on offer, they said, should be allocated on merit, not patronage. Above all, the reign of exploitation by self-interested politicians had to stop.

The 'Marshall'-Massop *rapprochement* was also instrumental in setting up a peace committee whose crowning glory was the organisation of the famous 'One Love Peace Concert'. The proceeds were to be used to make a start on improving living conditions in west Kingston.

Staged at the National Stadium on 22 April, the gig featured a star-studded bill including Big Youth, Dennis Brown, Culture, Jacob Miller and Inner Circle, ex-Wailer Peter Tosh, and the great man himself, Bob Marley – Marshall and Massop had personally courted Marley while he was still in self-imposed foreign exile; the legend's return being the first time he had set foot on the island since the 1976 assassination attempt.

The nine-hour extravaganza was a massive success. The star acts pleaded with the rudies to throw away their guns and live in unity. The festivities were capped by a most unlikely event. During an endless rendition of 'Jamming', Marley beckoned Manley and Seaga to come up on stage. As a crowd of 85,000 euphoric – and initially stunned – revellers looked on, Marley held their right hands, raised them aloft and joined them together in a symbolic grasp above his head. It was, by all accounts, a tear-jerking gesture. And that was about the size of it; an emotional and symbolic photo opportunity.

The strains on the gang truce showed throughout the summer and autumn of 1978. By the winter it was being frequently violated. Any hopes of rejuvenating it were dashed on 4 February 1979 when Massop and two allies were shot dead by JCF officers in controversial circumstances. In May 1980, 'Bucky Marshall' was gunned down outside a dancehall session in Brooklyn. Ironically, the reformed gun hawks had fallen prey to gun violence.

The Cold War climate returned all too quickly. Over the next few years there would be numerous incidents which smacked of JLP-organised and CIA-inspired efforts to destabilise the Jamaican Government.

These came to the fore in January 1979 with a wave of rioting over the (IMF-induced) tripling of petrol prices. The nationwide demonstrations were organised by a group calling itself the National Patriotic Movement (NPM), a shadowy JLP front used to whip up social unrest.

Its tactics worked; the ensuing riots all but para-lysed Jamaica. Banks, offices, schools and, at one point, the power station serving Kingston were shut down. Typically, shops were looted and burned. Tourism was disrupted by civilian-erected roadblocks, and bauxite production by unofficial strikes. In all, seven people including three police officers were killed; two of whom died in an attack by Rude Boy mercenaries on their station in Nannyville, near the national stadium.

Seaga accused the Government of employing armed bully boys to shoot at 'peaceful' JLP protesters, and alleged that the PNP was trying to second security force personnel for personal party uses. Both, he said, were part of a devious plan he dubbed the 'Reichstag Plan' to cancel the elections. Manley countered by saying the mayhem was part of 'an organised plot to overthrow (his) government'.

By the autumn, Seaga's American propaganda offensive had plumbed new depths of mischief-making. Whilst in the United States he circulated bogus reports of direct links between the PNP's top brass and the DGI and KGB. In truth, though, only the more hawkish of elected and public officials took them seriously.

For all the political mischief-making 1979 was, by Jamaica's standards, a relatively violence-free year. Just over 200 people were officially reported murdered compared with 381 the previous year. But by any standards 1980 was the mother of all bloodshed.

By 1980, it was no longer sufficient to simply shoot one's political rivals. Now, in order to make full sense of the political ramifications, it was essential that murders left a lasting impression of wanton ruthlessness. Increasingly victims were kidnapped, and gagged and bound with wire before being savagely killed – some unfortunates were even taken to torture chambers and 'interrogated' before execution. Mutilated corpses were dumped with crudely-written signs declaring them 'Labourite' or 'Socialist'.

In April, Manley was sniped at as he was canvassing in the JLP's Southside enclave of his central Kingston constituency. The attack triggered another of Jamaica's famed atrocities: the Gold Street Massacre.

The counter-attack took place at a JLP fundraising dance in Southside a few days later. About 400 revellers were dancing the night away when the session was stormed by about one hundred fatigue-wearing, machine-gun-toting PNP Rude Boys. Miraculously, only five people were killed and ten injured in the lightning attack just yards away from a police station.

May and June saw a wave of nasty, indiscriminate

shootings and murders. On 22 June Jamaica was stunned by the news that the army had thwarted an attempted military coup. The plotters had planned to seize the JDF armoury, kidnap and kill Brigadier Robert Neish, the army Chief of Staff, and force Manley to resign in a nationwide radio broadcast. Rumour had it that Seaga, who was in Washington at the time, was to be asked to take over the premiership.

In spite of its foundation within the military, the conspiracy's designs were attributed to H. Charles Johnson, the only civilian arrested. Johnson was the leader of the little known – and even less-supported – right-wing Jamaica United Front. A security company owner, he was something of a standing joke in Jamaican politics, until it was disclosed that he had fought with the American army in Vietnam.

Naturally, the incident only added to Jamaica's bad press, but even Manley was unconvinced about it being part of the dreaded destabilisation campaign. All he could be sure about was that: 'man and man meet; man recruit man; man and man plan.'

Yet the idea gained support from some unexpected quarters. Andrew Young, US President Jimmy Carter's black ambassador to the United Nations, had only recently warned of an alleged National Security Council plan to destabilise the Manley government. In Jamaica, the now defunct *Daily News* quoted Dr Fred Landis, an American *spy*chologist said to be an expert in CIA psychological warfare techniques. 'There is,' he said, speaking in Kingston, 'a CIA psychological campaign going on in Jamaica on the largest scale in the world since Chile.'

'Any suggestion that the Leader of the Opposition would have been asked to participate in a government takeover by undemocratic means,' stressed JLP deputy leader, Pearnel Charles, 'is a ficticious figment of their imagination.' Meanwhile, from Washington, Seaga rather rashly dismissed the entire affair as a 'comic opera'; a stunt to justify another State of Emergency. However, Jamaicans – and even sections of the American press – tended to agree with the highly-respected Brigadier Neish. This thing had been real.

The prevailing view was bolstered by Louis Wolff in July 1980. The editor of American spy magazine *Covert Action*, Wolff alleged that the CIA had fifteen agents in Kingston. He named N. Richard Kinsman, as station boss.

Two nights later Kinsman's Kingston residence was allegedly machine-gunned and bombed. Suspiciously, however, it was noted that he waited until the following morning to report the attack – to the by now rabidly anti-PNP *Gleaner* as opposed to the police. Also there were no visible signs of an explosion outside his residence. Another episode in CIA destabilisation? Many thought so.

Meanwhile, ruthless tribalism continued. In the early hours of 14 July JLP gunmen kicked off the door of a house in Greenwich Town, and executed seven occupants. A fifteen-month-old baby and a seven-year-old girl looked on as the assassins methodically shot each of the victims in the head.

The children were spared, but that was not the rule. During the same week, one in which at least twenty-five people were slaughtered, a two- and a five-year-old were gunned down as they played innocently in the street. Earlier that morning three women – all aged over sixty-five – were clinically snuffed out as they lay sleeping in their beds. Nobody was given immunity by the rudie merchants of death. Even hospitals, nurses and doctors were seen as legitimate targets.

Once again the situation was growing out of hand. And, once again, nothing the State and its forces did could stop the political warfare and criminal violence.

Liberal estimates put the death toll at 350 by mid-July. In fact, a minimum of 125 people had been slaughtered that month in Kingston alone. Manley and Seaga made a joint appeal for peace.

But a month later came yet another sign that political die hards were not interested in peace. A JLP 'supporter' was arrested during a police raid on a party constituency office. He was found to be in possession of a stolen gun; a gun which had been taken from the body of a police officer murdered the year before.

Day after day, week after week, month after month, the slaughter continued. By October 1980 it was virtually impossible to come up with an accurate estimate of how many people had been killed. Transparently clear, though, was the Rude Boys' acceleration of the killing spree as polling day approached. In the final weeks leading up to it, it was not uncommon to hear of thirty or forty murders. On Nomination Day, three weeks before the election, PNP MP Roy McGann became the first parliamentarian to be gunned down. Another fifty-nine were reported killed in the week leading to the election, bringing to 145 the tally for the month. Meanwhile, many people were simply 'disappearing', never to be seen again.

Polling day was the same as any other for the dedicated Rude Boy guerrillas. Kingston was set ablaze, and Jones Town almost burnt to the ground. Fire fighters were shot at, four JCF officers and two voters slaughtered. MPs were fired at, too.

The cover photograph shows one such incident featuring Edward Seaga – he is the one in dark clothing seen walking away in the right mid-ground. His chief bodyguard, Detective Sergeant Keith 'Trinity' Gardener, a legendary policeman, is the man at the firing end of the rifle (see back illustration).

There were no surprises on election day; the PNP

was crushed, only managing to win nine of Parliament's sixty seats.

In some ways, the long predicted PNP drubbing was coincidental – not least because the tribalism continued as outstanding scores were settled. Forty people were murdered in the first three weeks of November, a reduced rate but nothing to rejoice about. By the end of the year estimates of the annual cull ranged from a liberal 800 through a probable 1,100 to an unlikely 1,300.

So what part did the long destabilisation campaign, as opposed to his own political fecklessness and economic recklessness, play in Manley's demise? Whatever the case, Manley's loss was Seaga's gain. A former governor of the World Bank, he won his long-awaited chance to govern Jamaica. Interestingly, though, he was still Prime Minister elect when he gave his first indication of the path the JLP would not be following. 'When I am sworn in as Prime Minister,' he told a throng of reporters, 'my intention is to ask the Cuban Ambassador to leave Jamaica because he is *persona non grata*.'

At the end of the day, those who did best out of the mayhem were the rudie gangs, or posses as they were calling themselves. It has to be said that no real evidence exists to prove that Cuba and America trained the rudies. That said, though, it is difficult to imagine how they acquired the espionage techniques that they have used since to establish and protect drug gangs in the United States, Canada and Britain, without assistance from these outside forces.

Either way, the skills the Rude Boys acquired during Jamaican political and criminal service stood them in good stead when they began to wander off to foreign parts in the aftermath of the 1980 General Election.

CHAPTER FOUR

Frankenstein's Monsters

'The "don" of today is a drug dealer. Not a ganja pusher. He is a hard drug dealer. Cocaine is bringing tremendous potential money into the equation . . . The new drug don is a very ruthless and very smart person . . . He has big bucks to control, and is smart enough to use those bucks to spread money in a community . . . (to) look after the baby-mothers, and is therefore beginning to represent a very, very serious threat to the way Jamaica is going to develop.'

Prime Minister Michael Manley,
Weekly Gleaner, 10 March 1992

Michael Manley was once again Jamaica's premier when he offered the above analysis – the PNP having kept up the two-term government electoral tradition by trouncing 'Mr Eddie's' JLP in the 1989 General Election. His sobering comments provided the background to the unveiling of a government strategy designed to defeat the island's drug gangs.

What Manley had in mind was an all-out attack on poverty and its root causes allied to a more general assault on violent crime. 'We cannot surrender inner city poverty to anybody,' he declared, 'We cannot.'

Of course, the 'anybody' that had Manley particularly worried was the new wave of drug dons. He identified their emergence with chilling developments that had been taking place in Jamaica's drug culture over the previous fifteen years. During this period, narcotics (especially cocaine and crack, its highly addictive derivative) had, he said, become 'a whole new source of wealth' for indigenous drug overlords.

The benevolence of cocaine dons, argued Manley, had led to the creation of a worrying status quo in the ghettoes; a normality in which the poor had turned otherwise vicious criminals into heroes and saviours. To ignore this, said Manley, was to imperil the future of the nation's children. This deadly monster had to be destroyed once and for all to rescue Jamaica from a violent, drug-induced orgy of self-destruction.

Jamaica's drug culture had indeed undergone a serious transformation since the late 1970s and early 1980s. But the opening of new drug markets within the inner cities was only the tip of the iceberg. Crucially for the political establishment, associated changes had seen the vanquishing of their traditional influence over Kingston's inner city 'garrisons'. Chief amongst these shifts was the fate of their political 'appointees', the political don and his gang. In short, the once undisputed tutelage of the awesome political gang had been usurped by the forces of the almighty drug don.

Indeed, by the time Manley proffered his masterplan for the defeat of the drug don, that dark force had taken control of the 'garrisons'. The drug bosses and their soldiers ruled over the 'garrisons' like feudal lords once did their fiefdoms.

This is not to suggest that the politicians or their gangs have become a totally redundant force in the capital's badlands – fifty years of tribal war have caused too much 'cross-border' animosity for that to happen. Rather, their influence is now largely nominal and symbolic. West Kingston's traditional war-ravaged 'garrison' constituencies still fly the party flags, but today these flutter well below the skull and crossbones of the drug posses. In truth, with the exception of election time, the political don is dead. The cry of the ghettoes today is 'long live the drug don'.

The background to this crucial phase of transition is complex and multifaceted. Suffice it to say, Jamaica's politicos have done more than any other force to make the ascent of the drug don a reality. Like Frankenstein, Jamaica's fickle, corrupt and megalomaniac politicians have created a monster they cannot control; a monster which, at no small cost to Jamaica, follows its own destructive will.

Clearly, the ascent of the posses (a term that came into vogue during the dancehall reggae revival of the early 1980s) to ghetto omnipotence has not been achieved through their fiendish activities alone. In many ways the ground has been cleared for them by the failings of government (and Opposition), the security forces and the judiciary to defeat them.

The Government heads the list of culprits, though. Its incessant failure to correct Jamaica's economic demise has provided the drug dons with a fertile breeding ground to multiply their deadly practices. And through the sponsorship of tribal violence with its concomitant creation of 'garrison' constituencies, the Government has both 'legitimised' inner city gun terror and provided the druggists with well-defined areas in which to continue it.

As prime minister between 1980 and 1989, Edward Seaga made a telling contribution to the rise of the posses at home. Seaga is the antithesis of Manley; a dour, humourless and businesslike professional technocrat. Near-white in complexion, he hails from a well-to-do

Syrian-Jamaican background. A Harvard-trained anthro-
pologist, he went on to study folklore and revivalism in
Jamaica, where he used his studies to forge links with the
people in what is now his constituency.

Legend has it that Seaga was personally recruited
to the JLP by Sir Alexander Bustamante, the party's
founding father; he was said to have 'brains'. If so,
the young pretender did not betray his patron's faith
in him.

In 1962 the ambitious Labourite pulled off a political
masterstroke by winning the depressed Western Kingston
seat. A phenomenally popular MP – amongst his constituents – 'Mr Eddie' has held it ever since. A telling measure
of the respect he commands came at the 1980 General
Election where he polled an incredible ninety-six per cent
of the ballot.

Seaga continued to demonstrate his pedigree as a Member of Parliament after his infamous Back-o-Wall–Tivoli
Gardens adventure. In 1963 he was charged with the
responsibility of drafting the JLP's five-year plan. After
holding the portfolio for Community Development and
Welfare during the JLP's first term, Seaga was promoted
to the pivotal role of Minister for Finance and Planning
during its second and final stint. In 1980, six years after
his elevation to the party leadership, he found himself as
Prime Minister of Jamaica.

As in 1976, Seaga had focused his party's 1980 election
campaign on the theme of the mass suffering caused by
the PNP's catastrophic links with Cuba and communism.
Still, the manufacturing of the communist bogey did not
win him the election. Instead, all the evidence points to
Seaga being elected on the strength of his impressive
management record. When he had told the electorate
that 'Deliverance is Near', echoing the party's election
slogan, they took it to mean economic deliverance. If
anyone could honour his promise that 'money will jingle

in your pockets', it was Jamaican politics' cool-headed, technocratic whizzkid.

Needless to say, it did not pan out like that. Even so, Seaga cannot be faulted for his selfless efforts. An autocratic leader, like Atlas, he single-handedly shouldered the burden of Jamaica's responsibilities. Much to the distress of his fellow parliamentarians, the workaholic personally took control of the ministries of finance and planning, information, culture, and defence.

Seaga came up with a two-pronged economic 'deliverance' strategy dubbed 'Seaganomics', in deference to his recently elected American ally, President Ronald Reagan. The first plank was the transformation of the Jamaican economy into a model of state-engineered capitalism; Jamaica was to become a Third World laboratory for First World experiments in 'trickle down' economics.

The second arm of Seaga's economic strategy required an overseas crusade. More specifically, he envisaged an all-out assault to open up new markets in North America, especially the highly fertile United States. This, he reasoned, would bring in both badly-needed foreign exchange and increase jobs in Jamaica. It was therefore important to keep domestic wages internationally competitive; better low-paid than jobless, said Seaga. But by the time he had finished, Jamaican workers were amongst the most poorly paid in the Western world.

Ultimately, the success of Seaga's plans hinged on the country's economic viability. He needed friends in high places to back him, and found one immediately in the form of Ronald Wilson Reagan. Seaga's anti-Cubanism and pro-Western free-marketeering made him a firm favourite in Washington, initially at any rate. Reagan demonstrated this by granting Seaga the distinction of being the first foreign head of state to visit him at the White House. The President later awarded him the American Friendship Medal.

Crucially, Reagan's support of Seaga helped the latter
to curry favour with the world's powerful financiers, not
least the International Monetary Fund and the World
Bank. This allowed 'Mr Eddie' to renew Jamaica's
relationship with the IMF on highly favourable terms. In
all, Seaga borrowed a staggering US$1,096,000,000 alone
from the IMF, and paid for it by effectively relinquishing
his control over Jamaica's economic destiny. Meanwhile,
ordinary Jamaicans paid the price in new levels of
suffering.

At street level the feeling was one of *déjà vu*; a nightmarish scenario featuring broken promises and unforgiving hardships. The Seaga government cut protectionist
price controls. So whereas at the end of Manley's last
stand a family of five could just about survive on the
minimum wage, under Seaga the same family required
two and a half times their disposable income to put the
same rudimentary provisions on the table.

The Government slashed public expenditure on housing,
education, hospitals and roads to the tune of 400 per cent.
The price of imported raw materials and goods went
through the ceiling, causing, *inter alia*, thousands of
Jamaican small businesses to collapse. Seaga promised
more jobs but, by the end of his first spell in office in 1983,
he had succeeded in adding another 20,000 unemployed
to Manley's legacy of 290,000.

By 1984, the economic miracle worker was in need of
a miracle himself. Seaga's latest problem stemmed from
the JLP's failure to repay its IMF tranches. Now, like
a termagant wife, the Fund was making whining noises
about filing for divorce.

Seaga's solution was to implement a stringent programme of draconian measures, including devaluing the
Jamaican dollar and laying off 6,200 government workers.
By the end of the year close to half the population was
eligible for government food stamps.

By January 1985, a disaffected population staged a general strike, the first since the epoch-making struggles of 1938 – even the party's Bustamante Industrial Trade Union took part. And so the rounds of tax rises, job losses and overwhelming suffering continued until on 9 February 1989, the electorate put Seaga out of his governmental misery.

The economic 'guru's' legacy of economic failure was crowned by a more than quadrupling of Jamaica's foreign debt burden to US$4 billion, roughly US$1,600 for every Jamaican citizen.

The man left to pick up the pieces was a 'born again' Michael Manley; a man who still wanted to be friends with Cuba, but not at the expense of a fruitful relationship with the White House and the Western world. He even wanted to befriend Reagan's replacement, President George Bush.

Manley had been chastened by nine years in the political hinterland, a fact which came across in his prescription for Jamaica's economic future. If Manley's new approach resembled a near replica of Seaga's discredited one, it was because it was. Perhaps the biggest difference between them was that Manley's was a sort of liberal market force economics with a caring social face.

In this way, the individual needs of the people gave way to the collective interests of the nation. Socialism took a back seat to democracy. The IMF was to be worked with, not struggled against. There were to be no more lavish 1970s-style handouts. Still, 'Joshua's' was hardly the economic miracle Jamaica had been crying out for. In short, he and PJ Patterson – his successor after March 1992 – have done little to alter Jamaica's stormy economic course.

PJ Patterson, the PNP president, took over national and party leadership when Manley was forced to relinquish them due to ill health. Remarkably, he became the party's

first leader to emerge from outside of the Manley dynasty.
But his victory was all the more remarkable since he had
only recently been sacked from Cabinet over his alleged
role in a £1.5 million duty waiver scandal involving the
Shell Oil company.

A highly educated, British-trained lawyer, the MP for rural
South East Westmorland first became a parliamentarian in
1960. A man from humble country roots, PJ – as he is
popularly known – has filled a succession of important
party and government posts including chairman and
deputy prime minister, the ministries of foreign affairs,
production, development, planning, and industry and
commerce.

On 30 March 1993, a year to the day after his promotion, Patterson led the PNP to a sensational general
election victory over the Labourites. The nationalists
picked up fifty-three of the sixty seats, and remarkably
Patterson became the country's first elected black – in
the classic sense – prime minister.

For all the party's tremendous electoral popularity, the
PNP has failed to transform Jamaica's ailing economy.
This was amplified by the late Carl Stone, a professor of
Political Sociology at the University of the West Indies. In
October 1992, the part-time *Gleaner* columnist wrote that
voters who had supported the PNP's 1989 electoral bid
were 'angry that they have voted Mr Seaga out of power
only to find that the PNP is implementing his policies but
with less efficiency, competence and expertise.'

Under the Manley–Patterson regime Jamaica has suffered from runaway inflation; it rose to an incredible 106
per cent in the fiscal year 1991–92. Patterson's daring
devaluation of the Jamaican dollar while he was Finance
Minister saw it plunge from eight to one US dollar in 1990
to thirty-three to one in May 1995. Pegging wage rises at
less than half the rate of inflation (thirty-two per cent)
has resulted in a colossal upsurge in industrial disputes

and strike action. As ever, unemployment remains at chronically high levels. Consumer imports have risen, while vital money-making exports have fallen. In 1993 alone, the Patterson administration posted a record US$1 billion trade deficit, raising the country's foreign debt burden to US$4.5 billion at the time of writing.

Between them, Seaga, Manley and Patterson have guided the Jamaican economy from crisis to chaos. And it has been the people, especially the poorest and the most vulnerable, who have had to suffer the consequences. To those who recognise a correlation between socio-economic hardship and crime, it will be more than coincidental that crime – especially its violent manifestations – has travelled precisely the same troubled course. In fact, as Jamaicans have been asked to make more and more sacrifices for the sake of the national economic good, violent crime has orbited to new heights. Nowadays it has become to Jamaica what gambling is to Hong Kong: a cultural institution.

Unfortunately, the relentless rise in crime has not been the only consequence of governments' consistent failure to get the economy back on track since 1980. Another tragic by-product has been the usurping of some of its expected functions by the drug dons. Indeed, as the Government has struggled to meet its commitments to the needy, the posses have stepped into the breach to cushion the blow.

In truth, the drug gangsters' contributions have been limited. Still, without them, many impoverished ghettoites would receive no relief at all. Of equal importance is the fact that these contributions have tended to strengthen the bonds between the giver and the takers at the expense of the interests of law and order.

By itself Jamaica's economic collapse cannot explain why the drug dons have progressed to the stage of benevolent

feudal lords. The key to that lies in two distinct areas of
their business dealings. The first is the posses' mixed
fortunes in the role of international narcotics traffickers.
The second, the massively successful diversification of
their drug interests within Jamaica.

Like the previous decade, the 1970s saw the posses
continuing to flourish in their careers as ganja traffickers.
In what remained a highly competitive business, Jamaican
ganja barons managed to maintain their ranking by
substantially upping their cultivation and shipments of
the 'herb'. In fact, towards the end of 1984, US Drug
Enforcement Agency (DEA) officials placed Jamaica
(fourteen per cent) a distant second behind Columbia
(sixty per cent) as the major importer of ganja into
the United States. But that second spot had come at
the expense of the Mexicans.

The brainchild of disgraced US President Richard
Nixon, the agency reckoned that Jamaican gangs were
responsible for shipping almost 2,000 tons of ganja into
the United States on an annual basis. Federal officials
also reckoned that the narcotic crop was the major
revenue generator for as many as 6,000 Jamaican small
farmers.

Only a fraction of the earnings stemming from the
trade filtered back into the Jamaican economy. However,
in an industry worth an estimated US$1.4–US$2 billion
by the mid-1980s, that fraction will have been worth
hundreds of millions of dollars to Jamaica's foreign
exchange-strapped economy. In truth, the illegal profits
from ganja trafficking more than doubled those accruing
from the combined revenues of bauxite, manufacturing
and agricultural exports, and tourism. Seaga, who had
openly scoffed at the reliance Manley's government had
had on the illegal profits from ganja trafficking, found
his government in much the same boat.

The 'honeymoon' period between Seaga and Reagan

was over by 1984. Tensions were beginning to surface. A major source of American friction towards Seaga's regime was the increasing tonnage of ganja that was flooding on to the mainland from Jamaica. The Americans liked even less suggestions that top Jamaican government officials were also involved in the smuggling. Accordingly, the Reagan Administration insisted Seaga take steps to eradicate the cultivation of ganja altogether.

Determined to halt the trade, the Reagan Administration threatened to suspend scheduled flights between the two countries if tons of ganja kept on turning up on in-bound planes. This had last happened in February 1984 when a scheduled Air Jamaica A-300 airbus had flown into Miami from Kingston with three tons of ganja stashed in the hold. The plane was impounded; and Seaga's government was forced to pay a multimillion American dollar fine to retrieve the state-owned aircraft. On another level, there was talk of Congress axing about US$125 million in annual aid to Jamaica if Seaga failed to get his act together.

The whiff of sanctions was enough to force Seaga's hand. The Jamaican Prime Minister immediately stepped up what had been a frankly lacklustre fight against the ganja suppliers. He ordered the destruction of the estimated seventy illegal airstrips that littered the inaccessible hilly interior. He insisted that private airstrips be monitored more aggressively. He called in the military, and put them in charge of increasing surveillance at Jamaica's two international airports; a move followed by a major round of mass sackings of security and baggage-handling staff which claimed 164 airport jobs. Seaga even tried to pressurise the *Gleaner* into censoring stories about the drug menace because of the negative effect they had on tourism. Reports about the traffic itself were probably a lesser concern than those featuring the increased gun violence and murder it had spawned. By the mid-1980s gun battles between rival rudie gangsters, and with the overburdened security forces, had become regular news features.

By far Seaga's most controversial measure, however, was an attempt to tax the illegal gains of the drug barons. Studiously avoiding its moral implications, he likened his daring initiative to the one used by the legendary Eliot Ness and his FBI cronies in their battle to convict Al Capone. Twenty-four unnamed, alleged drug traffickers were singled out and presented with a combined tax demand totalling £22 million. None of them was ever arrested, although one reportedly took a contract out on Seaga's life.

The stimulus Seaga received for his vigorous anti-ganja crusade was translated into an effective response. In 1985, the Government reported that it had seized just over 200 tons of cured ganja bound for export during the previous year – double the quantity seized in 1983. In addition, more than a thousand acres of ganja crops were eradicated, and 4,500 drug-related arrests made. By the end of October 1985, the security forces had wiped out 1,700 acres of ganja – a significant improvement on the 1984 figure.

But the anti-ganja crusaders did not have it all their own way. When the forces of law and order clamped down on air routes, canny drug traffickers exploited the plethora of hidden coves and inlets that dot the rugged Jamaican coastline. Limited human, technical and material resources meant that it was virtually impossible for the small Jamaican coast guard to police them, and ensured that a massive tonnage of ganja continued to slip through the trafficking net.

Seaga's belated war on the drug smugglers led to his government sustaining heavy 'losses' in other areas, too. In 1985, another two aircraft belonging to Air Jamaica were impounded by US Customs officials after the discovery of huge ganja shipments. Again, in April

1989, the Government was slapped with a US$29million levy, one of the biggest fines in American aviation history, after two tons of ganja had been discovered on an Air Jamaica jet. It brought to 130 the number of seizures on the national carrier since 1980.

Meanwhile, back in 1984, as the security forces burnt down acre upon acre of ganja, Jamaican farmers and traffickers registered their opposition by doing the same to plantations of sugar cane. With American dollars so precious, there was considerable support in Jamaica for their defiant stand. A poll showed almost two-thirds of islanders to be opposed to Seaga's attempts to end the ganja export trade. Even the PNP, which wholeheartedly backed Seaga's offensive, believed there was room for quid pro quo. At the very least, they argued, austerity-hit farmers should be compensated for their loss of income as indeed Turkish drug producers had been.

Still, none of these setbacks distracted Seaga from his anti-drug mission. If anything, he was under renewed American pressure to continue it apace. In early 1986, JLP Transport Minister, Pearnel Charles, took the battle to the island's seaports. Charles warned shipping companies whose containers were used to transport ganja that he would run them out of business. His announcement came in the wake of the discovery of some eleven and a half tons of 'weed' awaiting export on the docks during 1985. In 1989 the traffic was so heavy that the Government was forced to shut down the island's docks for three months.

In the autumn of 1987, the JLP leader went on the offensive again. He unveiled an ambitious twelve-point 'action' plan. Chief amongst these points was the threat to use the military to shoot down illegal aircraft found violating Jamaican air space; seizing drug traffickers' assets; and setting up a fund to pay people prepared to inform on the drug bandits.

Luckily for Seaga, the backbone of his ganja eradication thrust was provided by the joint Jamaican-United
States Buccaneer programmes. In 1986, Buccaneer III
destroyed approximately 7,000 acres of ganja cultivation,
about half the total crop. And, deploying Blackhawk
helicopters to drop massive concrete blocks – the JDF
had no military aircraft – (temporarily) took twenty-two
illegal air fields out of commission.

The cultivators were becoming increasingly marginalised,
but there was no let-up from the buccaneers. Forced on to
higher and higher ground, Buccaneer IV used helicopters
to spray herbicides on their plantations, in spite of the
potentially debilitating implications its usage posed for
livestock and humans.

By the second half of the 1980s the combined Jamaican-
United States front against the international traffic in ganja
was very much in the ascendancy. But just when it seemed
as if victory was in reach, the crusade was distracted by a
new phase in inter-party bickering.

Towards the end of 1986, the JLP accused top PNP
politicians of having links with the big wheels in the
ganja business. The nationalists hit back in similar fashion a year later when Errol Anderson, the JLP Security Minister, reversed the charges. More than that,
he named Paul Burke, the head of the PNP's youth
wing, as the alleged culprit. Naturally Burke denied the
charges. However, not to be outdone, Michael Manley
weighed in with a ferocious attack on the drug dealing antics of dubious politically-connected characters in
Tivoli Gardens – the Shower Posse – the seat of Prime
Minister Seaga.

But the juiciest of all the allegations was saved until
last. Significantly, it emanated from the United States.
The allegation was that Edward Seaga, the man leading
the Jamaican anti-drug offensive, was a major force in
the illicit trade. The charge was made by a convicted

Jamaican drug dealer to a United States Senate sub-committee on 8 April 1988. Even though they had stemmed from a convicted felon, Seaga vehemently denied the accusations.

However, his cause was not helped by an American network television programme which linked both political parties to the drug trade. Around the same time, a raft of similar claims were made by other convicted, American-based posse drug dealers that they had made regular cash donations to, and purchased firearms for, their preferred political party at home in Jamaica.

Deeply shaken, the ebullient Seaga shrugged off the charges, and continued with his dogged resistance to the ganja traffic. But as luck would have it, he had been ejected from office by the time it reaped the ripest of its fruits.

In the 1990s as Operation Buccaneer went through instalments v, vi and vii, ganja cultivation was drastically reduced. In 1991, the Jamaican security forces seized some forty-seven tons of ganja, and decimated almost 2,000 acres of ganja plantation – about seventy per cent of the total output. This represented a reduction of a quarter over the previous year alone. In 1992, 2,774 acres of ganja were wiped out, and forty tons of the cured product seized.

In the course of a decade annual ganja production had slumped from a peak of about 2,000 tons to a 'derisory' 600. While still a player of note in the field of ganja growing and smuggling, Jamaica had been relegated to third place behind Mexico, the new market leader, and Columbia. Ganja, which for a long time had been grown in the open on low-lying plantations of up to fifty acres, was reduced to cultivation on one and two acre sites on the sides of sheltered gullies tucked away in the mountainous regions. Today, to keep one step ahead of the helicopters, ganja farmers are forced to harvest their produce before it is fully grown.

To make matters worse, trafficking has become a major bugbear, with narcotics gangs having to find ever more ingenious methods to freight their product. Air routes are still used, but the trade has literally been driven out to sea with fishing, commercial and pleasure boats bearing the brunt.

'Mules' or drugs couriers are now doing more of the trafficking. Apart from ferrying ganja on their persons or in their luggage, the more innovative have experimented with techniques such as plaiting it into hairstyles and wigs.

The bigger suppliers, too, have had to find new trade routes. Targeting the island's major legitimate exporters is one. In September 1992, for example, 700 pounds of ganja was discovered in Connecticut hidden in cans supposedly containing processed food. And in June 1994, Hanes, the premier Jamaican garment manufacturer, suspended shipments of clothing to the United States after 200 pounds of 'herb' were spotted in a consignment in Jacksonville, Florida.

On the surface, the relentless onslaught against ganja harvesting and smuggling should have sent the Rude Boy gangsters into a state of panic since it jeopardised their incomes. But the posses were not running scared. The main reason being the second and most important factor in their continuing rise: the diversification of their domestic business interests.

There has long been a thriving market for narcotics in Jamaica – the island has always been considered to have suffered from a drug problem. But during the 1990s the degree of that suffering has been compounded by major changes in the domestic drug market. If one compares the days when the island was gripped by a moral panic over ganja-puffing Rastafari and rudies, to the present, then Jamaica never really had a serious drugs problem.

Few people doubt that it has one now. 'The term drug awareness has come to signify something meaningful for the average Jamaican, especially the youth,' a *Jamaica Herald* editorial agreed. The timing of the commentary is itself indicative of how deeply Jamaican society has been struck by its latest drug menace. This observation appeared in October 1992, on the eve of an event which in recent years has become a national institution: the fourth annual staging of Drug Awareness Week. 'This is,' the editorial continued, 'perhaps ironic in a country that has historically had illegal drug use but has only recently found itself with a drug problem.'

A year later *Gleaner* columnist Tony Johnson put a more worrying spin on this awful development. 'Jamaica,' he wrote, 'is almost a classic example of how the international drug trade can enter a market, and wreck a nation's youth, before the authorities are even aware of what is going on.'

The situation that both articles were alluding to is the phenomenal growth in the abuse of cocaine – especially crack cocaine – a problem which in no small part has been engineered by the posses.

Not so long ago, Jamaica was largely immune from the anti-social scourge of this deadly duo. Cocaine entered Jamaica, certainly; nine kilos were confiscated in the inaugural Jamaican-United States Buccaneer operation in 1974. The likelihood, though, is that these narcotics were in transit, bound for the United States. Basically, Jamaica had still to develop a thriving market for hard drugs. Ganja, especially quality strains like redbeard, indika and sensimilla, remained the Jamaican drug of choice throughout the 1970s.

As Jamaica entered the 1980s, the island found itself being exploited as a trans-shipment point for cocaine

destined for the United States. To an important criminal
body of opinion it was a narcotics entrepôt *par excellence*.
Leading the charge were the Cosa Nostra, the American
Mafia, and the fledgling Columbian and Peruvian cocaine
cartels. They favoured Jamaica because of its strategic
location midway between the cocaine-producing countries
of South America and the money-spinning American
markets. Again, with a history of smuggling, Jamaica
was seen as ideal for refuelling craft and stashing drugs
before the final assault on the United States.

As the years rolled on, the affinity for Jamaica as a
stop-over point was registered in a growing volume of
cocaine seizures. In 1980, for example, Jamaica's security
services did not intercept one ounce of cocaine. Four years
later, the coastguard stopped an American ship on its way
back to the United States with a consignment of cocaine
valued at US$45 million. In the same year, Jamaica's
terrestrial law enforcers confiscated 130 pounds of the
substance. In the space of two years, the hauls had
rocketed to just over half a ton. A then record single
seizure of 800 pounds of cocaine was made by the coastguard in the waters just off Kingston in 1987.

The longer the mounting hauls went on, the clearer it
became that not all of the recovered drugs were designated
for trans-shipment; that a new generation of Jamaicans
had developed a taste for the 'champagne' drug. And
with that (belated) realisation came a new chapter in
Jamaican society's sorry saga of misfortunes, and the
posses' continuing success story.

The irony in all of this is that Jamaica's emerging
cocaine suppliers had been forced into experimenting
with the drug because of Seaga's damaging anti-ganja
crusade. (In fact, the overriding reason for America's
continuing insistence that Seaga do more to counteract
the drug trade was the increasing frequency with which
ganja supply lines were being used to transport cocaine.)

In this way, cocaine was almost reluctantly added to the domestic drugs menu.

Heroin was another addition. While 'H' has never been anything like as popular as cocaine, there is a small market for the narcotic in Jamaica. The narcotic is usually shipped in from Nigeria, a task which is made less conspicuous by that country's established links with Jamaica – there is Nigerian Consulate in Kingston. In fact, five Nigerians were arrested after smuggling the drug into Jamaica within the space of a week in October 1992. Three of those captured had brought a pound and a half of heroin with them.

Cocaine hydrochloride (to give it its proper name) first began to penetrate the domestic market in the mid- to late 1970s. The trade, though, was largely restricted to a small group of affluent Kingston go-getters, including those involved in the music business. In those days cocaine was still too high-priced to have mass appeal.

There was also considerable demand among hedonistic foreign holidaymakers in the island's prosperous north coast tourist resorts. As recently as 1992, a Jamaican survey found a clear correlation between the supply of drugs to these resorts and the big demand for narcotics amongst sojourners. Conducted by Carl Stone on behalf of the island's National Council on Drug Abuse (NCDA), it found that a quarter of all tourists polled admitted they holidayed in places like Ocho Rios and Montego Bay because they could 'score' hard and soft drugs with ease.

The early 1980s saw a dramatic broadening of cocaine abuse in Jamaica as the price of cocaine fell sharply on the international market. The American market, by far the world's biggest for the 'power' narcotic, began to reach saturation point. Consequently, traffickers and dealers were forced to look for new markets elsewhere. With its well-oiled links to the international trade, Jamaica was an obvious destination.

This is not to suggest that the big American players dispatched their emissaries to the island. What happened was that business-minded ganja dealers took advantage of the modest prices, and added the drug to their inventories. Some even exchanged their ganja shipments directly for cocaine.

Murmurs about the perils of cocaine abuse were starting to be expressed around 1983. One important area of complaint surrounded the noticeable increase in drug-related violence. Unlike ganja, though, the violence spread to users. A few years later, another reason for soul-searching focused on the destructive influence the narcotic was having on the nation's school-aged children.

The powers that be would have done well to heed the early warning signs. For today Jamaica is in the grips of an epidemic of cocaine addiction, one which has had particularly devastating effects on a great many of the country's youth.

Drug seizures aside, the scale of the problem of cocaine abuse in Jamaica can be gauged from a number of sources. Chief amongst them are the growing number of cocaine dependants; the significant appearance of a welter of crack houses; and the considerable demand for the narcotic among the country's educated élite.

In terms of addicts, work carried out by the NCDA in 1992 found that an incredible 20,000 Jamaican youths were abusing cocaine and crack. The figure had actually fallen from an earlier islandwide total of 22,000. But while rural users were beginning to beat the habit, the reduction was offset by a trend of mushrooming cocaine abuse in Kingston. The port city is literally awash with 'coke heads', the typical profile being one of an inner city-dwelling male aged between thirteen and twenty-five.

More stark evidence comes from an alarming increase

in crack houses. The Jamaican capital was reckoned to have sixty crack bases at the end of 1993. More worrying still, unlike countries such as the United States and Britain, the locations of these crack dens are usually an open secret. This has led – with good reason – to questions about how seriously the police take the problem. In October 1993, for example, *XNews*, a pseudo-satirical Jamaican weekly scandal sheet, conducted an impromptu 'investigation' into the location of some of the city's crack dens. The investigating team's afternoon 'stroll around town' uncovered ten such outlets, including one which 'police sources' said was one of the largest.

Another crack venue, located 'right under the nose of one of the largest and oldest police stations in the island', featured in an article penned by Lloyd Williams exactly a year later. 'Almost anybody' in the locale, he wrote, 'can give directions to the crack house in Sutton Street.' Apart from its close proximity to Central Police Station, the crack outlet also sits in the vicinity of Kingston Magistrate's Court, where a fair proportion of its habitués end up, and the headquarters of the powerful Police Federation.

Not surprisingly, though, most of Kingston's crack houses are situated well away from the scrutinous gaze of the boys in blue. The prime locations are buried deep within the city's depressed ghetto communities. A belt of flourishing crack houses are dotted across the capital from Rockfort and Dunkirk in the east through tough inner-city neighbourhoods like Southside, Rema and Tivoli Gardens to Waterhouse, Moscow and Olympic Gardens in the west. Many cater for rich and poor alike.

One would, however, be wrong to think that the main reason for their location in these God-forsaken pockets of neglect, misery and despair is simply to capitalise on a captive market – although that obviously helps. It is because the police seldom venture into these lawless areas, especially without the back-up of heavily-armed soldiers.

There is also the knowledge that, even when they do, they are highly unlikely to get much assistance from local residents. 'That's a big complaint,' says Williams, the posse specialist. 'When they go into an inner city area they can't get any information. It might be common knowledge that John Brown sells coke, but they can't get the people to say it in court.' This is not at all surprising. After all, these neighbourhoods are governed by posse law which expressly forbids co-operation with the police. 'See and blind, hear and deaf' is the motto that those who want to live live by.

No matter where they are sited, however, the crack houses themselves are well fortified, well organised and well protected. *XNews* dramatically asserted that the dens, which can net upwards of J\$150,000 a week (£3,000), are patrolled by 'tough-looking ex-cons who are not afraid to sling their guns, while others use seductive females'. Whatever the level of protection, it is more a reflection of the predilection of greedy rivals to raid, rip-off and decimate their competition, than it is a sign of any genuine concern about the anti-narcotic activities of the security forces.

What the *XNews* piece neglected to mention was that crack house security transcends shows of brute force. The drug dons also employ sophisticated techniques to protect their investments. Crack houses keep their in-house inventories to a minimum and dealers use two-way radios to order more stock, usually delivered by young children on bikes and lowly gang members.

Mention should also be made of the widespread popularity of cocaine and crack. It is, perhaps, to be expected that many of those who have nothing to lose will look for solace in alcohol and drugs. But, were it not for the fact that middle-class people do not usually rob, assault and kill to buy drugs, the problem of cocaine abuse among the affluent would probably be as severe as it is amongst their ghetto peers.

Proof that Kingston's 'stush' society is vulnerable to the ultimate 'power' drug can be gathered on an almost daily basis. When New Kingston's banks and insurance companies close for the day, one need only loiter along the Barbican Road to witness the popularity of cocaine amongst the well-to-do. The road, which services prosperous 'uptown' postal districts such as Cherry Gardens, is a popular destination for besuited business executives and office managers in need of a fix. The buyers need not even alight their vehicles to purchase their supplies. At the junction where the Barbican Road meets Jacks Hill, 'respectable' men and women in flashy Japanese cars – the sort of people who often frown at ganja-smoking – can be seen lowering their electric windows to make drive-by purchases from a flotilla of largely young female dealers.

Cocaine does not discriminate between race, class, gender, religion or anything else for that matter. Cocaine is simply pro-money.

The explosion of powder and crack cocaine was masterminded, and is controlled, by a triumvirate of powerful forces. There are the Jamaican individuals who returned to the island after spells abroad. This group includes fugitive posse members who have fled from American (or other) justice. It is complemented by deportees, many of whom were repatriated after receiving criminal convictions for drug-related offences. In fact, according to the grapevine, one shadowy deportee is said to control one of Jamaica's biggest cocaine operations.

The second cohort is made up of indigenous entrepreneurs; players who use their quasi-legitimate export-import businesses and impeccable credentials as a cover for their insidious sidelines. They are joined by, and frequently operate in tandem with, politicians and top public servants, the latter of which invariably rely on their influential positions and important contacts to conceal their criminal operations.

The likes of Gerald Tucker, a former JLP Member of Parliament for East Portland and ex-mayor of Port Antonio, fall into this sub-division. On 18 January 1994, he was found guilty of possession of, and dealing in, cocaine at the end of a mammoth 18-month trial. The verdict, which resulted in a Buff Bay court handing down a custodial sentence, came after a police raid on Tucker's Fairy Hill home in June 1992 had netted thirty-eight pounds of cocaine.

And finally there are the posses. This group comprises both indigenous drug gangs and posse members who have served 'tours of duty' overseas. The latter group is by far the most organised and deadly of the trio.

It is not uncommon for these groups to collaborate although, as Lloyd Williams points out, familiarity plays a significant role in determining how the indigenous traffickers and dealers operate in Jamaica. 'In Jamaica they would act far more discreetly than they would in Washington,' he says. 'Because people here would point them out – although not very often.' Certainly not, informing on them carries a terminal health risk.

The native posses' *modus operandi* is a major key to understanding how they have managed to create rampant cocaine abuse in Jamaica. The techniques were perfected by their namesakes in the United States during the early 1980s. Accomplished business organisations, the drug gangs invested in their products in the same way that a soap manufacturer might invest in a new brand of washing powder. The pushers literally hooked potential customers by giving them free samples of their latest product ranges or otherwise off-loaded them at well below First World market prices. Then, as soon as they had established a high degree of 'brand loyalty' (in the form of cocaine and crack addiction) the wily drug organisations set about recouping their investments by churning out their products at more realistic prices. Within the space of a few years the posses had created a legion of cocaine zombies. And, 'Presto!' as journalist Tony Johnson expressed it, 'Jamaica had developed yet another problem.'

Of course, wholesale cocaine prices vary from time to time, depending on considerations such as supply and demand. However, the narcotic has seen a steady decrease in its price for a decade or more now. In 1992, for instance, when a kilo of cocaine exchanged hands for US$23,000 (£11,500) in the United States, it cost a mere J$200,000 (£5,000) in Jamaica.

The posses' habit of cutting out the middleman helps to explain this. Instead, 'mules' are dispatched to the South American mainland, where the narcotic is up to six times cheaper than in the United States, to buy a 'ki' (kilo) or two of 'coke'. The only overheads then are the cost of flights and accommodation and a fee of up to US$1,000. As luck would have it, in recent years 'mules' have been able to take advantage of regular air services from Jamaica to Columbia, Panama and Curaçao.

Some couriers get caught, of course. In May 1992, a twenty-three-year-old Jamaican was arrested at Norman Manley International Airport after he tried to smuggle almost two pounds of cocaine into the country. The drugs were discovered in tins labelled Klim Milk powder – nice touch – after the 'mule' got off a regular flight from Panama. Still, because of the piecemeal quantity seized, the losses of the trip's sponsor were limited.

Within the last few years, though, Jamaican cocaine traffickers have been using Columbians to bring the gear to them. Every week two Sam Airline flights from Bogota, the Columbian capital, land in Montego Bay. The service, which started in December 1992, was intended to facilitate legal trade links between the countries.

But, according to the JCF, the Columbian national airline is an airborne paradise for cocaine smugglers. At least fifteen Columbian couriers were arrested in 1994, and since the service started the police have seized more than 120 pounds of cocaine from incoming passengers.

Jamaica's Third World standard of living, however, has meant its drug dons have had to compromise on profits – at minimum wages (roughly £12,) it would take a fortnight for a Jamaican to save enough cash to buy a 'rock' of crack at British prices. Because of this, the drug dons have striven to extract every available cent from their sales. Their ambition has been achieved through an ingenious pricing strategy. In short, the dealers have cleverly tailored their products to meet the pockets of individual users, making them affordable for everyone.

To use crack cocaine as an example, at 1994 prices, a 'rock' cost between J$40 (eighty pence) and J$100 (£2) depending on whether it was destined for a lower- or middle-class crack pipe. Lloyd Williams explains how the system works. 'Instead of selling to an uptown guy for J$200, you cut the stuff and sell it to five (downtown) guys for J$40 each.' Thus, Jamaican drug gangs have been able to have their cake and eat it, too.

The cocaine boom has made a significant contribution to Kingston's escalating crime rates. Since the early 1980s, the non-stop gangland war to win the right to fill the capital's crack pipes has led to a tremendous worsening of gun terrorism and murder.

This has not gone unnoticed by the island's politicians. On the eve of Drug Awareness Week 1992, Opposition leader Edward Seaga highlighted the considerable 'smoking of crack and cocaine in the inner cities' as a major factor in the upsurge of 'gun warfare and destruction' in Jamaica.

The problem – as the police will confirm – has seriously regressed since then. The JCF pinpoints the blame for the cataclysmic upsurge in violence, shootings, and murder at the inter-drug gang turf wars over the right to peddle cocaine. 'If a youth is selling cocaine here,' says Williams of the police's logic, 'he doesn't want another one invading his turf.'

Resistance has been registered in the form of a bloodbath. Jamaica suffered 656 murders in 1993, not including 'lawful' killings by the police. That figure had already been passed by November of the following year. With Christmas – a traditional Jamaican season for shootings and killings – conservative estimates suggested the homicide tally would break through the 700 mark before the new year.

This breathtakingly beautiful Caribbean island is now speeding towards levels of murderous violence unseen since the carnage of 1980. Only now, drug-related terrorism has replaced political tribalism as the principle cause.

But drug gangsterism is not the only cause of crime in Jamaica. The overall crime rate has also been significantly boosted by the hordes of cocaine dependants; addicts who have been pushed into commiting crimes, or more crimes, in order to satisfy their uncontrollable cravings.

Crack is the most problematic of the cocaine cousins. It offers a uniquely powerful high, but that high ends in minutes with a paranoia-inducing low. In order to repeat the high, users therefore need to repeat the dose. Significantly, though, unlike heroin, there is almost no physical limit to how much 'rock' the individual can consume. The purely psychological 'need' to keep a 'buzz' going can cost a junkie anything up to J$5,000 a day (£100). Weekend bingers have even been known to blow J$75,000 (£1,500) – more than two years on

the Jamaican minimum wage – in a single orgy of
crack smoking.

Unfortunately for Jamaican society, the only way a
great many 'coke fiends' – working and jobless – can
finance their habits is by resorting to crime. 'Once these
guys get hooked . . . they are going to find the money,'
explains Williams. 'They are going to grab the woman's
handbag. They are going to commit some other form of
crime to finance their habit.' A non-discriminating narcotic, one young middle-class 'coke head' even resorted
to organising a J$750,000 (£15,000) burglary of his
family's business to finance his habit.

Not all cocaine dependants are as passive in their
cocaine-financing habits. Almost every addict is a potential (or active) handbag or necklace-snatcher, mugger,
armed robber or murderer. 'I can tell you,' says Mr P., a
well-known figure in Arnette Gardens in a thinly-veiled
reference to his neighbours in Tivoli Gardens, 'those guys
do a lot of coke, crack or whatever . . . And whenever they
take the crack and the coke [they have] one thing on their
minds – to go and rob and kill, rob and kill!'

Colonel MacMillan, the Jamaican Chief of Police, has
repeatedly attributed the growth in violent offences over
the last few years to vicious crack addicts. He says crack
is Jamaican society's Number One problem.

Some of the stories associated with crack-related violence are particularly frightening. One twenty-two-year-
old, having stripped his family home of everything he
could sell to raise money for the narcotic, turned his
attentions to his mother. He held a knife to her throat, and
threatened to kill her if she refused to stump cash to buy
crack. Unfortunately, not all junkies content themselves
with threats. One young man killed his mother by slashing
her throat. Another went one step further. He went to the
home of his estranged mother asking for drugs money; she
refused him, so he stabbed her to death. After slaughtering

his mother, the desperate junkie went round to his father's place. And when he refused to give his son money for drugs, he, too, was brutally murdered.

In between the calculated violence perpetrated by drug gangs and the often opportunistic kind practised by their addicted 'victims' for the sake of cocaine, there is that which stems from a small army of chancers and 'get-rich-quick' merchants. In fact, it seems the further one penetrates the business, the more ruthless the players become. In an industry where the financial rewards on offer are so high, it is no surprise to find that violence is a dominant feature of doing business. Put another way, where there is a market for drugs, there is money. And where there is money, crooked deals, violence and death are not far behind.

All three played prominent roles in the demise of Stafford Douglas on 19 November 1992. A 'business-man', he had driven down to Kingston from the softly undulating red hills of Mandeville, a major market town in the parish of Manchester in the heart of Jamaica. His mission: to 'score' a million Jamaican dollars-worth (£30,000) of powder cocaine.

Douglas hooked up with three men in Old Harbour, on the eastern tip of the capital. Together they did a tour of the local bars before ending up in the would-be buyer's car on Goldbourne Lane. But just as the transaction was about to take place something went terribly wrong. The sample he was given to test was not cocaine; it was flour. Forty-two-year-old Douglas was understandably outraged, and made his feelings known in no uncertain terms. His protests were short-lived though. Douglas's body was found soon afterwards, slumped over the steering wheel of his car. He had been shot in the face.

The only unusual thing about Stafford Douglas's ill-fated drug buy was that he turned out to be the victim. In cases where conmen try to rip-off naive punters – and they are not unheard of – it is normally the former who wind up in hospital or the mortuary.

Three men used a similar ploy to that of Douglas's killers in an attempt to scam a group of Kingston businessmen out of hundreds of thousands of Jamaican dollars early in 1992. Posing as fishermen who had supposedly found a large quantity of cocaine drifting at sea, the men were wined and dined by the prospective buyers. However, when the time came to sample the merchandise, and it was discovered to be flour, the conmen got their come-uppance by slashing the bogus drug dealers with machetes. The conmen were later admitted to a Kingston hospital with serious injuries.

Against daunting odds, Jamaica's embattled security forces (and judiciary) have been left to eradicate the drug gangs, and prevent the welter of crimes associated with the cocaine industry. The signs are that the forces of law and order are fighting a constantly losing battle. The police, it has to be said, are not entirely blameless, but neither have they nor the courts been assisted by impuissant drug legislation.

In many ways, Sutton Street provides a microcosm of the problems confronting the JCF and the courts; it demonstrates how deeply entrenched Kingston's cocaine culture has become, and how difficult it is proving to efface.

Its well-known crack house is subjected to considerable police scrutiny, although for some unknown reason the officers based a stone's throw away pay it scant attention. Instead, that thankless responsibility has most often fallen on the awkwardly known Special Anti-Crime Task Force (SACTF), a specialist 'trouble-shooting' wing of the JCF.

Chief among the SACTF police officers who keep a vigilant eye on the crack den is Assistant Superintendent

Keith 'Trinity' Gardener. One of Jamaica's most famous, perhaps infamous, crime-fighters, he ranks amongst those who wonder why the local police ignore the crack house – rumours abound of corrupt police involvement in its dealings.

'Trinity's' squad has been responsible for filling the local magistrates court with a procession of suspected users and dealers, but the list of prospective defendants shows no signs of tailing off. Sutton Street magistrates are continually jailing the local crack den's habitués and dealers. During the autumn of 1994, for example, twenty-three-year-old Sharon Allen was jailed for two years and fined J\$15,000 (£300) for dealing in cocaine. For all that, she can be said to have been lucky on at least two counts. One, she had been acquitted on a similar charge the year before – the court having chosen to disregard evidence from an arresting officer to the effect that he had discovered nine pieces of crack in a matchbox inside her home in the Sutton Street crack house; she said the officer found it in the communal backyard. Two, she got off pretty lightly considering the gravity of her offence.

Incidentally, Allen was again fined and jailed after chalking up her fourth and fifth cocaine related convictions in April 1995. Significantly, though this time the magistrate did not offer Allen the luxury of an either/or sentence; she was jailed for two years and fined. The crack dealer was not alone; another nine residents of the Sutton Sutton crack den had been brought before the courts during the previous weeks.

And so it goes on. Photographer, Levy Kirlew, from Kingston's 'uptown' Mountain View Avenue was fined J\$120,000 (£4,000) for possession, importation and dealing in cocaine. He stepped off a twice-weekly flight from Panama City (a tremendous source of Customs drug busts) with three and a half pounds of powder cocaine concealed in a bag of sugar inside his luggage. Even Gerald Tucker, the disgraced ex-JLP Member of Parliament, only received twelve months imprisonment after being convicted of possession and dealing in almost forty pounds of cocaine. To add insult to injury, the court simultaneously gave him the option of paying a J$50,000 (£1,100) fine to avoid doing any time in jail at all.

These are hardly frightening judicial deterrents or ringing endorsements of the Government's commitment to crush the cocaine trade. No wonder then that Sutton Street magistrates have been bombarded with cocaine cases. As crack becomes easier to 'score' than a good 'draw' of ganja, one magistrate confessed that she was hearing more cocaine-related cases than ones for ganja. Indeed the volume of cocaine-related cases has grown significantly since 1993.

Both judges and police officers have strongly urged the Government to get tough on the drugs, especially the villains involved on the supply side. In August 1992, Detective Superintendent Osbourne N. Dyer, the head of the Police Narcotics Division, called for stiffer sentences for couriers. 'That's the only way we can deal with [smuggling],' he said. 'You have to jail them or fine them hundreds of thousands of dollars, so it hurts.'

In fairness to the Government, there has been a somewhat belated acceptance of the urgent need to inject venom into Jamaica's drug laws. In November 1992, Security and Justice minister K.D. Knight told an international conference that steps would be taken to prevent honest banks from being unwittingly drawn into laundering dirty drugs money. Ironically, Knight's pledge came at a time when Jamaica had still to recognise money-laundering as a criminal act. His attack came within months of the disclosure in the United States that posses there controlled banking operations in the Cayman Islands for that purpose. There was every reason to suspect that Jamaica's drug gangs were doing the same.

P. J. Patterson has directed his thrust towards the traffickers. October 1992 saw the Prime Minister use a Drug Awareness Week conference platform to spell out the nature of his attack. 'We must punish traffickers and traders where it hurts most – confiscation of their illegal gains,' he declared. 'We cannot allow the "get rich quick" mentality to . . . make the "don" a hero.' With that in mind Patterson announced that legislation 'in this regard is being drafted and is on the fast track to passage'.

Exactly a year to the day after Patterson's speech, PNP Senator Peter Phillips used the same gathering to reiterate his government's commitment to strengthening Jamaica's anti-drugs laws – P.J.'s 'fast track' legislation was (still) being prepared.

The need for the Jamaican Government to get a move on was highlighted by a delegate from another Caribbean island. Christopher O'Mard, Antigua's Home Affairs Minister, told the conference that Jamaica was now second to Columbia as the prime supplier of drugs to his country. (Jamaica had long been a major shipper, and international gateway for the transport of narcotics throughout the Caribbean, Europe and Canada.)

Another fourteen months passed before the Patterson government finally prepared the promised legislation. The new measures came as amendments to the Dangerous Drugs Act. Major provisions included the imposition of maximum sentences of up to thirty-five years for drug traffickers and/or a ten-fold increase in the permissable fine to J$500,000 (£10,000). There was understandably great concern about the relatively low ceiling put on fines, small change to any self-respecting drug trafficker.

To counter this 'loophole', K.D. Knight proposed the
Drug Offences (Forfeiture of Proceeds) Act in the summer
of 1993 to allow for the confiscation of convicted drug
traffickers' property. It became law just over a year later.
At the time of writing, however, it is understood that no
convicted drug trafficker had had their assets seized in
accordance with the Act.

On the whole, the 1980s and 1990s provided the rudie
drug gangs with a vibrant environment in which to trade.
Apart from making fortunes for many of the drug dons,
this period paved the way for the Rude Boy gangsters
to become economic 'heroes' in the communities they
preside over. To a certain extent this has helped them to
buy the loyalty of their 'subjects'.

That loyalty has come very much at the expense of the
old-time ghetto custodians – the political dons – and their
masters. In fact, there is a strong correlation between the
demise of the political don and tribal violence, and the
ascent of the drug don and drug-related violence.

The political gangster's nemesis began in the aftermath
of the tribal Armageddon of 1980. The nation had been
sickened by the carnage, and applied intense pressure
upon the political establishment and the security forces
to ensure there would be no repetition. Even Government
and Opposition made noises about uniting behind a
bipartisan approach to eradicating the menace.

The Government led a severe crackdown on the gangsters. Seaga's regime had no alternative but to stand aside
and allow the police to round up the gunmen – besides,
with another election out of the way, the mercenaries had
once again outlived their usefulness.

As a result, scores of Rude Boy gun hawks from both
sides decided to make their excuses and leave Jamaica
altogether. This was even more of an imperative for those
who had fired guns for the PNP. As electoral losers they

were destined to become the unprotected targets of both the police and the victorious JLP sportboys.

Numerous JLP and PNP gunmen were helped on their way by 'kindly' politicians. Letters of recommendation were sent to the United States and Canadian embassies to help with the granting of visas. This deceptive expedient turned out to be a costly *faux pas;* one that Jamaican society is paying the price for today. Put another way, many of those former political gangsters have returned or been deported from fruitful 'exile' in their host countries as experienced, ruthless drug gangsters.

With the exception of a 'blip' in 1987, tribalism fell off sharply as the 1980s wore on. This unlikely phenomenon was partly the result of a growing consciousness that there was little or nothing to fight for. The political rewards dried up as the economy sank further and further into recession. In a strange way, though, the reduction was aided by events surrounding the 1983 General Election.

Universally denounced as bogus, it was won by the JLP – an uncontested election was probably the only variety the hugely unpopular Seaga could win. Controversially, Seaga had called the election at short notice after unilaterally reneging on a cross-party agreement to update the outdated electoral register, even though by statute he still had another two years in which to reform it. Rather than participating in the fraud, Manley decided the PNP would boycott the election on principle.

The unopposed election paid a heavy peace dividend, but sporadic outbreaks of tribal violence remained a fixture of the Jamaican democratic process. In January 1984 JLP and PNP gangs joined battle during demonstrations against another rise in petrol prices. Four or five people were killed, including an off-duty police officer and his lover who were gunned down in a bar. May 1984 brought the famous Rema incident involving

Jim Brown. In both instances, the police were once again joined by the army to patrol the streets and enforce curfews.

As always, elections brought the tribal devil out in those people who wanted their side to triumph. In spite of a joint appeal by Seaga and Manley for peaceful local elections in August 1986, polling day and the following week saw eight politically-motivated killings. In one, an alleged PNP supporter was dragged from her home and stoned to death after the party's overwhelming success. The overdue General Election of 1989 also resulted in a rash of killings. This, in spite of the fact that 'Mr Eddie' and 'Joshua' put their signatures to an historic peace accord in August 1988.

Predictably, Seaga tried to whip up public panic. Opposition PNP supporters, he claimed, were 'being organised for a massive campaign of violence, to become full-blown on election day'. He was proved wrong, of course. The death toll stood at seventeen for the three-week run-up to the election – a number had died in confrontations with the police.

Fifteen people were reported to have been slayed in the run-up to the 1993 General Election, Prime Minister Patterson's first as party leader. They included a nominations officer and a political bodyguard. In another incident, an innocent man was wounded by a stray M-16 round that smashed into his bedroom during a street shoot-out between tribal gangs.

The reduction in violence was again helped by the pacifistic posture of the leading politicians. Building on the relative success of the previous election pact, Patterson and Seaga had signed a 'Code of Conduct' for the 1993 election.

The pre-election period saw stage-managed roadblocks, inter-party scuffles, arson attacks on political offices and sniping at the security forces. But the most sensational indication that rudie political terrorists were still at large came on 27 March, three days before polling. Unremarkably, it followed the discovery of 2,000 rounds of ammunition and some false police uniforms by a routine military patrol in Tivoli Gardens. The clear implication being that JLP gunmen, disguised as policemen, were going to shoot their opponents and lay the blame on unruly JCF officers.

Seaga expressed his 'disgust', before going on to criticise the media for its alleged bias. The discovery of a 1,000 bullets in a PNP community hall during the previous month, he said, had not elicited the same level of frenzied outrage. The PNP described the arms cache as sinister, and the police lamented the implications it had for 'the nature of the political violence being experienced'.

P.J. Patterson won the election by a landslide. And, as the scale of his victory became apparant, he manfully declared that the time had come for reconciliation. This would be the last election to feature political killings and injuries, he said.

It was a wonderful sentiment, but one wonders about the basis for its utterance. Had he been alive, Carl Stone would certainly have disputed it. For, by the 1990s, the political duopoly's grip on the political gangs was at its weakest. As Stone eloquently pointed out a year before the election, 'We continue pretending that JLP and PNP politics created the gangs and have the power to end their life and that just cussing the politicians over their history of connection with violence will solve this problem.' This notion was, as the great man bluntly put it, 'Absolute rubbish. If this is not wishful thinking I don't know what is.'

So, tribal violence has remained a permanent feature of the Jamaican political process – regardless of the politicians' stomach for it. Importantly, though, it has never returned to the apocalyptic levels of 1976 and 1980;

nor is it likely to. In fact, more people were massacred in the final week of the 1980 election than in the whole of the period just reviewed.

For assorted reasons, the era of the political gunman seems to be drawing to an end. These include fundamental changes in the patronage system, and dwindling popular support for tribalism.

'You get the impression that it is over,' says Lloyd Williams of the final factor. 'People who used to indulge in it are saying to themselves, and to one another, that it's senseless.' With the exception of 'the hardcore political activists', he continues, 'people are distancing themselves from party politics and that tribal approach to solving anything. [The] poor, hungry, shelterless black people [who] are killing one another [are saying] "it's time we stop that".'

Opinion polls of late have endorsed this theme. Such is the disenchantment with the politics of tribal warfare, and the role of the JLP and PNP in fomenting it, that Jamaicans have been calling for the establishment of a totally new, third political force.

The demise of the political patronage system is another indicator. Over the past decade it has been increasingly perceived as a pursuit that does not pay – financially or politically. 'In a situation where scarce benefits are scarce, the politicians have nothing to offer,' explains Williams. 'The [1998] elections are not due for another three and a half years, so the political dons have no contracts to get.'

In the face of this, new recruits have dried up since the 1980s. They have sought new money-making ventures: crime. In turn, the loss to the political gang has become the gain of the criminal one.

Back in the early 1980s, political madness tailed off as criminal madness increased. A total of 371 and 376 murders were committed in 1981 and 1982, respectively. These figures were much reduced over 1980, but they represented a major upsurge in organised criminal violence, especially the drug-related strain. Crimes such as rape, armed robbery, mugging and bus hijacking also took a turn for the worse.

Since 1981 the better part of the JCF's time has been absorbed in the fight against violent organised crime. Driven by the turbo-charged engines of economic collapse, runaway inflation, endemic social deprivation and chronic unemployment, the crime crisis has matured with age.

As the problem began to take hold, JCF officers found themselves shooting it out with large criminal gangs. In June 1981, for example, the police managed to rid society of eight gangsters in one go. At the finale of a shoot-out in which two officers were injured, they gained a notable scalp in Anthony Tingle. Until that point Jamaica's Public Enemy Number One, he had been wanted for questioning in connection with a string of murders.

In Kingston and the major cities, 'uptown' business-types came under constant attack from violent robbers, many of whom preferred to leave no evidence in the wake of their crimes. Shops, businesses, bookies and banks became regular targets for heavily-armed, trigger-happy bandits. It seemed that violence was a key component in every crime they committed; that wherever there was quick money to be made some gun-toting smart alec would kill to exploit it.

Violent crime had got so out of control by 1983 that a host of private security firms emerged to fill the void left by the overstretched police. Many were oversubscribed.

Meanwhile, 'downtown' areas came under sustained fire from a host of undesirables: rapists, burglars, robbers, street robbers, drug dealers and a growing posse of (often criminal) mendicants.

These were perilous times for west Kingston. Tactics
once used by political gangsters gained currency amongst
the new criminal rudie class. Flimsy doors were kicked off
in the middle of the night, but instead of shooting or killing the occupants because of their political persuasions,
the intruders shot or killed them for their possessions.

Naturally, besieged ghetto residents did not have the
means to hire private security companies to patrol their
crime-ridden streets. The police could do little, and were
not welcome, anyway. Starved of government contracts,
gang members and weaponry, the political dons were not
best placed to protect them, either. So the ghettoes and
shanties began to look to the increasingly powerful drug
gangs for protection.

It is difficult to date this transition with precision. Matters are only confused by the chameleon-like propensity of
political dons like Jim Brown to metamorphose into drug
dons – with a commitment to the political 'struggle'. But
the second half of the 1980s is a good point from which
to chart it. From this period there occurred a significant
shift in the politics of traditional ghetto control. Where
once political gangs had fought each other to protect their
'garrison' constituents from merciless enemy insurgents,
drug dealers now battled amongst themselves for the right
to sell cocaine to them.

Graphic evidence of this fundamental shift has been
on display throughout the 1990s. Note Professor Stone's
worrying observations on the progress of the problem.
'Jamaica,' he wrote in March 1993, 'is on the verge of
developing a vicious level of narco-terrorism that could
easily mature into the kind of Columbian situation where
drug gangs operate as a state within a state and can dictate
terms to governments, communities and whole societies.'

Stone's point was supported after his death. Statistics
showed that close to 10,000 *violent* crimes were committed in 1993 – 9,000 occurred in Kingston's 'garrisons'.

'Jamaica,' claimed popular *Gleaner* columnist, Dawn Ritch, was now 'the murder capital of the world, ahead of the United States and Singapore.'

Raging gang warfare played no small part in creating that impression. For example, cross-border clashes arising out of a longstanding feud between Eastern Kingston's One Ten (110) Land and South St Andrew's Top Road posses accounted for eighteen murders in 1993. By the summer of 1994 the JCF had compiled a list of no less than fifty-five ruthless criminal gangs comprising up to 3,500 members who, they claimed, were holding Kingston to ransom. Sharing the limelight with the warring crews above were oddly-named outfits such as the Saddam, Bibow, and Chi Chi Boy gangs, and Willie Hagheart's fashion-setting Black Roses Crew. Meanwhile, heading the list of veteran gangster crews were the Shower, Spanglers and Jungle posses and the late 1970s PNP gunman, Radcliffe Rowe's Crew.

The 'unlicensed' gunplay of these assorted drug deal-ing interlopers brought them into direct conflict with their 'official' political cousins in the 'garrisons'. Their erstwhile influence coming under heavy fire, the political hardmen were to lose out badly. 'The drug gangs are independent of the political gang,' explains Williams, 'and are even seen as rivals.'

Rivals yes, equals no. Ultimately, the old guard's inability to challenge the superiority of the new breed of narco-terrorist resulted in a loss of their local political influence; throughout the 1990s, the political dons have seen their fragile hold over the 'garrisons' peter away. The lunatic drug dons have taken over the political dons' ghetto asylum.

It is deeply ironic that the loss of the 'garrisons' to the druggists has badly affected the standing of the Rt. Hon. Edward Seaga, the man cited by many as the architect of modern political tribalism. He certainly seems a changed

man. 'The violence must end once and for all,' announced
Seaga the peace maker. 'I will take every step possible
to ensure that residents of Western Kingston and the
neighbouring communities are free from fear.'

To that end, on 27 September, in much disputed circumstances, the JLP leader sent a list naming thirteen
alleged criminal gang leaders resident in his constituency
to Colonel Trevor MacMillan, the Police Commissioner.
Moreover, Seaga promised a J$25,000 (£500) bounty for
anyone who helped to bring in the man he singled out
as the *capo di tutti capi* ('don of the dons'), Michael
'Dudus' Coke.

Another of the late 'don dadda' Jim Brown's sons,
'Dudus' was quickly eliminated from police enquiries.
In fact, in a clear snub to Seaga, MacMillan maintained
that the JCF's investigations had been prompted by
intelligence from a police informant. Implicit in the
Colonel's rebuff was the idea that 'Mr Eddie's' actions
had been triggered by some personal political agenda.
Remember, the man trying to help the police had played
prominent parts in the funerals of Messrs Jim Brown and
'Jah T'.

Seaga's motives were impugned more overtly by the
PNP, and at least one of his seven Members of Parliament.
While the Opposition leader allegedly stated that by
ridding his constituency of these thugs he ran the real
risk of losing his seat at a future election, his opponents
were adamant that his actions were wholly self-serving.
A common argument was that by eliminating the alleged
gangsters, Seaga was at once disposing of men who had
become his mortal enemies.

Pious indignation was the order of the day for Marjorie
Taylor, the PNP Member of Parliament for East Kingston
and Port Royal. 'The difference between me and Mr
Seaga,' she bragged, 'is that I do not know the criminals.'
She continued: 'I do not associate with such people.'

Esteemed members of Jamaica's Fourth Estate joined in the feeding frenzy, (mostly) at Seaga's expense, including Morris Cargill, the greatly respected PNP politician turned pro-JLP *Gleaner* columnist. 'I suspect Eddie was not above making a virtue out of a necessity,' he wrote, on his way to stretching the local libel laws to their limit. 'His old trusted gang has over the years been replaced by young men, just as criminal but far less committed to the welfare of the J.L.P. Serving no longer any useful purpose, but a squalid criminal nuisance nonetheless, it must have seemed sensible to Eddie to rid his constituency of them if he could.'

Dawn Ritch levelled her mighty pen at Seaga in person, and the political system as a whole. Seaga's list was the result of his loss of control over the new wave of gang leaders, she wrote. In an article aptly entitled 'Chickens Come Home to Roost', she noted that 'the same thing has happened to all politicians in the garrison constituencies'. The reason for this was simple: 'They have no money and no jobs to give out, and cocaine barons now rule the roost.'

'These people were causing a lot of violence in his constituency, and they had no political connections at all,' adds Williams. 'These are just guys who get their money from drugs, levelling violence on the community, terrorising the community.' With Jim Brown dead, Seaga's political influence in his own constituency was now pared to the bone. 'They wouldn't listen to a Seaga,' Williams continues. 'They wouldn't listen to a Manley . . . These guys are just free-wheeling drug dealers.'

Not only would they not listen to 'garrison' Members of Parliament, the rudie drug dons have the all-round clout to shut them out completely. Social provision is one area where they have exerted their influence, the politicos' failure to sponsor urban terrorism having cost them dearly. 'They drive Lexus and Benz,' observes Williams of the new-age narcotics overlords. 'They have a lot more money than the political don of olden times. Again, the political don only had money at election time, but the drug don has money all through the year.'

Not only have they taken over as providers for the elderly, single mothers, children and the vulnerable, their immense capital reserves have allowed them to capture the hearts and minds of the youth. Observes Williams again: 'Some of these guys . . . can outfit a whole football team, buy the latest Chicago Bulls jerseys – which a political don cannot.'

The poisonous liaison between big money, cocaine, firearms and terrorism has had profound implications on another sphere of the political don's traditional ghetto influence; one which strikes at the very heart of political donmanship. At one time when ordinary ghettoites came into conflict with one another they would turn to the local political don to resolve their differences. Today the same people seek an audience with the drug don, and submit to his judgement. At best, then, where he still exists, the political don of today is a king without a throne or a kingdom.

What this implies is that the ruthless Rude Boy narco-terrorists have dislodged the political don in the role of ghetto lawmakers. Worse still, they have become glamorous role models for the youth, and Robin Hood-type heroes for the needy. Now, short of assuming the kind of influence that the late Pablo Escobar, the Medellin cartel cocaine kingpin, exerted over the Columbian Government, the rise of the rudie drug don is complete.

CHAPTER FIVE

The History of Violence

'We here today stand surrounded by an unseen host
of witnesses, the men who in the past and through all
our history strove to keep alight the torch of freedom
in this country.'

Norman Washington Manley
Independence Day, 6 August 1962

Lloyd Williams leans back in the cosy-looking swivel
chair that adorns his New Kingston office, and confides
his controversial views about Jamaicans. 'A Jamaican
doesn't usually brook any foolishness,' he explains. In
fact, he adds in typically understated tones, 'Jamaicans
tend to be aggressive'.

The posse specialist is alluding to the well-established
trait of Jamaicans to challenge authority – whatever
the odds. His opinions are not likely to win many
friends among fellow Jamaicans, but the mild-mannered
Williams speaks from considerable experience. He has
followed the Rude Boys' activities for more than a
decade.

Williams employs an anecdote to qualify his sombre
observation. The story concerns a Jamaican farm worker

employed in the United States. The seasonal contract worker and his colleagues were returning to their digs after an exhausting day in the sun-drenched fields of Florida when their bus was stopped by a lone highway patrolman – the bus driver had apparently been speeding. Annoyed about the hold up, the labourer approached the police officer and, pointing to the patrolman's gun, enquired how many bullets it contained. 'Five,' came the curt reply. 'And how many bullets you have in the pouch? Ten? Fifteen?', enquired the Jamaican. 'Well,' he continued, 'there are twenty-five of us! So what you going do?'

In spite of the real threat of violence nothing became of the incident. But, to Williams, it highlights the no-nonsense mentality that has become synonymous with Jamaican people. When Jamdowners get involved, seemingly trivial encounters can escalate into potentially life-threatening situations.

Even the massed ranks of law-abiding, hard-working, God-fearing Jamaicans are not immune from this national idiosyncracy. (Remember the Seventh Day Adventists who lynched an armed robber in their church?) Indeed, this trait is so pronounced that 'death before dishonour' could easily be substituted for the official Jamaican national motto.

On a different level, this attitude helps to explain the reasons for the disproportionately high success rates humble Jamaicans enjoy on the world stage. Jamaicans might acknowledge that obstacles stand between them and the fulfilment of their goals, but they do not allow that knowledge to deter them; obstacles can be overcome. One need only look to the spheres of sport, art and entertainment, and politics for confirmation. The record shows that Jamaicans have achieved international greatness far in excess of their country's modest population and frugal resources.

In sport, this will to win has thrown up gold medal-grabbing athletes such as the sprinters Don Quarrie, who represented his country at five Olympic Games, and the world's greatest-ever female sprinter, Merlene Ottey; boxers like Trevor Berbeck and Mike McCullum – who won several world titles (in 1986, Berbeck, McCullum and Britain's Jamaican-born pugilist Lloyd Honegan, respectively held the three world titles in their weight division at the same time); cricketers like the legendary batsman Lawrence Rowe; and the bowlers Courtney Walsh and Michael 'Whispering Death' Holding. And basketball is represented by New York Knicks and US All-Star legend, Patrick Ewing – he even has a range of sports shoe named in his honour.

Jamaica also boasts citizens who have greatly enhanced the island's literary and artistic reputations. The late Edna Manley, ex-wife of former Prime Minister, Michael – himself an accomplished writer – is famous for her sculpture; Roger Mais, Mervyn Morris, Vic Reid and Andrew Salkey for their novels; Karl Parsboosingh for his paintings; and Louise Bennett for her giant contributions to poetry.

Reggae is a Jamaican invention, and the idiom's vanguard are internationally-acclaimed writers and performers. Bob Marley and the Wailers did more than anyone to internationalise reggae music (and Rastafari) in the 1970s and 1980s. Now, a decade and a half after Marley's death, Jamaica's first musical superstar is one of only two deceased recording artists whose catalogues are annually oversubscribed – Elvis Presley being the other. Bunny Wailer and the late Peter Tosh (the other lead Wailers) both enjoyed high-profile solo careers. Today Ziggy Marley has taken over as the standard-bearer of his late father's 'one love' message. Meanwhile, Shabba Ranks and Buju Banton have developed international fan clubs through their masterful ability to use ragga to articulate the mood of present-day ghetto Sufferers.

In politics Michael Manley is one of the most respected statesmen Jamaica and the Caribbean have ever produced. The winner of a United Nations medal for his militant anti-apartheid stand, the retired politician's diplomatic skills are still in demand; he was invited to lead the delegation of international observers during the historic free elections in South Africa in 1994. And one of Jamaica's seven National Heroes, Marcus Mosiah Garvey, is viewed by the Rastafari as the prophet of their living god, Haile Selassie. But Garvey, who died in London in 1944, also stands out as the founder and leader of the Universal Negro Improvement Association, the largest black mass movement in history.

There are also the children of Jamaican immigrants who have made their names in the West. Whether Jamaican-born and foreign-raised or first-generation foreign, their Jamaican 'heritage' is a feature common to many of the biggest names in their fields: Linford Christie, British men's athletic team captain and Olympic sprint Gold medallist; television company boss, charity organiser and renowned comic actor, Lenny Henry; John Barnes, ex-Liverpool captain and England football team star; Lennox Lewis, Canadian Olympic Gold-winner and former British world heavyweight boxing champion; and General Colin Powell, the American Purple Heart-honoured, multi-war hero, former White House Chairman of the Joint Chiefs of Staff, and heavily-tipped candidate to become the first black president of the United States.

Fiercely patriotic, the citizens of the 'old country' have delighted in their diverse achievements every bit as much as the people of their respective homelands. Indeed, implicit in the Jamaican jubilation is the idea that their inherent 'Jamaicanness' has made a major contribution to their success.

'Winners' are often the ones who are the best at

channelling their adrenalin – nature's aggression – into their chosen activity. In this sense, the disproportionate success enjoyed by Jamaicans the world over is inseparable from their 'aggressive' disposition; Jamaicans are simply 'conditioned' to achieve.

Even Ben Johnson, the twice-disgraced, steroid-abusing Canadian sprinter, succeeded in this for a while. And the poor example he set provides a fitting introduction to the Rude Boys, a group of Jamaicans whose irrepressible determination to succeed has cast a dark shadow over the good name of their country.

The Rude Boys' aggression has contributed a great deal to the making of the Jamaican gangster. And when wedded *inter alia* to a willingness to use ruthless violence in pursuit of his ends, it helps to explain the sensational international rise of the rudie and his gang.

But why, as Williams sees it, do 'Jamaicans tend to be aggressive'? Is it to do with the environment or the specifics of their colonial experience? Possibly. But the island's British Caribbean neighbours in Barbados and the Republic of Trinidad and Tobago share very similar conditions and experiences, and they have certainly not attracted a reputation for violence like Jamaica and its criminals have. Indeed, far from it. Barbadians are more renowned for their prowess in hitting a cricket ball than they are for 'hitting' rival gangsters. Similarly, the citizenship of Trinidad and Tobago is famous for staging Mas, the Caribbean calypso carnival, and not for staging violent drug rip-offs.

The answer to this riddle – or a considerable part of it – is to be found in the Jamaican legacy. In short, the tradition of violence that sets the Rude Boys – and their law-abiding peers – apart is contained in the peculiarities of Jamaican history.

The roots of the rudie's aggressive manner are buried deep in the soil of Jamaica's historical development. The seeds were planted centuries before Jim Brown turned it into an art form. And the shoots were growing long before Jamaican advertising creatives came up with 'Jamaica: No Problem', a famous tourist industry slogan.

In truth, violence more than passivity has been the standard currency of the majestic island's progress from plantation slave colony to independent state. Far from conforming to Western textbook stereotypes of indolent, happy-go-lucky peasants, the island's inhabitants – black, white and brown – have shown an unerring willingness to take up arms to achieve their goals; to stand up for their rights, as Bob Marley eloquently put it.

In this context, the violent excesses of rudies like Jim Brown are merely the most extreme manifestations of a condition that is as old as Jamaica itself. Indeed, in one way or another, each of the nation's élite band of seven National Heroes has secured that rare distinction through their participation in, or proximity to, serious violence. For, if there is one lesson we can learn from Jamaica's history, it is that violence pays.

Long before Jim Brown's birth or that of his slave progenitors, Jamaica set off on the violent course that dominates its turbulent social and political scene today.

The Arawaks, Jamaica's first inhabitants, were its first victims. Amerindian tribesfolk, they settled in Jamaica around the eighth century AD, arriving in Jamaica armed with little more than paddles, spears and seeds. Clearly awed by its natural abundance, they named their tranquil haven *Xaymaca*, the land of wood and water. But, seven centuries after their arrival, their idyllic existence was to change forever.

As his ship straddled the breathtakingly beautiful coral reefs off Jamaica's north coast, Christopher Columbus remarked that it was 'the fairest island that eyes have ever beheld; the mountains seem to touch the sky'. On 4

May 1492 the explorer dropped anchor at Discovery Bay. His initial relations with the island's estimated 100,000 Arawaks were more than cordial; they worshipped and fêted the Spanish, believing them to be walking gods; they even lavished their golden treasures upon them.

The Indians' generosity was not reciprocated. The Spanish colonists, who began to establish permanent bases on the island in the early sixteenth century, met kindness with misery and cruelty. Writing the island off as useless because of its apparent lack of gold and silver deposits, the Spaniards decided to exploit their hosts. The Indians were forcibly enslaved, made to work on plantations, or serve as perpetually indentured domestics. Those who could not or would not comply with the Spanish diktats – and there was small-scale resistance – were brutally punished. Countless Arawaks were massacred; numerous died from being overworked; others committed suicide in protest at their inhumane treatment.

The effect on the Arawaks was catastrophic. By 1598 Arawak numbers were dwindling at a phenomenal rate. So much so that the erstwhile Governor of Jamaica, Fernando Melgarejo, was driven to propose protective measures. Melgarejo's suggestion was for a 'reserve', where the simple Arawaks could live by their own laws, customs and traditions, unmolested by the sophisticated colonists. However, the embryonic but influential Spanish plantocracy could see no collective benefit. After all, they reasoned, they had introduced crops. Who would tend them if the Arawaks were freed? So, Melgarejo's plan, probably the last chance for Arawak survival, was unceremoniously shelved. By the time the British captured Jamaica half a century later, the indigenous Arawaks had become extinct.

After decimating the Arawak slave population the Spanish set about importing replacements from Africa.

However, Spain's importation of African slaves into Jamaica was to be short-lived. Like the Arawaks, its cruel stranglehold on Jamaica was coming to an end.

The seventeenth century marked a watershed in European political and economic relations. In 1493 Pope Alexander VI granted Spain and Portugal the right to exploit the New World. A century and a half later the cosy bilateral arrangement which had allowed the two all-conquering nations to carve up large tracts of the new territories was in mortal jeopardy. The Iberian duopoly found itself under attack from its emergent sea-faring and increasingly hawkish European neighbours: Britain, France and Holland.

Jamaica was ripe for the picking. The island's economy had regressed by the end of Spain's tutelage. The Spaniards had treated Jamaica like a seventeenth-century motorway café; a place where seafarers stopped off to take on provisions or repair their craft. Worse, with a population of only 3,000 – half being African slaves – its defences were rudimentary and inadequate.

The opportunity was finally seized by the British on 10 May 1655. A hundred and fifty years after Columbus's 'discovery' of Jamaica, an 8,000-strong British invasion force breezed into the port of what is today the capital, Kingston. Meanwhile, the Spaniards freed their slaves and livestock, and headed for the aptly named Runaway Bay on the north coast, before sailing to nearby Cuba.

The greatest resistance to British hegemony during this period came from the Maroons, the African slaves who had fled or been freed from Spanish captivity. 'Maroon' is derived from the Spanish word *cimarron*, meaning 'wild'. Originally used to describe feral cattle, by the mid-sixteenth century Maroon came to mean African runaway slaves.

In all, the British spent the first eighty years of their occupation in a futile and costly attempt to re-enslave the escapees. The Maroons might have been considered wild but, as the British soon discovered, the Africans they encountered were an extremely brave, calculated and sophisticated foe.

Importantly, Jamaica's Maroons differed significantly from their counterparts on other Caribbean islands. This group hailed from the Akan-speaking peoples of the Gold Coast; predominantly the Ashanti and Fanti nations. These slaves were collectively known as Coromantes, the name stemming from Cormantine, a small British fort on the Gold Coast constructed in the 1630s. Descended from noble warrior castes, the Coromantes were athletic and strong in build, thought and enterprise. Significantly, they were feared by their African peers and European slave traders alike; the Coromantes did not think twice about killing their foes.

In spite of the reputation they developed for riotous behaviour, the Coromantes were the British plantation-owners' preference of slave. Their intelligence, durability and raw strength made them highly-valued slave stock. Jamaican plantation owners even turned down offers from prosperous merchants for them. Partly because of this, Jamaica soon provided the biggest penitentiary for the Coromantes.

Not content to merely evade recapture, the Maroons began a process of positive engagement. Such aggressive behaviour was to typify Maroon-British relations for the better part of the next hundred and thirty years. Not infrequently bands of Maroons would descend from their mountainous retreats to attack and pillage local plantations for livestock, provisions, weapons and ammunition. But civilian sites were not the only targets of Maroon raids. The British militia was equally vulnerable to attack.

Predictably, the British authorities viewed the Maroons' lawless, quasi-autonomous settlements with contempt; they were inimical to the interests of the *status quo*, and had to be destroyed at all costs. The British unilaterally declared a genocidal war on them.

In practice, however, the British found a formidable enemy in the Jamaican Maroons. The colonial forces were fighting an invisible army, one that was expert in using Jamaica's unforgiving topography to wage guerrilla warfare on the British Redcoats. For all that, the British prevailed in the early battles. But the hostilities did not end there. Their numbers augmented by a succession of slave rebellions, the Maroons went on to wage two almighty wars against the British.

The First Maroon War took place between 1690–1739. The African 'soldiers' fell under the command of Cudjoe. The son of an Ashanti who had himself escaped the tyranny of plantation slavery, Cudjoe co-ordinated the various Maroon communities' attacks on the invaders.

Cudjoe worked in concert with Nanny, the chief of the Maroons in the Blue Mountains. Her contribution to the Maroon war effort led her to be canonized as one of Jamaica's National Heroes, the only woman. Like Cudjoe, Nanny was an Ashanti, but unlike him she had never been enslaved. The Maroon heroine was said to possess supernatural powers which immunised her from the effects of the enemy's bullets.

Like earlier Maroon combatants, Cudjoe's guerrillas mounted hit-and-run attacks. During the midnight skirmishes they razed plantations, liberated slaves, destroyed crops and stole livestock. In addition, they lured the Redcoats to mock villages where they were surrounded and attacked.

Embattled and despondent, the British were compelled to import specially-trained tracker dogs from Cuba to sniff out the enemy. They also enlisted the services of free slaves and 200 Indians from the Mosquito Coast to fight alongside them.

In the end, the hostilities were brought to a close at the behest of Colonel John Guthrie, the Commander-in-Chief of the hapless Redcoats. The endless succession of Maroon victories were demoralising his men, and emboldening the slaves. So, in 1739, the humiliated Colonel sat down with Cudjoe beneath the sprawling branches of a cotton tree in Cockpit Country and put his signature to 'a treaty of peace and friendship with . . . Captain Cudjoe and the rest of his captains'. The pact was sealed with the blood of its co-signators.

Crucially, the peace treaty guaranteed Cudjoe *et al* land, hunting rights, and, most importantly, the right to self-determination. In return, the Maroons agreed to desist from harbouring fugitive slaves and, equally significantly, to help the British track down and recapture escapees in future. In 1740 the British struck a similar deal with Nanny's Blue Mountain Maroons, but it is said that she steadfastly refused to return runaway slaves to an uncertain fate.

The war ended in a notable victory for the Maroons, and soul-destroying defeat for the British. The extent of the British climbdown can be seen in one of the terms it signally failed to get the Maroons to ratify: the imposition of taxes. The Maroons refused point blank, arguing that if they were living in their own lands the British had no jurisdiction over them.

The Maroon-British peace held for fifty years until the British violated it. The Second Maroon War was sparked by a seemingly trivial event: the public flogging of two Maroons in Falmouth, Trelawny. To make matters worse, the lash was applied by a runaway slave, who the victims' group had previously recaptured and returned to his owner's plantation.

The war began in earnest when Maroon insurgents

burned down Trelawny Town. The conflict raged on for
a year, following a similar pattern to previous Maroon-
British encounters. The Africans adopted guerrilla tactics,
the British sustained heavy and demoralising losses.
Once again, the colonists were compelled to import
man-hunting dogs from Cuba. And finally the war ended
in the signing of a peace treaty proposed by General
Walpole, the British Commander-in-Chief.

During the early years the Maroons were not the only
ones to successfully use force against the British to realise
their ambitions. At times, and in their own ways, both
Jamaica's slave and buccaneer populations replicated the
Maroons' example.

The buccaneers were a motley bunch of lawless,
stateless transients who inhabited the coastal regions
of Hispaniola, Cuba, Jamaica and thereabouts around
the mid-sixteenth century. A combination of runaway
servants, opportunists, deserters, marooned sailors and
criminals, they began their careers as indigent traders;
hunting animals, smoking their meat over grills called
boucans – hence the term buccaneer – and selling the
product to passing ships.

In time, the increasingly prosperous buccaneers got
into piracy, for which they are infamous. They hijacked
ships and used them to terrorise the waters around the
region.

British buccaneers set up shop in the fort at Port
Royal, the first British capital of Jamaica, shortly
after the island was taken from Spain. The 8,000-
strong settlement was to achieve international notoriety
as the 'pirate capital' of the world. It became the
adopted home of legendary pirates such as Calico Jack,
Bluebeard and Henry Morgan.

The most famous of all the buccaneers was Henry
Morgan. And he, more than any other, exemplifies the

tradition which has seen Jamaica reward violence with success. Morgan was the son of a wealthy Welsh farmer. He sailed originally to Barbados, where he was to be an indentured servant. However, his greater ambitions got the better of him, and he fled to Hispaniola. The young Morgan joined the buccaneers there, but his career took off in Jamaica.

Within a few years of his arrival at Port Royal, Morgan was appointed 'admiral-in-chief of the confederacy of the Jamaican pirates'. And, through his exploits on the high seas, he went on to attain the reputation of a nautical superstar.

Initially the buccaneers were viewed with open disdain by the British authorities at Port Royal. A parasitic and ungentlemanly threat, their lewd behaviour led the settlement to gain the unsavoury reputation as 'the wickedest city in Christendom'.

The buccaneers were tolerated for two reasons. One, their piratical money-making ventures turned Port Royal into the richest city in the entire Caribbean. Two, by allowing the buccaneers to settle in Port Royal, the British authorities afforded themselves an insurance policy against piratical attack – the buccaneers seldom pillaged from their adopted settlements.

But it was the dual demands of war and empire-building that finally cemented the relationship between the buccaneers and the British authorities, and gave rise to the fame of pirates such as Henry Morgan. In the 1660s, with Britain's forces depleted by war with Holland and conflict with Spain, Britain found a ready outlet for the buccaneers' dubious skills. The British officially sanctioned the buccaneers' criminal activities; effectively reinventing the buccaneers as glamorous British mercenaries. Privateering, as it was known, became a glorified form of piracy. Moreover, by recruiting the buccaneers, the British constructed a buffer from behind

which they could pursue their designs on imperial expan-
sionism. The British even licensed the practice, requiring
privateers to pay for the privilege.

Henry Morgan's infamy stems from his ruthless
privateering attacks against Spanish settlements. He ravaged Puerto Principe in Cuba; pillaged the town of
Maracaibo; and tortured and slaughtered the inhabitants
of Porto Bello and Panama City. Moreover, Morgan
returned to Jamaica with hundreds of thousands of silver
'pieces of eight'. He became a Jamaican hero.

Significantly, Morgan received royal approval after his
'heroic' destruction of Panama City; he was knighted by
King Charles II. In the slash of a sword, Morgan the
bloodthirsty barbarian was transformed into Morgan the
respectable gentleman.

Sir Henry Morgan used his sumptuous wealth to build
himself a showpiece mansion in Port Royal, and invest
in several sugar plantations across the island. His new
status finally saw him elevated to the rank of Lieutenant-
Governor of Jamaica, the island's second highest office.

If Jamaica's colonial establishment initially viewed the
buccaneers with hostility, then its volatile slave populations were seen as a perennial danger. Indeed, scarcely
a year passed between the seventeenth and nineteenth
centuries without a major slave rebellion – or at least the
threat of one. In truth, the whole of the Jamaican slave era
was one long black struggle against white oppression.

When Britain conquered Jamaica it continued Spain's
African slave-importing tradition with a vengeance. By
the time the slave trade was abolished in 1808, in
excess of one million slaves had been imported into
Jamaica.

The increasing demand for African slaves was stimu-
lated by a fundamental shift in Jamaica's agricultural
activity. The cultivation of tobacco, cotton and other

small-scale crops had been superseded by the large-scale, labour-intensive cultivation of sugar. Indeed, sugar became the prime currency of commerce in the New World during the eighteenth century, and was central to the expansion of Britain's coffers.

This transformation can be gleaned from the rapid growth of the island's large sugar plantations. In the mid-1670s there were less than sixty. Seventy years on, there were at least 430. Indeed, during the eighteenth century Britain was to become the world's largest single producer of sugar, making it the jewel in Great Britain's imperial crown.

Sugar's ability to generate obscene wealth was apparent in the rising fortunes of the entrepreneurs involved in its trade. Suffice it to say that the Lloyd and Barclay families made enough capital out of the trade to set up the banks which bear their names to this day.

But the slave trade was not without its drawbacks – the biggest being the unpredictable temperament and behaviour of the slaves themselves. Needless to say, the Africans resisted enslavement from the day of capture onwards. Violence both circumscribed and underpinned the relationships between African and European from the outset.

British slave traders (and their European competitors) drew their supplies from the populous West Coast of Africa. Africans were sold into slavery in their millions. The whole experience from capture to plantation was one of pronounced humiliation, fear and brutality for the African. They were force-marched in chains to slave compounds. Before shipping, they were stripped and had their heads shaved; many were then branded with their owner's stamp. Once aboard ship, the Africans were chained together, and stored on shelves in the often insanitary hold. At best, each slave was allocated a space smaller than an adult coffin.

Mortality rates among slaves in transit went as high as fifty per cent. It is estimated that of the fifteen million Africans enslaved from the shores of the Dark Continent, between a third and a half died along the 'middle passage'.

Death stemmed from a number of causes, including suffocation and overheating, contagious diseases and malnutrition. A great many, especially the Coromantes, died in the course of resisting their captors. Countless were beaten to death by merciless sailors. Other mutinous slaves were thrown overboard.

Proud African females were also included in the death toll. Pregnant women often killed their babies at birth, rather than have them grow up in captivity. Others ended their own lives by hunger strikes, hanging or jumping overboard.

Slavers took between two to three months to complete their 6,000 mile voyages. On arrival – even before the slaves were auctioned off – the brutal process of 'seasoning' was set in train. 'Seasoning' was the practice of domesticating new slaves into the plantation existence; and of conditioning them to believe that all Africans were inferior, and all whites superior.

The process could take up to three years – an eternity given that the life-expectancy of the average plantation slave was only nine years. The copious use of the whip formed the mainstay of the 'seasoning' process. Slaves could expect to be whipped, often by their peers, for the most minor infraction.

In some respects, though, whipping was the least of their worries. The most sadistic plantation owners would decree that rebellious or otherwise disobedient slaves should have a limb amputated, or be executed. Not surprisingly, up to a third of all slaves died during the 'seasoning' process. The tacit message – one that lives on to this day – was that a black life was cheap.

With or without plantation discipline, the slave's existence was punishing. The average slave could expect to
toil anywhere up to eighteen hours a day, beginning at
4 a.m. Land was set aside for the slaves to tend to their
own provisions during breaks in their work. After slavery
this practice was to provide the new peasantry with an
essential tool for their independence and survival.

Yet, for all the violence perpetrated against them, the
slaves resisted. The passive form manifested itself in
techniques such as playing dumb – after all, slaves
were supposed to be limited intellectually – murdering
newborn babies, committing suicide, tacitly working-to-
rule, sabotaging machinery, and – for those who could –
running away.

Rebellion, however, remained the ultimate expression
of resistance; every slave lived only to win his or her freedom. One of the most organised and ruthless attacks on the
plantocratic structure came in 1760. It was masterminded
and led by a runaway slave named Tacky.

Tacky, another Coromante, had two bold and clearly-
defined objectives: genocide on Jamaica's white population; and, the imposition of a black colony. The warrior's
offensive began with an attack on Port Maria in St Mary
but quickly spread throughout Jamaica. The fighting,
which lasted six months, embraced a thousand slaves
across the island. Tacky's freedom fighters killed sixty
whites, and destroyed thousands of pounds worth of
property. Before he was killed, Tacky and his followers
sought refuge in the mountains – only to be pursued by
the Maroons. His eventual death left a leadership void
and, rather than be re-enslaved, several of his followers
chose death by their own hand.

The bloodletting did nothing to dissuade other slaves
from hatching freedom plots; there were a further twenty
during the twenty-five years after Tacky's death. However, 1832 marked the island's last significant slave

rebellion. The Christmas Rebellion was short-lived but had an unquestionable bearing on the future shape of black-white relations throughout the British Empire. In the two weeks that it was active, the rebellion accounted for more than £1 million-worth of plantation damage, and, involved 20,000 rampaging slaves.

The plot was hatched as early as August 1831 by Sam Sharpe, a Baptist lay preacher and town slave. Yet another of Jamaica's hallowed band of National Heroes, Sharpe went on to win the honour through his violent deeds.

Known affectionately as 'Daddy' Sharpe, the holy man used his 'spiritual' credentials as a cover to clandestinely enlist the support of slaves across four western parishes. As a preacher he had the freedom to wander unmolested from plantation to plantation, spreading the word of God to the downtrodden slaves. But Sharpe used his privileges instead to foment rebellion.

The cleric's plan was to use the Christmas break – when the plantocracy's guard would be at its lowest – as a launch pad for a full-scale rebellion. He succeeded. In the days that followed plantations were razed and their slaves released to join the battle, a dozen whites were butchered, and martial law declared.

Martial law was followed by a promise of amnesty. Thousands of slaves responded only to be subjected on surrender to what amounted to 'kangaroo' court justice; they were expeditiously executed. Those fortunate enough to escape the quasi-judicial lottery were given up to 500 lashes of the whip.

Meanwhile, the self-confessed plotter was sent to the gallows in Montego Bay on 23 May 1832. Unrepentant to the last, Sharpe's final words sum up the spirit of the slave, past, present and future. 'I would rather die on yonder gallows,' he told his executioner, 'than live in slavery.'

The significance of the Christmas Rebellion cannot

be understated; it catapulted the issue of slavery to the top of Britain's political agenda. 'Moral', 'ethical' and 'Christian' sentiments aside, the benefits of slavery were agreed to be outweighed by the violent volatility of the slave masses. The only safeguard against future volcanic slave eruptions was to abolish the practice altogether. On 1 August 1834, the British Parliament outlawed slavery in its territories. Jamaican violence – or the threat thereof – had paid off for all British slaves.

The Christmas Rebellion was not the only violent episode in Jamaica's bloody history to be rewarded with overwhelming social and political change. Only thirty years after the Emancipation Proclamation transformed the status of slaves across the British West Indies, an epoch-making rebellion took place which had profound repercussions, on the day-to-day government of Jamaica.

By 1865 the recently emancipated Jamaican slaves were suffering under a new form of bondage. The abolition of slavery had triggered the rise of a new black peasantry; a population which was toiling against the odds to make a fresh start away from the stigma of plantation labour. However, through no fault of their own, their efforts bore little fruit.

Once the overflowing font of Britain's economic fortunes, Jamaica was now on the breadline. And with Britain now one of the world's undisputed leading maritime, financial and industrial nations, its interest in the loss-making Old Empire had waned.

Ironically, the abolition of slavery itself contributed to their overall problems insofar as it precipitated the terminal decline of Jamaica's plantation sugar economy. Emancipating the slaves meant paying them for their labour, something the struggling sugar plantocracy was not in a position to do. Subsequently production costs spiralled out of control, while the global price of sugar tumbled.

Jamaica also suffered from internal ailments. Disease killed thousands. Drought caused crops to fail, inducing an overreliance on imported foodstuffs. In fact, by 1865 Jamaica was importing most of its provisions from the United States – fatally, at the very moment America was in the throes of its Civil War, pushing the price of its exports through the ceiling.

The Jamaican peasantry felt the privations of everyday life the most. Unemployment was chronic. The cost of living had risen out of all proportion to increasingly devalued wages. Worse, no-one seemed to give a damn about their wretched condition. The House of Assembly, Jamaica's semi-autonomous legislature, was unmoved. Controlled by a coterie of powerful, white sugar interests since its inception in 1664, its only salient change had seen the inclusion of a few rich, bi-racial Jamaicans. Most of them mimicked the white class's views and acts; they were definitely no friend of the black masses.

The autocratic Assembly imposed exacting taxes on the disenfranchised peasantry with no regard for their inability to pay them. Laws were enacted to meet the planter class's needs alone; justice was that thing that served the white oligarchy's interests.

The island's Governor was central to the Jamaican peasantry's dilemma. In a previous incarnation, Edward John Eyre had immortalised himself as a formidable explorer and brave Protector of Aborigines in Australia. But that was then and this was now.

To him, the poor's dire condition was brought about by their own indolence and fecklessness. Or, as Eyre put it: 'The utter want of principle or moral sense . . . are quite sufficient to account for any poverty or crime which may exist amongst the peasantry of Jamaica.' This was endorsed by the Colonial Office, which 'advised' that the peasantry's prosperity depended on 'their working for wages, not uncertainly, or capriciously, but steadily and continuously . . .'

The sum of this black suffering and white indifference was to set the stage for a duo of Jamaica's National Heroes to come to the fore in the context of the Morant Bay Rebellion. Those heroes were George William Gordon and Paul Bogle.

Gordon was the product of a liaison between a wealthy Scottish planter and one of his slave mistresses. A member of the Assembly, he rejected the comfortable niche of 'respectability' his immense wealth and property could have afforded him. He opted instead to champion the rights of impoverished Jamaicans. An autodidact and talented orator, he saved his choicest invective for Governor Eyre's maladministration of Jamaica; this ultimately cost Gordon his life.

A magistrate – until Eyre disbarred him – Gordon had ordained Paul Bogle as the Baptist deacon of a settlement called Stony Gut. He, more than Gordon, was the true leader of the Morant Bay Rebellion.

Bogle was a farm owner and first-generation free black man, descended from a slave who was also a Baptist deacon. Bogle's considerable business interests resulted in his being one of only a hundred-odd men to be given the franchise in St Thomas. Still, wealth and privilege did not dent his enthusiasm for black equality and justice.

Like Gordon, Bogle used his influence in an attempt to improve the lot of his followers in Stony Gut. He vociferously demanded improved wages and working conditions, reductions in the price of staple foods, and access to land for cultivation by his people.

Suitably, the prelude to the rebellion was a local court case over disputed land involving one of Bogle's congregation. The defendant had refused to pay rent on land he occupied in Stony Gut, arguing that it was the

common property of the villagers. In the event, Bogle
and his supporters disrupted the trial. In turn, the Custos
(the governor's representative), a German immigrant by
the name of Baron Von Ketelhodt, issued a warrant for the
arrest of Bogle and twenty-one members of his posse.

Bogle's men kidnapped the police party that was sent
to arrest the felons, and cajoled them on pain of death to
pledge their support for him. The next day Bogle and his
cadres staged a protest march on the Morant Bay court
house to lobby for black equality. By the time the group
arrived in town its ranks had swollen, and events took a
dramatic turn for the worse.

From inside the court room the petrified baron read
the riot act. But even before he could finish, he and his
men came under attack from the rampaging protesters.
Seven Boglites were shot dead. Meanwhile, Ketelhodt
was murdered, and thirteen of his men perished when the
insurrectionists set fire to the court-house. In the fray that
followed prisoners were released, and the police station
was raided and weapons seized.

Emboldened by his success at Morant Bay, Bogle led
a party of insurgents on to local plantations where they
liberated the workers. Reactionary servants and barbaric
planters were singled out for execution. For the next
three days Bogle's 'liberation' army marauded through
the estates of St Thomas imposing their own brand of
equality and justice.

Eyre's response was as swift as it was brutal. A dicta-
torial and unpopular man, he declared martial law. The
Governor dispatched *HMS Wolverine*, a British gunboat,
from Kingston to the troubled area. The soldiers aboard
pursued a scorched earth policy, shooting or hanging 600
rebels. A similar number was flogged, and a thousand
dwellings were burnt to the ground.

As the dust settled, Gordon – in Kingston during the
affray – was illegally returned to Morant Bay on Eyre's

instructions, to stand 'trial' for fomenting the rebellion. No evidence existed against him, but within hours of his return Gordon was hanged. (Incidentally, in a Victorian *cause célèbre*, Eyre was recalled, dismissed, tried and eventually acquitted of Gordon's murder at the Old Bailey.) Bogle, who protested Gordon's innocence, was captured by Maroon forces, and hanged aboard HMS *Wolverine* on 24 October 1865.

News of the Morant Bay Rebellion had a profound effect on the British Parliament. Its causes became the focus for a 900-page Royal Commission report which concluded that Jamaica had suffered from incompetent government. The only solution was radical constitutional change.

Accordingly, the island and all British West Indian interests save Barbados became a Crown Colony; Jamaican government falling directly under the control of the British Crown. For the first time since 1664, Jamaica's plantocratic oligarchy found themselves with wealth, but little power.

The new constitutional arrangements paved the way for beneficial reforms in areas like education and healthcare, and marginal improvements in the condition of the masses followed.

Race – or perceived racial differences – increased in importance as Jamaica rolled into the millennium. However, Jamaica stumbled forward in relative peace until riots erupted in 1938, and all but plunged the colony into anarchy.

The workers' riots were in no part due to Crown Colony government. The new regime was as disinterested in the needs and aspirations of the disenfranchised masses as it was their former political masters. At best, the new leadership merely removed the pronounced pro-planter bias from previous legislation. This enabled the poor, almost by default, to make limited progress. But, for the most part, the only lasting contribution successive Jamaican Governors made was in the form of uninformed legislation and vacuous leadership; like Nero the hierarchy fiddled while Jamaica burned.

Jamaica's terminal plight was brought into sharp relief by the Sufferers. The vast majority of the island's burgeoning population had no votes, no protection and no rights. And the void showed – wages had not been raised since emancipation. They lived in substandard accommodation, were malnourished and highly susceptible to disease.

It was amongst this dispossessed group that the 1938 workers' riots drew their intellectual inspiration and physical power. Emboldened by the teachings of Garvey *et al*, black people throughout the Caribbean Basin began to rise up violently in search of their rights. As with its British West Indian peers, the outbursts of street violence marked a crucial turning point in Jamaica's political and economic development. They represented the populace's first faltering steps along the difficult road towards national independence; and the end of the plantocratic reign. The riots culminated in the formation of trade unions and black-led political parties.

The first in a rash of disturbances which lasted for six months took place in St Thomas in January 1938. Some 1,500 workers at Serge Island went on strike for improved wages and conditions. Predictably, their demands were met with State resistance. However, Jamaica's poor were undeterred, and the small island was quickly swallowed up by a tidal wave of similar strikes.

Those disputes were soon to have fatal consequences. In April, Sufferers at the Tate & Lyle plant in Westmorland withdrew their labour. Management responded with a bid to employ 'scab' labour from Jamaica's huge pool of reserve workers. Not unsurprisingly, major violence flared in which a handful of Sufferers were shot dead by the police.

For the next three months strikes ran along the gamut of Jamaica's working classes: dockers, domestic servants, banana cutters, cane workers. Strike-related violence claimed the lives of a dozen or so Sufferers.

It was during this period that the remaining twosome of Jamaica's National Heroes came to prominence, the middle class mulatto cousins, (Sir) William Alexander Bustamante and Norman Washington Manley. Both were also central to the later struggle for Jamaican self-government and independence.

Born Alexander Clarke, Bustamante was the son of an Irish father and a brown-skinned mother. After a succession of jobs, he settled down to work as a money-lender. However, neither Bustamante's mixed parentage nor chosen profession precluded his involvement in organising black workers and leading strikes; an involvement which caused the authorities to imprison him during the 1938 riots.

A charismatic extrovert, 'Busta' was an unrivalled champion of the rights of the black poor. His considerable popular appeal emanated from his readiness to cross the dual racial and class divide and use his station to stand up to the employers, the authorities and the police. His dedication won him a mass black following. An autodidact, it also enabled him to found Jamaica and the Caribbean's first trade union, the Bustamante Industrial Trade Union, in 1938.

Norman Washington Manley, KC, was the antithesis of his older cousin. Where Bustamante was ruled by his passionate emotions, Manley was governed by his considerable intellect. A First World War hero, Manley was a distinguished athlete and Oxford-educated Rhodes scholar. In fact, he won first class honours at the Bar at Jesus College, and was Prizeman at Gray's Inn.

Jamaica's finest lawyer, Manley stepped into the breach as a mediator when his cousin was imprisoned. He was able to use his polished communication skills to relay the bigger picture to ordinary Jamaicans. Namely, that their aspirations for a brighter future were inexorably tied to their overall ability to influence it. With this in mind Manley, a staunch nationalist, helped to found the People's National Party in 1938 as a vehicle to mobilise the masses. In the constitutional changes that accompanied the 1944 elections it was his agitation that led to the introduction of universal suffrage.

Both Manley and Bustamante made their mark during the unrest, and were to dominate the national political scene for the next three decades. But, significantly, neither man could claim to have resolved the strikes. That distinction was held by the workers, the ones who stood to gain most from it. Not only did they win substantial wage increases, they also forced the local government to pass legislation to improve their rights and conditions, and legalise trade unionism.

How conscious the workers of 1938 were of the historical precedents for their actions is unclear. But there can be no doubt that violent aggression has been the most impressive weapon in the armoury of all of those – the Spanish, the Maroons, the buccaneers, the African slaves, the peasants and the workers – who have striven to make their mark in Jamaica.

Similarly, the willingness of Rude Boys like Jim Brown to apply ruthless violence in pursuit of their goals has been central to explaining their global rise. For all that, though, they are not unique. Jim Brown and Co. have merely revolutionised a practice that has been used by equally ambitious Jamaicans for the past 500 years.

CHAPTER SIX

A Culture of Violence

'Guns are more important than sex. Once you have a gun you can have all the sex you want. Guns give you anything you want – money, food, TV, car. No girl can say "no" when you hold a gun to her neck. No man can say "no" when you say "gimme or else". Once you have a gun, you have happiness.'

Father Richard Ho Lung, commenting ironically on the mentality towards gunmanship in the ghetto. From his 'Diary of The Ghetto Priest' column in *The Daily Gleaner*, 1 October 1993

'Some of the incidents that trigger violence in the ghetto are frighteningly trivial: casual remarks about women or clothes; an accidental stepping on someone's foot; approaching the Don's lady for a dance; accidentally spilling beer on someone; not showing enough respect and deference to bad men. All of these trivial circumstances are the stuff of which dances are shot up, families massacred with M-16 assault rifles, youths are shot and put in garbage bags and houses are invaded and burned down.'

Carl Stone, *Weekly Gleaner*, 3 November 1992

Violence is not new to Jamaica. Mass violence has been a hoe in the hands of generations of down-trodden African-Jamaicans; the tool they used to clear the weed-choked

ground in which the seeds of an independent Jamaica
were planted, and have struggled to grow.

Ironically, since Jamaican independence, another species of violence has taken root; a virulent, weed-like strain
which with every passing day threatens to undermine the
roots of independent nationhood. This new species is not
to be confused with the infestations of criminal violence
and political tribalism, although their effects have been
equally divisive and destructive.

In keeping with its criminal and political cousins,
this parallel form of violence has ravaged entire ghetto
communities. In essence, it is – for want of a better term
– wholly social. Arguably, this oxymoronic practice has
always been part of everyday Jamaican life, especially
amongst those whose lives are played out beyond the
margins. But over the past three decades in particular,
violent social crime has reached plague proportions in
Jamaica's festering ghettoes and shantytowns. It has
become what one Jamaican commentator called 'a socio-
spiritual cancer which is rapidly spreading'. Like an
all-pervasive mental illness, it has spawned a generation
of psychotics and psychopaths; men and women whose
violent behaviour has become something of a rule, rather
than an exception.

Nobody has expressed this doomsday scenario more
eloquently than Diana McCauley. In the autumn of 1994 she
passed judgement on her fellow Jamaicans in an article aptly
entitled 'A Culture of Violence'. 'We are a violent people,'
asserted the accomplished *Gleaner* columnist, 'and crime is
rampant in our country because we believe in violence. We
believe it gets us what we want.'

Of Jamaica's estimated 700 murders in 1994, about
four in every ten victims died as a result of some
domestic, often drug-related, altercation. The Jamaican
belief in social violence is an axiom that extends to all
sections of society, the well-heeled and educated middle

classes included. The pull of violence is such that it has been institutionalised into the language and culture of Jamaica. For instance, people who contract sexually transmitted diseases often talk of getting 'shot'.

However, reggae music has perpetuated this trend more than any other aspect of Jamaican culture. One need only survey some of the stage names adopted over the years to appreciate the force violence has in popular culture: Dillinger, (Dennis) Alcapone, Louie Lepki, Josey Wales, Bounti Killa and the oddly-named Gun John Crow. Until a recent clampdown by the Jamaican police, Ninjaman, a top DJ (rapper) had carved a profitable international career out of preaching gun lyrics. At the same time, dancehall sessions have been a frequent venue for real-life violence and murder. And a welter of the genre's leading exponents have been consigned to an early grave as a result of it.

The social acceptability of violence combined with the harsh political economy of ghetto life has given rise to some of Jamaica's most ruthless criminal killers. Simultaneously, it has prompted generations of Jamaican ghetto teenagers to idolise the gun and gunmanship in the same way that Western youth deify the latest rock band or football star. Even the supposedly 'good guys' – the church-goers, the police, the politicians and generally law-abiding citizenry – have been highly susceptible to this contagious disorder.

And it is precisely because of the indiscretions of Jamaicans like these that one can better understand the social acceptance, deification even, of the Rude Boys. The fact is that Jamaican society as a whole has capitulated in transforming ruthless gangsters into latter-day heroes because of their capacity for violent disorder.

'Compared to the Jamaica I grew up in,' lamented the Hon. Carl Stone, a few months before his death, 'our country has become an arena of violence, aggression and lawless behaviour.' But this, wrote the distinguished fifty-two-year-old scholar in November 1992, was 'really just the tip of the iceberg'. A far bigger problem was Jamaican society's general 'proneness' to acts of aggression and violence. Stone identified these traits in the all-too-common practice of 'Verbal abuse and forty shilling words', and the obvious fact that nobody respected 'rules anymore or the rights of others'. 'Bullyism,' he complained bitterly, 'is now the norm.'

Few were better placed to comment on the subject than Carl Stone. In the same article he confessed to once holding a lorry driver at gun point until the police arrived after the motorist 'ran into a lady's car and was insisting on driving away'. Stone also allegedly lawfully shot and killed two men in separate bar room incidents. Jamaica really had changed beyond recognition since the Professor's youth – although his analysis was no doubt coloured by an overly romantic recollection of the 1950s and early 1960s.

Indeed, juvenile delinquency had begun to surface as a serious problem during the first half of the 1960s, when Stone was in his early twenties. More and more young, dispossessed, city-dwelling Rude Boys were embarking upon careers as petty criminals. This showed up in a significant upsurge in theft, burglary, shop-lifting and robbery. It was not until the 1970s, however, that many of the same, by now recidivist, criminals started graduating into violent crimes such as rape, mugging and armed robbery.

The first signs of Jamaica's shift towards a culture of violence came as early as the late 1960s. One of the earliest indications that this was not just a criminal 'thing' came in the guise of an outbreak of mob violence.

It was in 1974, for example, when the Seventh Day Adventist lynch mob struck. There were thirty-five such lynchings in 1984 alone. And Jamaica's press still report stories about violent vigilantism today.

Almost anyone, it seems, is liable to take the law into their own hands. Age is certainly not a factor, as a group of Kingston College students demonstrated in the summer of 1993. A group of teenage students 'disciplined' one of two prowlers on the campus who had attempted to rob one of their classmates. According to the *Gleaner*, the robber was given 'a fine beating before he was rescued'. But his ordeal did not end there. As the news spread, a posse of irate local citizens descended on the seat of learning to issue 'a second beating'. Fortunately for the villain, they were prevented from doing so.

In an earlier, ghoulish illustration, a group of country folk took a leaf out of South African township 'justice' to settle a score. Having apprehended some suspected cattle-rustlers, they promptly 'necklaced' them in blazing petrol-soaked tyres.

As horrific as this incident was, there is a great deal of public tolerance – even sympathy – for displays like this. Take, for example, the case of a neighbour-hood watch scheme operating in crime-infested central Kingston. In August 1992, the group was alerted to a violent, attempted armed robbery – two knife-wielding desperadoes were trying to hijack a British tourist's hire car. The agreement holder bravely resisted, while his niece sounded the alarm – she was slashed across the face with a knife for her pains. Seeing the attack on his niece, the petrified visitor ran away, only to be chased by the lowlifes. Within minutes a posse of watch groupers had descended on the scene like a ghetto cavalry, and the hunters became the hunted. In no time, the volunteer force had corralled the thieves. How-ever, rather than making citizens' arrests, the volunteer force opted to exact street revenge. One of the villains managed to escape with a beating and a stabbing. His hapless accomplice, by contrast, was unmercifully beaten to death.

The significance of this event is derived from the way it was covered by the local press. A report of the incident was plastered across the front page of the *Star*, Jamaica's evening tabloid. A popular paper, the reportage is particularly revealing insofar as it further endorses McCauley's view about the disturbing Jamaican social acceptance of violence; that the means, no matter how lawless, justify the social results. What is most astonishing about the *Star*'s account, however, is both the tacitly reverential manner with which it reported the watch group members' 'heroics', and the matter-of-factness with which it dealt with their lawless brutality.

'Quick action from Neighbourhood Watch . . . ' appeared above the almost triumphal banner headline, 'THIEF BEATEN TO DEATH.' The story went on in glowing terms to refer to the swiftness of the group's response 'which led to the *apprehension*' (author's emphasis) of the thieves. Incredibly, it reported, 'within a few minutes' of hearing the tocsin, Lockett Avenue 'was filled with people armed with machetes, knives, iron pipes and pieces of wood'. As for the man they killed, well, he was tracked 'by the residents, caught beside the income tax building and beaten to death'. End of story.

From the article's tone one might be forgiven for thinking that the 'residents' were seen as heroes. As if to underline that point, the tabloid published a half-page photograph featuring the 'trophy' lying curled up in a pool of his own blood – most of which, we are informed, 'flowed from the right ear and the back of the head'. In short, what amounted to a beastly killing committed by a frenzied lynch mob became a topic for celebration.

It is this type of mentality and behaviour which helps to explain why Rude Boys are top dog in Jamaica. For if anyone has displayed a capacity for taking the law, reshaping it to fit their specific needs and administering it, it is the rudies.

The rudies are the kings of the ghetto jungle, a status attained largely through ruthless acts of criminal and political terrorism. Because of them, the gangsters are both feared and hero-worshipped in the ghettoes and shantytowns over which they reign supreme.

Moreover, through the Rude Boys' various exploits, a vibrant, all-embracing subculture has been built up around them over the years. The dons, their 'ranking' lieutenants and 'soldiers' have become the role models that many of their young male 'charges' aspire to, and female ones pursue. Their violent exploits have been immortalised on record, and have provided the musical entertainment for many a dancehall session. Even fashion has paid homage to gangsterism.

Crucially, though, the rudies' 'badness' is merely the most vivid expression of that which surrounds them; it is a cultural thing, and the gangsters are simply the pace-setters. To make full sense of this anomaly, one needs to understand the mechanics of their environments. It is simply not enough to know that the people are poor. Or that they live in wretched conditions. Or that their communities are often divided on tribal lines. Ghetto life transcends the material and the party political; it is about survival – and survival technique is one of the rudies' many strong points.

Naturally, these factors come into their own in Kingston, the location of Jamaica's major posses. It is appropriate therefore that the search for clues to their strength is confined there. But, before the search begins, a poignant clue.

The character of the ghetto jungle is summed up by a few of the informal names given to sections of it. Enclaves like Tel Aviv, Beirut, Dunkirk and Angola tell a collective story of horrendous violence. As does

Moscow, a volatile area on the outskirts of Waterhouse, although this battle ground was actually named after Tony Moscow, a gangster who was shot in half by a woman soldier.

There is, however, no such thing as a typical ghetto. For example, the communities of Jones Town, Arnette Gardens and Waterhouse are no where near as depressed as those of Riverton City, Shanty and Callaloo Bed, the latter being the glorified squatter camps that mark the end of Jamaica's socio-economic line.

Jones Town is one of the many areas that make up the South St Andrew constituency in west Kingston. A PNP stronghold, it houses about 8,000 residents and is situated about two miles from the bustling city centre. Compared to the air-conditioned, pastel-shaded shopping malls, exclusive multi-storey hotels and business corporations of the city's commercial district, Jones Town resembles a vermin-infested slum earmarked for demolition.

Jones Town is a maze of narrow, potholed streets. Small heaps of untendered rubbish line the streets giving the appearance of markers along the road toward some unspecified treasure. Several of the roads are bordered by six-feet-high corrugated tin and zinc fencing. With the vicious dogs that lurk behind them and the occasional burglar bars, this fencing represents the first line of defence against the hordes of burglars and gunmen that prey on the area.

There are no shortage of trees and lush greenery, but, in Jones Town, the beauty of nature offers little relief against the seemingly endless expanse of rusting metal and crumbling concrete. The environment is truly a mess. Just off the Slipe Pen Road, one of the main thoroughfares between the city centre and downtown market area, sits a piece of wasteland that resembles a large bomb crater. In spite of the culvert that runs through it, it is the closest thing Jones Town has to a park. Local children play football or gangsters there on their way home from school; groups of unemployed men gather there to chew over the latest gossip, and avoid the oppressive heat of the wooden and tin huts they call home; and, bordered by a few shops, mothers come to purchase their meagre, daily provisions. Lying in the shadow of Jones Town Police Station, it is at least a relatively safe place to hang out.

Whatever the state of Jones Town now, the area has developed significantly since the poor first began to populate it. As recently as the 1970s, Jones Town was a part of Trench Town, the lawless area immortalised on record by its most famous son, Robert Nesta Marley. In those days the area was an out-and-out squatter settlement. The sole amenity the six hundred or so settlers had was a single stand-pipe to clean, cook and water themselves and their animals. The area was not developed until Anthony Spaulding, a populist Member of Parliament and one-time resident, was appointed Minister of Housing in Manley's PNP government in the 1970s.

The homes themselves blend well into their environment. The housing stock falls loosely into two categories: single-storey bungalows and crudely-constructed government-built housing schemes or estates like Greenwich Farm. In reality, there is little difference in quality; both are fairly decrepit.

The interior of the typical Jones Town home does not fill one with jealousy. Living conditions for the often large families that occupy them are cramped. This is especially so where small bungalows have been converted to house two families. Perhaps only a crab would feel comfortable moving around inside them.

Personal possessions are limited. A few changes of clothing – including a party or 'Sunday best' outfit; the odd piece of inexpensive jewellery and a Casio-type watch; a few pots and pans and, in some cases, a clapped-out fridge-freezer; sundry cheap ornaments; a radio/cassette recorder and, maybe, a television set. Luxury items do not exist in Jones Town.

There are, however, distinct advantages to living in what people in Britain would call council accommodation. 'The houses are built by the politicians,' says Mr P., a long-time Jones Town resident. 'And people hardly ever pay water rates, rent or whatever. They just live.'

Still, nobody gets anything for nothing, and the beneficiaries are called to account with their votes come election time. 'The first line the politicians use on these people,' is, says Mr P. of politicians as a whole, '"see, I give ounu (you) free house and free dis," whatever. So they are being used.'

A well-known and popular figure around Jones Town, Mr P. insisted he remain anonymous. 'The truth have to come out somehow,' he says. All the same, he fears that 'maybe word goes out I'm saying the wrong thing', making him a marked man among the underworld figures who rule over his area.

What little money Jones Townians possess tends to go towards paying school fees and their children's lunch money, buying khaki school uniforms, and feeding the family. Putting food on the table is a major headache. 'You eat today, you can't eat tomorrow,' complains Mr P. 'That is bullshit. It should never go on in a country like this, a country that is so fruitful.' Jamaica is indeed an extremely fertile country. Yet the typical ghetto diet is poor, and many suffer serious health problems as a consequence.

Beef is out of the reach of the pockets of the vast majority. Mutton is for special occasions. Fish is more affordable, but not on a daily basis. And the prime portions of chicken are reserved for middle-class stomachs. The poor make do with chicken neck and back, while the better-off 'take it and feed their dogs,' fumes Mr P.

Worse still, 'chicken back reach a price now that some poor people cannot buy it'.

Education is a sporadic affair in Jones Town. Children only attend primary school when their families – invariably a single mother – can afford to pay the modest fees. And with providing food a priority, it is common for pupils to miss their classes two or three times a week. Needless to say, combined with an inadequate diet, this retards the children's ability to make academic progress, and hinders their already limited chances of eventually breaking out of the ghetto. Perhaps the only saving grace is that the city's Comprehensive Clinic is located on the edge of the settlement.

For most of the residents of Jones Town earning an honest living is what other people do. This is not to suggest that the majority are criminals. Rather, it is to state a hard fact of ghetto life: most people are neither educationally equipped nor socially acceptable enough to compete for the limited supply of unskilled jobs on offer.

But, even if the openings were available to them, many locals would turn down the offer of a steady job. The work ethic has been beaten out of them by decades of disaffection and social neglect.

Besides, to be 'somebody', one needs the type of money that these jobs cannot provide. 'Even a guy who goes to university and study, have all his degree and whatever behind his name,' explains Mr P., 'if he does not have any money, he's nobody. Because that's what runs Jamaica, money. Everything, money. From the top to the bottom, money.'

In Jones Town, the quest to secure money assumes a number of guises. For the unemployed it is reducible to living from hand to mouth; an endless cycle of trying to raise enough dough to get through to the next day. It is not uncommon to see men 'investing' their limited resources at the bookies or on their skill at ludo or dominoes.

Children, the eldest especially, are under parental pressure to help with the family's upkeep. By the age of nine or ten many are forced out on to the streets in a bid to make a 'raise'; to find urgently needed funds. Their efforts range from collecting returnable soft drinks bottles to washing windscreens and begging.

Nevertheless, Jones Town boasts people in gainful employment. A handful of artisans make a humble living as tailors, seamstresses, mechanics, electricians and the like. The tradeless majority, however, depend on hustling and higglering to survive.

Higglering is the buying and selling of goods in the informal business sector. The higgler is a middleman – or, more commonly, middlewoman – without the overheads. Their ability to undercut regular retail prices has seen them become the quintessential vendors of goods to the ghetto poor. For the same reasons, however, higglering is an extremely precarious means of existence.

Another less sophisticated and profitable form sees women on street corners sitting patiently behind large wooden trays stocked with an assortment of water biscuits, chewing gum, individually wrapped boiled sweets, cigarettes and Rizla papers. In this world, profit margins are based on breaking up a packet of Wrigley's chewing gum or Craven 'A' cigarettes, and selling their contents by the unit. As such, the profits are barely worth talking about.

Hustling – a favourite of the young – is slap bang in the middle of the criminal world. Mr P. explains how it operates in Jones Town. Some of 'the male sector, they try to deal with drugs like ganja, cocaine,' explains Mr P. of the Jones Town experience. Others, he says, barely concealing his disgust, 'are homosexuals – they sell their body to men . . . to survive'. Some of these rent boys have even been known to boost their incomes by robbing their clients of cash, jewellery and even designer sports shoes. They tend to get away with it, too; few males in this rabidly homophobic country would own up to being gay, let alone having sex with a male prostitute.

Women are also deeply involved in the drugs world, especially as 'mules'. By Jamaican ghetto standards they are well paid for their hazard-filled services – up to J$25,000-a-trip (£500) plus flights and expenses. Avoiding detection carries its own dangers. Mr P. recalls a recent case in which a local female smuggler 'was carrying drugs, and the cocaine burst up in her vagina, and she died eventually'.

Prostitution is a more common way for a minority of Jones Town women to scrape together a living. The females involved (some as young as fourteen or fifteen) dare not openly ply their trade in Jones Town, though. A devoutly religious people – Jamaica has more churches per square mile than any other – Jamaicans frown on the world's oldest profession.

Nearby New Kingston, which houses the city's major international hotels, and the area in and around Mandela Park in Half Way Tree, are popular haunts for nocturnal prostitutes.

Soliciting at night helps the working girls to reduce the inevitable stigma of being spotted by people from their area. Unfortunately, though, this does not always work out in practice. 'I even came across a case where I was in a prostitute joint [go-go club] just looking around,' confesses Mr P. He was surprised to see 'about three chicks from my area. And when they saw me, they tried to hide because they are involved. I know some of them are ashamed of what they're doing; they don't want to do it but, in some cases, they are forced to for survival.'

Go-go clubs like the famous Chelsea in New Kingston provide another outlet for prostitution, a place where exotic, strip-tease 'dancers' can meet punters. Still, danger is never far away. It is not unknown, for example, for 'tricks' to be robbed at gunpoint by a prostitute's accomplices. Alternatively, pimpless girls have been beaten up and even killed by punters who refuse to pay up.

Selling sex is not confined to the unemployed, however. Even relatively educated working women have been known to turn to it. These women come into contact with their 'clients' in the course of their regular work routines; for example, middle-aged businessmen who have frequent dealings with a bank or an insurance company. Strictly speaking, these women are not prostitutes. But the fact remains that they are prepared to perform sexual acts in return for gifts and money that will enhance their poor standard of living.

That, more or less, is the social and economic reality of Jones Town. But at the other end of the spectrum, right at the bottom of the pile, there is Riverton City.

The 'city's' fortunes are a far cry from those of the places that surround it. The irony is certainly not lost on one of the few people to tend to the needs of these forgotten people, Monsignor Richard Albert. 'The worst poverty in Jamaica exists just across the [Spanish Town] road from Wray and Nephew', one of the richest companies on the island, says the priest. 'From Six Miles to Rockfort you've got the boardrooms of the wealthiest companies in Jamaica, and right across the street, the worst poverty and malnutrition.'

The contrast could certainly not be greater. The location of Riverton City, Kingston's most neglected and poverty-stricken community, is itself a metaphor for the people who are forced to live there. The settlement is centred around Kingston's principal municipal rubbish dump.

Based in PNP Member of Parliament O.T. Williams's West St Andrew constituency on the western fringe

of Kingston, Riverton City is 'home' to about 7,000
Sufferers. Like a 'problem estate' in a British city,
the 'city' has become an unofficial dumping ground
for Kingston's most hopeless and vulnerable cases: the
mentally and physically disabled; the elderly homeless;
young victims of domestic abuse and so on.

Living conditions here make Jones Town seem luxu-
rious; Riverton is like a Sowetan township or a *favela*
in Rio de Janiero transplanted to Kingston. Up to
ten-member families occupy crudely-constructed shacks
patched together from wood, tin and even cardboard
scavenged from the dump. The more fortunate live in
shacks supplied by Father Albert's fund-raising drives
or concerned foreign Christian charities. Either way,
these rudimentary structures are highly susceptible to
the vagaries of the weather.

The interiors are just as bleak: stark, dark and often
insanitary. At best, there is only enough room for one
or two rickety beds – if their residents have them
– a primus stove and the few belongings the family
possess. In the midst of these dreadfully claustrophobic
conditions, it is common for members of larger families
to sleep in shifts.

Basic amenities such as tarmac roads, running water,
electricity and sewerage are at a premium. The average
toilet is a shallow latrine excavated behind the dwelling.
Supplies of electricity and water have invariably been
tapped from the city's supplies. For the majority, running
water is provided by a communal stand-pipe.

That said, Riverton City is more fortunate than some of
its counterparts in that it has its own communal showers,
provided by a foreign charity. But like everything else
in these communities, access to such facilities is strictly
rationed. Girls shower one day, boys the next and so on.

There are no health, social or welfare services located in
Riverton City. The urgent need exaggerated by the filthy

environment which the poverty-stricken must endure. The threat of disease and infection is an everyday hazard. In March 1991, Father Albert told an international poverty alleviation conference in Holland, that it was not uncommon 'to find elderly people with maggots coming from sores on their bodies'.

What little relief the residents of Riverton City receive invariably comes from Father Albert. An expatriate Roman Catholic priest from Peekskill in New York State, he decided to dedicate his life to ministering to the Jamaican poor soon after his ordination in April 1976. A charismatic character and consummate hustler in his mid-forties, the Monsignor has used his ebullient personality to secure funds from foreign governments, local businessmen and a variety of charities to assist his flock. In fact, in spite of his white skin and religious disposition, Father Albert is all but worshipped as a saviour-God by the people of the three parishes he ministers to in Riverton City, Olympic Gardens and Waterhouse. Even the vilest of the gunmen respect him. Fluent in the working-class Jamaican patois, he literally speaks his flock's language.

Monsignor Albert's immense popularity also stems from his highly controversial political stand against the people he deems responsible for causing his parishioners' distress. Pronouncements like the following put his notoriety into perspective: 'This is structural poverty. It's come about because of [government] corruption, because of bad management. It's come about because of unfair distribution of the wealth of the world,' he says. 'And, y'know, we're suffering as any Third World country from that massive debt that our leaders incurred.' Albert's outspokeness and good works have turned him into Jamaica's God's Don.

Father Albert is responsible for providing Riverton with a source of primary education. The Monsignor has erected the Riverton City Basic School, a large, brick-built, one-room school in the belly of the settlement. His parish churches pay for the teachers' salaries.

But still Monsignor Albert cannot do everything. The handful who pass Jamaica's Common Entrance Examination have no guarantee of securing a cherished secondary school place. Entrance is based on a lottery system, one in which only one child in six secures one of the 10,000 places.

With a minimal education behind them, the majority of Riverton's dwellers are barely equipped to speak proper English, let alone read and write it. And saving the young from falling into a life of crime and exploitation becomes more difficult as time progresses. Says Albert: 'Once they get to twenty-three or twenty-four there's nothing you can do with them. They're set in their ways.'

Employment opportunities are alien words in communities like Riverton. And it shows. 'Fifty per cent are unemployed or unemployable,' says Father Albert. Moreover, 'Most people are not mentally, physically or emotionally prepared for the market economy.'

In the main, economic survival is founded on charity, crime, subsistence and the hustle. The most popular hustle revolves around scavenging among the refuse for garbage with a cash value. But with so much at stake, even down among society's pariah, a strict pecking order has evolved, backed up by the threat of violence.

So, as the rubbish trucks hurtle in, groups of able-bodied adolescent men clamber aboard to be in pole position when the containers regurgitate their contents. Surrounded by the nauseating stench of rotting matter, aggravated by fierce sunlight and clouds of polluted dust, the youth trawl through knee-deep refuse in search of zinc, returnable soft drinks bottles, and anything else that might net a few dollars.

Meanwhile, like vultures waiting for the lions and

hyaenas to clear the scene, small children, the mentally and physically vulnerable, and the elderly wait in the burning sun for their moment to feed off Kingston's rotting carcass. This cohorts' foraging is driven by subsistance; gathering enough chewed-over food to get them (and their families) through to the next day. 'They used to say in Jamaica people queue to sleep,' remarks Father Albert. 'Now they say they queue to eat.'

These people are used to leaving the dump empty-handed; hunger is a fact of life in Riverton City. Father Albert recounts a pitiful anecdote concerning a young member of his staff by way of illustration. 'I got 5,000 patties from Coney Island, a local amusement arcade, which I distributed to the [Riverton] kids. One of them, Redman, cried. When I asked him why he was crying he said it was because it wasn't his turn to eat that day. It was his sister's.'

Others lower down the shanty pecking order try other means to find sustenance. Some have secured grants to raise pigs on the rubbish dump. (On more than one occasion the army has had to be called to slaughter pigs suffering from swine fever because the threat of violence from their owners has been too much for the police.) Other resourceful types try their hand at fishing. Fishing for mullet with impromptu tackle they stand beside the stream that straddles, and is no doubt polluted by, the rubbish dump. There is no need to elaborate upon the potential health risks involved.

Riverton City's women, typically young, single mothers, do the best they can to provide for their children. Some take in washing or work as domestics for meagre wages. Inevitably, others turn to prostitution.

Away from the perpetual fight for survival, the people are left to their own devices. In the mercurial worlds of Kingston's ghettoes and shantytowns, social and domestic violence are dominant features of everyday life. People are quick to hit back at those who bother them; some, as Diana McCauley points out, to the point of paying 'contract killers to eliminate anyone [they] have a dispute with.'

Mr P. confirms this. 'Oh yes,' he says, 'if you want a guy killed right now, you just put a price on his head' and someone will gladly do the job. But it gets worse. 'When I say price,' Mr P. continues, 'a man can be dead for even a spliff . . . A man beg you a spliff, and he'll do the job for you, easily.' Life is cheap in the margins.

These problems are compounded by a lack of social outlets to relieve the pressure. Riverton City has no formal entertainment escape routes. Barefooted, sometimes naked, children cavort about the contaminated wasteland, making up games as they go. For most adults, the concept of home entertainment is just that, a concept. Some adults own transistor radios and cassette recorders, but few possess a television set. Drugs and alcohol offer the best diversions, and both are severely restricted by the lack of funds.

The range of entertainment outlets is much larger in Jones Town, but the pattern is much the same. People shoot the proverbial breeze or go to the stream of small bars that litter the area or the Odeon cinema at Cross Roads. The privileged few car owners might take a date to the drive-in theatre at Harbour View or New Kingston. Failing that Jones Townians tend to stay indoors behind the relative safety of their zinc fences and guard dogs and chat, play music, dominoes or ludo or watch television.

Naturally, sex is another temporary release. But lately, even this poses potentially devastating dangers. One is the traditional poverty trap problem of teenage (and generally unwanted) pregnancies; a syndrome Mr P. refers to as 'children having children'. The fact is that, raised in cramped surroundings, with minimum privacy,

young children are exposed to sexual relations from an
early age.

In later years, many are subjected to the violence of
sexual abuse; sex becomes something that is given and
taken freely. Thus, teenage pregnancies are accidents
waiting to happen, and rape is sewn into the fabric of
the ghetto culture.

In Riverton City getting pregnant is seen by some as
a panacea. 'As soon as she gets a little breast on her,'
notes Monsignor Albert, '[men] start to get interested in
her. She sees it as a way of getting out, maybe, and she's
pregnant, and she's out of the school, and the whole thing
begins again!'

Sexually transmitted diseases (STDs) are another major
ghetto problem. The dreaded duo of the HIV virus and
AIDS have become a real danger; one augmented by the
prevalent belief among ignorant heterosexual males that
they are 'batty' men – homosexual – complaints.

Recent estimates put the number of virus carriers at
10,000 – the vast majority of whom were ignorant of
the fact that they are carrying and spreading the virus.
Two-thirds were men over the age of fifteen. Meanwhile,
a Kingston survey suggested that ten per cent of the city's
prostitutes were also infected.

The best chances of letting off steam come on Friday
nights – Jamaica's traditional party night. After dark,
the ghetto streets are literally swamped with young men
and women dressed up in their fineries. Decked out
in glittering boob tubes and 'batty riders' (hot pants)
topped off with extravagent gold costume jewellery and
outrageously elaborate hair-dos, many of the women leave
very little to the imagination.

Many are simply 'modelling'; trying to stand out
and have their good appearance complimented. This
might seem like an exercise in sheer, uninhibited vanity.
But for those who are not at all valued by wider

society, 'modelling' offers a weekly opportunity to be
a 'somebody'.

Some go on to 'model' at a dancehall or open-air
ghetto sound system sessions. For a cover charge of
about J$50 (£1), they flock to venues like city-centre
Kingston's famous House of Leo to hear heavyweight
sound systems (mobile discos) such as Stone Love
Movement, Metromedia and Bodyguard. Whether singly
or in a sound 'clash' (competition), the systems thump out
a mind-numbing mixture of the latest dancehall singles,
reggae classics or 'revive 45s', and 'specials', customised
recordings used to extol the 'champion' virtues of their
outfit. However, even these essentially peaceful and
fun-filled events are not immune from violence. In
fact, from the earliest days of the sound systems, the
dancehall reggae culture has been beset by outbreaks of
crowd violence.

Sound systems started off in the early 1950s playing a
diet of sanitised American doo-wop and R&B. Always a
fiercely competitive 'industry', owners tried to distinguish
their sound by making regular trips Stateside to exclusively obtain the best releases. The competition is just as
fierce today. However, the rivalry is usually played out
through the medium of violent lyrics; vocals that wallow
in the maiming and murdering of rival 'sound boys'.

The music policy changed dramatically with the advent
of ska during the early 1960s. Top sound systems owners
like Duke Reid and Coxsone Dodd began to dabble in
producing tunes by indigenous ghetto talents. Although
a largely instrumental idiom, ska performers began to
reflect the stark realities of ghetto life, a sort of social
commentary which has continued to the present day.

It was in this era that the first militant, ghetto protest
songs hit the Jamaican market. By 1967, with the West
Kingston Wars in full swing, Dudley Sibbles released
'Gunman', the first of many offerings of what are now

called 'gun lyrics'. 'Gunman' was so controversial that Jamaican radio refused to play it.

Even before its release, real-life violence had become a firm fixture of the sound system scene. Competition to be the 'champion' sound was frequently played out in brawls and knife fights between followers of rival sounds. The rationale for acts of violence at dances has changed over the years, but it remains a feature of the dancehall culture.

For a couple of years after about 1966, reggae music mellowed into what was called 'Rock Steady', a sort of Jamaican soul music. However, Rock Steady turned out to be a musical respite.

In the late 1960s, reggae (proper) emerged to spread the word about Rastafari, critique the state of the black existence, and reflect the culture of the ghetto. Apart from singers like Bob Marley and Burning Spear, this militant, bass-driven musical form spawned a host of 'toasters' or rappers such as I-Roy, U-Roy and Big Youth. The latter launched successful recording careers by crude and comical extemporisation over current vocal releases or 'dub plates', specially-recorded acetates.

Sexually-explicit lyrics or 'slackness' also became a part of the early reggae idiom, again reflecting the moral malaise afflicting the ghettoes. But it was not until the origins of dancehall music in the early 1980s that 'slackness' and 'gun lyrics' became a major force in the reggae music and sound system cultures. Dancehall – so named because its stars made their names by improvising lyrics over records during dancehall sound system sessions – surfaced around 1981. Without doubt the undisputed king of dancehall was Yellowman, a black albino with a unique line in 'slack' lyrics.

By the mid-1980s, dancehall had entered a digital phase known as 'ragga' or 'raggamuffin'. More than any other expression of reggae music, 'ragga' has been the cause of lasting controversy on account of its uncompromising lyrical content. The controversy has centred on the deification of gun violence. Ninja Man, a current DJ (rapper) sensation is to 'gun lyrics' what Yellowman was to 'slackness'. But he is not alone. DJs Super Cat, Beenie Man, Mad Cobra, Gun John Crow and Cutty Ranks are just a few of the many to have jumped on this highly popular bandwagon.

An arbitrary survey of the type of lyrics in question is sufficient to explain why they have aroused so much controversy. If Bob Marley shot the sheriff in self defence, his successor did so for the hell of it. In 1993, for example, Echo Minott had a worldwide reggae hit with a number entitled 'Murder Weapon' in which he encouraged rudies to shine their guns in preparation for a showdown.

In fairness, Minott's contribution was tame in comparison with the graphic gun violence depicted by various DJs. In 'Limb by Limb', for instance, Cutty Ranks boasts about shooting somebody's eyes out. They only get more sadistic from there. Lyrics abound about murder victims' brains and bone marrow being splattered all over the place, and so on.

The fact that numerous DJs earn a handsome living out of 'bigging' up (gun) violence and lawlessness is the least of their critics concerns. The major bone of contention is the belief that 'gun lyrics' help to 'justify' and perpetuate the carnage. 'People look upon those guys as idols,' argues Mr P., 'and maybe if they were doing something more cultural, then you would find the atmosphere change with these [ghetto youth]. But everybody is talking about the gun.'

Over in Waterhouse, Monsignor Albert echoes Mr P.'s observations about the 'gun talk'. 'What I am concerned about,' he says, 'is the effect the dancehall culture has on the mind of the youth, talking about guns, talking about warfare, talking about slackness.' Furthermore, the ghetto priest believes this focus on negativity spells danger. 'Dancehall, unfortunately, too often is slackness, is indiscipline, is in glorification of what's the weakest in man. Whether it be his sexual drive, whether it be his desire just to fill himself with drugs and to feel good with drink, or to feel powerful with a gun, you know. That's what the danger is in dancehall.'

The pro-'gun lyric' lobby argue that the songs are being taken too literally. They stress that they are dealing with 'reality', merely reflecting the way the ghettoes are, and the way the people think. Even so, the lives of several of the offending DJs have strayed away from straightforward accounting.

The vulgar antics of Winston Maragh, the Indo-Jamaican DJ sensation better known as Super Cat, were the cause of a violent incident during one of Jamaica's major concert festivals. It unfolded on stage at the 'Sting' event on Boxing Day in 1991.

Mr P. was there. 'Super Cat came on stage,' he recalls, 'and the first thing that came out of his mouth was "kill the pussy, kill him for fun". Now, we're talking about the gun. Well, someone in the crowd didn't like it, and they fling a bottle on him. And the first thing he said: "Pussyhole [female sex organ], fling another bottle again and I will shot ounu down right now." And it cause a disturbance. Matter of fact, it mash up [ruined] the whole stage show.' Super Cat later apologised for his behaviour.

In February 1993, Shabba Ranks (the current king of 'slackness' and the winner of back-to-back Grammys in 1991 and 1992) appeared in court on an assault charge. A Kingston fisherman claimed that in 1990 the Epic recording star had attacked him after he expressed a preference for Ninja Man. The alleged attack caused him to lose a testicle, he said. Ranks, real name Rexton

Gordon, admitted the assault, but was cleared by the magistrate on the grounds that it had been aggravated.

More ominously, though, apart from receiving numerous convictions in Jamaica and around the world for possession of drugs, many leading DJs have come to the attention of the police and courts for more sinister reasons.

In March 1992, Desmond John Ballantine alias Ninja Man (the king of 'gun lyrics') was fined US$5,000 by a New York court for illegal possession of a gun. A maid had spotted it whilst cleaning his hotel room. Back in Jamaica just over a year later, he was arrested on charges of illegal possession of a firearm and shooting with intent to kill. His arrest followed a shooting incident at a Kingston recording studio. Ninja Man was remanded in custody, before being booked to appear before the Gun Court.

Mark Myrie a.k.a. Buju Banton has also landed up in court on a gun charge. Twenty-one-year-old Banton confessed to illegally possessing a .45 calibre handgun and firing it after a concert date in the Cayman Islands. He was reported to offer in his defence that 'sometimes it happens that people [in Jamaica] with a licensed gun shoot it off as a salute'. True enough. He was fined US$875 and given a six-month sentence suspended for two years.

All too often, however, acts of violence have spelt disaster for many of Jamaica's singers and DJs. Several have been the victims of robberies or have had their houses burgled, causing some to go into voluntary exile. Others have not been so fortunate. The pantheon of leading reggae performers snuffed out by the gun includes: General Echo, Big John and Fluxy, shot together by the police in 1980; Carlton 'Carly' Barrett, the Wailers drummer, and Peter Tosh, one of the group's leaders, shot dead by gunmen in separate incidents in 1987; DJ Nitty Gritty, shot dead outside a New York record store in 1991; and DJs Pan Head and Dirtsman, the brother of another DJ star, Papa San, 'outed' by gunmen in 1993.

Most of these murder victims were products of the ghetto who decided to stay there. But social violence is also a frequent visitor to the venues where their music is played. In fact, even without physical violence, the atmosphere in the dancehall is one that all too often celebrates it. It is, as Banton suggested, common for revellers to fire live rounds into the air at dancehall sessions. Known as 'gun salutes', these are a way of showing appreciation for an entertaining sound system, DJ or tune. One of the greatest ironies is that often inebriated, off-duty police officers are some of the biggest culprits.

Regrettably, though, the dancehall is both a venue for social violence and the source of conflicts that lead to it. In August 1992, for example, in the early hours of the morning an unidentified man was gunned down during a session at the House of Leo. He was shot in the eye, and his body had scarcely stopped breathing before a crowd of on-lookers decided to rob him of his shoes and gold necklaces.

A year later Mr P. attended a ghetto session featuring the mighty Stone Love which led to more killings. Apparently, one of the revellers had lent another his gun with the proviso that it be returned before the dance was over. Unfortunately, the borrower reneged on his promise. 'So,' says Mr P., all the lender did was to wait until 'everybody go and retire to bed in the early morning . . . and just go [to the borrower's home] and shot the people who was inside there.' The 'offender' and an innocent man were killed on the spot, while a woman was left battling for her life in hospital.

Such is the force of social violence in the ghetto that Mr P., while regretting the unnecessary casualties, had not one iota of sympathy for the 'guilty' murder victim.

'You see,' he explains, 'guns are precious to these guys – that's their livelihood, that's what they use to live. If a man lend you a gun you have to give it back to him, or else you're in a problem.'

The multiple problems associated with the dancehall music culture have led to an all-embracing backlash. In 1994, Stone Love (the undisputed champion sound) and Stone Love Productions, its record label, decided to boycott 'gun lyrics' altogether. (If anything, though, they have merely toned them down.)

Away from the industry, Colonel Trevor MacMillan, Jamaica's hardline Police Chief, had barely taken up his new post when he announced a clampdown on the purveyors and broadcasters of violent records. In his own words: 'I do not care if you are a Grammy winner, Emmy winner or any kind of international star – if you preach violence and it is against the law, you must be dealt with.'

MacMillan was particularly peeved by records which appeared to encourage people to shoot law enforcers. Echo Minott's 'Murder Weapon' will certainly not have earned him any friends down at Police Headquarters – he boasts of shooting deputies, sheriffs and police officers.

As Mr P. says, 'guns are precious' to their ghetto owners. Guns are not just about doing crime, they are objects of desire which help to define one's status. To own a firearm is to be a 'somebody', to be respected and feared. Hence, almost every young man wants to own one.

Jamaica's culture of violence has been kept alive by a flourishing gun culture. The fascination with and craving for firearms starts at an early age. Says Mr P., a father who has raised a small army of children, 'Everybody speaks about the gun – even the little baby coming up. As he has his little hands he's trying to make dirt guns out of

clay. And . . . so it's like born inna him – just the gun
he speak about.'

As the boy approaches his teens he will yearn to lay
his hands on a real gun. Opportunities are never far away
in the ghettoes. 'They have a thing called "gun baggage",'
says Mr P. 'Gun baggage' refers to the youth the rudies
offload their weapons on to when the security forces are
around, the police being less likely to search a minor for
a firearm.

From the age of eleven onwards these boys need guns
like a junkie needs a fix. 'Now that youth is getting a gun
from you – as a big man – to carry, and respects you as
the don,' intones Mr P. 'Same as you he want his own
'cos he get used to that. So, it's an ongoing phenomenon,
the "gun ting".'

Indeed, as he enters his teens, and the stark realities
of his bleak future unfold before him, the boy will make
an effort to learn about the various types of firearms in
circulation. He will fantasise about what type of gun
he will carry. A light-weight, user-friendly piece like a
Glock 17? Or perhaps an AR-15 assault rifle, the civilian
equivalent of an M-16?

At this crucial stage in his young life, the youth's circle
of friends will more than likely be swollen by peers who
originally harboured dreams of earning a legitimate living.
The newcomer is the High School graduate who has had
a secondary level education, but cannot find a job. His
solution? 'Simple!' says Mr P., 'Him join a gang. For
that's where he's sure to get some form of aid or help;
some form of money must run his way.'

The 'gun ting', is extremely difficult to escape. The
pressures on the ghetto youth to get involved are unrelenting. Witness one of Father Richard Ho Lung's many
ghetto experiences. The ghetto priest, whose sardonic
quotation opened this chapter, once eavesdropped on
a conversation-cum-lecture between 'Long Arm', an

experienced gunhawk, and a group of budding gun-men.

According to the priest's account in the *Gleaner* in October 1993, 'Long Arm', like a ghetto Fagin, implored his audience to 'get a gun if you don't have one. Then learn to jump walls, learn the streets, the back of the houses, run for cover in the broken down buildings.' The point was to be prepared. Because, as the lecturer said, 'If you don't graduate in this gun business, you can't survive.'

The need to be handy with a 'shooter' is something of a self-fulfilling prophecy in the ghettoes. Even if the gun owner has no intention of becoming a ghetto bad boy, the onus is on him to get 'tooled' up for personal protection. Moreover, according to 'Long Arm', he would be a fool not to because everybody has a gun: the police, friends and associates. And who is to say that 'your baby mother' does not have one which she will turn on you one day. Therefore, the moral of 'Long Arm's' cautionary tale is 'get handy with a gun' because 'when you dead you can't learn'.

The overwhelming evidence is that 'Long Arm' was preaching to the converted; the 'gun ting' has been claiming the lives of increasing numbers of young people during the 1990s.

Seaview and Olympic Gardens are notorious areas for gunplay, a problem that was highlighted in a 1993 news-paper article which also pointed to one of its unfortunate by-products: 'law-abiding' youths buying weapons for protection. One self-confessed 'decent citizen' justified his need to arm himself by saying that 'it's no use playing sweet boy an' get dead. Me not going to make a youth jook me [shoot] down and gone.' At any rate, not when he could 'get a gun for J$400'.

The youth in question was saving up to buy his treasured weapon. Others compensate – literally – by

turning to their own devices. For the longest time,
ghetto youths have been manufacturing primitive, but
lethal, home-made weapons using easily accessible parts
like bicycle pipes and household springs.

Weapons seizures provide another indication of just
how potent a force the gun is in Jamaica. In the first eight
months of 1992, JCF operatives managed to confiscate
157 illegal firearms. The awesome arsenal included two
M-16s, three sub-machine guns – an AK 11, Ingram
and Interteck – and an array of powerful hand guns
and home-made weapons. In excess of five weapons
every week were recovered in 1993, including eight in
one forty-eight-hour period in October. The police even
recovered an M-16 with 'Property of the US' stamped on
it with several stickers of pop megastar, Michael Jackson.
Two hundred and eighty-six weapons had been recovered
up to the end of September 1994. These included a Desert
Eagle pistol and three M-16s, one of which was found
pegged to a clothes line during a raid in Tivoli Gardens.

Naturally, the gun culture has been responsible for
producing some of Jamaica's most fearsome gunmen.
Two of them, Natty Morgan and Sandokhan, have been
immortalised on record by Super Cat. Both hailed from
Monsignor Albert's volatile west Kingston parishes. Over
the years the trusted ghetto priest has managed to persuade
five wanted gunmen to turn themselves in to the police,
but not these two desperadoes.

In both cases Father Albert was persuaded to try by
his beleaguered parishioners. Both were on the run after
having broken – that is to say, bought – their way out of
prison, and precipitated large-scale security operations to
hunt them down.

According to Father Albert, in both instances the
security forces strongly believed the fugitives were being
harboured by members of their communites. In retaliation,
he says, they subjected the residents of Waterhouse and

Riverton City to a reign of brutal terror in a bid to get them to divulge the fugitives' whereabouts. He says their tactics ranged from arresting octogenarian grandmothers to 'taking little children, putting them against a wall, and telling their mothers they're going to shoot them' if they failed to 'inform'. He even alleges physical torture, arms being broken and the like.

One of the gunmen was Wayne Smith, a.k.a 'Sandokhan', a cop killer from Waterhouse. In July 1988, the JCF's excesses prompted petrified locals to plead with Father Albert to meet with the felon, and beg him to turn himself in. 'So I did,' says the priest. In fact, the embarrassment caused by Father Albert arranging three open-air meetings with Jamaica's Public Enemy Number One caused him to be admonished by the Minister of National Security.

'So now I start to meet with him, very easily,' recalls the priest. 'Meetings are set up and I try to convince him that it's best for him, the community and everyone, if he turns himself in.

'And the same thing happened with Natty Morgan,' says the priest of the other gunman, who topped the police's most wanted list in 1991. But Morgan, a product of Riverton City where his dreadlocked father still lives, was a different kettle of fish. He was a don with a large, well-organised and heavily-armed posse behind him.

Monsignor Albert's first meeting with Natty Morgan aptly demonstrates the point. 'I thought I had been set up,' he recalls. 'Eighteen men came with three point men all dressed up in fatigues, hard helmets, the whole business. I thought it was an army patrol come to kill me . . . It turned out to be Natty and his men,' he says. 'Grenades, canteens, M-16s, the whole business. Right there in Riverton, just by the school.

'Fifteen minutes from the Governor General's residence eighteen, twenty men were going around like that, and were able to hide from . . . the police for almost one year . . . Can you imagine eighteen men in London going around like that? It's impossible!'

Monsignor Albert's supplications eventually came to nothing. Both Sandokhan and Natty Morgan, he says, were 'blown away!'.

The prospect of getting 'blown away' by the police goes with the territory of being a gunslinger. But the situation is slightly different in Jamaica, where the police have acquired a reputation for going over the top in their encounters with violent criminals. 'The Jamaican policemen,' explains Lloyd Williams, 'aren't going to . . . read them their rights. Police here are guys who carry AR-15 or the M-16 routinely. Weapons . . . that the SWAT teams in New York or Chicago have to get special permission to carry.'

To many, it seems the police wield them with impunity. It would not be stretching the point too much to suggest that the Jamaican Police are regarded by many to have adopted a tacit shoot-to-kill policy.

But even when the police are not recklessly dispensing bullets in shoot-outs with armed criminals, there is a widely-held perception that they display a brutal streak in their everyday dealings with the people, especially the poor. According to columnist Tony Johnson, as a result of Jamaica's violent social streak 'considerable numbers of policemen have taken the view that the people must be treated with extreme violence, or they will not have any respect for law and order.'

Ironically, this is not a view that is disputed by the JCF. Within a week of taking up the post of Commissioner of Police, Colonel Trevor MacMillan vowed to stamp out the more unsavoury practices of his underlings. 'They have to stop what they are doing – beating up people,' insisted the twenty-seven-year JDF veteran. 'They have to.' In the six months leading up to MacMillan's directive, the public had lodged two hundred separate complaints of brutality against JCF officers.

And, as recently as November 1994, Deputy Commissioner Francis Forbes freely admitted the charge to a *Gleaner* reporter, but stressed that the police were now reforming their anti-social habits. 'It will take some time for it to reach a level where there will be no force at all – if we ever reach that level,' he rather ominously confided. 'But I think that there is a definite trend, in a positive way, against police using a lot of excessive force.'

The problem for the police, however, is that the longer they have brutalised the population, the more those people have turned against them. So, instead of being seen as a part of the solution, they have become a part of the problem. Moreover, for the people most affected by police brutality – the Sufferers – this trend has positively driven them to look to the Rude Boys for protection. This has only cemented the rudies power.

In fairness to the island's security forces – particularly the 125-year-old JCF – the fight against crime is a thankless task. Like the public sector as a whole, the 10,000-strong JCF contingent is hugely under-resourced, understaffed, insufficiently trained and overworked.

Jamaican police work is an axiom for danger. In 1980, for example, twenty-two officers were murdered. After a few 'quiet' years, another thirteen were killed in 1983. In 1984, another score was added to the fatalities. By the end of the decade, a total of 120 police personnel had been killed in the commission of their duties.

If there is one incident that sums up what the Jamaican Police are up against on a day-to-day basis, it is that which the *Weekend Star* labelled 'one of the most barefaced and brutal attacks on law enforcement officers in Jamaica's history'. This particularly horrific incident occurred in broad daylight on one of Kingston's busiest shopping streets in the summer of 1992. A callous attack, it claimed the lives of two plain-clothed detectives, united the nation in shock and sorrow, and sparked an explosion of public cries for a renewed drive against the gun terrorists.

On 20 July 1992 Constables Desmond Thomas and Quenston Williams had been called to South Parade in response to the reported sighting of two gunmen. Williams was in the process of searching a man when the suspect suddenly grabbed him, and pinned his arms to his sides. As a small crowd looked on, another man – who had been seen sitting nearby – sauntered over to the scene, drew a handgun and shot Williams in the back of the head at point blank range. The cool killer then turned his weapon on Constable Thomas, shooting him in the back. Both detectives died at the scene.

There was also an equally chilling postscript to this tragedy; one which speaks volumes about the insane culture of violence that thrives in modern-day Jamaica. The police launched a nationwide search for three suspects, but before progress was made a vital eyewitness to the killings was shot dead. A higgler, 25-year-old Donald Copeland was gunned down by an unknown assailant at a Maxfield Avenue address. Nobody knows why.

Tragedies like the murders of Constables Williams and Thomas result in universal sympathy for the police, but only postpone the barrage of abuse hurled at the JCF for its apparent failure to defeat the rudie gunmen. Moreover, the Jamaican Police Force is much maligned on the grounds that it is inefficient, ill-disciplined, unmotivated, badly organised, criminally inclined and terminally corrupt. (In 1992 and 1994 it was disclosed that serving officers were illegally selling gun permits to convicted criminals.)

Equally disturbing is the well-documented involvement of JCF officers in the drug business. In one notable instance, K.D. Knight, the Justice Minister, had to step in to prevent a mob of irate ganja dealers and villagers from beating a quartet of crooked, low-ranking JCF officers to

death when their rip-off failed. At the other end of the
scale an Assistant Superintendent was caught *in flagrante
delicto* in a US Drug Enforcement Agency sting – he was
trying to sell them a large consignment of cocaine.

Other officers are known to work for criminal deportees
and fugitives from foreign justice. 'In some of the slum
areas,' explains Lloyd Williams, 'some of [the criminals]
have links with the police, [who] run these crack houses
for them.' And others still are known, even by the
police themselves, to run flourishing and deadly drugs
operations.

In May 1994, Williams published the fruits of an
intensive investigation into what he called 'untouchable
cops' in the *Gleaner*. 'Untouchable' because, according to
one of Williams's sources, 'they are protected by several
other lawmen and high-ranking politicians who get some
spoils from the trade'. The officers in question were said
to use legal business outlets as a cover for their insidious
practices while, according to Williams, acting as major
league national and international players in 'a network
which involves illegal money trading, importation of
firearms and narcotics'. One of the rogues was claimed
to have stashed J$30 million (£682,000) in a single bank
account. The lucrative dealings were underpinned by a
posse of armed ghetto youth who acted both as 'base
protectors', keeping rival drug organisations at arm's
length, and 'hitmen when the need arises for a rival to
be eliminated'.

The fact is that for a long time the public has had
compelling reasons to question the police's function as
protectors of their interests.

Police violence began to surface as a major social (and
political) issue in the late 1960s. Indeed, many trace
the origins of a 'shoot-to-kill' policy against Jamaica's
criminal element to a speech delivered by former JLP
Prime Minister, Hugh Shearer in 1967. In the midst of

his now notorious presentation, Shearer announced that he had given 'orders to the police to proceed without reservation and without restrictions to tackle the problem of violence and to bring the wrongdoers to justice in whatever way it can be done.'

Of course, Shearer did not openly give JCF officers a license to kill at will. But, at the same time, his comments were hardly an endorsement of the principles of human justice. And so, even before off-duty police officers in Brazil founded their notorious 'death squads', uniformed JCF officers were all but sanctioned to remove Jamaican society's anti-social elements.

Seventeen years on, Winston Spaulding appeared to endorse this view in a speech to Parliament. In 1984, the Minister for National Security and Justice put the JCF's crime-fighting antics into perspective. 'The fact that so many of these criminals have been killed by the police in shoot-outs,' he maintained, 'is clear testimony that the police are fighting regardless . . . It is not the inactivity of the police that is the problem. It is the activities of these widespread gangs.'

No matter when it started, the JCF's institutional brutality has attracted widespread criticism from within and without Jamaica. As far back as 1983, E. George Green, the Parliamentary Ombudsman, was vocally condemning the high incidence of police violence. He was compelled to reiterate this in 1985.

The JCF's extrajudicial activities have also made them the subject of several reports by human rights organisations in Jamaica and overseas. In 1986, the Americas Watch Committee (AWC) published a highly condemnatory report on JCF human rights abuses in which it referred to police killings as 'an open secret in Jamaica'.

The investigation which led to the American-based human rights organisation's report came about at the request of the Jamaica Council for Human Rights. One of its major findings vividly reflected the scale of the problem of police violence: 'the Jamaican police have killed an average of 217 of their fellow citizens in each of the last seven years.' (The Committee believed the real total to be higher.) In 1981, the worst year in the survey's ambit, the JCF killed 319 Jamaicans.

The AWC report went on to unequivocally reject the typical explanation given by the JCF for the staggering death toll: 'shoot-outs with armed and dangerous criminals'. A more appropriate scenario for the killings, it said, was simply that 'the Jamaican police engage in summary executions'.

Eight years on, the same damning conclusions were reached by the General Council for Human Rights Watch. Speaking for the Washington DC-based Council in April 1994, Juan Menez emphasised the findings of the (usually conservative) US State Department's 1993 report on human rights to support his own group's analysis. He concluded, 'the JCF engages in summary executions of suspects under the guise of shoot-outs' with the police.

The universally-acclaimed human rights group Amnesty International also added its considerable weight to the argument. Targeting the ill-fated Anti-Crime Investigative Detachment, a special JCF task force, Amnesty International accused the squad of conducting extra-judicial killings. It was the only way the organisation could logically explain why, according to police accounts, more 'suspects' (91) had died in 'shoot-outs' with the police than were injured (67) by them in 1993. Another source reckoned that the JCF killed more civilians on an annual basis than almost any other police force around the globe.

That the JCF has official support for its murderous exploits is further evidenced by the paucity of officers brought to justice on account of them. Sufficient evidence is seldom gathered to secure prosecution or disciplinary proceedings against errant police officers. Prosecutions like that of Acting Corporal Leonard Austin are a rarity. He was sentenced to hang in March 1992 after being found guilty of murdering a witness against three policemen allegedly involved in the illegal drug trade. Even then, the evidence against Austin was water-tight. Two investigating officers had spotted his car outside the murder address. And, later on the same day, Austin absconded to New York where he was immediately detained and deported.

Rather than facing prosecution, Jamaica's most celebrated and violent officers – the terms are often inseparable – are placed on a public pedestal; and their excesses are often trebly rewarded with immunity from prosecution, promotion, and induction into the cult of the personality.

No more striking an example of this bizarre practice is available than that of Keith Gardener. Gardener is a living legend in the JCF and Jamaica as a whole.

Known throughout Jamaica as 'Trinity' – some say on account of his being shot and stabbed on three separate occasions, others that he took it from a spaghetti western called *Trinity Is My Name* – Gardener earned his fearsome reputation as a junior officer back in the 1970s and 1980s. In those heady days, he was said to operate as 'a one-man strike force', and was drafted on to Edward Seaga's personal protection team in recognition of this during the tragic 1980 General Election.

Gardener's celebrity status was apparant in his dress code. In his heyday as a detective, the six feet two inch legend sported black clothes and gold chains, and drove around in a black car. According to the AWC report, Gardener would show up for court cases 'wearing two pistols and carrying a rifle'. He was more like Shaft, the mercurial black private eye of 1970s blaxploitation films, than a real-life detective.

'I've lived a life of glamour,' admitted Trinity during a break in his part-time university course in management studies in 1994. But that did not come about without significant human cost. 'Trinity' left a trail of death and destruction in his wake.

According to a file on him in the AWC report, there were at least four occasions where 'Trinity's' violent behaviour resulted in the Government being forced to shell out substantial damages to his victims or their surviving relatives. One involved a man who had to have his legs amputated after being shot by the famous gun-toting officer. A court awarded him J$80,000 in compensation. Another victim was beaten to death by the 'seasoned officer'.

In yet another case, which seems to have escaped the law courts, 'Trinity' shot at a jogger. He allegedly mistook the victim for someone who was thought to have been fleeing from the scene of a crime. According to the AWC, 'Trinity was about to execute the man, when the victim called out and Trinity recognised him as someone he knew'.

Trinity's senior rank has not ended his shooting days. A man who not so long ago was tried and acquitted of his wife's manslaughter, 'Trinity' made the Jamaican headlines again in April 1995. The police were still investigating the precise circumstances surrounding his shooting of a man in a Kingston bar where the officer was drinking, when the news surfaced. Meanwhile 'Trinity's' latest victim was critically injured.

In spite of, or maybe because of, his violent background, 'Trinity' has scaled the ranks of the JCF; he is currently Superintendent attached to the Special Anti-Crime Task Force in central Kingston. Even now 'Trinity's' reputation still precedes him. The *Weekly Gleaner* reported that 'Trinity's presence in these communities has sent a number of criminals underground.'

The problem of police violence is not isolated to individual officers. Over the years a number of specialist police squads have earned the ire of the common people, too. One was nicknamed the 'Eradication Squad'. This highly-trained, forty-strong unit was created by, and answered exclusively to, Edward Seaga in 1981. Its members were accused of carrying out numerous murders, and it was insinuated that one of the squad's tacit functions was to intimidate and kill the residents of PNP strongholds.

Another squad, the Anti-Crime Investigative Detachment, came into existence in the wake of the carnage of June 1993. Indeed, in the same week that Operation Ardent – a much-vaunted, but essentially ineffectual, islandwide joint police-military task force, was disbanded – Jamaica's criminal element went on a killing spree that claimed twenty-five lives. In fact, many considered the activation of this latest detachment to be a knee-jerk response to a particularly horrific incident which claimed three of those lives.

The incident in question was the grotesque triple murder in the troubled Hannah Town district of west Kingston. Like the cold-blooded murders of Constables Williams and Thomas before them, these sadistic slayings galvanised the Jamaican public to demand improved action to wipe out the gun terrorists. If more evidence were needed, then the chilling murders provide ample testimony to the omnipotence of ruthless violence in Jamaica.

It was minutes before dawn on Tuesday 29 June 1994 when a posse of a dozen men armed with powerful guns descended on Hannah Town. The group, which allegedly included Devon 'Trevor' Morrison, one of Jamaica's most wanted men, promptly cordoned off Drummond Street.

At No. 20, sixty-five-year-old Harold Hines lay in bed asleep. The same was true of young siblings Lamar Mitchell and Audrey Anna Collins, and their mother, Valerie Barrett. In no time, the veneer of peace and tranquillity was shattered when gunmen opened fire on the address; the paper-thin wooden walls offering scant resistance to the high-powered bullets that ripped through them.

The probable target was Hines, a shoemaker, who was due to give evidence in a forthcoming murder trial. There is confusion over exactly what happened next. But what is clear is that at least three men entered the building and by the time they left the siblings were dead. One eyewitness tearfully recalled hearing seven-year-old Lamar make a pitiful plea for his life. In the event, he was shot through the heart with an M-16. His five-year-old sister, Audrey, met a similar fate; the whole of the left side of her face was blown away. Their mother survived the barbaric attack, although her right arm was left maimed by the gunfire. For better or worse, she agreed to be drafted on to Jamaica's less than secure Witness Protection Programme.

In an extremely rare sequence of events, the police went on to arrest a notable suspect for the murders. Charges were preferred against Christopher Mark Coke, one of deceased Shower Posse don Jim Brown's sons.

Coke was brought to trial on 30 March 1994. Valerie Barrett, the mother of the slain children, emerged safely from protective police custody to give evidence. The sole prosecution witness, she was able to identify two of the three gunmen who had broken into her house on that fateful morning. In fact, she testified that Devon 'Trevor' Morrison and Everald 'Run Joe' Carby had stolen some of her belongings before ruthlessly turning their weapons on her and her defenceless children. (Both of these men had been killed in separate 'shoot-outs' with the police before they could be charged with the Hannah Town murders.) Barrett did not, however, identify Christopher Coke, represented by Tom Tavares-Finson, as one of the killers, and he was acquitted.

The trial lasted one day, but the homicide officers on the case could claim a Pyrrhic victory. After all, Barrett's evidence had 'cleared-up' another three of Kingston's catalogue of unsolved murders.

The JCF has a pitiful record of bringing the island's murderers to justice, and this has only helped to strain further their already taut relationship with the general public. In fairness to the JCF, their difficult task is hampered by the understandable reluctance of potential prosecution witnesses to air their testimony in court. Ordinary citizens fear reprisals, and the police are rarely able to persuade witnesses that they will be safe under the island's Witness Protection Programme.

Public reluctance reflects, but by no means fully explains, the annual tally of homicides that remain unsolved every year. Incredibly, figures from Jamaica's 1990 Social and Economic Survey show that in an average of 200 murders a year, JCF detectives fail to charge any suspect(s). Of the 449 murders committed in 1986, for example, more than half (264) did not result in charges being preferred. This sorry pattern was repeated through the late 1980s and into the 1990s. In 1987 there were 442 officially-recorded murders and 263 arrests; in 1988, 414 and 227, respectively. There were 439 homicides in 1989 with only 207 arrests. And in 1990 the murder toll stood at 542 – some estimates put the figure as high as 700 – with 313 arrests.

None of the above is to suggest that there is anything disingenuous about the Government and police's over-all commitment to overthrowing the tyrannical rule of Jamaica's violent gun criminals. P.J. Patterson's Anti-Crime Investigative Detachment is a case in point. Theirs was to be an exercise in State muscle-flexing. The gun bandits and posses were to be met head on, albeit it only in the 'killing fields' of the Corporate Area. In fact, the detachment of 127 JCF policemen and women was remitted to target known Rude Boy gunmen and posses.

Star columnist, Calvin Bowen, pondered whether Patterson's new law and order strike force would fare any better than Operation Ardent. 'Or will it,' he asked, 'burn itself out after a few corrosions?' The squad is still functional, so a definitive answer cannot be provided here. But Bowen was not alone in believing that forming 'another "death squad" . . . can hardly be a permanent solution'.

Since July 1993, however, the squad has been dogged by a series of damaging scandals. To begin with the public and media were understandably outraged by the Anti-Crime Investigative Detachment's acronym, ACID. It was not just the term's corrosive connotations that caused offence. It was more the fact that in real life acid – like guns, machetes and knives – is used by Jamaicans to exact revenge or settle disputes, especially by women.

Amid the howls of public derision, the authorities wisely decided to rename the squad; it is now known as the Special Anti-Crime Task Force (SACTF). But even before its name could be changed, the antics of certain ACID officers had already started to burn a massive hole in whatever public support the police hoped the unit might win.

There are few surprises in the SACTF's record of crime fighting. The detachment has recovered several weapons, made numerous arrests and, according to accounts, 'killed some wanted men in shoot-outs'.

There have also been some notable success stories. In one, SACTF officers seized half a dozen deadly weapons during a raid in Spanish Town, and reportedly foiled a planned orgy of violent robberies in the process. Three M-16s, two high-calibre pistols – a Sig Sauer and a Pietro Berretta – and a .38 revolver were recovered. Still, SACTF's efforts have not so much as caused a ripple across the bloody surface of the Corporate Area's gun-filled, ghetto reservoirs.

Another similarity between SACTF and its myriad predecessors – and one which more than any other has turned the public against the police – is its appalling record of shooting innocent people. Within the first few months of operation, ACID and SACTF officers had shot and killed three people. In August 1993, for example, an ACID squad sergeant was suspended after shooting an innocent woman in Spanish Town.

But it is not the nature of the events alone that the people object to, as much as the alleged circumstances under which they frequently occur. Indeed, police and civilian eye witness versions of events are often contradictory. That was certainly the case in the death of forty-one-year-old Everald Carby in west Kingston.

In what has become a typical scenario since the late 1960s, police reports later claimed that SACTF officers had been 'greeted by gunfire' in Bowens Road whilst on patrol in the Waltham Park Road area. The account went on to state that the officers in question had returned fire, and Carby was killed in the ensuing shoot-out. The Police Information Centre (PIC) report noted that a .45 semi-automatic pistol and two loaded magazines had been recovered from the scene. It added that Carby, who used the alias Run Joe, was on the police's most wanted list in connection with a number of unsolved murders, including the gruesome triple murder in Hannah Town.

Independent eyewitnesses told a different story. One typically anonymous female eyewitness reportedly told the *Sunday Gleaner* 'wi nuh know nothing . . . go ask

ACID, a dem murder di man'. Meanwhile, the *Jamaica Herald* reported Bowens Road residents saying that there had been no shoot-out; that Run Joe's 'running' days were ended when the police arrived at his home at No. 19 at 7.15 a.m., took him out into the backyard, and shot him. The residents also pointed to the fact that there were no bullet holes in Carby's home as one might expect to see after a shoot-out.

Controversies like this are ten-a-penny in the history of Jamaican police–civilian relations. The JCF seems to display an arrant, if not arrogant, disregard for the sanctity of human life and the rights of the people it has been entrusted to protect.

Consider, for example, the police's response to the actions of a group of concerned by-standers one night in Kingston in May 1993. The incident involved a group of selfless citizens who came to the aid of an injured taxi driver who had been shot in the face and chest after being held up by gunmen. Obviously seriously injured, the good samaritans decided to rush him to hospital. They were intercepted by a JCF patrol.

Believing, it appears, totally without reason, that the occupants of the speeding vehicle had committed an unspecified offence, the patrol did a U-turn, and promptly made after them. On catching up, the trigger-happy patrol officers directed their M-16s at the car, and opened fire. The driver was hit in the face and shoulder, but was fortunate to survive the 'shoot-first-ask-questions-later' attack.

The crisis of confidence in the Jamaican Constabulary Force is not confined to the public and the odd police officer. Clearly concerned by the abysmal image the JCF has acquired over the years, the Security Minister was drawn to add the weight of his voice to the debate. In March 1993, K.D. Knight assured the general public that 'all persons, who . . . bring the force into disrepute, must, and shall, be separated from the force, whether by way of discipline or criminal procedure'. To that end he sacked eleven errant officers for either negligence or receiving criminal convictions. The disgraced group joined the ninety JCF officers who had been sacked on similar grounds during 1992, and the eighty-five from the year before that.

In truth, it is only recently that serious steps have been taken to curtail the JCF's irregular practices. By early 1994, Colonel MacMillan had either sacked or suspended thirty-nine corrupt, indisciplined or inefficient officers. In addition, he stripped another twenty-five of their detective status.

MacMillan underpinned his strategy with a more novel ploy. He created a police unit nicknamed the Never Never Division. It was set up to accommodate police personnel whom he suspected were unworthy of the distinction. After internal investigations failed to turn up sufficient evidence to support disciplinary or criminal proceedings against nine officers, an undeterred MacMillan simply 'assigned' them to the new division.

MacMillan made it publicly known that he had lost all confidence in the Never Never Division officers. 'They are sent there to do nothing,' he declared. 'And the best thing for them is to leave the force.' To that end, the solitary functions the disgraced officers perform is showing up for work in the morning, and returning home in the afternoon.

Understandably, the hardline disciplinarian stance adopted by Commissioner MacMillan has not endeared him to a number of his charges. His new broom tactics threaten to sweep clean away the JCF's 'canteen' culture of violence and abuse. So, it was no surprise to hear that disgruntled officers have apparently been prepared to use extrajudicial methods to curtail MacMillan's enthusiastic house-cleaning programme.

One of several stories relates to a 'well-to-do' Corporate Area sergeant who allegedly took out a J$ one million (£23,000) contract on the Police Chief's life. The plot came to light in May 1994 when, instead of carrying out the contract, the alleged hitmen apparently reported the matter to the police. Predictably, the sergeant – who continues his duties – denied the claims, and passed the matter off as a vendetta against him.

Prime Minister Patterson is one of many leaders to have called upon the Jamaican public to end its history of non-co-operation with the JCF in the interests of defeating violent crime. However, if the odious catalogue of police brutality and malpractice cited above is anything to go by then, what he neglected to explain to them was, why, of all people, they should assist – let alone put their trust in – the JCF.

Patterson is not the first Jamaican premier to find himself in this quandary. Arguably, every prime minister since Bustamante in 1962 has faced a similar dilemma. And perhaps the only tangible difference between the problems encountered by successive Jamaican leaders is one of scale. That is, with the passage of time, the culture of police illegality has become bloated and more deeply entrenched in the structure of 'normal' police work. Indeed, there is a strong argument to suggest that the problem is so far advanced that it is now almost impossible for the Jamaican public to distinguish between the two.

But there is another, not unrelated, pressing problem. In school, we are taught that for every action there is an equal and opposite reaction. If that is the case, then the generation-long failure to substitute (political duplicity and) police lawlessness with the rule of law has had a frightening counter-effect. In short, it has created a perilous vacuum in the defence of (legitimate) law and order; a vacuum, more to the point, which, in the ghettoes and shantytowns at any rate, has been filled by the ruthless Rude Boys.

CHAPTER SEVEN

Confessions of a
Spanglers Posse Gangster

'Sometime dem say dem can't really understan' if
we a revolutionist or we a PNP or Labourite. But
you see we? We have PNP live inna our area . . .
But you see most of I-n-I [us]? We a no politician.
We is just straight-up [out-and-out] gangster. Strictly
gangster world we deal with.'

Bigga Knee, veteran Spanglers Posse gangster

June 1992. The blisteringly hot summer sun beats down
on downtown Kingston's Heywood Street Market. At
ground level, the hundreds of higglers and market-goers
who crowd the venue seem oblivious to the sun's merciless rays. A handful of vendors deflect the worst of the
heat with flimsy black umbrellas.

For all, the common aim is to entice hard-up shoppers
with the 'best' and 'cheapest' Kingston has to offer.
To that end, spread out across the cratered wasteland
that doubles as the market-place, there is to be found
an abundance of fresh produce and wares; everything
from bargain-priced yams, pimentos and green bananas
to cloth, kitchen utensils and even coal.

Luke Lane is one of several that trickle down a gentle slope into the Heywood Street tributary. At first sight, there is very little to distinguish this lane from any of the others that border the market. It houses a small primary school, but were it not for the conspicuous presence of a tiny concrete playground penned in by a tangle of meshed fencing there would be little to separate it from its surroundings.

For the most part, the hundred and fifty-yard stretch of disintegrating tarmac provides a thoroughfare to an array of overcrowded, rickety, paint-stripped, one- and two-storey timber-framed dwellings. With small piles of smouldering rubbish dotted along its length, the scene resembles Beirut without the rubble.

At the bottom of the lane on the corner where Heywood Street meets Luke Lane, half a dozen adolescents hold court outside in the cooling shade of a bar. Between swigs of ice-cold Dragon Stout or Heineken and drags on outrageously large spliffs, the young men talk animatedly about 'matters of consequence'.

Football is one – in particular John Barnes's prospects of making England's European championship team. The Jamaican-born son of a former ranking Jamaica Defence Force officer, Barnes is a favourite amongst these self-confessed football addicts; they keep up to date with the Liverpool star's fortunes via the sports pages and televised highlights. Girls – that is, sex – are another lively topic of discussion. 'Bigga Knee', the eldest of the group, and a man noted for his insatiable libido, takes the lead in this debate. And then there are the latest dancehall 'licks' (tunes) and 'champion' sound systems.

To the casual observer there is nothing particularly special about these young men. Certainly, what little casual clothing they adorn seems a little more expensive than that which one normally sees. And they do not seem to be short of ganja or beer money. Still, they are young – which in these parts is coterminous with being ill-educated, unemployed and (generally) unemployable – physically able and appear to have nothing constructive to do with their time.

It does not take long, however, to discover that there is something peculiar about them; a difference which sets them apart from the *hoi polloi*. One of the group, a youth of about twenty years, breaks off from the conversation to beckon a passing higgler. 'Eh, bwoy! Eh, eh, pussyclaat [an expletive for which there is no literal translation]!' he thunders. The street trader, a middle-aged, pot-bellied man wearing dusty cut-off trousers and a badly sweat-stained vest, stops dead in his tracks. 'Eh,' the adolescent continues, 'me no done tell ounu [you], ounu no fi come 'bout ya?'

The 'transgressor' nods vigorously sending trickles of sweat racing down his shiny brow; he had indeed been instructed to keep away from Luke Lane. 'Listen, ounu better run before me drop two kick inna you backside, seen [understand]!?', orders the youth. 'An' no bodder come back, ouno hear!?' Shaken, the higgler scurries off like a maltreated puppy on his swollen, shoeless feet, and the group pick up their stalled conversation.

Even before this unexplained verbal assault on the trader, there was a tacit indication of this group's sep-arateness. While his pals chatted a few feet away, a seventeen- or eighteen-year-old youth had been standing on the corner in the full glare of the sun hawkishly surveying the area. Of particular interest was the fifty-yard expanse of unpopulated terrain between the edge of the market and the construction site of what looked to be a warehouse beside a tall brick wall. His head completely shaven save for a large dollar sign shaped out of his remaining, close-cropped hair, the adolescent maintained a lonely vigil. The youth was specifically on the look-out for armed interlopers attempting to breach the wall's considerable defences. For the wall and the area in front of it mark one of the no-man's-lands separating Tivoli Gardens, the province of the Shower Posse, and the Matthews Lane stronghold of the Spanglers Posse.

'Shabba', the 'sentry', and his friends are Rude Boys; Spanglers Posse gangsters to be precise. Still, the look-out would tell you that his surveillance was geared as much towards thwarting a pre-emptive Shower strike against his counterparts, as it was to prevent them from harming the market people. Indeed, being a Spanglers gangster carries a tremendous amount of responsibilty outside the sphere of commiting crime. Being a Spanglers gangster entails policing and protecting the community, too.

The irony behind Shabba's activities is that they occurred during a mutual truce between the posses. It had been agreed soon after a round of bloody 'frontline' skirmishes in February 1992 which had left at least a dozen people dead. And those 'troubles' had been triggered by the gun slaying of Jah T., the previous Shower don and son of Jim Brown, the one before that. Incensed Shower members (and Tivoli Gardens as a whole) – quite correctly – had blamed Jah T.'s death on their traditional foes in the Spanglers.

'It's a fact,' confirms Mr P., who lives a mile up the road. 'He come in our area and firing guns all over the place . . . and all them stuff deh. So somebody just plan for him, and when he was leaving they just shot him.' Retribution is swift and invariably final in these parts; you live by the sword, you die by it.

Six months later, armistice or not, the Spanglers chose not to relax their long-established system of round-the-clock monitoring of the Spanglers-Shower borderlines. Shabba, whose naked torso tells the story of his long involvement in gangland warfare – five bullet wounds and countless knotted knife and machete scars – put it thus: 'Garden Man a plan fi we [have got it in for us].'

In truth, Shower blitzkriegs have been a fact of life here for nigh on thirty years.

The situation has changed slightly since the interviews for this chapter were recorded, although the essence remains intact, in some ways; only some of the names have been changed. Built up over three decades, the Spanglers-Shower enmity continues apace. But its tribal political foundation and that of the gangs involved in it has all but crumbled away, leaving a hardcore confrontation based almost exclusively upon rival drug interests. In this way, 'garrison constituencies' have become drugs turf.

'You hardly hear these days of one side going against another because of politics,' agrees posse expert Lloyd Williams. 'The reason is more likely to be somebody trying to take over somebody else's turf.' By the same token says Williams, 'You never hear a guy talk about he's from Shower or Spanglers or Tel Aviv or Rema or Waterhouse. He'll talk about his links with those [drug] posses in Miami or New York.' Indeed, in the last couple of years posse names have become something of a flag of convenience for the drug gangsters who lay claim to them.

Leaving aside these important changes, the picture of the Spanglers Posse's culture and operations painted by Bigga Knee, the principal interviewee, is as vivid today as it was when he described it.

'Me no really sorry fi people, [so] me no want nobody sorry fi me,' declares Bigga. 'Me will fuck up anyone as quickly as possible, y'unnerstan'. A so me stay [That is the way I am]. Me no have no mercy fi nobody. So you see when tings [have to] happen, me [will] do it.'

In spite of the uncompromisingly provocative bent of his sentiments, Bigga actually comes across as being quite 'normal'. He certainly looks and sounds it. In fact, although he is a bit on the lean side – at about five feet nine inches tall, the hundred and fifty pounder looks like he borrowed a bigger brother's Marina string vest, 'shot-up' jeans and black Ewing hi-tops – he is quite a darling with the ladies. 'When you say girls now,' he boasts. 'Excess amount.'

The tone of Bigga Knee's prose owes a great deal to a life played out in the ghetto badlands, more than half of which, he says, has been spent in the ranks of the Spanglers. If there is a culprit for his hard edge, it is what the rudie and others refer to as 'reality', the lessons absorbed in the university of ghetto life.

At thirty-one, Bigga is a veteran Spanglers hardman, a 'ranking lieutenant' in his own right. To youthful adherents like Shabba, he is a don-figure comparable to the OGs – original gangsters – of Los Angeles' fabled Bloods and Crips. And in keeping with the African-American hoods, Bigga Knee is a rare commodity, a gangster who has lived to relatively ripe old age. He is also something of an exception, having arrived at where he is without ever having been imprisoned, or even convicted of any offence.

On the one hand, to reach this point and remain involved in gangsterism, he has had to inculcate the idea that life is intrinsically worthless. On the other, more practical, hand, Bigga has also had to develop a range of skills, including the will and the ability to shoot, stab or beat his opponents to death.

Together, these traits have left him with a Devil-may-care attitude to life and death. 'Yeh, well some people die young and some die old,' he says matter-of-factly. 'Me no mind for me understand say people must have to go one of the day.' Hence, his tragic indifference to either. Rather, Bigga's activities are channelled into living life to the full – for as long as he can.

This is not to suggest that Bigga has been complacent with regard to his personal safety – the Rude Boy sleeps with a 9mm Beretta handgun under his pillow. Rather, the certainty of death has had a liberating effect on him. Moreover, it has been the guiding light in what amounts to his life's work. With a grin that exposes a full set of sparkling white teeth he explains: 'Me just go and live life, and have fun making money.'

'Making money,' the universal dream, is a common ambition of the present-day dons, lieutenants and soldiers or 'fryers' who make up gangs like the Spanglers. It is a far cry from the original purpose of such cohorts. In fact, the Spanglers have had to go through a series of major transformations to reach this point since their genesis.

'Spanglers Posse a come from Back-o-Wall, which is Tivoli Gardens. Lizard Town. But a Regent Street the gang form,' advises Bigga. The gang actually came into existence around the beginning of the 1960s. At that time it was one of only a handful of Kingston ghetto gangs. And, unlike the others – busily perfecting the arts of pickpocketing, counterfeiting, shoplifting and theft – the Spanglers were not renowned for taking part in crime. In fact, the first phase of the posse's history was defined by their members' love of popular music and style; the Spanglers were nothing short of gangland Kingston's fashion victims. That said, Spanglers members were not immune from participating in violence. At a time when it seemed that every gang followed a favourite sound system, the Spanglers fell in behind Duke Reid's Trojan sound.

A liquor store owner, Reid was an obvious choice. A giant of a man, he was 'larger than large' in every way imaginable. When his set played out it was common to see the Duke dressed up in an expensive, tailored suit, carrying a shotgun over his shoulder, a .45 on his hip and a cartridge belt draped across his chest. Reid's superstar 'badman' image was topped off by a crown he wore as he was carried shoulder high to the turntable. A chanting DJ and, along with Coxsone Dodd and Edward Seaga, one of the pioneer reggae record producers, Duke Reid was the epitome of 'rudeness'.

Competition between the early sound systems for the mantle of top dog was fierce. One way of demonstrating one's worthiness was by keeping an exclusive and up-to-date playlist. Hence, sound system owners made frequent trips to the United States to exclusively acquire the latest R&B hits.

Another method – and this is where members of the Spanglers came into their own – was to rubbish rival sound systems and disrupt their sessions. The sounds actually hired their own hecklers to attend rival dances and loudly criticise the competition's music policy. Often in situations like these, or when two big sounds 'clashed' in the same venue, heckling would degenerate into open conflict. To prove how 'bad' they and the Trojan sound were, Spanglers would lay into followers of the competition with fists and knives. In a way, this practice served as training for the coming political battles which marked the second phase of the gang's history.

The Spanglers were products of the ever depressed streets of Back-o-Wall, so it is perhaps to be expected that their members indulged in violence. That their violence did not extend to criminal activities, initially at least, is accounted for by the fact that, like most gangs, the Spanglers were formed on a rigid set of principles. The founding fathers' now largely nebulous, unwritten rules were quickly adapted to suit the prevailing times, allowing the gangsters to participate in crime.

Away from the rest of his group – and with a few more beers inside him – Bigga is happy now to expand on the history of his outfit. He perches casually on the hind legs of a white plastic chair in an empty bar, an obligatory bottle of Dragon Stout on the table in front of him. Glossy, colourfully-painted murals adorn the walls somehow subduing the meticulously clean, bright red tile floor. The legally-owned premises of an unnamed Spanglers member, above the bar hangs a framed photograph of a dreadlocked man in his mid-twenties. A small, tarnished engraved brass plate beneath it records the portrait as belonging to 'Early Bird', a PNP youth leader who was 'martyred' for the tribal cause. According to Bigga, he was one of the men who 'set the foundation', the Spanglers' 'constitution'. 'One and few dead,' says Bigga, gesturing in the direction of Early Bird's photograph, 'but most of them alive. Mosta dem deh a foreign, y'understand. America. Edgecombe [in Manhattan], Brooklyn, New York. Spanglers gang run the whole a dem turf deh.'

The gangsters Bigga refers to left Jamaica in the late 1970s and early 1980s, leaving the day-to-day running of the gang in the hands of younger affiliates like himself. But long before they journeyed overseas, they were forced to evacuate the area where the Spanglers were founded.

Tribalism was the cause of the Spanglers' exodus from Regent Street. Up until the early 1960s, Kingston's apolitical youth gangs lived in relative harmony. The entente cordiale was based on the fact that each had its area, and was happy to stick to it.

Unfortunately those areas were defined on another level by forces outside their sphere of influence. In short, they were either PNP or JLP bases of support. And in the JLP areas, which included Back-o-wall (Tivoli Gardens as it had become after Seaga's ruthless redevelopment purge) the pressure was growing to take sides. Falling under the sway of politicalisation and patronage, some like the Tivoli Gang (the forerunner of the Shower Posse) opted to join the JLP.

By 1966, just as the first organised political battles featuring handguns were about to kick off, the Spanglers declared their loyalties to the People's National Party. Although on friendly terms with the non-partisan Denham Town-based Park gang – they carried out armed robberies together – by the late 1960s both gangs were coming under constant bombardment from the recently-formed, JLP-sponsored Tivoli gang. Even as the PNP won the 1972 General Election, the last pockets of Spangler resistance were being forced out of the area. 'Then,' says Bigga, 'lickle [little] by lickle, war, war, war. Til it happen dat [the Spanglers] leave that section deh completely – Labourite did have the more power.'

And so the gang regrouped to the PNP's Matthew's Lane enclave, and entered the political struggle with a vengeance. Matches Lane, as it is widely known, quickly became a launch pad for armed, cross-border raids into Tivoli Gardens, and the target of mutual attacks.

Bigga was still in his early teens when he joined the Spanglers shortly after the upheaval, and on his way out of them when he saw his first sustained political action. The occasion, of course, was the terrifying run-up to the 1980 General Election. He remembers it vividly: 'In '80 you have de big war now wid Gardenist [the Shower Posse] an' we. Big, big ting! Every day people dead. Police a no touch [enter] dem side deh. Whole a town lock down when war a gwan [go on].'

Even before the mighty Spanglers-Shower war of 1980, Bigga's gang had become a big wheel in the drug trafficking business, the third phase of the posse's development. As time has passed, however, the preoccupation with tribalism has tended to become of secondary importance. The political struggle exists only in as far as it is foisted upon the gang. Nowadays, left to their own devices, the Spanglers would gladly bid it good riddance. To Bigga and his colleagues gangsterism is about making money; anything else is an inconvenience.

*   *   *

Bigga Knee's background made him classic material for a career in gangsterism. While not from a textbook, poverty-stricken family, he was brought up away from the socialising influence of his parents; they left Jamaica when he was an infant to seek a better life overseas. 'Me grow stubborn,' the rudie confesses. 'Hard tribulation. Granny beat me regular.'

Bigga has no complaints about what amounts to a traditional, beating-filled, Bible-based Jamaican upbringing. He does not blame anyone – not even himself – for the way he turned out. But even as he recounts his early childhood, there is no escaping the effects that growing up in a violent ghetto environment had on shaping his development.

Bigga hails from Concrete Jungle or Trench Town as it was known when he was born there in 1961. 'From me lickle bit [small] me know say me'd a come [turn out] bad,' he admits. By the age of fourteen 'coming up' he had tired of his Granny's well-meaning ways, and began moving with the wrong crowd. 'Me lick me head [fraternised] wid me bad brother a Waterhouse, and from deh so me just start to be a hardcore. Sleep anywhere – piece a cardboard 'pon house top or anywhere available – where you know say you headback safe [protected]' from gunmen.

'So you see inna dem time [those days] now? Pure wanted man me walk with, pure big man. When me a walk with them [I also became] wanted – and me no do nothin' fi [to be] wanted. Well, you know, when you and the Feds buck up, dem nah go separate [distinguish between] you. [They] just a say "everybody wanted". So you know say, well, [it will lead to] probably a big shoot-out, y'understan'.'

Perhaps the only surprise was that Bigga chose not to 'link up' with a Jungle gang. He attributes his rejection of this course of action down to the 'bad attitude' of gang members in Jungle at the time. '[If] You live a Jungle,' the Rude Boy recalls, 'or you come in . . . crisp [well-dressed] and a spend you money, you good [might] a lose you life. Just so. Ordinary so. Dem kinda corrupted; just kill out dem one another and dem bullshit deh. So me no really stay round deh so.'

Determined to become a gangster all the same, Bigga plumped for the Spanglers. His youthful jaunts around town had taken him into various 'garrisons', but he liked the more orderly Matthew's Lane area the best. So, at the age of fourteen, when other boys dream of being football stars and music legends, Bigga moved to Matthew's Lane to become an apprentice professional gangster.

Bigga Knee was not the only outsider to find comfort and protection in the Spanglers. Over the years the posse has made a reputation for itself through its progressive approach to recruiting and retaining members from all over the place. Unlike tribes like the Jungle and Shower posses, says Bigga, 'We no kill out soldier, we recruit.' (His pronunciation of recruit sounds like recute.) 'People dem love Spanglers,' he says.

This forward-looking approach has paid dividends in terms of the posse's strength. One of the bigger sets, all told there are probably about 120 Spanglers in Kingston.

Interestingly, this number includes an affiliate group from Rema, the decaying, JLP-controlled government housing project on the other side of the derelict Old Ambassador Theatre, within shooting distance of Jungle. Appropriately known as the Rema Spanglers, they have had to fight for their right to exist behind 'enemy lines'. Says Bigga: 'Through [because] dem live box on [sandwiched in] a Seaga area, dem man no really response [responsible]' for the violence.

Still, the Rema Spanglers find solace in visiting their namesakes downtown. 'Dem man dem come round

[Luke] lane 24-7 [twenty-four-hours-a-day, seven-days-a-week),' explains Bigga. 'We no hurt dem, we love dem. And dem love we. So we an' dem haffi live good. So Spanglers dem nuff [plentiful], nuff, nuff, man.'

In keeping with many of their contemporaries, the Spanglers are not a structured gang in the traditional sense of the word. They are probably best described as a loose confederation of semi-autonomous cells. Hence, Bigga's dual standing as a veteran lieutenant of the overall 'federation' and the don of his own 'battalion'. It is truly a complex situation with, on the one hand, cell members free to pursue their own devices and, on the other, every Spanglers' cadre being subjected to the tacit code of conduct laid down in the cryptic 'foundation'.

'A we [we are] overall [boss] fi we self, man. Straight up,' explains Bigga. The only exceptions, he says, are certain respected 'big man' in the area; the Spanglers' 'elders' and esteemed PNP political activists. Such hallowed figures are given 'respect to the max. Anybody try fi hurt him, fi hurt we,' adds the veteran gunslinger. 'But otherwise we no use boss inna our area. Y'know . . . you is a free man.'

By all accounts, this was the complete opposite to the state of affairs in neighbouring Tivoli Gardens, especially when Jim Brown reigned supreme. 'Jim is a man [who would] just give out order, and people dead,' the rudie says clicking his fingers. Not surprisingly, this policy bred a certain amount of resentment and fear amongst Shower soldiers. Not to mention the disruptive influence it had on the Shower Posse's operations. This, according to Bigga, is yet another reason why 'we no work offa [submit to a] boss . . . Boss ting we no inna [interested in].'

For all the implied freedom, though, Spanglers still have to submit to a rigorous set of dos and don'ts – or face the consequences. For the most part, Bigga is vague about exactly what constitute group offences. Still, he is chillingly clear about how many are punished. 'Well,' he asserts, 'if dem nah obey the rules or from them nah [do not] behave certain way . . . we a go watch you. And any lickle [wrong] move you mek, you a go dead.' However, gangsters who cannot take the 'system', he says, are free to 'just leave go mek it 'pon dem own'.

Whatever else they choose to do, the main thing is that disaffected members must not violate the posse's code. 'You must understand what I mean,' Bigga continues. 'Like, suppose you nah leave now, and you coulda wan' turn all like [become an] informer. Like, carry you name [defect] to another side of gang, or you'd a want set up some man. You must have fe dead [have to die], for you is a stumbling block.' This aspect of Spanglers regimen, at least, is as plain as black and white.

The Spanglers Posse form the ghetto 'government' of the Matthew's Lane 'precinct'. They are the leading 'industrialists' and social carers, security forces, lawmakers, judges, juries and jailors. And their members are folk heroes and role models for many a wannabe gangster. The Spanglers are feudal lords, and the general population their vassals in the Matthew's Lane 'garrison' fiefdom.

The Spanglers' hegemony has been built up over the years on, and is held up by, the twin pillars of organised crime and tribal politics. That said, the tribal factor today is a shadow of what it was even fifteen years ago.

On the tribal front, the Spanglers have grown from being mere pawns in the political chess battle to all-powerful queens. As self-avowed 'straight up' gangsters, this is not a position of responsibility they particularly relish. Either way, though, they realise the tremendous power they wield over prospective parliamentary candidates. For the harsh reality is that they control the hearts and minds of the local electorate. Moreover, without their say-so, the electoral ambitions of any

The burnt body of Lester Lloyd Coke, alias 'Jim Brown', being viewed by employees of Roman's Funeral Home in Kingston.

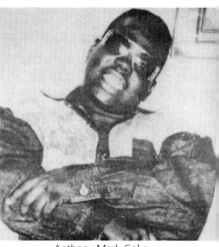

Anthony Mark Coke 'Jah T', son of Jim Brown.

Camilla Coke (*left*) stands beside her mother, Beverley, viewing the open casket of her father, Jim Brown.

Helmeted police search an auto at a barbed wire roadblock in a western Kingston street during an intensive search for weapons and bombs in October 1966. *(Associated Press)*

Edward Seaga (*seated, left*) surrounded by glum supporters after his Jamaican Labour Party's defeat at the polls (1977). *(Camera Press)*

Ghetto gunmen Claudie Massop and Bucky Marshall make peace. Their truce signals the end of a ten-year curfew in the Kingston ghetto, and is regarded as something of a miracle (1978). *(Camera Press)*

Rastamen and whites get round the table to discuss conditions in the ghetto. Pictured on the right are Claudie Massop and Bucky Marshall. *(Camera Press)*

Before a crowd of 20,000 at Kingston's National Stadium
Bob Marley joins Michael Manley (*left*) and his arch-rival
Edward Seaga (*right*) in a symbolic handshake. *(Camera Press)*

Bob Marley with Bucky Marshall. *(Camera Press)*

Prime Minister-elect
Edward Seaga being
hoisted by his party
workers at the party
headquarters after
defeating Michael
Manley in the national
elections (1980).
(Popperfoto)

Jamaica under Edward
Seaga. Election slogans
are splashed on Kingston's
walls: rival People's National
Party and Jamaica Labour
Party factions crossing out
each other's handiwork.
(Camera Press)

President Reagan meets with Prime Minister Edward Seaga in the Oval Office (1988). *(Range/Bettmann/UPI)*

Jamaican politician Michael Manley, during the 1989 election campaign. *(Lennox Smillie)*

Prime Minister-elect Michael Manley, during his first press conference after his victory in Jamaica's 1989 elections. *(Popperfoto)*

Jamaican Prime Minister, P. J. Patterson of the People's National Party, before the 1993 elections. *(Popperfoto)*

Ranking Dread.

Yardies in Britain *(Topham Picture Point)*

candidate would be severely jeopardised, if not totally dashed.

Bigga Knee maintains that the Spanglers do not have formal links with any political parties, including the PNP, whom they openly favour. In fact, by the time Bigga spoke about them, the posse was completely independent of the political establishment. As the august rudie points out: 'You see inna our area, politician no really have nothin' fi do with [its running]. We work and build our area by ourself. Gun! We buy dem . . . We no have no gun fi no politician [the politicians don't give us guns]. Pure drugs man sell and buy dem guns [drug dealers buy their own].'

There is, however, another side to the story, one which vividly illustrates the ties between politicians and the Spanglers. In June 1992, for instance, the smart, spray-painted graffiti on walls around Matthew's Lane boldly declared the solidarity between 'Earl Spencer P.N.P Spanglers'.

And so, up to a point, did Spencer himself. During the summer the former Labourite communed with the Spanglers on a regular basis in Luke Lane. The PNP's 'caretaker' and prospective parliamentarian for the West Kingston constituency, he spent several hours 'reasoning' with these hardened criminals in what one can only imagine was a bid to encourage the gangsters to mobilise their 'vassals' on his behalf.

'You see him now,' says Bigga with a trace of militancy in his delivery, 'as an MP, we [will] vote him in.' However, the acid test of how Spencer would fare subsequent to an electoral victory depended on his posture to the posse. Poli*trick*ery (as the Rastafari call political deceit) would not be tolerated. Says Bigga: 'If him come around and . . . bullshit, him have to leave and can't come back nowhere 'bout ya. For we will kill him, you understand.'

As it happens courting the Spanglers did not help Earl Spencers' electoral ambitions – Seaga kept his seat. In fact, Spencer's political fortunes only went downhill from there. A year after his 1993 election defeat, he narrowly escaped a prison sentence after being convicted of unlawfully 'rescuing' a prisoner from police custody and attempting to pervert the course of justice. Apparently, he had used his political clout to stop a group of special constables arresting a chain-grabber in July 1992. Spencer was fined J$3,000 (£68). He could have been jailed for six months.

Of course, the fundamental reason why the Spanglers are able to maintain a stranglehold over the PNP in the tribal arena is that, for all their criminal gangsterism, they still protect the political borderlines. They are the vanguard of resistance against the area being overrun by pro-JLP clans such as the mighty Shower Posse. Not that the Shower of today is any more interested in turning the Matthew's Lane enclave into a valuable piece of JLP real estate, than the Spanglers are in keeping it PNP. On the contrary, the Spanglers' primary concern is to prevent their domain from becoming a thriving drugs market for Shower dealers. But for hopeful Members of Parliament and councillors the fact remains that the area contains a precious reservoir of potential PNP voters, one which they rely on the Spanglers' influence to secure for them.

However, as is always the way in this complex and confusing world of narco-politics, tribalism is easily confused with drug-related violence. 'You see inna de West now,' explains Bigga, 'as you quint [squint] is war. If [the Shower] kill a man from over my side, we a go kill anyone from dem side: man; woman; pickney [children], anybody at all. Cah you see, through [because] dem a cokehead . . . dem just do a lot of bullshit.'

But the bottom line, says the rudie, is gangsterism. 'We

no really deal with [tribal] war. We deal with money. Money! So, you see, if anyone touch [troubles] our corner, wicked tings happen.'

The criminal pursuit of money, then, is the driving force behind the activities of gangsters like Bigga Knee. Although vocationally a career criminal, Bigga believes that Jamaican society as a whole is geared towards crime. 'Everybody wey [who] work deal with racket,' he claims. 'A so Jamaican deal wid it – dem love fast money.'

Bigga is, however, mindful of the fact that not everybody involved in crime enters into it for the same reason he did – sheer love. Indeed, he concedes that, apart from those attracted by wanton greed, a combination of social privations, economic hardship and lack of opportunity account for a reasonable slice of the country's criminal classes. 'You have man wey a bad man, and him still want to work – for him have him education – and can't get a work [job],' the Rude Boy explains. 'So you find say him go the other way around.'

To Bigga this sad state of affairs is reducible to the miserable condition of the country, and the failings of the political establishment. He points to the lack of employment opportunities as a cause of rising school drop-outs. Similarly, he ponders the effects of large-scale lay-offs in contributing to the crime wave.

The collapse of the health system is a case in point. 'For right now,' he argues with a passion that belies his ruthless activities, 'you go to all a hospital, you hardly see nurse, you hardly see doctor – you haffi definitely go a private doctor. A patient deh deh [is there], she stay there til she die. Nobody no deh fi [there's nobody to] assist her. So you see through dem lickle ting deh [and because of this], that's why nuff fights gwan a Jamaica. Cah Jamaica people dem no like the bullshit.' Jamaican history bears him out on this point.

'And I tell myself,' he continues, 'that, if them don't

pressure it [if they didn't put it under pressure], this
country would be a lovely country – less gun-shooting,
less people dying, less robber, all of those bullshit. If
money a run [is plentiful], man deh 'pon him corner nah
have time [people wouldn't have time] fi sit down an' a
study evil, y'know; fi go shoot a man. For everyday he
can find himself with a money.' But – and it is a major
imponderable – when money is scarce, hungry men are
driven into committing crime. 'As him get up, him good
all [might even] kill a man out deh so . . . So that's why
you find so much [crime] gwan a Jamaica.'

Naturally Bigga apportions the major share of the
blame for this dire state of affairs to the political establishment. He is convinced that the JLP and PNP's historically
disastrous mishandling of Jamaica's political economy
has contributed greatly to the country's present anarchic
crime wave. Apart from that, though, the senior Spanglers
gangster maintains that political interference by, and the
corrupt greed of, certain parliamentarians have only made
matters worse.

One target of Bigga Knee's criticisms is the on-going
anti-drugs crusade. Or, as he puts it: 'See inna Jamaica,
weed and coke mek much people survive – hold up
the country with foreign money.' But ever since the
Government joined the Americans to cripple the narco-
trafficking industry, he points out, 'Jamaica kinda in a
certain bankruptcy.'

Bigga clearly takes a dim view of his country's political
duopoly. The Rt. Hon. Edward Seaga is singled out for
particular criticism. Bigga is particularly scornful of
the contribution Seaga's policies have had in creating
a generation of Jamaican cocaine dependants at home.
He alleges that the one don of the JLP posse, as he once
described himself, freights drugs to the United States 'by
the container', and hides his shadowy dealings behind a
cloak of terminal violence.

For all his admonitions, though, Bigga inwardly admires the JLP boss for his type of ruthless leadership. 'Seaga is a man wey, probably, if we did have a type man like that fi run our team, nothing stop we inna de world, man,' says the rudie. 'Me a tell you!'

As for his personal involvement in the criminal underworld, Bigga confesses, 'Me nah work inna life [I've never worked]. I rather deal with the smuggling, and when I done [finish] I use that money and start over something I can invest offa, which is a legal business.' To that end, he describes 'downtown' as a 'goldmine', and admits to a number of profitable sidelines. These range from running protection rackets to dealing in guns. However, the most lucrative outlet for his talents is drugs trafficking.

Protection rackets prosper especially during times of gang warfare. With the police unwilling or unable – or both – to restore the peace, says Bigga, 'You find say de businesspeople dem love gunman'. Local shopkeepers willing to pay the (unspecified) premiums are provided with armed 'soldiers' to protect their property and premises and, more importantly, to safeguard their lives. The point being that 'when war a gwan, anybody can dead, anybody at all', the Rude Boy says. 'Every man you see is a gunman, you see. So we protect our area, people inna our area.'

Guns, although largely used for posse business, are another money-spinning sideline. 'War tools,' as Bigga refers to them, come into Jamaica in a number of ways. One method is through donations (often murder weapons) from Spanglers in the United States. 'See a man lef' offa him corner, an' him deh a foreign an' him mek money [If a man goes abroad and makes money],' observes Bigga. 'Him [He'll] just buy all three gun and send 'pon him corner, and dat di deh [they are there]. Him coulda buy some more and send. The group a just get bigger and bigger. Him just buy and buy til you find you have X amount.' At which point surplus stock is sold on at a huge profit.

Firearms are also obtained through tourists. In fact, holidaymakers provide a useful conduit for a range of trafficking services. 'You see Ochie [Ocho Rios] now? You see tourist?' exclaims Bigga. 'Tourist a someone who bring guns come a Jamaica come sell. Bring [take] weed go a foreign, coke, anything! Dem run dem shit deh. So if you deh a [are in] Jamaica, you no have fi fly out. If you link with all a good tourist you can do business. You can just buy your stuff . . . and you get you money. She get fi her own. And if you tell [her] "bring ten guns", she a bring it.'

And it is not just any old guns, either. Given that they are every rudie's tool of the trade, it is not surprising to find that gangsters are both knowledgeable and particular about their weapons of choice. Because of their contacts and preferences, rival posses tend to fire different makes of firearms at each other. 'We is a youth now wey like draw fi de war tool [firearms] like Russian, Germany, Vietnam. Dem gun deh we like,' explains Bigga.

Generally speaking, when it comes to trafficking, Bigga *et al* will smuggle in anything there is a market for. So, for example, they are always on the lookout for car parts – a precious and heavily-taxed commodity throughout Jamaica. But whether car parts or handguns, Bigga's set have made some useful friends at the island's ports. Poorly-paid customs officials are easily corrupted. At the time, the rudie was doling out one-off payments worth J\$10,000–J\$20,000 (£250–£500) and monthly retainers of J\$5,000 (£125) to his Kingston airport staff in return for them turning a blind eye to certain incoming cargo.

Without a doubt the biggest money-earner for Bigga and his crew is the traffic in drugs, cocaine in particular. Jamaica's position as the premier Caribbean entrepôt for narcotics means that, wherever illegal drug cargoes are bound for, they invariably pass through Jamaica on their way there. And, when they are not using tourists to 'mule' them, gangsters like Bigga make extra cash by acting as middlemen for other drug operations.

So cocaine comes in from 'Panama, Curaçao, Haiti and dem places', but, explains the experienced smuggler, 'when it come here, it reach England, America, those places' because they know the best routes and channels to transport it. Even certain consignments of narcotics bound for Caribbean states are routed through the Spanglers.

Surprisingly, perhaps, there is little call for Bigga's expert services from his namesakes in the United States. Naturally they enjoy close and cordial relations with Spanglers branches in the States – the Jamaican wing provides new recruits, for example – but these do not normally spill over into the realm of cocaine trafficking. 'More time [usually] dem have the connection where dem get . . . good stuff. So dem buy it' themselves, explains the Rude Boy. 'You have man up deh who have dem connection where dem no have fi link by [deal with] us fi get it.'

For all their adeptness in the field of illegal activities, Bigga's 'division', and the Jamaican Spanglers as a whole, are not swimming in riches. In fact, while they 'get by' handsomely, they are poor relations by comparison with some of the newer all-drug crews, and sometime-political posses, like the Shower Posse.

Ironically, the explanation for this curious anomaly is to be found in the Spanglers Posse's experiences with the cocaine trade in the United States. In turn, this enlightenment has had far-reaching consequences on the scope of the original posse's abilities to make money from crack and cocaine in Jamaica itself. In short, the Spanglers have added some new rules to the mystical 'foundation': they have prohibited the sale and consumption of hard drugs in their Matthew's Lane enclave; and banned their members from abusing them. 'You see, through most of our man go a foreign [have been abroad] dem know what coke is [can do],' explains Bigga. 'So dem no really want nobody inna our area turn vampire [addict].'

Putting the Spanglers' seemingly 'responsible' stand against their members indulging in cocaine to one side, cynics might argue that it simply amounts to good business practice. After all, it is not one or two posse drug dealers who have become so enamoured of their 'nose candy' or 'Scotty' (as in the famous Star Trek line, 'Beam me up, Scotty') that they have neglected to sell it, choosing instead to consume it themselves. Invariably, in some instances, this has led to the abusers' deaths. But in every case, it has compromised the efficiency and profit-making ability of their group.

Indeed, as self-appointed lawmakers and arbiters of 'feudal' justice, the Spanglers are determined to ensure that their turf does not fall prey to the lure of cocaine. As Bigga expresses it: 'We lick [clamp] down 'pon it hard.' This is apparent both in their efforts to keep alien drug dealers at bay, and their equal conviction to stop members of the Matthew's Lane community from indulging in hard drugs. The penalties for both are severe.

'If a man in our area an' him a sniff [snort cocaine], him can't mek we know,' says Bigga defiantly. 'Cah if we know, an' him no stop, him have fi leave the area complete [completely]. If him no stop we going kill him, for we don't want him bring the rest inna it fi mash dem up [we don't want him to infect and ruin the rest] . . . for one bad seed spoils all . . . Strictly weed [ganja] we deal with, y'understand?'

With cocaine providing a route to fast cars and fancy living for a plethora of accomplished local cocaine dealers, it is not surprising that the more ambitious among them have tried to set up bases of operation in the Spanglers Posse's principality. These have been repelled with customary force by the local warlords. 'One time dem open a coke shop [crack house] a Luke Lane,' recalls Bigga. 'And we give dem orders fi lock [close] it down, and dem no lock it down. Well, we go turn on a gunshot [went in with guns blazing] . . . and lock it down. Silence it. It no open again.'

Keeping the cocaine kingpins off Spanglers 'corner' is no easy task. The Spanglers' kingdom stretches north for a couple of blocks along Rose Lane – one of the borderlines with the Shower Posse – before turning west into Beeston Street for a block and heading north again up Oxford Street. Following the same northward course, the boundary continues into Upper Rose Lane and Upper Oxford Street, parallel to the Tivoli Creek, before turning east into Studley Park Road behind the Comprehensive Clinic in Arnette Town. From there the border runs southward along Slipe Pen Road through Drummond Street to Orange Street (the site of Kingston's famous Ward Theatre) before finally heading west again through West Queen Street and the Spanish Town Road. The entire territory is approximately 1,200 metres long by 400 metres wide, and houses about 8,000 'subjects'. Policing it is a full-time job.

The Spanglers are more liberal than most in their government, but they still subject the area to a policy of iron-fist control. 'Anyting we say stand,' demands Bigga. 'You see [if] certain tings [problems] harass the neighbourhood? We can't deal with that.'

Crime, other than that of their own making, is a definite taboo. Spanglers Posse members take a particularly dim view of resident criminals who feast off, or intimidate, the charges they protect. They take an especially hard line against local freelance gunmen. 'To me,' the veteran gun 'hawk' says, 'dem Third World youth deh dem crazy. Most a dem a just badness dem a deal wid . . . For you have some crazy youth inna my area right now – every day and night dem a fire gun, y'know?

'Them ting deh can't work [are unacceptable]. When a man mess with you dat different.' Indeed not. Those who insist on committing crime are encouraged to do so beyond the boundaries of the Matthew's Lane stronghold. Failure to do so results in torture and imprisonment in a Spanglers' 'jail cell' or instant execution. It is as simple as that.

In keeping with all ghetto gangs, petty thieves are definitely considered *persona non grata*, and subjected to vicious punishment for practising their trade on Spanglers' turf. The general feeling is that such anti-social elements give the areas they operate in, and therefore the people who control them, a bad name. 'Tief?' barks Bigga disdainfully, 'We no like dem system deh [we don't like theft]. If a man thief and him a run through [operate in] our area, him a get him two foot broke and him two hand broke, and then we get a [hand]cart an' sen' him up by the [nearby Kingston Public] hospital. We no response fi him again.'

Earlier Shabba had recounted a recent incident involving him and some Spanglers Rude Boys in which they had apprehended a local thief. According to Shabba, while he and others set about breaking the unfortunate victim's limbs, one of the enforcers jumped on his chest. 'Me no know how him survive,' chuckled the young rudie.

The punishments meted out to ordinary, law-abiding citizens seldom, if ever, regress to the level of bestial savagery. However, locals are still liable to physical punishment for putting the 'peace' in jeopardy. The difference, if anything, is that the iron-fisted rudies don a glove.

In this way, the Spanglers have completely supplanted the police as the keepers of law and order. No matter how trivial or grave an alleged incident, local people are instructed to report it to the posse. 'Whether you stab somebody or anything, we can deal with the case more than even a police,' asserts Bigga.

It is not simply that residents are advised not to liaise or co-operate with the JCF – it is a directive; those who defy it effectively criminalise themselves. '[If] you live in our area and anything happen and you go a [police] station, you have fi leave,' the Rude Boy continues. 'We no like see police inna our area . . . Them will more come fight 'gainst we [they're more likely to harrass us], y'understand?'

Avoiding the police like the plague, and referring one's problems to the Spanglers, are not of themselves a guaranteed passport to a painless resolution of those situations. In some cases, both 'plaintiff' and 'defendant' lay themselves open to disciplinary proceedings. 'If two somebody [people] a fight,' explains the veteran Rude Boy, 'the two a ounu [both of them] a get beaten. One nah get, whether [or not he] did first start it.'

Unjust it might seem, but the Spanglers' policy is extremely effective. 'You find say people understand themselves, and they know what is what,' says Bigga somewhat euphemistically. 'So dem fi carporate [co-operate], y'understand? We no really pressure our people dem. A just dem fi [they just have to] know and under-stand themselves: "See and blind, hear and deaf." That's how we really deal with our area.'

In spite of everything else, the Spanglers accept that their responsibilities transcend the maintenance of local order. By their own admission they see themselves as local benefactors, too. Benefaction comes in a number of forms, but, significantly, its dispensation is as much about reducing hardship, as it is undermining the need to resort to crime.

Special efforts are made to cater for the elderly and

the young, particularly during the holiday seasons. But, generally speaking, all the needy in the area are provided for. 'You see like Easter?' enquires Bigga, 'every home get money, bun, cheese, flour, all type of ting. Or more time [alternatively], you have store people who give them tings for the community – specially the old people dem – offa our heading [instruction] . . . We mostly give them the benefit cah we no want know, say, them inna the area and dem hungry . . . and disaster. We no really like that. It better me hungry.

'What worse, we live inna market area, again. Dem place deh now, fresh food [is in abundance]. For as de truck come in, we can get stuff offa de truck or what have you. [Sugar] cane, all fruit, anyting at all. Fresh . . . Through we live deh so now [because we live here], you nah normally say, well, hungry. We can deal with our tings ourself, y'understand. Politician no know none a dem ting [it's got nothing to do with the politicians].'

The young receive similar treatment. 'We keep treats [parties] for kids,' explains Bigga Knee. 'Everybody get presents – no matter how lickle you is . . . You get your book, pencil, pen, dolly, all types of tings you get . . . And like the school now [as for the school] . . . we have store man [owners] wey support our school, say, with anyting at all the teacher want. An' a we pay de teacher dem.'

In fact, as much as the Spanglers' 'straight-up' gangsters are role models for many a youthful, would-be rudie gunslinger, they try to keep children and teenagers on the straight and narrow. Bigga maintains that even if he has to give away his last penny to a teenager, he will gladly give it. The reason is because 'me no want him go outta road, go see somebody with them tings, beg it, or probably [he] can't get it, an' then [he] a go steal it . . . which is trouble. So we stick out [stand up] fi dem.' With most of the area's parents abroad, this is truly a mammoth undertaking.

More and more, however, the burden of providing has been eased by the charitable instincts of infinitely more prosperous Spanglers gangsters abroad. (Sensible) foreign-based gangsters tend not to burn their bridges; they never know when they might be forced to return to their home turf. While they frequently ship guns to their stablemates in Matthew's Lane, they also double as providers for the general population. 'A man go foreign now,' observes Bigga, 'an' him a mek money. Him send money, an' mek everybody eat food. He may sen' on some clothes, an' a no [they are not] cheap clothes him a buy. Him buy dear clothes, mek everybody live up [well].'

Finding an explanation for the immense power the Spanglers Posse wields in relation to the populace of their Matthew's Lane territory brings us full circle. But where once the Spanglers' lawlessness was sanctioned – bankrolled and armed – by megalomaniac politicos, it is now backed up by the awesome armouries they have acquired independently through dealing drugs.

Their weaponry, fearlessness and ruthlessness have made them a formidable foe, one which has kept the police at arm's length. And one, moreover, the police certainly do not rush to take on. Bigga explains why: 'Right now in Jamaica, the freedom fighter – which is we – have gun more than what the [police] force have, and more than what the army have.'

Indeed, Bigga Knee believes that the Spanglers are so well equipped that 'if right now a political war or a revolution war should [break] out in Jamaica, the police and the army can't hold it back – them have too much people fi fight, and you have X amount of gun inna Jamaica.'

A tragi-comic illustration of the power the Spanglers display over the police appeared in the *Weekly Gleaner* in May 1994. It concerned the second day of demonstrations staged by angry higglers and market vendors over the JCF's removal of vendors from illegal downtown pitches. Carrying placards bearing legends such as 'No vendors no stores' and 'We want justice', the protestors set about blocking roads and bringing local traffic to a standstill.

As the situation hotted up, police in attendance called in the JCF's Mobile Reserve (officers equipped with tear-gas) to disperse the crowd. But before the trouble-shooting task force could swing into action, they were ordered to stand aside. The directive came from a Matthew's Lane don who was reported as saying: 'Boss, ounu just leave and gwan [leave and go away], we wi [will] tek care a tings.' Meanwhile, the police were made to look on helplessly as 'a group of dons' grabbed the protestors' placards and 'boxed' (punched) some of them in their faces before finally ordering them to vacate their 'manor'. In light of this, it will come as no surprise to learn that, while he has a grudging respect for the army, Bigga wholeheartedly believes 'police a coward'.

As always the Spanglers Posse's biggest threat ema-nates from the arch-enemy, the Shower Posse. Because of its location as a gateway to the city, its political sympathies and its cocaine-free environment, the Shower have made repeated attempts to wrest Matthew's Lane away from the Spanglers.

According to Bigga, because Shower soldiers are cokeheads to a man, they cause unnecessary conflict. This in turn impairs their effectiveness. 'If dem did conscious,' he explains, 'I feel them woulda tek over Jamaica.

'Everybody in Jamaica 'fraid a dem, 'fraid a Garden Man. Well you see now? We no 'fraid a dem for dem is we neighbourhood [they're our neighbours]. We know fi dem background . . . We know everyting 'bout dem, just like dem know everyting 'bout we. For we a neighbourhood.'

Over the years these bloody encounters in the 'Wild West' have seen the death of hundreds of people, many of them totally innocent. This is in spite of basic precautions taken by the Spanglers to ensure the safety of their charges – wooden walls are no match for stray M-16 bullets. When the latest war erupts, the order immediately goes out for the streets to be cleared – not that it takes much persuading – especially of children. 'We have to secure the kids dem,' opines Bigga, 'so when we say "in", dem have to [go] in. Anybody at all, when we say "in, in," cah we no want nobody get no shot. We out deh a fight de battle day and night, you understand?

'When all war a gwan, see all [in] a day?' remarks Bigga. 'Probably all ten, fifteen, twenty [people are killed]. Sometime one. Sometime none. Sometime a war may go on fi all like a month, and inna de month you coulda find all fifty people dead, hundred all get shot up and batter fi life. It up to dem if dem cover it [seek retribution].'

'Spanglers no nurse [don't have mercy on] people,' says Bigga, 'dem love fly head [shooting off people's heads].' He had only recently been involved in a fierce gun battle, which, he says, was only stopped by the intervention of a joint police-military task force. Had the State's forces not intervened the rudie boasts 'we'd a clean out the whole a Garden, for dem start it'. According to Bigga, 'Them a come from [political] meeting and fire shot 'pon we lane. People get shot [so] we haffi discipline them back. The two a we a gangster [we're both gangsters], and we can't look soft for we name is big.'

One thing is for sure, Bigga has done his fair share of gunslinging and killing over the years. So much so, in fact, that he seems genuinely unsure of how many notches he has carved into his gun. 'Well,' he sighs, 'I don't really know the amount for more time shot a fire [you're shooting] and, probably through the range, you might shoot a man an' him run go dead in a field.' The only thing he is certain about is that 'nuff man' have died by his hand.

For all his drug dealing, shooting and killing, Bigga Knee does not have much to show for spending more than half of his life as a gangster. Home is a one-room wooden shack partitioned into two small rooms, only one of which is occupied by him. It has no toilet, only a communal latrine out back. It has no bathroom, only a communal stand-pipe in the yard out front. It has no kitchen, either.

Apart from sundry fading posters from past sound system 'clashes' and semi-naked women (many of which are British Page Three models reprinted in the Jamaican press) a double bed, a large, beat-up case full of clothes, an array of expensive-looking shoes and trainers, a few pairs of flashy sunglasses, a plethora of audio cassettes, a top-of-the-range ghettoblaster, a shadeless light bulb and his trusty Beretta, Bigga Knee has nothing, or at least nothing visible.

Bigga likes being a 'somebody'. Although he is modest about it, he clearly enjoys the glamour and celebrity that goes with being a dangerous, Rude Boy gangster. He thrives off the 'respect' he receives from fellow rudies. He is empowered by the immeasurable influence he holds over the local community. He loves the girls – and they love him – the money, and the danger.

Yet still there is something missing. Bigga wants to set up in business (a legal business) but he is hamstrung by a lack of funds. With the Spanglers' strict rules against dealing cocaine within the community, the only way he is ever going to get the finances he needs is by applying his skills in the West; he needs to go abroad.

The most likely way of getting there is through the time-honoured tradition of being 'sent for' or recruited by a fellow Spangler who has planted his roots. Bigga himself yearns to carry on that tradition of providing opportunities for the ghetto underprivileged. 'If me deh a foreign now,' he says. 'A man send fi me, an' me deh deh an' a mek money [a man sends for me, and I'm there making money], me can send fi ten man. And . . . whether [or not] him family, but him have fi send fi somebody, y'understand? For is a man send fi him, so him haffi send fi somebody.

'An' every man do dem business; every man have dem own money. Me no bring send fi you, and mek you come work fi me. When you come [you get] a lickle half pound [start]. A your start that. That mean you start from deh so, an mek youself be a man.'

The funny thing is that Bigga had an open invitation to join a friend in London. But he was wavering, uncertain about what to do. 'I get a Brixton call from a Spanglers,' he explains. 'Him a tell me say mi fi come inna de place. But me no really like England – me would go there still – but just 'Merica fi me all the while. I like crazy country. England no crazy enough. I like 'Merica. 'Merica is a crazy country. I like that country.'

America beware!

CHAPTER EIGHT

Exodus – Movement of the Posses

'I think [the posses] carried their violence with them to the United States, and wherever they go. I don't think they're gonna act any differently whether they're in the United States, Canada, Britain. It probably just depends on the accessibiltiy of firearms.'

'Anne', Intelligence Analyst,
Bureau of Alcohol, Tobacco and Firearms

The nucleus of what were to become the posses began to converge *en masse* on the United States after the carnage of Jamaica's 1980 General Election. The story of the posses' successful colonisation of the United States from thereon is deeply ironic. For what was, first and foremost, a desperate attempt on the part of the political gunslingers to escape the attentions of the Jamaica Constabulary Force, actually ended in the beginnings of the most lucrative phase of their criminal lives.

When Edward Seaga became Jamaica's latest incumbent in the Prime Minister's office, he was put under intense public pressure to bring the mercenary Rude Boy gunmen to justice. In order to make them expiate for their political sins, Seaga ordered the police to round them up without delay. At best, this meant the gunslingers faced prosecution for their murderous, politically-sanctioned deeds. At worst, it exposed them to the very real danger of becoming the victims of potentially fatal 'shoot-outs' with the heavily-armed and deadly Jamaican police force. Thus, leaving Jamaica (a task facilitated in part by grateful political paymasters) seemed the best bet to the political gun hawks at the time.

Yet within five years of their enforced mass exodus, the gangs or posses and the Yardie 'refugees', would go on to carve an indelible, blood-stained scar across the face of America, their supposed safe haven. Their members' savagery would smooth the way to the gangs themselves becoming one of America's most profitable, widespread and feared criminal entities, ever. In fact, by the mid-1980s the posses would be identified by American law enforcers as the most ruthless and deadly, alien criminal organisation ever to hit the nation's streets.

Inexplicably though, in spite of their fanatical penchant for often public exhibitions of violence, the posses would achieve this dubious status without the host country's local police and federal agents being aware of their organised presence.

Relating the story of how thousands of homicidal Jamaican gangsters and their gangs managed to elude the attentions of probably the world's most sophisticated and organised law enforcement establishment for so long is not easy. For one, in establishing a foothold in the United States, the posses were clearly not what one would call subtle. Intimidation, violence, torture, and murder reigned supreme in everything they did, and was evident everywhere they settled. Suffice it to say that at this stage, the gangsters' knowledge of Cold War-style espionage techniques learnt during their 'apprenticeships' in Jamaica's political gangs contributed more than anything else to concealing their operations. Indeed, as we shall see, by the time the American authorities got wise to the activities of the posses, their leading gangsters were heading towards 'untouchable' status.

So how did they get to that point? In terms of their initial associations with the United States a great deal depended on the ability of the new arrivals to conceal their presence. To a man, the gangsters achieved this by heading for the country's long-established Jamaican (and African-Caribbean) communities.

Since the 1880s, America has been perceived as the ultimate land of opportunity by countless groups of poor immigrants. The Italians, Irish, European Jews and, more recently, the Koreans, are but a few to subscribe to this notion. Ambitious and industrious Jamaicans were no exception, either. In fact, whether skilled and educated or simply impoverished, Jamaicans have been heading for the United States for longer than most other immigrant groups. So much so, that bustling metropolises like New York and Miami boast Jamaican-based communities running into the tens of thousands.

America is estimated to house about 400,000 legal Jamaican residents. In New York City, areas such as Flatbush and Crown Heights in Brooklyn, North Bronx in the Bronx and the aptly named Jamaica in Queens have become 'home' to Caribbean immigrants from English-speaking islands like Trinidad and Tobago, Antigua, Barbados and Jamaica for almost a century. In fact, one in ten, or 200,000, inhabitants of Brooklyn hail from the Caribbean.

When it comes to Jamaicans, predictably the single largest Caribbean grouping, Crown Heights, is something of a mecca. Along Utica Avenue and its environs are to be found a plethora of Jamaican-owned businesses ranging from specialist clothes and music shops to shipping companies and travel agents, and restaurants that serve mouth-watering Jamaican delicacies like Jerk chicken, and ackee and saltfish. In many respects, Crown Heights has grown to become home from home for the Jamaicans who reside there.

It was, therefore, to areas like this that a new wave of Jamaican immigrants flocked during the late 1970s and early 1980s. Typically, a great many of the new arrivals were illegal immigrants. Indeed, it is thought that well over half of the Big Apple's estimated Caribbean population of between 750,000 to one million people entered the country under false pretences. Either way, during the early 1980s the Immigration and Naturalisation Service (INS) began to notice a sharp increase in the numbers of Jamaicans showing up with bogus travel documents (a posse trademark) or permanently overstaying their temporary visas.

That, however, was only one of the many major differences to distinguish this influx from previous ones. Another was that, unlike their predecessors who went to the United States with marketable skills and law-abiding ambitions, this group was made up largely of terminally work-shy wannabes and violent narco-political criminals. From the very beginning these undesirables had their sights set on making their fortunes in the world of crime.

By all accounts, the members of this new cohort did not waste any time in displaying their criminal credentials in the adopted communities. 'Those guys went up there with their traditional sort of gunslinging, and naturally they are not going to line up at employment agencies,' explains Lloyd Williams. The Jamaican journalist, who has closely followed the career of the posses in the United States, reckons the Jamaican *gundeliros* fell into the criminal underworld as soon as they had arrived. 'So they'll hang out with some of their friends [from back home] who are selling dope for the black Americans, and, in some cases, the Columbians,' he adds.

For all their illegal activities, these political mercenaries (and the apolitical criminal aspirants from Jamaica who frequently teamed up with them) were not immune to the promise of the much-vaunted American Dream. No different from any other newcomers, they wanted to make it big in the USA. Add to that, though, the fact that, probably more than any of their immigrant predecessors, the rudie gunmen were used to wielding tremendous influence – and firepower – in Jamaica, and one had all the ingredients for an impending power struggle in the drug business. In short, the gangsters were not content with being tenants, they wanted to be landlords.

The impending battle for control of the ganja business was not long in coming. 'These guys have just come from a tradition where they shoot first and ask questions after,' points out Williams. That deadly feature of their behaviour proved particularly damaging for their Dominican, Columbian and African-American employers. 'They were pretty ruthless,' explains Williams, 'and they killed a lot of their quote "bosses" unquote, and literally just took over their operations.' Round One to the posses, then.

Other like-minded newcomers simply banded together to form their own posses. Still political fundamentalists at heart, the membership of these groups both reflected and kept the tribal rivalries of yore alive in the United States. More than that, the posses tended to recruit from friends, acquaintances and allies who hailed from the same neighbourhoods back in the 'old country'. The crafty gangsters' knack of producing phoney travel papers also meant that they were able to draw in fresh blood from those same ghettoes with impunity.

However they were formed, though, the results were exactly the same. The posses set out, guns blazing, to capture the local ganja business lock, stock and barrel. This ambition was obvious in a number of other ways including the unrelenting efforts of Jamaican drug barons at home to export increasing tonnages of ganja on to the United States mainland during the late 1970s. As a consequence, between 1978 and 1979 Jamaica's share of the American marijuana market rose by two percentage points to eight per cent, still a distant third behind Columbia (eighty per cent), but gaining on second-placed Mexico (twelve per cent).

With increasingly larger tonnages of the 'herb' flooding in from Jamaica via ships and planes, there was also a marked increase in the number of interceptions made by the American authorities. Newark and Miami were the sites for two multi-ton seizures of ganja in 1979. Also, while American law enforcers were aware of only one plane crash or accident involving ganja from Jamaica in 1978, they came across twenty in the following year. And over the same period, ganja-related arrests jumped from ten to thirty-three.

The pattern of increasing ganja-related arrests continued into the 1980s. By 1982 American law personnel were arresting hundreds of Jamaicans for possessing and selling ganja. But, more than anything else, it was their shocking violence which made the ruthless Rude Boys stand out. Indeed, as tribally intact posses shot it out with each other for the right to control ganja markets, the death toll and homicide arrest rates rose sharply up and down the country.

Still, in spite of the serious upsurge in Jamaican-related violence the American authorities failed to diagnose the condition as what it was, inter-posse feuding over drug turf. Indeed, it is estimated that posse violence resulted in the slayings of anywhere up to 1,500 (mainly Jamaican) victims in the half decade to the mid-1980s before its organised basis was recognised. In truth, it is a mark of the posses' success in hiding their activities that the federal authorities did not begin to tally such killings until 1985, shortly after they became aware of the gangs.

*   *   *

So how, with all this overt violence including public execution-style homicides, did posses like the Shower, Spanglers, Waterhouse, Jungle and countless others manage totally to elude the United States' substantial forces of law and order for such a long time? The secret, or the best part of it, lies in the way the posses are organised and structured; features which make them unique among their criminal peers. These aspects also provide vital clues as to why the gangs managed to increase their market share of ganja sales, and have generally proved so difficult to 'search and destroy' since their official discovery.

The make-up of posse personnel has changed significantly over the years. For example, the need for more and more labour arising out of the post-1985 crack revolution led the posses' executive command structures to make more use of Jamaican women and African-Americans. However, the basic structure of these organisations has remained intact.

When they first sprang up in the early 1980s, the posses' organisational structures immediately distinguished them from any previous criminal enterprise. To begin with American-based posses are not structured in the way that, say, a social scientist might define a 'structure'. So where intra-Mafia group relationships are punctuated by rigid family ties, the posses' were based on loose associations of like-minded gangsters with a common interest in 'doing business'. There was seldom an overall posse don; such Napoleon-types invariably end up dead at the hands of one of their aspiring lieutenants. In truth, rather than conforming to a strict demarcation of responsibilities, it was routine for posse members to perform various, often interchangeable tasks.

The closest one could get to an authentic posse structure was through a tripartite pyramid of responsibility. The upper tier, the dons, handled the group's leadership functions. It was their job to co-ordinate the supply and distribution of drugs to the cartel's branches and outlets wherever they existed in the United States. Other important duties included maintaining overall control of the organisation, shaping its development and, of course, counting and laundering its drug profits.

Then, as now, the members of this stratum usually operated out of New York or Miami, the 'source' cities or nerve centres where the 'parent' posses maintained their bases of operation. It is no coincidence that these cities also contained America's largest concentrations of lawful Jamaicans. Like parasites, the narco-gangs sought shelter, protection and sustenance for their nefarious activities in a welcoming environment. Generally speaking, a don's only physical contact with his, or occasionally her, underlings in outlet cities usually arose out of some major problem or dispute that they were called upon to resolve.

Day-to-day posse management was handled by a middle echelon, the overseers. In the early days the trust factor was a key criterion in meeting this job's specifications. Usually, the dons and the overseers originated from the same neighbourhood in Jamaica, where they will no doubt have brandished guns under the patronage of the PNP or JLP. The overseer's tasks included ensuring their street dealers were well stocked, collecting drug receipts for the dons and recruiting 'workers' – which after the mid-1980s increasingly meant African-Americans – to perform the posse's menial tasks.

The bottom tier was made up of 'workers', a posse's lumpenproletariat. They performed the 'shit work', everything from selling drugs to providing protection, acting as 'look-outs' and 'mules' for drugs and drug money to purchasing weapons, and renting apartments and vehicles.

In reality, though, the situation has not been anywhere near as straightforward as this. Like any successful business organisation the posses' survival and prosperity has depended on their ability to behave like chameleons; to adapt effectively to environmental changes and life-threatening circumstances. This is a point not missed by the people who track them. 'Jamaican posses, more than any other criminal group,' concluded an ominous US Federal report on the gangs, 'have continually demonstrated an ability to alter their methods of operation to avoid detection.' More than any other feature of their operations, this uncanny ability to adapt quickly to perilous situations has enabled the Jamaican bandits to keep one step ahead of the law.

This tendency actually dates back to the posse cohorts' days as political gunmen in Jamaica during the island's US-Cuban Cold War years. In short, the leading posse gangsters' organisational adroitness was part of the legacy of political 'training' bestowed upon them during their 'apprenticeships'. And, as we have seen, the probability is the rudie mobsters learned these valuable lessons directly from agents of the CIA and Cuba's DGI. Either way, the posse gangsters left Jamaica with a substantial working knowledge of political espionage techniques; the sorts of machinations that were more readily associated with the novels of John le Carré.

This expertise, in turn, is crucial to an understanding of why the posses were not detected earlier. And the headstart they gained also goes some way to explaining why the posses have proved so difficult for American law enforcement agencies to nail down since. So, even before the crack craze, in the days when they operated as exclusive ganja traffickers, the posses were able to establish themselves in major cities and towns without the local police being aware of them. Of course, local peace keepers would know Jamaican gunslingers had been around – the increasing intake at city morgues proved that much. However, what appeared on the surface to be opportunistic guerrilla attacks on local drug dealers or frenzied shooting matches between Jamaicans were, in fact, well-planned pushes to take over new or existing market-places for ganja sales.

The first phase of these occupations would begin with a don dispatching a trusted 'spy' to stake out a potential location. The infiltrator would report back on the strength of the host drug dealing organisations, the local users' drugs of choice, suitable retail outlets and so on. If these diverse factors measured up, a crack squad of 'soldiers' and 'enforcers' would be dispatched, guns in hands, from New York or Miami to seize the new territory. The gunmen would then return to their base city only to be replaced by a low-profile 'cell' comprised of overseers and 'workers'. After that, almost like a bear in hibernation, the posses would remain dormant until their organisation's safety was jeopardised by competitors.

In those halcyon days, the posses outwitted many a local militia. 'They understand compartmentalisation,' argues Con Dougherty, a twenty-year veteran Bureau of Alcohol, Tobacco and Firearms (ATF) agent. These people were around for years almost unnoticed, and where they were noticed, misdiagnosed,' adds the experienced crusader in the United States longstanding 'War on Drugs'. 'I saw reports personally in Hartford, Connecticut, that talked about a strongarm group for the Rastafarians called the "Shower Posse". Now, I don't think there could be anything less related than the Rastafarians and the posses.'

'Compartmentalisation', as Dougherty awkwardly refers to it, is one of the many tricks of the trade applied by posse overlords to safeguard the organisational integrity of their gangs. Its implications go beyond mere misdiagnosis. They shape the whole fabric of a posse's operations by shrouding them in secrecy. And, as a consequence, augment the difficulties of infiltrating, not to mention, smashing them – two tasks which have become increasingly imperative since the crack boom got under way.

The practical application of compartmentalisation found its zenith during the crack boom. Still, it was an equally indispensable weapon in the posses' clandestine armoury during their formative years in the United States. In short, it helped them to set up the ganja distribution networks that would later service the traffic of firearms and narcotics like crack. Initially, in terms of their ganja dealings, compartmentalisation enabled the posse kingpins to keep a healthy distance between the operations they directed and the people who carried them out.

So, for example, a New York don would instruct a trusted overseer to supervise ganja dealing operations from, say, four locations in Washington DC. The supervisor would then employ a fleet of street dealers in that city; dealers, more to the point, who would be answerable only to him. Indeed, to all intents and purposes, the dealers would consider the overseer to be their ultimate boss, and have absolutely no knowledge whatsoever of the New York connection.

As if keeping the worker stratum in the dark were not sophisticated enough, the overseers themselves would take steps to protect their own identities. Like Lon Chaney, leading rudie posse members were the men of a thousand faces. Thus the mythical Washington-based overseer might use a different name with every worker he came into contact with. So, in the unlikely event that a dealer was apprehended and considered 'helping the police with their enquiries', they would only be able to identify their putative boss as 'Longers', 'Stick', 'Billy' or whatever. Again, had law enforcement officers got wind of the organisation and attempted to infiltrate it, they would have been none the wiser about who the big players really were.

'They may just know him by a nickname or a street name. And that same person may have a different street name in every area of the country that he goes,' asserts 'Anne', an ATF intelligence analyst. 'So identifying anyone of any real significance in the organisation is very, very difficult. And because they're so mobile they are literally in Dallas tomorrow morning, and back in New York a couple of hours later . . .' An anonymous drug agent offers an even more fatalistic prognosis: 'You can't track these characters,' he says. 'The Jamaicans come and go so quickly, they change up their people. It's hard to track them. It's harder to keep pressure on them at a Federal level.'

Again, the dons and overseers learned the value of bogus identities, aliases and travel documents in Jamaica. So, even when they were stopped by the police they would be able to produce 'genuine' drivers licences and the like bearing the identities of other people. Even then the posses' activities did not stop at manufacturing fake identification documents. 'If you come into the United States from Jamaica . . . with a legitimate entry document,' explains Dougherty, 'among the posses it's not unusual for you to "lose" your Green Card, to go to the INS and get a replacement. And all of a sudden there are two Geoff Smalls, perfectly indentified, one in Miami, one in Hartford, Connecticut.'

On a broader, organisational level, the posses also managed to conceal their presence by assuming a holistic approach to their business dealings. Once again, the posses distinguished themselves by being the only nar- cotics syndicate to use this technique.

What it means in effect is that with regard to ganja, for example, the whole process from wholesale to retail was centralised. The beauty of this was that the entire operation was kept in the family, so to speak. Thus, there were no middlemen to remunerate or who could be compromised by the police and federal authorities. And, generally, there was a much diminished threat of the operation coming to the attention of the authorities.

Dougherty is no fan of the posses. But he has a grudging respect for their organisational genius. 'The way they would move dope,' he explains, 'they would buy it at wholesale, move it through the chain, distribute it on the street and no money was due back up until the street sale had been made.' However, Dougherty's admiration stems less from the system itself and more from the fact that it worked. 'That implies a lot of control. That implies exercising a lot of discipline,' he continues, tongue in cheek, 'because people tend to forget in the criminal business to send that money back from time to time, and they have to be discouraged from doing that.'

Given their reputation for ruthless violence, the rudies probably had less to worry about in that department than most crime syndicates. Indeed, those most likely to 'forget' about their responsibilities came mainly from the ranks of African-Americans recruited by the posses to help service the crack boom. They were lowly functionaries who underestimated, or were simply unaware of, the vicious force they were taking on.

The story of the posses' initial colonisation of the United States then, is one of the hand of primitive, gunslinging brute force hidden in the glove of sophisticated organisational secrecy. The former in particular became more and more evident after the mid-1980s. Meanwhile, the latter has continued to make the posses very difficult for the combined forces of United States law enforcement to defeat. And together, the unlikely liaison has catapulted the posses into the top division of American organised crime.

CHAPTER NINE

The Posses: A Problem Identified

> 'Any time I hear of any homicide in the United States
> where there are multiple victims, where they're bound
> in some type of way or it has some type of torture –
> might be little kids there – the first thing that comes
> to my mind is that it's the posses. Our other groups
> tried to be like the posses, but I don't think they
> can do it.'
>
> 'Anne', ATF Intelligence Analyst

The second chapter of the posses' colonisation of the
United States can be divided into two distinct stages. The
initial period, the posses' heyday, fell roughly between
the mid-1980s and early 1990s. This era witnessed the
meteoric rise of the Jamaican drug gangs both in terms
of their organisational strength, creation, capture and
share of profitable drug markets, and national expansion.
Indeed, for a short while it seemed that wherever crack
was being retailed, the posses were either selling it or
controlling its sale.

The second phase runs up to the present, and has seen
the posses very much on the defensive. Their share of
the nation's narcotics markets has crashed, especially
in major metropolises like New York, Los Angeles and

Miami. And the membership of the gangs has shrunk because of a combination of sustained law enforcement pressure, inter-posse splintering, and the ascendancy of well-connected rivals. Together these factors have forced the posses' hands, and led them to make a number of tactical alterations in the way they approach the business of doing business.

Still, both halves of this tale of mixed fortunes are united by one common denominator: ruthless violence. On the one hand, the posses' predilection towards extreme violence helped to underpin their phenomenal success during the glory years. On the other, the posses' overkill of the use of violence later helped to precipitate their partial downfall; the Rude Boys literally shot themselves in the foot.

While today's Jamaican narcotics outfits are by no means yesterday's gangs, they have nevertheless struggled since the early part of the 1990s. All in all, the Jamaican crime lords are a shadow of the force they once were. In fact, a number of telling parallels can be drawn between the status of the posses and Great Britain today: both once ruled over, and profited handsomely from, mighty empires; both command respect and invite fear from certain quarters; and both have seen the better part of their 'greatness' drain away over the years.

Similarly, in the same way that people seldom talk of 'Great Britain' anymore, so, too, the term 'posse' has lost its customary currency. 'Posse' has become a simple suffix; a term used to round off the name of a gang of avaricious Jamaican criminals, as opposed to a feared and respected Jamaican narco-political outfit. Thus, over the past few years, the Shower and Spanglers Posses, the one-time twin towers of US-Jamaican possedom, have given way to a shower of wholly US-formed fly-by-nights. New York's Fuck Everybody Posse is a prime example.

Jim Brown would doubtless turn in his grave.

Ironically, Jim Brown – or the Shower Posse at any rate – played an unwitting part in America's formal introduction to the posses. In early 1984, about a year before the Jamaican 'exiles' smashed their way into the money-spinning world of crack cocaine, American law enforcement was on the verge of sighting them for the first time.

The 'vision' came fully five years after the Rude Boys had begun to flock to the United States *en masse*. And even then the 'revelation' was more the outcome of a dark odyssey through uncharted waters, than a voyage of deliberate discovery. In fact, in much the same way as the Watergate scandal began with an apparently innocuous attempted burglary, the road to unearthing the posses started life with a mundane minor weapons find.

The trail goes back to the spring of 1984. It began when an INTERPOL agent in Kingston, Jamaica, requested an officer at the ATF in the United States to assist him in tracing the origins of a dozen handguns. The deadly cargo, which was intercepted *en route* to the Shower Posse in Tivoli Gardens, had been discovered in a shipping container at the Port of Kingston. The bureau's National Tracing Center duly followed the paper trail back to a gunstore in Florida where Americans flock to buy their firearms.

However, the discovery posed a further conundrum, and only in solving it did the real story behind the posses begin to unfold. In checking gun store records in Broward and Dade counties in south Florida, the ATF agent discovered that the handguns were, in fact, purchased as part of a consignment of over a hundred firearms. The whereabouts of the remaining weapons was a mystery that needed to be cleared up.

It did not take long. The industrious ATF investigator

found the weapons were being used as exhibits in numerous drug and murder investigations all over the States. 'They found them in homicides in [Washington] DC, in New York, in Kansas City. They found those guns in Dallas, Texas . . .' explains Agent Dougherty. And, the official conclusion was '"holy smoke, the guns are telling us a story here": we'd got a network of associations and areas of activity all laid out; kinda like turning on a fluorescent light trail on a map, you could see all these different places.'

Here, then, were the first pieces of a jigsaw puzzle that in piecing together would eventually reveal a vivid picture of violent, organised Jamaican narcotics and gun trafficking across the nation. In this particular instance, the pieces – guns, drugs and homicides – formed a ghostly image of several thousand Shower Posse gangsters. It was discovered that the posse's operations were allegedly being directed by one-time professional footballer Vivian Blake in the United States, and the infamous Jim Brown in Jamaica. Much to the amazement (not to mention embarrassment) of the American authorities, it was also found that the posse's lethal web of operations covered a dozen major American cities.

Over the next few years, the ATF made further enquiries into posse activity at local, State and national levels. Through painstaking detective work the Agency managed to identify scores of expatriate Jamaican posses. The Spanglers and Waterhouse each turned up in twelve cities; the powerful Rema Posse in seven; and the Riverton City and 'Junglists' in five each. Finally, in 1987, when the ATF had an acute understanding of what was happening some seventy posses with between 20,000 and 40,000 operatives had been identified nationwide.

In New York, which set the trend for the country, several posses were 'discovered' with city-wide memberships of over a thousand operatives. Subsequent law enforcement drives drastically altered that picture. Even so, until the beginning of the 1990s, four of the nation's biggest posses – the Shower, Spanglers, Jungle and Dunkirk – boasted payrolls running into four figures.

By 1987, getting on for a decade after the posses had begun their mass exodus to the United States, American law enforcement was acutely aware of the force it then faced. The potency of that force was summed up in two, somewhat bland, sentences from a major Bureau report entitled, 'Jamaican Organized Crime'. They read: 'Jamaican posses are bold and aggressive bands of criminals who traffic in large quantities of narcotics and firearms, reaping a billion dollars annually from their drug proceeds. These groups are also involved in money-laundering, fraud, kidnapping, robbery, burglary, assault, and murder.' Somewhat belatedly, the ATF, by now spearheading the federal drive against the rudies, was forced to acknowledge the rudie gangs as, in its own words, 'a national epidemic'.

Despite their recent setbacks, the wily and ruthless posses continue to be 'a national epidemic'. However, the nature of the Rude Boy plague has changed markedly since the posse problem was first diagnosed. If anything, in the decade since they came to official notice, the drug-dealing killers from Kingston have become even more ruthless, deadly and sophisticated. To affect these changes the rudies have had to undergo significant, sometimes costly and painful, transformations; ones which, however, have helped to keep their organisations on a firm business footing.

One feature of the posses' activities has been largely unaffected by the welter of changes: the rabid predisposition of the Rude Boys towards bestial violence. In truth, posse violence has got quantitatively and qualitatively worse since the wraps were taken off them. This trend is explained in large part by the heightened stakes and competition generated by the gangsters' movement into the world of crack cocaine. The Jamaican *gundeliros* are without doubt the most frightening and bloodthirsty group of organised villains ever to set foot on the American mainland.

Cornelius J. Dougherty should know. Sitting behind his stately desk in a spacious air-conditioned office, the ATF operative sighs and makes a revealing confession: 'We thought in 1980 that the worst thing we'd ever seen were the Mariel Cubans,' he says of the exiles who were part of the 125,000 Cubans boat-lifted to the United States in 1980. 'They would fight it out with the police, had organisational identity, had been in prison together, many of them had been in the military together.'

The Cuban drug barons he refers to were criminal anomalies. The underworld element among the Marielito refugees totally disregarded the 'moral' code that, until their arrival, had defined how far American mobsters could 'legitimately' go in the commission of their crimes. Still, Dougherty admits that for all their violent anarchy, the Mariel Cubans were 'pretty tame' compared to the phenomena that followed them: the Jamaican posses.

After twenty years of 'frontline' service in America's vaunted, perennial 'War On Drugs', Dougherty has a wealth of personal experience to draw upon. Nowadays, Con (as he likes to be called) is a public affairs officer at the ATF's headquarters in Washington DC but his veteran status commands that his opinions be given respect. And when it comes to the posses, a cushy desk job in a safe, semi-palatial office cannot temper the obvious hatred he feels towards them. 'Some of the homicides are truly disgusting,' he opines, without attempting to disguise his contempt, 'even to experienced law enforcement professionals. Gratuitous violence. Gratuitous slaughter.'

The impact of Rude Boy violence on the United States cannot be understated. To appreciate how truly barbaric the rudies are, it is revealing to rank them against their antecedents and competitors in the American violence and murder stakes.

Everyone is aware of the exploits of the cowboy gunslingers who laid siege to the Wild West in the late nineteenth century. But, in all honesty, history has imbued characters like Billy the Kid and 'Doc' Holliday with a posthumous importance far beyond the scale of their actual crimes. So even before Sheriff Wyatt Earp rode in to clean up Dodge City in the 1870s, only thirty-three gunfighters had been laid to rest. Pah! Compared to the posses, the cattle rustlers, train and bank robbers were only toying with their six-shooters.

The same is true of the Tommy-gun-toting gangsters who terrorised Chicago during the Prohibition era between 1919 and 1933. The vicious, and up to that point unparalleled, excesses of mobsters such as Al Capone sent shockwaves across the world. They have left us with an image of torrential rivers of blood flowing through the lawless streets of the Windy City. For all their undeniably barbaric violence, however, the reality was quite different. In their deadliest year, Capone and his cronies only managed to 'snuff out' seventy-six fellow gangsters. New York City suffered more than three times as many posse fatalities in 1990.

Murder Incorporated (MI), the corporate killing machine masterminded by the evil genius of Jewish gangster Louis Lepke in association with Mafia *capo* Albert Anastasia, had a similar record. At the height of its activities in the mid- to late 1930s, the New York-based enterprise boasted a string of two hundred or so high-class executioners on its books. MI's assassins commanded annual five-figure retainers for their services, but between them they probably averaged about sixty murders a year. In fact, MI's

greatest contribution to the history of criminal killing was
the instrumental role its corporate ethic played in adding
three new terms to the lexicon of murder: 'hit'; 'hitman';
and 'contract'.

The figures who hang in America's current Rogue's
Gallery are definitely more ferocious than their predecessors. However, in spite of more awesome arsenals
and increasing pressures to utilise them, these players are
also-rans when pitted against the Jamaican crime lords at
their bloodiest. This includes the posses' competitors in
the nation's illicit, multi-billion dollar drug industry; the
arena in which most lives are lost.

When one thinks about violent, organised American
crime, one's thoughts invariably stop at the Mafia. But
the legendary godfathers of American syndicated crime
are not at all like the images we see of them in the mov-
ies. Indeed, Hollywood stereotypes aside, the traditional
Mafia killing is actually quiet, clinical and focused. The
Cosa Nostra (and in some ways this complements the
film industry's romanticised notions) tend to specialise
in symbolic 'hits'. Their killers prefer to send a 'clean'
message to their adversaries by tucking objects like fish
or money into their victim's bodily orifices. In summary,
the Mafia are not wholesale killers, and certainly not
ruthless ones.

Where Mafia enforcers exhibit 'a touch of class' in
their murders, the Mariel Cubans and the Columbians –
another key faction in the American narcotics empire –
have proven themselves to be tactless thugs. In effect,
the God-fearing Italian-Americans are candidates for
beatification by comparison with their South American
rivals, and latter-day saints when it comes to the posses.

The propensity of the Columbian drug gangs for
barbarism is well documented, especially in their native
land. Between the late 1970s and early 1980s the embryonic cocaine cartels held the unenviable title of being

America's grandmasters of savagery. In fact, their promotion into the first division of American drug trafficking was tainted by a passion for hitherto unimaginable expressions of mindless, bloody violence.

'There was a famous case in New York,' recalls a drug enforcement agent. 'They killed a whole family – women and children – and hung them up in an old supermarket for the police to find.' In their early days, the cartel bosses seemed oblivious to the chagrin of the American public, police and media. However, their overt displays of hideous aggression were limited and short-lived.

The Mariel Cubans were even more despicable than their Spanish-speaking cousins. Their killers literally went straight for the jugular. Fidel Castro's wayward former subjects boasted a chamber of horrors that included a little number dubbed 'the Cuban neck-tie': a slit throat with the victim's tongue pulled through the wound. In keeping with the Mafia and the Columbians, though, once they had established their niche in the world of syndicated crime, the Marielitos also exercised considerable self-restraint. Even on the rare occasions that Cuban enforcers assassinated entire families, says Dougherty, 'that would take place in an apartment; that would take place out of the public view for the most part.' Publicity-seeking, and the attendant dangers it posed for unnecessarily attracting the attention of the police, was deemed bad for business; it was to be avoided at all cost.

During their heyday, and for several years after it, the posses were a different kettle of fish. To all intents and purposes it was as if they worshipped shocking violence. Murder to the rudies was the same as spinach is to Popeye: a source of physical strength and confidence. To quote the sober prose of a Federal report into their dealings in the late 1980s: 'Jamaican posses are responsible for a disproportionate number of murders committed by one criminal group.'

One needs only to peruse the relevant homicide statistics to appreciate the report's sentiments. In the period since statistics have been collated more than 5,500 posse-related homicides have been recorded. The rudie narco-terrorists killed 1,048 people between 1985 and 1987. 1988 saw a record 1,094 posse-related homicides. In 1989 and 1990, the tally dropped to 773 and 612, respectively. Yet, while the rate of Jamaican-related slayings has fallen off considerably during the 1990s, American crimefighters still caution that 'the rate continues at an unacceptable level'.

These murders occurred wherever there was a significant posse presence, but heavily-populated metropolitan areas bore the brunt, especially those with visible Jamaican communities. Of late, the big American cities have seen a welcome dimunition in the number of Rude Boy killings they experience. Still, in terms of sheer numbers New York had 250 posse homicides, Washington DC 100 and Miami one for every week of 1990.

The posses' wholesale killing spree was to be expected. Not simply because the rudies were archetypal ghetto desperadoes; young men who were prepared to kill to get ahead, and expected – wished even – to die a violent gangster death themselves. No. It was inevitable for one thing because, when it came to the 'art' of killing, no one knew better than the Rude Boys how to affect it. In this light, if the posses had had a collective motto it might have read: 'have (the right kind of) gun, will kill'.

Without putting too fine a point on it, the average Rude Boy is a weapons expert. 'They love guns,' says Dougherty. 'These guys wear guns like we [journalists] wear pens,' adds Williams. Importantly, the rudie's knowledge of guns extended to an ability to acquire them while maintaining a discreet distance from the obvious perils posed by law enforcement.

Given a choice, a typical posse would purchase its guns from a licensed firearms dealer, especially those in Florida. That way they could be sure they were buying the genuine article, and reduce the risks of purchasing defective weaponry. This approach also meant the Jamaican *gundeliros* could bulk buy from a range of favoured makes and models.

The obvious drawback with acquiring firearms in this way, though, was that it made it easier for American law enforcers to identify the buyer. Federal law requires that forms have to be filled out recording the purchase, and the last thing a posse gunman or associate wanted to leave in their wake was a paper trail. But, as we shall see, no problem was insurmountable for the posses. One method they applied to circumvent the legal obstacles was the traditional resort to using bogus identification.

Another, later, departure was 'straw' purchases. It sounds sinister but it boiled down to hiring intermediaries or 'strawmen' to do the dirty work. Even here, the posses demonstrated characteristic cleverness. To avoid detection they recruited specialists from outside their immediate racial group. The players included white Americans and Jamaican-born Chinese, whites and Indians. Following this route, the posses found a novel way to acquire their weaponry.

Of course there were still potential pitfalls. By working with 'outsiders', something that for the longest time the 'Yardies' were loathe to do, the Jamaican gangs actually increased the risks of detection. In this instance, though, the pros clearly outweighed the cons. The object of this particular exercise was simply to keep as far away from law enforcement agents as possible.

These were the most favoured, but certainly not the only means by which the posses acquired their huge arsenals. The Rude Boys also bought large quantities of brand new firearms from private individuals at flea markets or gun shows. Unlike licensed gunstore owners, these individuals were never under a legal requirement to record their transactions. In fact, the sellers were not even called upon to ask the purchaser for identification. Another source, was the stockpiles of weapons appropriated during residential and commercial burglaries, or traded for drugs.

Favoured posse weapons covered – and cover – a wide range. However, in the main, the posse gunslinger's weapons of choice were the variety they could conceal in a jacket pocket. The most popular types were inexpensive, compact, high capacity, 9mm, semi-automatic pistols. American-made Intratecs (TEC 9s) topped the 9mm chart. 'It's not a particularly good arm,' according to Dougherty, himself a weapons expert, 'except that it looks intimidating, and when loaded it carries a lot of bullets.' Given their reputation for ruthless violence, that was generally a good advertisement for the Rude Boys.

Guns of this sort have become indispensable tools in posse business dealings. They are both cheap and highly deadly. Israeli-made Uzis, another favourite, partly because of their ability to 'let off' 600 rounds per minute, were retailing at £500 each in 1990. TEC 9s sold for around half the price.

Moreover, guns like these can fire thirty-six bullets without reloading, and literally tear a human body apart at close range. Over the years, numerous law enforcement agents have learned this lesson at their cost. Some have been killed outright; or else caught off guard when the officers have had to reload their more conventional firearm.

Other posse favourites included high-powered assault rifles like AK-47s and Colt-manufactured AR-15s which can discharge eleven rounds a second. The rapid fire

Heckler and Koch HK91, KG-9, and the MAC-10, which fires 1,100 bullets every sixty seconds, also found favour. American handguns such as Smith and Wessons and Colt 45s were also highly prized. But, with a few aberrations, the emphasis was always on quality. 'Where they get a choice, they make very informed selections in the weapons they choose,' says Dougherty. 'And they tend to choose them the same way that the military and law enforcement agencies would choose theirs. They know their guns and they do like them.'

Proof of this was graphically illustrated following the arrests of two Jamaican nationals on Federal firearms violations in July 1987. The arrests, in Tampa, Florida, led to one of the largest single seizures of a posse's weapons. The Alcohol, Tobacco and Firearms agents concerned recovered sixty-five handguns including Austrian-made Glocks, Ingram mini-MACs and mini-TEC 9s ('Baby Uzis'), two AR-15s and eighty-eight boxes of ammunition.

'We had one instance,' recalls New York based ATF Group Supervisor, Bill Fredericks, about his part in the Shower Posse's demise, 'where [a Shower Posse player] went to a gun store and bought US$40,000-worth of guns in one go, and basically told us he had delivered them to Vivian Blake.'

Arguably, the Rude Boys also liked killing. And when it came to protecting their drug investments from rivals and law enforcement, certain among them were prepared to commission the use of explosives and arson as another line of defence. As they spread out from their 'host' communities to conquer new drug territories, the posses discovered that they could make their presence felt more acutely with (fire)bombs and hand grenades. Indeed, the use of explosives and arson became so synonymous with the posses after crack arrived that law enforcement agencies came to view them as Jamaican 'trademarks'.

Competing drug traffickers whose apartments and vehicles were 'torched' certainly got the message. In an episode from 1987, a gangster lobbed a hand grenade into a crowded Chicago lounge bar frequented by opposing posse operatives (and innocent bystanders). For once, no one was killed or seriously injured. Meanwhile, in Maryland, another band firebombed an 'illegal' crack house set up on their turf by a rival faction. Three people, including a crackhead, died as the fire engulfed the premises.

But the posses also found a defensive motivation for the use of bombs. Already fortified crack houses were booby-trapped to give further protection against unwelcome intruders. In a tragic instance of this kind, the ploy backfired. A firebomb planted in a crack house in Evanston, Illinois, was accidentally detonated. The fire blocked the route to the apartment's reinforced steel front door. The windows had been fitted with burglar bars. Five people perished in the blaze.

Not only did the Jamaican gangs thrive on wholesale and mass murder, they were totally disdainful of the impact their murderous antics had on those whose job it is to investigate them.

In Dougherty's estimation, it is not simply the fact that their violent crimes were more plentiful or heinous *per se* – although they were – it is the manner in which their 'badmen' carried out those atrocities that made them distinct. 'These folks tend to like to go public,' he says. 'They're more willing to express their message, not only to their opponents or to the disloyal, but to the community generally, about how strong and powerful, and how free they feel to act with impunity.'

The Jamaican gangsters did not care about who, where or how they murdered. If one happened to be in the vicinity of a Rude Boy shooter's intended victim(s) during an assassination attempt, too bad. 'They do drive-bys, and just shoot everybody in the opposing neighbourhoods. Innocent. Guilty. Its irrelevant,' adds Dougherty. 'They just drive down the street and start shooting people.'

This ruthless indifference towards innocent by-standers was brutally demonstrated one sunny afternoon at an open-air reggae concert in Newark, New Jersey. The event was attended by thousands of music lovers who paid a minimum US$25 for the pleasure of seeing a star-studded bill of Jamaican performers. Then the shooting started. 'Consider it,' exclaims Dougherty, 'hundreds of people running for their lives while some posse members blaze away into the crowd at a few people with whom they have a problem!'

This attack was premeditated, but social events are just as likely to be settings for exhibitions of random rudie slaughter. That posse operatives carry guns into dances and concerts – on social grounds – only adds to the potential for mindless violence. Fuelled by petty jealousies or drugs and alcohol, impromptu shootouts at such occasions are not uncommon. They account for many of the perfectly innocent people who are killed or injured by the posses because they happen to be in the wrong place at the wrong time.

This was the background to a fatal shooting incident at an all-night 'blues' party in Boston in 1989. A lone gunman sprayed the revellers with an Uzi sub-machine-gun. He left three dead and fifteen wounded. There was no apparent reason for his attack.

The motive behind the 1987 shooting of a New York nightclub-goer was crystal clear, although no less impossible to comprehend. The hapless victim was unfortunate enough to inadvertently step on Delroy 'Uzi' Edward's foot. Edwards, a one-time JLP gunslinger and the Renkers Posse don, promptly pulled out his 9mm revolver and executed the man with a single shot to the head. Even though the venue was packed to the rafters, homicide detectives were unable to find any eyewitnesses to the slaying. Doubtless those who saw the cold-blooded execution remembered the ancient Jamaican posse code: 'See and blind, hear and deaf'.

And, in August 1992, members of two competing posses clashed at a discotheque in Miami, Florida. Subsequent police reports suggested that the carnage was triggered when a Rude Boy from one of the posses 'dissed' (disrespected) the 'woman' of a Rude Boy of the other. In any event, the ensuing shootout claimed four lives and left seventeen wounded, three of them critically. Two of the deceased were later identified as posse operatives. The other two were complete innocents; revellers who went to the wrong nightclub on that particular evening. 'It's a classic, textbook example of the way posses settle disputes,' was the reaction of Captain Al Lamberti, on whose turf the shootings occurred. 'The Mafia does it cleanly. The posses make big messes. They don't give a damn about anybody.'

There has always been considerable debate among American law enforcement agencies about where the posses slot into the nation's organised crime league. However, there is unanimity about their top ranking as America's most ruthless mass murderers. What sets the posses apart from the rest of the pack is an almost total – if not complete – absence of any notion of the sanctity of human life. Raised on a diet of sordid political, and arbitrary criminal violence in Jamaica, the rudies quite simply do not give a damn about life and death. In fact, extreme violence to the posses has been what the ideology of non-violence was to the movements of Gandhi and Martin Luther King: a philosophy of life; the ultimate expression of a lust for respect, money and power.

The signal failure of the posses' criminal peers to mimic the scale of their atrocities is perhaps best explained by the fact that, like 'Uzi' Edwards's shameless nightclub 'execution', many of the rudies' acts of savagery fall into a grey area. Put at its simplest, there is often no rational or logical explanation for Rude Boy violence. So killings often transcend the interests of business or group discipline. Murders of this kind are perpetrated in the name of machismo and face-saving, personal retaliation and retribution. At their most extreme, they find the 'Yardmen' fulfilling their own sadistic prophecy. For example, fellow human beings are 'wasted' for no other reason than an aspiring posse gunslinger's desire to cultivate a violent reputation. The only certainty in this nebulous underworld is that it is generally easier to lose one's life than it is to preserve it.

The Rude Boys' willingness to carry out indiscriminate shootings, use of high-powered firearms, bombs, arson, and other violence, showed that the posses would stop at nothing to achieve their ends. The rudies rewrote the rule book governing American crime. Not surprisingly, their amended version made it legitimate to silence law enforcement officers.

As America's law enforcers gradually began to close the net around the murderous Jamaican cartels, they found that the latter's guns and bombs were being deployed against them. By the late 1980s, the hunters had become 'legitimate' prey for the hunted. Where most criminal organisations baulked at the idea of killing cops, the posses threw themselves headlong into it, a bloody tendency that stemmed from their well-rehearsed practice of shooting Jamaican police officers. Of course, some confrontations with law enforcement officers were unavoidable; they occurred in the 'line of duty'. When posse gunslingers are trapped with their backs against the wall their fearless mentality often dictates that they fight it out to the death, rather than surrender.

This was the scenario of an attempted drugs rip-off in Florida in October 1990. Four heavily outnumbered 'Yardie' mobsters were penned into a warehouse by a joint ATF, FBI, SWAT team and Metro Dade undercover police task force. The bandits resisted repeated demands for their surrender, and opened fire on the authorities. Two were killed outright, the other two were too seriously wounded to return fire. There were no injuries amongst the task force team.

Other law enforcers were not so fortunate. American crimefighters venturing into the posse underworld have been murdered by mistake or as a warning to others. On 1 February 1992, a Florida police officer became a statistic in the former category. James Fulwood, a Florida Highway Patrol Trooper and fourteen-year veteran, was blown to bits when he triggered a car bomb during the course of a search. He had stopped the vehicle, driven by his two assailants, for speeding. (The bomb was actually intended for a woman who was going to testify against the posse about a murder they had carried out.)

Without doubt, one of the vilest examples of a posse police killing involved Kenneth Burns, a New York officer. Burns was an experienced officer nearing retirement, and a father of four. On a blustery night in March 1990, the officer was assigned to what on the surface must have seemed like a cushy job. He was to guard the entrance to a building in Crown Heights, Brooklyn, where two Jamaican prosecution witnesses in an imminent posse drug and murder case were being kept under round-the-clock police protection.

In the event, Officer Burns probably never knew what hit him. 'They simply killed him as he sat in his police car in front of the building,' says Agent Dougherty. More galling still, the posse assassins made no attempt to penetrate the building and kill the potential witnesses. 'The message was delivered when they killed Officer Burns,'

concludes Dougherty. 'The message' was clearly understood. The would-be witnesses decided not to testify, and
Officer Burns's killers were never apprehended.

Burns and Fulwood were tragic posse statistics; men
who just happened to be in the wrong place at the wrong
time. However, other posse attacks bear all the hallmarks
of their true intentions – a clinical desire to wipe out any
vestige of resistance to their narcotics interests.

The firebombing of a police officer's vehicle in
Cleveland, Ohio, was a perfect example. The officer,
whose persistence was causing a local posse considerable
headaches, was meant to die for his professionalism. He
narrowly escaped death by jumping clear of his blazing
vehicle.

Wedded to attacks like this were annual reports of
contracts or rewards for the killing of specific law
enforcement agents. Similar to the officer in Cleveland,
these were lawmen who consistently put local posses
under pressure.

In March 1992, four posse operatives, arrested in
Charleston, South Carolina, for drug trafficking offences,
were further charged with soliciting a contract on the
police officer who affected their arrest. In another case,
from the same year, an ATF agent received information
that a posse don wanted him dead. The don's plan was to
use a female posse member to set up a meeting under the
cloak of offering information about him. She would then
carry out the 'hit'. The plan was only thwarted because
the ATF agent got wind of it in time, and declined the
meeting.

The passion for violence that circumscribed the posses'
activities in the United States into the early 1990s came
into its own during the mass marketing of crack in
the mid-1980s. Moreover, the unlikely alliance between
ruthless barbarism and sophisticated organisation were

key components in the posses' momentous promotion
into the ranks of America's premier drug trafficking
league table.

For a while, these disparate qualities enabled the posses
to rule the crack-dealing roost with an iron fist. Their dark
force was such that ordinary people dared not inform on
them. It was such that no other criminal faction had
the psychological equipment to take them on. Excessive
violence permeated every aspect of the posses' activities
from opening new markets to enforcing group discipline,
settling business disputes to empire-building. Indeed, it
was something of a posse trademark.

Numerous lives were sacrificed in the quest to build
crack-dealing empires. Witness the career of a posse
don who was vying for control of the drug market in
south Florida. In less than two years, the rudie overlord
orchestrated more than twenty murders in his quest for
ultimate hegemony.

Or, the equally vicious alleged aspirations of Eric
Vassell. At the beginning of the crack boom, Vassell's
Gulleymen Posse had pretensions of controlling the narcotics market in the Crown Heights section of Brooklyn,
New York. In those days, it was common knowledge
that if a murder victim's remains were discovered in the
lobby of 1357 or 1367 Sterling Place, the don had either
contracted the killing or carried it out himself. Seventeen
corpses were recovered from these addresses before a
Federal warrant was finally issued for Vassell's arrest.
(At the time of writing Vassell is fighting a rearguard
action from a Jamaican prison against American attempts
to have him extradited to stand trial.)

The posses' growing territorial ambitions also swelled
the list of fatalities. In 1989, for example, the quest
to control new markets resulted in seventeen posse-
related homicides in Boston. The tally almost doubled
to thirty-three dead in 1990. But 1991 saw competition

between established drug outfits and the posses increase. Moreover, the incumbent Columbian, North Vietnamese, Chinese and Dominican gangs fiercely resisted the Jamaican advances. The result, a record fifteen homicides in January alone.

The picture was much the same in the unlikely setting of Hartford, the capital of Connecticut, where a recently-arrived posse was fighting it out with two resident African-American drug crews. In 1989, the Hartford police department investigated forty-two drive-by shootings with the loss of nineteen lives. Evidence from 1990, however, suggests that the posses were beginning to win the war of attrition. There were fewer drive-bys and a minor reduction in the murder rate.

That said, 1990 was a bad year for some smaller urban centres which, until then, had been posse-free zones. Bridgeport, Connecticut; St Petersburg, Florida; Raleigh, North Carolina; and Tucson and Phoenix, Arizona, were among a long list of unfortunate cities which got their first taste of the posses' ever-increasing ambitions to control America's expansive narcotics industry. Like a terminal cancer, the posses colonised these unsuspecting bodies and began to suck the life out of them. The evidence from Tucson and Phoenix is that resistance was slight – there were only three fatalities. As a rule, though, the posses were willing to kill as many opponents as it took to further their ruthless ambitions.

And then there was the catalogue of horrific posse-related mass murders that emanated from the arena of group discipline. Put simply, posse overlords are unforgiving of the treacherous and the disobedient. The cast in this category includes informers and fifth columnists, members of failed coup attempts and those who unilaterally decide to take more than their allotted due. In May 1990, two 'enforcers' from a Brooklyn outfit were dispatched to Dallas, Texas to sort out a problem of the latter variety. The Rude Boy 'troubleshooters' fulfilled their remit to the letter. They rounded up five renegade African-American teenagers suspected by their don to be holding back on the proceeds of their drug sales. The quintet were driven to an apartment, ordered to strip naked, herded into a bathtub, and riddled with Uzi sub-machine-gun fire.

A different offender was lined up against a wall and shot sixty times with eight different weapons. His body was deliberately torn to shreds. The idea being to prevent the customary opening of the victim's casket at his funeral. This type of killing is designed to send a clear signal to anyone else who might have been considering following his course of action.

As with other ethnic criminal organisations, the nebulous world of drug disputes created more work for undertakers and gravediggers. In May 1991, for example, a posse massacred five members of one family during an armed attack in Brooklyn. The unfortunates included a pregnant woman (who was also shot in the stomach for good measure), two boys aged two and twelve, and a seventeen-year-old woman. The latter, the pregnant woman's niece, was actually on vacation from Trenton, New Jersey. Another person whose premature death echoed to the familiar refrain of being 'in the wrong place at the wrong time'. All five were executed; shot in the back of the head at point-blank range in what has become one of the posses' grim 'calling cards'.

A few days later, again in New York, five more people were murdered in a similar attack. This time there was a clear drug connection. The police recovered a kilo of cocaine worth US$20,000 on the street, US$7,000 in cash and two semi-automatic pistols from the run-down flat on Synder Avenue, East Flatbush. Two of the victims, Michael Johnson and André Edwards had convictions for possessing crack, but, once again, innocent women and children were among the dead. They included Johnson's common-law wife, Andrea Vega, and their three-year-old son, Nicholas. The other victim, a neighbour by the name of Sharon Davis, made that familiar mistake of visiting her friend's apartment at the wrong time.

Had a manual been written for trainee posse gangsters it would have emphasised the need for indiscriminate public shootings and killings and the wholesale slaughter of innocents in random situations. On the subject of planned homicides, a chapter on the application of torture would have been highlighted as required reading. Indeed, on their way to the top, the typical premeditated or organised posse homicide invariably involved some form of torture.

A creative bunch, the Rude Boys were never short of ideas about how to extract information out of their victims. The most popular components of posse torture comprised: 'torching' the victim; shooting them in the face; playing Russian Roulette; slashing their throat; and dismemberment.

In one celebrated example, Spanglers Posse members tortured and killed a young rival before dismembering his body and scattering the remains all over New York City. It is customary in this type of murder to leave the deceased's head where it will be found as a warning to the community. Accordingly, the west Kingston butchers dumped their victim's head in an open trash can, where it was discovered by a drifter searching for fragments of crack. Soon after, two NYPD patrolmen spotted the hobo 'kicking the head down the street like a soccer ball'. Its mouth still bore the gaffer tape that was stuck across it to stifle the torture victim's futile screams. The gruesome findings did not stop there. The house where the corpse had been savaged contained a blood-stained bathtub with so many different DNA samples ingrained in it that profiling for the identity of other victims was rendered useless.

The posse executioners often exhibited tremendous sophistication in covering their tracks. In fact, the more thoughtful rudie posse members went to extraordinary lengths to confuse their pursuers. One intrepid New York outfit turned to buying excess barrels for their 9mm Beretta's. After their 'enforcers' carried out a murder they promptly switched barrels and disposed of the one used in the killing, thus dashing any chance of the weapon being subsequently identified by ballistic examination.

American law enforcers also noticed a tendency for posse killers to alter the scene of their crimes. Members of a big posse in Rochester, New York, routinely removed all the bullet shell casings after their assassinations. Another group, who set aside a room in an apartment complex for the sole purpose of carrying out executions, went a step further. After 'wasting' a victim they would coolly remove the spent cartridges from the walls, and call in a carpenter to fill in the bullet holes.

The epidemic drug trafficking, ruthless gun terrorism, communal intimidation, merciless torture, and indiscriminate murder by the posses, became as vividly defined in the demonology of American crime as it is in the Jamaican psyche.

They became so pronounced over the years that in October 1992 the Prime Minister of Jamaica was dragged into an undiplomatic row with the American media over posse criminality. So fierce was the opprobrium that P.J. Patterson was forced to make an unscheduled defence of his fellow islanders during an official visit to New York City. He conceded that 'a few Jamaicans' participated in what he euphemistically termed 'unacceptable forms of anti-social behaviour'. Clearly worried about this stereotypical image, however, Patterson went on to warn the American press to 'not lose sight of the fact that there are many more Jamaicans performing with honour'.

The sense of outrage quickly spread to Jamaica. Meanwhile, in downtown Kingston, the ghetto streets were consumed with protests of a different kind. In recording studios and sound systems all over the sprawling slums of west Kingston, dancehall DJs were churning out militant denials of the American rhetoric. Top dancehall star, Buju Banton, released a smash hit single called 'Yardie'. In it he laments the fact that, to his mind, every shooting, rape, or person found with their head bashed in was attributed to the 'Yardies'.

So much for the Mafia, Columbians and Mariel Cubans. Even now, in the couple of years since they began to tone down their antics, the rudies are still the clear front runners in the American violence and murder stakes.

Sheer, unadulterated violence was merely the unacceptable, public face of the posses' early activities. Behind that image of bestial savagery, and helping to better understand their monumental American success story, lurked a keen sense of business acumen. Moreover, the foundations of the posses' rise were underpinned to an equal degree by their sophisticated organisational structures and state-of-the-art *modus operandi*. After all, the rudies had been killing their rivals and each other for years before they were finally identified as belonging to organised crime syndicates.

Moreover, these self same features had afforded the posses the luxury of a breathing space, which they needed to institute and expand their ganja operations across the United States. So, when the crack boom finally got under way, the Jamaican gangsters benefited from having a ready-made and finely-tuned distribution network in place. And this showed up to devastating effect from the very start of the crack craze.

One would be making a grave error to underestimate the importance the posses' structure and method of operation

had on their early crack-dealing exploits. Indeed, the
posses composed the vanguard of the crusade which
spread the narcotic across the United States. 'For me,'
says Fredericks, 'the posses were primarily responsible
for spreading crack.' Fredericks is not alone in believing this. An earlier ATF report also credited – or
blamed – them for being primarily 'responsible for the
onslaught of crack cocaine on the eastern seaboard of the
United States'.

In terms of the crack boom, the tripartite pyramid of posse member responsibilities remained largely
unchanged. What did change was the make-up of the
people in the middle and lower tiers. Organisationally,
the posses metamorphosed with the advent of crack- or
gate-houses. In spite of this, the organisational integrity
of a drug gang's operations was maintained through
the application of Cold War 'compartmentalisation'
techniques. So, for example, a New York-based don
might have employed a trusted overseer to manage
three street-level crack- or gate-houses (A, B and C) in,
say, Detroit. According to 'Anne', the ATF intelligence
analyst, 'the people at [gate-house] A do not necessarily
know about B and C; and none of them may really know
that they're working for one individual.'

In turn, the overseer might use a number of different
runners to ferry small amounts of drugs and money to
and from the crack-house. (No runner was ever trusted to
carry more than about three ounces of a class A drug or
US$ 2,000 in cash.) This, another ploy gleaned from their
Jamaican days, proved an effective safeguard against the
inherent dangers of the don having his 'property' hijacked
by rivals or confiscated by crime fighters. It also lessened
the risks of the runners themselves making plans to rip off
the posse.

Crucially, the use of runners also showed that posse
overlords understood the importance of what Dougherty

terms 'diminishing the exposure to resources'. That is, keeping a respectful distance from guns, drugs and drug money – the sorts of things that long prison sentences are made of. Significantly, during the posses' 'salad days' especially, this technique was an ideal means to reduce the exposure of their organisations to detection. For even when runners were caught *in flagrante delicto*, the small hoards they were concealing prompted overworked law enforcers to classify them among the small-fry dealers.

The hypothetical runner might also take a new worker (probably an African-American) to the crack house. African-Americans began to be recruited in earnest around 1986. The innovation was an inspired piece of posse cunning. It tended further to insulate top- and middle-ranking posse activists from the close scrutiny of law enforcement officers. The Jamaican kingpins started to 'put the American blacks up front to take the jail time', says a drug field agent.

Beyond this, however, the staffing trend signalled the posses' rapid expansion. It was a tocsin for law enforcers; a warning that the dons and their lieutenants were actually attaining 'untouchable' status. The longer this situation has prevailed the further some of the 'big fish' have swum away from the Federal net.

The posses' push into crack sales emanated from an almost prophetic realisation of the drug's market potential. It was a highly potent and addictive narcotic. It was cheap, quick and easy to manufacture and distribute. In fact, all the budding 'chemists' required was a batch of high-quality cocaine, some bicarbonate of soda, a Bunsen burner or microwave oven, and a bunch of ruthless gunmen. And, to cap it all, infinitely larger profits could be made from crack than could ever be made from marijuana. Says Fredericks: 'It was natural to flip over into the crack situation.'

From that point onwards, the posses' well-oiled marijuana marketing and distribution machine went into overdrive. The point is underlined by a nameless drug enforcement agent: 'They treated their dealers as if it was a [legitimate] business, and they worked shifts.' In fact, the explosion of crack addiction led to its merchandising becoming a highly-organised, twenty-four-hour-a-day, year-round obsession.

The discovery of crack was like celebrating Christmas every day of the year for the posses. Potential profit margins were astronomical. But, once again, the narcoterrorists' holistic or exclusively in-house approach to selling drugs propelled even those gains into another galaxy.

In practice, what happened was that wholesale quantities of high-quality cocaine were purchased by the dons (always from a number of sources to protect supply lines) who then filtered them down through the organisation to their street dealers. No money changed hands before a street-level sale. Without go-betweens to pay off, profit margins rose to as high as 1,000 per cent *above* what the posses' rivals were making.

The mid-1980s crack boom provided the posses with an invitation to the big time, one which they gladly accepted. But in taking it they had to undergo a number of sometimes painful, revolutionary changes. These alterations inevitably affected their structure, organisation, personnel and business relationships. In fact, about the only thing to come out the process intact was the craving for respect, riches and power. In some ways this period of perestroika also marked the 'Americanisation' of the posses; the point at which the only similarity between the American-based posses and their Jamaican 'parents' became their common names.

One of the first, and most nerve-wracking, changes concerned staffing matters. For the first time since their arrival, the posse heavyweights were forced to look beyond their trusted 'old Rude Boy networks'. In fact, the dons knew that in order to reap the full rewards of the crack onslaught, a process which involved nationwide expansion of the posses' dealing operations, they would inevitably be forced to look outside of their ethnic milieu.

African-Americans, employed in visible street-level jobs, were taken on as much as anything else to insulate the big posse players from the risk of jail time. However, even before indigenous blacks were put on to the posses' payrolls, the dons had exhausted a source closer to home: their women.

When they had first come into existence the posses were almost exclusively Jamaican male preserves. However, in the same way that the Second World War emancipated millions of women, albeit temporarily, from the despotism of the kitchen sink, the demand for the posses' products led to women taking on positions of real importance within them. Beyond mere expediency, the recruitment of Jamaican women reflected a trust 'thing' among the dons and overseers.

In truth, prior to 1985, Jamaican women were little more than posse pariahs. Among chauvenistic Jamaican males, women were – and are – chattel: casual girlfriends, molls and 'baby mothers', the unwed mothers of a rudie gangster's children. At best, they did the 'shit work' designated for 'workers'.

Even now, the liberation of female posse members is far from complete. However, those who have broken through the glass ceiling have often assumed prominent positions. Female posse members were, and are, to be found working as assassins, back-up shooters for male drug couriers, and bodyguards for high-ranking cohorts. American intelligence has reports of 'Yardie' women either directing specific operations or asserting their influence over the whole posse. In the mid-1980s there was even a report of an all-female Jamaican gang, the Classic Posse.

Nepotism and sexual relationships were often an integral factor in deciding these latter arrangements. Take Sharon Tonge, Delroy 'Uzi' Edwards's lover. In the late 1970s, when his Renkers (it means stinking) Posse was raking in US$100,000 a week from assorted drug sales in Brooklyn, Baltimore, Philadelphia and Washington DC, Tonge was entrusted to keep the 'company's' books in order.

'Uzi' Edwards's faith in his 'woman' – he was also married – was repaid in kind. When his luck finally ran out, and he was put on trial for various offences including racketeering and murder, Tonge was the only other of the twenty-three co-defendants convicted with him to plead not guilty. Edwards was sentenced to 501 years imprisonment; Tonge beat a cocaine possession charge, but was sentenced to eight years on a conspiracy charge.

By enlisting and promoting Jamaican women, the dons underlined the importance they attached to keeping their operational secrets 'in the family'. When the success of the crack plague caused them to turn towards Americans of Jamaican descent, they were doing the next best thing. This line of recruitment had its problems, though. 'You could have a young Jamaican-American, second generation,' says Agent Dougherty, 'who would wind up in the Shadow Posse in the United States, who had never been in a posse.' Still, there was a clinical logic to choosing novice Jamaican-American gangsters. The idea being that what they lacked in experience, these wannabe gunslingers would make up for with an inherent knowledge of the 'runnings'; the ethos of ghetto gangsterism at 'home'. In other words, 'See and blind, hear and deaf'.

But it was the final source of posse recruitment that

was most startling. Not only that but it signalled a major diversion in the philosophical direction being taken by the posses. When the Rude Boys first began to arrive in the United States they formed small closely-knit associations on the basis of old neighbourhood friendships, kinships and, of course, political affiliations. But the move into the crack enterprise virtually put an end to these clannish cohorts.

More to the point, the mid-1980s onwards saw the deification of Jamaican party politics give way to an equally fanatical worship of the Almighty Dollar. 'Originally it was thought that a lot of the drug dealing was to provide money back to the political parties [in Jamaica],' argues a Washington-based drug enforcement agent. 'My own personal feeling is that it's now a group of people, who just happen to be Jamaican, who see it as a form of lifestyle and a way to make a lot of money, and they couldn't care less what happens in their former homeland.'

Lloyd Williams confirms the point from Jamaica. He argues the posses finally realised that the benefits they used to get from Jamaican politicians were 'chicken feed'; that 'the thousands of Jamaican dollars they were earning for slinging guns there was nothing to the thousands of US dollars they were earning' from dealing in drugs in mainland America. 'So they grew out of the sphere of politics, and set themselves up as drug dons,' he concludes.

The radical departure in posse recruitment policy was based on a simple premise: to progress in the American drug industry what the posses needed most was people with experience, not political devotion. Accordingly, the rudie narcotics networks began to recruit tried-and-tested operatives from across once rigid party political lines. They literally went on headhunting expeditions; it was like Wall Street meets the drug market.

These days, 'the colour is green' (as in dollar bills), is

how one federal agent interprets the shift. 'If someone was, say, a Dog [Posse member] who relocated to an area that was Spanglers or Shower predominantly, he would become one,' adds another. 'You know, there's no animus towards him. No, "gee, in New York you were on the competing side of us, so we're gonna take you out and kill you." Nope! It's "you're Jamaican, you know the business, you're there"'.

This tendency both marked the complete 'Americanisation' of the posses, and the permanent relegation in importance of their Jamaican namesakes. American business interests were put before Jamaican 'national interests'; American money before Jamaican politics. The time had come for the Jamaican poor relations to look after their own interests.

The bold recruitment policy adopted by the posses during the nationwide expansion of their crack-dealing enterprises offered a solution to a pressing internal difficulty. It enabled them to keep the momentum going, but only up to a point. Other difficulties lay ahead; external problems over which they had much less control. And if they were to continue their progress, the posses had to tackle these problems head on.

As the posses fanned out across the United States in search of new narcotics markets to conquer, they found that the force of arms and a reputation for ruthlessness were not always enough to ensure victory. Their rapidly growing success had stunted their organisational capabilities; they simply could not grow quickly enough to organise the gunpower and expertise they required to sustain their operations in any and every piece of drug territory that took their fancy.

This uncharacteristic impuissance pushed the wilier posse dons into adopting a more 'mature' approach to doing business. One alternative saw enterprising dons setting themselves up as wholesale brokers. They bought surplus amounts of cocaine and held them until a buyer could be found.

The most profitable sources of extra revenue, though, came from forming alliances, and striking compromises, with erstwhile enemies. In one sense, the movement towards these kinds of arrangements was somewhat inevitable. After all, in order to obtain their supplies of cocaine and, to a lesser extent, heroin, the dons had had to sit down in negotiations with Columbians, Mexicans, Cubans and Nigerians. Forming closer 'partnerships' then, became an almost natural progression.

But, the posses had not succumbed to the *glasnost* bug; if they were 'born again' it was only because the prevailing circumstances demanded a more cooperative reincarnation. In short, the posses still wanted it all for themselves. With that ambition out of reach, though, they resigned themselves to the next best thing: making as much money as they could with the minimum effort. And when it came to making 'crazy' amounts of money, the posses were prepared to team up with just about anyone. 'If you're a Wendy's, and I'm Burger King and [another agent] is McDonald's, that's fine,' an undercover ATF agent says, explaining the logic behind the posses' neoteric business philosophy. 'We can all dominate these four corners of the market.' This is precisely what the posses set out to achieve.

Thus, rather than 'turning their guns on fully' in an all-out offensive to eradicate the competition, the posses tried to muscle their way into rival drug operations instead. So, for example, in cities where Guyanese mobsters had a stranglehold – Tidewater, Virginia; Charlotte, North Carolina; and President Clinton's hometown, Little Rock, Arkansas – the posses set themselves up as middlemen. (The Jamaican narco-terrorists had no qualms about working as intermediaries for other drug syndicates.)

However, posse employees were also enlisted to do 'shit work' like street dealing and 'muling'.

Similar relationships were forged with smaller groups like the Panamanians and the Nigerians. Meanwhile, in Houston, Texas, reports surfaced of posse members entering into arrangements with the Triads. A Triad was supposed to have supplied the posse with arms, while a contingent of rudie sharpshooters were said to have made up the supplier's personal bodyguard.

These, however, were minor examples of the posses' co-operative spirit. If the posses had had their way they would have taken over new drug markets without so much as a second thought, but their often disastrous attempts to do just that in areas like the south-west frontier put paid to such notions. In California, in particular, a vicious posse push to break into the state's extravagantly lucrative drug centres was thwarted by two major obstacles: the Bloods and the Crips, Los Angeles's notorious street gangs.

Unable to shoot them into submission, with character-istic guile, outfits like the Shower, Spanglers and Dunkirk posses forged profitable ties with the LA gangs. The precise reasons for, and degree of, these associations varied with each interaction.

The Spanglers and the Crips agreed to divide ter-ritory in Venice, California, simply to avoid a rep-etition of the mutually fatal confrontations that had heralded the posse's arrival. In Los Angeles, the Dunkirk Posse sought permission from the Crips to open a 'rock-' (crack-) house in the heart of the gang's ter-ritory in return for 'protection'. Up the west coast, in San Francisco, the Oak Park Bloods supplied a newly-arrived posse with weapons in exchange for mari-juana. 'They're calculated,' says Dougherty alluding to yet another manifestation of the inter-drug cartel relationship. 'The Jamaicans are perfectly willing to serve as wholesale suppliers and allow the street gangs to run the retail distribution. In that sense, they're pretty sophisticated.'

The extent of the posses' 'sophistication' (or love of money) at a time of revolutionary change was graphically illustrated by a most unlikely relationship. Not content with poaching experienced drug players from across once rigid 'garrison constituency' and party political lines, rival posses began to co-operate with each other in the common interests of accumulating cash.

At its most extreme, this policy found the Shower Posse, fanatical supporters of the JLP, working alongside their mortal enemies and the PNP's star enforcers, the Spanglers Posse. (There were even unsubstantiated reports that the posses had merged in certain areas.) Whatever the case, the ability to slice up drug territory helped to prevent mutually costly 'wars', and, crucially, raise profit margins.

The sophistication of the posses, and their ability to adapt effectively to organisation-threatening situations, reaped massive rewards in terms of their narcotics market share and profitability. Within the space of a decade, the posses' cunning had seen them amass a drug empire that extended to every corner of the United States. In fact, during their heyday, it was easier to pinpoint where the rudies' operations did not exist, than where they did.

These included conservative Delaware, Rhode Island and the far northern states along the east coast, and the sparsely-populated, rural farming states of the north and midwest – Washington, Idaho, North and South Dakota, Nebraska, Wisconsin, Wyoming, Montana, Iowa and Minnesota. Meanwhile, markets (and suspected markets) for the posses' narcotics arced from their east-coast strongholds all the way around to Alaska in the far north-west.

And it was not just their spread that emphasised the

success of the posses, it was the manner in which they consolidated their interests within the areas they spread to. By 1990, the posses, the relative newcomers, collectively controlled at least twenty-five per cent of the narcotics markets in over thirty major American cities.

The trade remained strongest on the east coast; and crack continued to be the posses' brand leader. The Rude Boys managed consistently to reach figures of thirty per cent or more of the market in areas where they dealt crack. In some places, though, they surpassed even that respectable percentage. In the major New York City and Philadelphia markets, for instance, the posses accounted for thirty-five per cent. That rose to a two-thirds share of the smaller Washington DC's market. The figures rise to seventy per cent in Hudson, New York State, and eighty per cent in Bristol, Connecticut.

A snapshot of the situation around the country showed a similarly healthy picture. In the Southeast the posses managed half of Florida's lucrative Miami and Fort Lauderdale markets. In addition, they supplied at least seventy-five per cent of crack sales to users in Pensacola, Florida; Piedmont, South Carolina; and Kingston/Goldsboro in North Carolina. In Jacksonville, North Carolina, the posses distinguished themselves by controlling the entire market.

In the Midwest, the posses accommodated a third of the crack trade in Cleveland, Ohio and more than twice that in Johnson City, Tennessee. Down in the Southwest, the posses managed to dominate sixty per cent of the market in Dallas, Texas. And finally, in the West, the posses were the biggest single suppliers of crack to Inglewood, California.

For all that, the posses also built up a substantial trade in powder cocaine, heroin, marijuana and sundry narcotics in their strongholds. Wherever ganja was on the drugs menu, the narco-terrorists catered for at least ninety per cent of the retail market.

Crack was like manna from Heaven. The stupendous

profits it generated transformed one-time poor Rude Boy gunmen from Kingston's violent, vermin-infested ghettoes into multi-millionaires. Nevertheless, most dons and 'lieutenants' continued to live a low-profile existence, preferring to stay close to the inner city areas of New York and Miami. For many the only concessions they made to their spartan lifestyles came in the form of designer clothing, luxury cars and twenty-four-carat gold jewellery.

The bulk of their ill-gotten gains were secreted into off-shore bank accounts. Banks in the Cayman Islands, which lie off the north coast of Jamaica, remain particular favourites. In a typical laundering operation the don would set up a bogus corporation and deposit his millions in it. The money, now 'clean', would then wend its way back to him in the form of a 'loan'. One ambitious don applied a more novel approach to laundering his ill-gotten gains. He assumed a Jewish-sounding surname, and employed 'respectable' Jewish frontmen to run his legitimate real estate ventures for him.

Invariably some of the proceeds of drug crime wend their way back to relatives and friends in Jamaica where they are spent on luxury items like cars and houses. One big-time New York don built a multi-million dollar mansion for his elderly mother in Cherry Gardens, a fashionable Kingston suburb. 'Most of them have property, have invested the money – until the day of asset seizure catches up with them,' says Jamaican journalist, Lloyd Williams. The welter of unfinished, deserted multi-million dollar mansion developments that currently litter Jamaica is testament to that.

Shrewd dons tended to put their considerable wealth into land and property. Building shopping malls and hotels, and opening shops were popular ventures. In both the United States and Jamaica, it was also popular to open nightclubs to facilitate the laundering of 'dirty' money.

*   *   *

Back in the United States, the character of many a fragile
inner city neighbourhood was savaged beyond recognition
by the activities of the Rude Boys who lived and worked
in them. The Jamaican invaders almost single-handedly
changed the face of urban, low-income, black America.
Apart from the thousands of victims of drugs and drug-
related violence, the rudies left a legacy of familial and
communal disintegration.

The 'ghetto' family was one prominent victim. At best
brittle, the 'traditional' (black) family role model – a
strong-willed, dominant single mother – was replaced by
a new figurehead in thousands of households: a pre-teen
or teenage drug dealer.

The process was gradual. It started with rudie 'scouts'
plucking African-American inner city youngsters, some
as young as eight-year-olds, from the streets and enlisting them into their drug operations. The children were
taken on as (well-paid) look-outs. If they performed this
function well, the overseers used them as runners of small
quantities of crack and drug money. The wages improved.
Later, the budding criminals were handed a few 'rocks'
to sell. And finally, if the proceeds came back, the youth
'graduated' into fully-fledged drug dealers, turning over
thousands of dollars a day. The end result saw teenagers
and even younger children supplant their matriarchs as the
head of the family household, according to one anti-drug
agent, 'simply because he's the biggest wage-earner
through the sale of crack'.

The changes also registered on the street. 'At one time,'
the informant continues, 'the most respected man in the
community was the pimp. He had the women; he had the
cars; he had the money. He was the big guy on the block.'
That syndrome came to a halt in the mid-1980s. Today,
he says, 'the pimp has been replaced by the crack dealer.
The guy who was a pimp at nineteen to twenty-five has
been blown away financially by a fifteen-year-old who is

making more money than the pimp could ever imagine was available to him.' And the beauty of it is, the crack dealers do not need a stable of prostitutes to earn them their riches; they can do it all by themselves.

America's inner city communities were not alone in suffering the effects of the posses, their products and services. By the late 1980s and early 1990s things were beginning to fall apart for the posses, especially those at the top. The posses were beginning to come under intense law enforcement pressure and, ironically, many of the attributes that had cleared the way for their ascendancy were coming back to haunt them.

The fall was gradual. In fact, it can be strongly argued that it started even before the mid-1980s when the posses came to national attention.

It began with the splintering process, whereby the big posses were broken up into smaller outfits. This was caused by two phenomena: the desire of ambitious 'lieutenants' to 'run tings' under their own banner; and the later impact of law enforcement drives against big posses. In both cases, splintering precipitated the breakdown of the organisational strength, influence and profitability of the posses.

The origins of the crack generation in the mid-1980s, in particular, tended to exert a catalytic influence over the splintering process. Naturally, as the profits from crack poured in many a top-ranking gangster wanted a bigger slice of the action. This left many incumbent dons in a quandary: to kill (or run the risk of being killed by) their ambitious, trusted and skilled right-hand men, and deplete their strength and effectiveness in the process; or to allow them to go their own way to much the same end.

More often than not the drug overlords opted for the latter of the two evils, or an ingenious version of it, anyway. They allowed their pretenders to go it alone with the proviso that the new groups purchased their drug inventories directly for the 'parent' posse.

But another, more profound and damaging, reason for the upsurge in splintering, was the increasing advances of American law enforcement. As a posses' leadership was identified and removed, the management void prompted ambitious underlings to try to wrest control of the remaining organisation. Alternatively, they took the cream of the remaining workforce and began to deal under their own flag.

Splintering had a marked effect on the landscape of Jamaican organised crime. Indeed, it is true to say that some of the most deadly American posses started out as splinter groups. This is particularly true of those that broke off from Jim Brown's Shower Posse.

The up-and-coming Strikers Posse was a ruthless breakaway faction. The outfit was headed by a former ranking Shower gunman believed to have been involved in a string of murders in Jamaica, the United States and Canada. A gaggle of Shower gun hands also joined the Strikers crew.

Amongst other things, the Strikers were thought to have been behind three gruesome bank robberies in Chicago and New York City. Apart from systematically killing the workers at these outlets, they claimed the lives of two Chicago policemen who responded to one scene, and a retired, have-a-go-hero New York cop who happened to be at the scene of another.

The growing propensity of certain posses to specialise in violently ripping-off or stealing their narcotics led to the loss of credibility of the whole of posseism; something from which the 'community' has never fully recovered.

'They're doing a lot of drug rip-offs now,' says Anne, the ATF intelligence analyst. 'I don't think the drugs are scarce. It's just a way to get the money and the drugs because they don't care about killing.' 'I don't know if they're doing it out of desperation,' adds Bill Fredericks, 'but they are big into rip-offs. They set up their suppliers and knock 'em off.'

The tendency has become so acute that it has become a by-word in the rudies' lexicon of 'causes of death'. One of the cases Fredericks had on his books at the time of his interview concerned a Jamaican crew who had systemati-cally ripped-off a group of passive Nigerians for heroin, and Columbians for cocaine. 'We got fifteen homicides attributable to them as a result,' says Fredericks.

A measure of how important drug rip-offs have become to the posses is seen in the lengths to which the Rude Boys are prepared to go to set them up. 'Within the US, there are international rip-off guys,' explains Fredericks, a man who was once described as a 'walking encyclopedia' on the posses. 'They actually move out of the US specifically to do rip-offs. They even try to lose their accents because it's become synonymous with the Jamaican posses.'

Drug rip-offs have cost the posses dearly. Naturally, it led to endemic suspicion amongst their big suppli-ers, especially the Colombians. 'The Jamaicans,' says Fredericks, 'would always decide, "let's rip 'em".' And this, in turn, led to the emergence of a new power base in the world of mid- and street-level drug dealing, the Dominicans. In fact, the Dominicans, who are singled out by some as having developed crack for mass consump-tion, are now to street-level distribution of narcotics what the posses were a decade ago. Alternatively, the posses' avarice and violence has been responsible for them losing the greater part of their drug empire.

When it comes to cocaine, for example, the Columbians have taken to dealing with their cultural and linguistic cousins instead of the alien and untrustworthy posses. The Dominican gangs then service the needs of the Jamaicans and African-Americans. Arrangements like this suit wholesalers like the Columbians even more. Apart from distancing themselves from the Jamaicans, the Columbians benefit more because the Dominicans tend to purchase a hundred or so 'kis' of product a week, compared to the piecemeal two or three kilos a day the posses would buy.

The dramatic displacement of the posses as a major narcotics distribution force was not the only consequence of their love of appropriating other people's drugs. Increasingly, the victims of their 'crimes' have decided to fight back.

Willie Hagheart, the dancehall-loving, alleged leader of the Kingston-based Black Roses Crew would probably agree. Allegedly a major league rip-off artist, Hagheart's sister was murdered by a Columbian death squad in the Bronx after she allegedly set them up for a rip-off. Her body was flown back to Jamaica for burial, but, unbeknown to her grieving relatives, the Columbians had tailed it in the hope of catching up with Hagheart. As a result, Munerlie, Hagheart's brother, was also murdered. Now, the word is that Willie Hagheart walks around armed to the back teeth in preparation for Columbian reprisals.

In spite of the rip-offs, probably the biggest reason for the posses' downfall was their own excessive violence. That is, one of the major factors that propelled them into the big time, signalled their downfall. 'What happened,' explains Fredericks, 'was that the big posses – the Shower, the Spanglers, the "Kirkies" – attracted so much attention that the Feds homed in on them. It's deadly now. As soon as the Feds hear the word "posses", they begin to focus on them.' In short, the Rude Boys were too violent for their own good.

Once the Feds had targeted the posses, a combination of policing methods, tailor-made laws and, much later, a network of informants did the rest. A vivid reminder of the force the posses grew to become is provided by the anti-posse industry that pursues them. Today, wherever the posses exist, there is a plethora of specialist task forces designed to put them out of action. The ATF has its own Jamaican Task Force in branches throughout the United States. On a more general footing, the Justice Department has also developed the National Jamaican Posse Data Base in Washington DC to buttress their own efforts and those of local, State and Federal operatives.

The first real victories against the posses stemmed from the 'Operation Rum Punch' series in 1987. The Shower Posse was urgently targeted in the first strike. Amongst other things, their rudie gunmen were believed to have committed over 600 murders between 1984 and 1987.

When the purge came on 19 and 20 October 1987, after a year of behind-the-scenes investigations, it was quick and fast. A task force comprising hundreds of Federal, State and local insurgents launched a series of simultaneous raids in fifteen American cities. One hundred and fifty-seven people were arrested and charged with a wide variety of criminal offences. And, as if to underline the posse's skill at 'importing' ethnic Jamaicans, a staggering seventy-five per cent of those detained were found to have entered the United States illegally.

The effort of the Dallas task force was typical of those that struck in the other fourteen cities. Their agents had been involved in investigations since November 1986. During that period the Shower Posse was linked to forty-four murders in three years. Its city-wide branches were estimated to make US$400,000 in profit every day from crack-houses alone.

On the day the counter-offensive was launched, 115 officers comprising the city's police and County Sheriff's Department deputies, the ATF, DEA and INS staged a series of aptly termed 'cluster fucks' on fourteen separate locations across Dallas. The intention was to overwhelm the Rude Boys with their sheer weight of numbers and raw firepower. It worked. Fifty-four Shower suspects were arrested. (A second, even more labour intensive Operation Rum Punch attack netted 304 suspects.)

Over the years, the Shower has been decimated by drives like these. In fact, misfortune after misfortune has rained down on the gang's members. What with Jim Brown's mysterious death, the 'accidental' extradition of Richard 'Storyteller' Morrison to the United States and a concomitant generation-long prison sentence, and the ongoing attempts of alleged co-leader, Vivian Blake, in Jamaica to wriggle out of extradition proceedings which would see him standing trial for a host of serious criminal offences, the Shower's leadership has been taken out of circulation.

Experienced operators who might have filled that leadership void have also been disqualified. In the cases of Blake's brother, Black Tony, and his step-brother, Earl 'Kong' Hussing, disqualification has come about via arrest and detention as they prepare to answer racketeering charges in Florida.

Bill Fredericks was instrumental in the New York purge against the Shower Posse. The story of his involvement is revealing, not least because it captures the air of incredulity that surrounded the events leading up to the lid being taken off the posses. But it also highlights the relationships between some of the leading players.

Fredericks is typically New York blunt about his initial view surrounding rumours of the Shower's presence in the mid-Eighties. 'I didn't believe them,' he says. 'I thought these guys were bullshitting us. This is *really* an organisation?' he adds, feigning disbelief. A part of the credibility problem, he explains, 'was conceptual. We were used to talking about Italian organised crime. Apart from anything else . . . nobody gave a shit, anyway.' In short, they could

not see the big picture in terms of organisation, violence
and allegations of political affiliation.

The Shower's name was first mentioned by the
Jamaicans he and his colleagues had been arresting at
that time on federal gun charges; people who were likely
to say anything to help lessen their jail time. However,
Fredericks changed his tune when the ATF began to
cultivate three key informers comprising a man and two
women – one of whom acted as a concubine for Jim Brown
and Vivian Blake. 'They started to tell us how a lot of
this [ganja] money was being shipped back to Jamaica to
support Seaga's people,' he says, 'and how Jim Brown
was a link between people here dealing drugs and Tivoli
Gardens. Then we began to hear about competition with
the Spanglers – they were mainly Manley people – and a
lot of money going back to Jamaica, and some high level
political people associated.'

Even so, pinning down the identities and roles of those
involved proved a major headache. One of the first big
breaks came with the apprehension of a rudie named
Cecil 'Modeller' Connor; a man who had fled a Kingston
hospital where he was being treated in 1978, while serving
a life sentence.

A prosecution witness in Kong's trial, he was initially
one of ten rudies arrested during a drugs raid in New York.
The raid netted 100 pounds of ganja and two handguns.
But, for some unknown reason, Modeller coughed about
what the ATF knights had overlooked. 'He says we
missed a phoney shaft that had US$100,000 and twenty
guns,' recalls Fredericks. 'Those guys – we let them go
– within two years those ten people had committed ten
murders.'

Kong inadvertently turned out to be a mine of information. 'He was out in the open,' explains the agent,
'not as sneaky as Vivian Blake.' More importantly,
'Black Tony and Kong pretty much did [Blake's] dirty

work on the streets – shootings, murders and drug distribution.'

As for Vivian Blake, he 'was a John Gotti-type person with the ability to attract people to him; they fashioned themselves after Mafia dons,' argues Fredericks. 'They had these characteristics of leadership, organisation and enforcement which either make you a genius or a criminal.'

Still, Blake was no criminal genius; he made mistakes. 'Blake was a much more hands-on guy,' explains the ATF supervisor. 'He connected himself too much to people at distribution level, particularly in the distribution of firearms, not just in the US, but back to Jamaica to support political aspirations.' Inevitably this led to the law enforcement spotlight being turned on to him.

Looking back Fredericks maintains that for all their adroitness at setting up their ganja-crack distribution network, and guns and money operations to Jamaica, rudies like Jim Brown and Vivian Blake were 'made bigger than what they really were – drug dealers.'

Many would no doubt dispute this view. And even Fredericks confesses to the 'frustration' he and his operatives experienced over their inability to bring the duo to book. Jim Brown was never tried by a US court, and while federal agents arrested crateloads of Shower rudies, the ubiquitous Blake was not one of them. In fact, he fled back to Jamaica in 1989. Whether or not he was going to be forcibly extradited to the United States to answer federal guns and narcotics racketeering charges was scheduled to be decided by a Jamaican court on 25 May 1995. If returned and convicted, Blake faced the prospect of up to 390 years in jail – plus a multi-million dollar fine.

There are still gangsters who refer to themselves as Shower, but the Shower they have in mind is but a shadow of the one that sent pulses racing across America a few years back. 'They're all gone now,' says Fredericks. 'It's just not the same anymore.'

Through co-ordinated task force assaults like the ones on the Shower Posse, law enforcers have been able to reclaim some of the ground they lost to the Rude Boy parasites. After admitting it had a serious drug trafficking problem – the prerequisite step in any cure – Kansas City was able, albeit briefly, to exile the posses following an Organised Crime Drug Enforcement Task Force (OCDETF) case.

The investigation, which started in May 1986, included major players from the ATF, Customs, DEA, FBI, INS and the Kansas City Police Department. On a lesser level, the city's own government departments – sanitation, public works, tax assessors and so on – were seconded into the all-hands-on-deck effort.

The Kansas City initiative, says a participating drug enforcement agent, was 'a whole new concept in law enforcement'. Indeed, the rest of the city was ignored as the task force engaged in 'storm trooper tactics'. Roads were sealed off; sub-police stations were opened up in the heartlands of previously rampant drug-dealing neighbourhoods; derelict buildings and other potential drug-dealing outlets were demolished or, failing that, handed over free of charge to police officers who were willing to move their families into them for a minimum two-year period. Such officers, or high sheriffs, were even given a direct 'hotline' to the mayor's office.

The pilot operation was a huge success in all but one respect. The Crips and Bloods moved into the territory vacated by the posses. Such is the fickle nature of America's War on Drugs.

The demise of Eric Vassell's Gulleymen Posse was one of the most spectacular task force triumphs. But beyond that, it highlighted the clever and deadly forces

that the posses represented, and underlined the lengths
to which America's law enforcement battalions had to go
if they hoped to stop for good the menace of Jamaican
gangsterism.

From their humble origins in McGreggor Gulley in
Kingston, Vassell and his Gulleymen rose to run an
American drug empire that netted an estimated $1m
every ten days. As early as 1979, the gang had begun
to distribute and sell heroin, cocaine and freebase in the
Crown Heights section of Brooklyn.

By the mid-1980s, when the local market was swamped,
Vassell, like other enterprising dons, spread his operations
to less competitive outlets. Rochester, New York and
Dallas, Texas featured prominently. He was dispatching
between three and four kilos of cocaine to Dallas on a
weekly basis. On top of their drug dealings, Gulleymen
operatives were involved in subsidiary offences like
illegal firearms trafficking – it was routine to send
guns with drug consignments – illegal million dollar
wire transactions, armed robberies, rapes and at least
twenty-two murders.

The Gulleymen's vicious reign finally ended on 6
December 1990 after an eight-month investigation. It
culminated in a joint ATF, INS, Brooklyn South Homicide task force and Dallas OCDETF identifying forty-four
posse suspects. Twenty-four were arrested in a series of
co-ordinated swoops.

Sadly, Vassell himself was among the twenty who
slipped through the task force net; he was placed on the
United States' 'Most Wanted' list. However, Vassell was
arrested in September 1994 in Jamaica, and extradition
proceedings started against him. The District Attorney's
office in the Eastern District of New York is anxious that
he stands trial on charges ranging from drug trafficking
and conspiracy to distribute cocaine and heroin to running
a criminal enterprise, homicide and conspiracy to launder

money. At the time of writing, Vassell was trying to avoid extradition.

The official drive against the posses (and other organised gangs) has been boosted by the introduction of a number of laws which carry lengthy prison sentences. Furthermore, some of these same laws have been amended to make it more difficult for the drug and gun traffickers to evade punishment for their offences.

One such law is the Comprehensive Crime Control Act of 1984 (CCCA). This stipulates a minimum mandatory five-year to life sentence for anyone carrying a firearm in the commission of a drug crime. The Gun Control Act of 1984 is another. Worse still, these amendments mean there is no scope for probation or parole, and all sentences run consecutively with those imposed for actual offences. The Armed Career Criminal Act (1984) is particularly severe. The three-strikes-and-you're-out statute demands a mandatory fifteen-year to life sentence (plus a US$250,000 fine) to any offender with three previous convictions for serious drug offences.

And then there are the laws pertaining to the running of criminal enterprises. The Continuing Criminal Enterprise Act (CCE), a favourite with the DEA, is specifically geared towards addressing drug-related crimes. By definition a gang leader with five or more followers who participate in three or more offences are liable to prosecution under CCE.

But the Racketeer Influenced and Corrupt Organisations Act (RICO) is the jewel in the legislative crown, and the law most widely used against the posse members. 'Federal agencies love to use RICO and CCEs because they're great statutes to cover any organisation – including labour unions,' admits Fredericks. Indeed, Jim Brown would have stood trial, and Vivian Blake can look forward to standing trial on these latter two statutes if he is ever extradited.

One of this particular law's idiosyncrasies is that it allows for one person to be declared an enterprise. Apart from lengthy prison sentences and heavy fines, the Act allows for the forfeiture of all the proceeds of 'dirty money'. A drug enforcement agent stated the advantages of these laws: 'When you come in with CCE and RICO [it's] mandatory life on some of these counts for a whole posse of people. It's not just one individual. That's the way to go!'

The members of a fledgling Florida posse would probably agree. They belong to the same outfit that (allegedly) blew up Florida Highway Patrol Trooper James Fulwood. The fourteen defendants (ten Jamaicans, four African-Americans) charged under the auspices of RICO face possible life sentences under several of its provisions. They include: racketeering; conspiracy to distribute narcotics; and death by explosive device. The gangsters also face a mandatory minimum thirty-year prison term for 'possession of an explosive device during a drug trafficking offence'. All convictions run consecutively.

Richard 'Storyteller' Morrison would definitely agree. He was convicted on Count II of the RICO statute: conspiracy to distribute narcotics.

However, for all its assistance, RICO has its detractors. 'RICO is a particularly effective tool where they're exposing their wealth and their ill-gotten gains,' says Dougherty. But the Rude Boys, he says, 'have not gone the big house route in the United States, they're not ostentatious spenders ... By and large, you're better off charging them with everything but electricity and convicting them on the substantive charges.' RICO's supporters might ask him to try and convince 'Storyteller' Morrison about that.

*   *   *

For all the sophisticated innovations, punitive laws and dedicated law enforcers, the posses are still a force to be reckoned with. 'We've smashed up enough to limit their visibility,' explains Fredericks, 'but not to say there's not a lot of them out there.'

As for rounding up their members, a federal report concedes that 'fingerprint checks and photographs are usually the only way to determine the actual identity of a posse member'. Indeed, in the final analysis the report concludes, 'It is only through an unrelenting, unified and flexible approach by all levels of law enforcement that we can combat the threat by Jamaican posses'.

Even so, the character of the posses has changed markedly over the past several years. Today, the Jamaicans who band together to form a posse are mindful of the need to keep their organisation small. 'I would say the m.o. has changed,' confirms Supervisor Fredericks. 'They no longer seek to have gigantic organisations – the bigger the outfit, the more suscep- tible they are to capture. The typical operation now is out of New York to four cities, say, Baltimore, Columbus, Ohio and Detroit.'

In this respect, the posses are into niche marketing. The Rude Boys know that they cannot compete on equal terms with the distribution networks set up by the Dominicans, but that they can boost their profits by targeting cities and towns where crack sells at much higher prices than New York and Miami. With the exception of the Deep South where there is no known posse presence, this 'interstate' approach to doing business has enabled the rudies to maintain a strong presence in cities all over the United States.

In keeping with this new-found inconspicuousness, the posses have toned down their violence considerably. Or, as Bill Fredericks puts it, 'They don't want to do too many murders because it attracts a shitload of law enforcement attention. The more killing you do, the more attention you get.'

In the final analysis, then, the Americans have, at long last, got their posse problem 'under control'. Still, as long as there is a market for illicit drugs and the posses continue to keep their heads down, there will always be a demand for their services. But while American law enforcement can congratulate itself on its success in tackling the posse menace, that success augurs ill for other countries.

Over the past few years, the Rude Boys, following much the same pattern that they adopted in the United States, have redoubled their efforts to conquer neighbouring Canada. Canada, with its British heritage, has been seen as a much easier place for the 'Yardies' to expand into than the Dominicans and Latin Americans.

The United States's recent success in driving the posses further underground or out of the country completely is also a potentially portentous development for Britain. 'It's good news for us,' says Fredericks, 'but bad news for you – the English.' 'Watch out,' adds Anne, 'that's all I can say.'

CHAPTER TEN

The DC Experience

'In my experience, over the past several years of working with the Jamaicans, they came in – [mainly] from
New York – they taught the [African-] Americans
how to take a community, how to run it [as] a drug
organisation. They ran it with efficiency and a lot
of fear and terror. Now it's gotten to the point that
the Jamaicans have settled down *per se*, and the
Americans will shoot without reason.'

Sgt. 'Beetlejuice' Beadel, Washington DC police

Washington DC has a considerable posse problem,
although today it is nowhere near as acute as it was
up to the early 1990s. In fact, the capital has undergone
something of a revival.

No more aposite a symbol of that resurgence is available than the political reincarnation of Marion Barry Jr.
Barry, a former student civil rights activist and apostle of
Martin Luther King, was DC's Mayor for twelve years
from 1978–90. A giant of local politics, Barry's heroic
efforts to increase housing and jobs had made him the
darling of the city's poor and dispossessed. Then in
January 1990 his world was torn apart by a sensational
drugs scandal. Barry was videotaped during an FBI

'sting' operation smoking crack and making rather embar-
rassing sexual advances towards a woman (who was
not his wife) in room 727 of the Vista International
hotel in Washington. The Mayor's shameful criminal
misconduct cost him six months in prison on a cocaine
possession charge.

However, the disgraced ex-Mayor emerged from prison
having 'seen the light'. A 'born again' African-American,
he even began to don traditional African robes and became
as determined as ever to make a meaningful contribution
to public life. Cured of his alcohol and drug addictions, the
rehabilitated Barry picked up the pieces of his shattered
political career and in January 1993, he was re-elected to
the DC city council as a member for the impoverished
eighth ward. By May 1994, in spite of the stigma of a
criminal record, Barry was ready to reclaim DC's top
job. Indeed, the way he saw it, no candidate was better
qualified to run the city. 'Who better to say to our young
people,' he asked a crowd of well-wishers, 'Yes, you can
fall down . . . But what is more important is that you can
get up. Look at me. I got up.'

DC's predominantly African-American population lapped
it up. And, as a result of their votes, Marion Barry Jr was
inaugurated as Mayor of Washington DC on 2 January
1995. He might not have revolutionised the lot of the
mass of poor people since then, but at least one aspect of
the capital's sorry condition has changed since his return:
Washington DC has relinquished the unfortunate title of
the murder capital of the United States. (That mantle
has now been passed to the world's jazz capital, New
Orleans.)

In terms of his addiction, Barry pulled himself back
from the brink. Largely by default, the city he presides
over has managed to do the same with regard to its
drug-related mayhem. Yet the posses, the villains whose
activities have made a major contribution to both rampant

drug dependency and drug violence in Washington DC, continue to lurk in the wings. Only time will tell whether Barry goes into relapse. But the question of whether DC will once again succumb to the extraordinary influence of the posses is largely out of his and the city's control. For now at least the posses' guns are silent, and Washington DC's fate lies in the hands of the rudies from Jamaica.

A city of about 600,000 souls, DC might have experienced chronic posse-related drug and violence problems, but its suffering is a shadow of that which exists in much larger, importation and distribution metropolises like Miami, New York and Los Angeles. Indeed, the scale of the drug problem in Los Angeles was highlighted in November 1994, when it was estimated that getting on for eighty per cent of the City of Angel's paper money supply had traces of cocaine or other drugs embedded in it. Yet DC remains a microcosm of the nationwide impact of the posses.

Probably as much as, if not more than, any other major American city, DC has done everything it can to rid its streets of the scourge of the posses. Yet, in spite of a string of innovative and costly local and federal initiatives, and a number of high-profile convictions against big-time drug traffickers and dealers, the city remains firmly in the grips of an overwhelming drugs-related crisis. One, moreover, which over the past decade and a half has been shaped and directed by the posses down to the last vial of crack, 9mm semi-automatic handgun and hollow-point bullet. In this sense, the Washington DC experience is very much the American experience.

It is a nauseatingly humid ninety-five degrees as portentous black clouds converge over DC's stunted skyline. A mighty storm is brewing above the mother of Western democracy. Meanwhile, down on the city centre streets, in the nerve-centre of American justice, liberty and equality, it is business as usual. Politicians, civil servants and lobbyists jockey with each other for the privilege of getting their interests addressed. The visitors and corporate delegates who contribute to the capital's $2 billion-a-year tourist industry soak up its facilities: the picture-postcard landmarks, expensive restaurants, fancy nightclubs and bars. Around the six-lane Beltway, DC's cornucopia of air-conditioned shopping malls are deluged by people of every nationality; their every need serviced by battalions of mainly black workers. DC is the epitome of the Star Spangled Banner; the essence of the American Dream.

Yet Washington DC is a Jekyll and Hyde city. An oasis of politics, government bureaucracy and commerce surrounded by a desert of urban neglect. The Hyde section is populated in the main by poor blacks. In fact, DC houses more black people proportionately and absolutely than any other American city. It is home to almost a half a million African-Americans (accounting for three-quarters of its population) and a great many ethnic blacks. Hence DC's nickname, Chocolate City.

Within a half-mile radius of the White House, the run-down neighbourhood streets are 'governed' by vicious drug gangsters, and the nights resound with the crackle of semi-automatic gunfire. This is the other side of DC; the side that does not appear on the postcards and in the tourist brochures. Until recently, no other city in the Western world had a higher per capita murder rate.

Needless to say, the vast majority of the victims of this nightmarish violence are black – murder is the most common cause of death for black American males aged between fifteen and thirty-four. Indeed, of the city's 372 homicides in 1988 only eight of the victims were white. It is also the case that the lion's share of DC's murders (sixty per cent in 1988) take place in the gun-laden arena of the illegal multi-million-dollar drug industry. Not that surprising when one considers that some ten per cent of the city's population habitually abuse drugs.

Drug-related black-on-black crime is not new here, but over the past few years it has become more frequent and increasingly sordid. Prior to the onslaught of the posses, Washington was fighting a losing battle against the problem of drug-related violence. Compared to the post-posse arrival period, though, the slaughter of those days had something of a 'rustic' quality to it. Everybody knew what the drug business was about in those days. Everybody knew where they fitted in, what was permissable, what was against the 'law'. Life was much simpler before the posses arrived.

In the late 1970s, shortly before the Rude Boys first arrived, DC's narcotics of choice were heroin and the hugely popular PCP or Angel Dust, a powerful hallucinogenic. A hardcore of African-American dealers cornered the supply market. Meanwhile, less adventurous drug abusers got their kicks from smoking mary jane, ganja.

With regard to the distribution and sale of ganja, DC experienced the same kind of problems with violence and murder as other American cities at the beginning of the 1980s. Using the city's estimated population of 10,000 law-abiding Jamaicans for cover, Rude Boy gunslingers moved in with a traditionally blinkered determination to control the market. The subsequent inter-posse violence unleashed between factions like the Shower, Spanglers, Waterhouse, Riverton City, Tel Aviv, Super and Banton Posses quickly brought the Jamaican bandits to the attention of the local authorities.

It was not only the increased level of gun warfare that attracted the police to the presence of the rudies. As ever it was the manner in which much of it was perpetrated: public shoot-outs and execution-style slayings with high-calibre, rapid fire weapons. However, like their counterparts elsewhere in America, DC's police were unaware of the organisational force behind the carnage.

The breakthrough in the police's understanding came on the eve of the crack explosion in 1984. But it was a couple of years before the reconstituted posses made a play for the city's embryonic crack market. In fact, the narcotic was actually introduced to the city by wily local dealers who immediately recognised its immense profit-making potential. This group literally went out of their way to supply the DC market with crack. They would take the shuttle up to New York, where powder cocaine and crack were dirt cheap and readily available – crack was selling at between US$5–US$10 a vial – fly it back to the capital and offload what was still a rare commodity at US$25–US$30 a vial. The profit margins were so healthy it was like making money out of waste paper.

But when the New York drug scene became swamped with crack, the posses hungrily searched for new outlet cities in which to retail it. Washington DC was one of the first on the list, and the rudies were not about to allow any small-fry local dealers to stand between them and the grand designs they had for it. Crack would combine the 'kick' of cocaine with the financial outlay of ganja; crack was destined to become the people's drug.

By early 1987 Washington DC was plunged into a full-scale drug war as the posses took on the PCP kingpins, and battled amongst themselves for control of the choicest drugs turf. Interestingly, though, it seems that even though the posses behind the city's ganja traffic were often the same as those involved in the crack-related warfare, the players were totally different. 'One thing that is a little unique about the Jamaicans,' explains a Washington-based ATF agent, 'is you'll either find a group of Jamaicans who sell marijuana or they will sell crack.'

The scale of the crack conflict was graphically reflected in the rapid growth of the city's annual homicide tally. In 1986, for example, DC buried 197 murder victims. By 1988, that figure had almost doubled to 369. In the three years to 1988, rudie mobsters were responsible for at least sixty murders – and in all probability a whole lot more – in the DC area.

As is inevitably the case, a great many of the victims were rival posse members. In fact, it got to the point where whenever a 9mm weapon like a Tech-9 was found to be the weapon used in a fatal shooting, local homicide detectives would immediately form a mental link between the posses and the attack. Moreover, the upper echelon of DC's 4,000-strong police force was so alarmed by the appeararance of this lethal weaponry and its callous usage that it considered issuing officers on patrol with similar firearms to better protect themselves.

The other primary source of murder victims came from the ranks of local African-Americans. Between them the Rude Boy gangs' ruthless savagery eliminated the African-American competition. The rudies' goal of taking over DC's lucrative crack markets was given a welcome boost by the fact that the majority of the African-American dealers who controlled them were unused to carrying arms to defend themselves on the streets; although that was hastily rectified to some extent. By contrast, the vast majority of Jamaican dealers would never have dreamed of leaving home without a 'strap'.

The onslaught of the posses was similarly reflected in the cavalier style of the atrocities carried out. In one week in November 1987 – a week which witnessed the killings of six Jamaicans in DC – a posse member was shot to death in front of his wife by two gunmen who burst into their home. A friend of the deceased narrowly avoided probable death by leaping through an apartment window. In a typical act of Rude Boy bravado, the victim's wife was left to mourn her husband, completely unmolested by the killers.

Two months later, five Jamaicans were slaughtered by a trio of posse enforcers from Brooklyn in an apartment in Landover in neighbouring Prince George's County. Of the four men and a woman 'terminated', three of the men were known players in the open-air drug markets that prospered around the notorious Mayfair Mansions and Paradise Manor housing developments. Just over a month after that massacre, two Jamaican women were ruthlessly executed in front of their four infant children in the Meridian Place area of north-west DC.

Pretty soon the crack trade and, to a lesser extent, the attendant violence and murder, spread out of the city centre and into white, middle-class districts like Virginia and Maryland. Oblivious to the real dangers of detection by the police, Jamaican dealers became a common sight in the predominantly white, rural confines of small suburban Washington towns. Disturbingly, by 1988, within two years of their DC crack campaign, the posses had made crack the drug of a new, raceless, ageless, genderless and classless generation.

But posse-related violence and murder is not as bad as it used to be in DC. Now the Rude Boys rule the roost there is much less call for it. However, this is of little comfort to federal agents like 'Forrest', and his long-time partner, 'Dave'. An experienced ATF agent in the Washington Field Division, Forrest knows that he and his colleagues in law enforcement still have an Everest to climb before they can talk about ending the posses' rule. 'The city needs to be taken back,' he frowns in a way one imagines reminiscent of Wyatt Earp in his first day on the job in Dodge City. 'Period!'

Across the Potomac River, on the other side of the White House, it is easy to see why. In the shadow of the city's famous all-black Howard University campus, a young African-American member of the Nation of Islam is engaged in animated conversation with a group of scruffily-clad 'brothers'. Decked out in an inexpensive, but smart, grey suit and standard-issue red bow tie, the apostle of Minister Louis Farrakhan tries to interest the gaggle in the latest edition of *The Final Call*, the religious body's highly professional publication. But whatever else the black Muslim's audience is interested in, it is not a crack at spiritual redemption.

This is DC's 4th District. One of the capital's largest precincts, it is a cosmopolitan lower- and middle-class area which covers parts of the city's north-east and north-west sections. In fact, multi-million-dollar town houses owned by diplomats can be found within two blocks of some of the capital's roughest and toughest housing projects. Geographically, the district borders the Rock Creek Park nature reserve to the east, Harvard Street to the north, the railroad track to the west and the Potomac River to the south.

In terms of demography, the district's timber-framed, three-storey town houses are home to an exotic cock-tail of Dominicans, Hispanics, Salvadorians and African-Americans. Jamaicans also feature prominantly, especially in the 600 block around 13th and 14th streets and Gerard, Euklid, and Morton. And, as in any other area of significant Yardie settlement, the population has its own grocery stores, restaurants, bars, and nightclubs like the Hummingbird and the Clubhouse.

White faces, with the exception of authority figures, are few and far between in these parts. The streets of the 4th District are awash with black people: queueing for buses, pushing babies in buggies, carrying big brown paper 'sacks' piled high with groceries, and loitering in groups on street corners.

Just up the road from the luckless member of the Nation of Islam, on the corner of Kennedy and Georgia to be

precise, a white, plain-clothes detective is engrossed in
an encounter of an altogether different nature. In what is
one of the city's notorious drug-dealing areas, Sergeant
Beadel is interrogating and publicly searching four adolescent black Jamaican males for drugs. An officer of
considerable experience with regard to posse members,
the first thing Beadel does is to instruct the men to take
their hands out of their pockets. When they first came
into DC, he says, there were occasions when he would
question them for ten minutes or so, and, when he frisked
them, would find a gun in their waist. The rudies were an
unknown quantity then, but nowadays Sergeant Beadel
knows more than enough about them not to endanger his
life like that.

One of the men he is searching now, a twenty-three-
year-old who has identified himself as Anthony Williams,
is found to be in possession of a 'dime bag' ($5) of ganja.
During his thorough search (it includes checking under
the suspect's testicles) Beadel makes another important
discovery, a birth certificate. There is a problem; the tattered photocopy bears the name of one Michael Anthony
Clarke.

A call to the 4th District's dilapidated police HQ reveals
that Clarke, or whoever he is, has a bench warrant out on
him stemming from an earlier non-appearance in court on
another marijuana possession charge. Meanwhile, Beadel
clears the offender's compatriots to leave, which they
do without so much as a backward glance. Beadel, a
middle-aged detective whose vast experience is etched
across his face, radios for a patrol car to take his quarry
to the precinct. Compared with most of the Jamaicans he
deals with this particular felon is a minor irritant. He will
deal with him later.

Beadel, or 'Sergeant Beetlejuice' as he's known to local
posse operatives, has 'worked Jamaicans' since they

began to arrive with their guns and narcotics in the early 1980s. He and federal agents like Dave and Forrest have seen it all, and are, as such, uniquely placed to give a first-hand account of the minutiae of the posses' reign of terror over the city.

Beadel is anything but surprised by his latest arrest's reluctance to divulge his true identity. It is, says the seasoned street cop, symptomatic of the way that even honest Jamaicans have come to view their nationality since their villainous counterparts converged on DC. 'Jamaicans will lie to you about where they're from,' he says. 'A lot of them will tell you they're from the Virgin Islands or Guyana just to take away the stigma of being Jamaican.'

Judging by the posses' colonisation of the nation's capital, lawful Jamaicans have every reason to disguise their true origins. The frightening story mirrors that of other major metropolitan centres. Like those of nearby Baltimore or distant Bristol, Connecticut, and Johnson City, Tennessee, it is a saga of terror, torture and murder united under the umbrella of an irresistible drug epidemic.

But in keeping with everything else they do, the posses' colonisations were well planned and organised, business-like even. Even though the decision to seek out fresh markets was somewhat foisted upon them by prevailing circumstances, the Rude Boys exhibited a great deal of nous when they approached cities like Washington DC. 'They began to approach it like a genuine business,' says Lloyd Williams, the Jamaican posse specialist. 'They would go to some little city and scout out the place. And they'd decide "OK, let's get some men in here and open up shop."'

Because of their meticulous planning, when some of New York's big-time posses arrived, the local population (including the criminal fraternity) simply never knew

what they were up against. 'You will find some organisations that will come over and suddenly in a week or
two you'll have a complete organisation set up,' remarks
Beadel. 'When they come in to take over an area, they
come in very fast and very violent.'

However, the posses' first step was to find suitable
bases for their trafficking operations. Posse strongmen
went in with their typical ruthless flair, and literally
annexed local people's homes, especially those belonging
to the most vulnerable: drug dependants and welfare
cases. 'They go in and just intimidate,' says ATF agent
Dave, Forrest's partner. 'They'll go into someone of low
income . . . and they'll tell them exactly what they expect
them to do: "You're outta here. We own this now."'

Alternatively, posse 'scouts' would find someone,
usually a welfare mother on crack, and pay them off
with regular drugs. The gangsters would even compensate
the occupants for the thousands of dollars worth of phone
calls that they ran up during the course of their nationwide
business dealings.

Yet, as easy as it was to find suitable premises, the
rudies' unwelcome intrusions were sometimes accompanied by a streak of sheer vindictiveness. 'In one of the
cases we had, they came in – there were three of them
with guns – they made everybody strip down, sexually
assaulted two of the girls and then kicked them out,'
says Dave with more than a hint of incredulity. 'Kicked
them out of their apartment!' For one of the evicted rape
victims, the unbelievable ordeal did not end there. The
posse in question soon turned her into a crack 'vampire',
and then press-ganged her into selling the narcotic for
them. There are no shortage of examples like her.

Ruthlessness of this order was also extended to dealings
with ordinary customers. For example, in another memo-
rable example from Dave's casebook, after displacing the
rightful occupants from their home, the new 'landlords'

installed 'a couch, a chair and a coffee table', he recalls. 'They put the crack on the table. They'd let one person in at a time – they had two guns on 'em. [The crack buyers] took what they wanted and put their money down. There was never any dispute. If there was they'd either get beat up or they'd be shot. We had these homicides down here as a result.' Contrary to popular belief, when it comes to the posses' dealings with crackheads, the customer is not always right.

Not that the crafty posse members outstayed their 'welcome'. One abiding secret of their success at avoiding police scrutiny has been the way in which the henchmen employ a system of rolling colonisations. Almost as soon as the Rude Boys had annexed a property, they would move on to a new location. An apartment could be a family home today, a flourishing crack-house tomorrow, and a home again the day after. And, given DC's epidemic inner-city poverty and the rudies' method of acquiring retail outlets, there were no shortage of prospective bases in the capital.

After a couple of weeks, when the new arrivals had got their infrastructures in place, posse combat soldiers launched their offensives to take over the streets. Not surprisingly, given their mentality, they were more than a match for DC's incumbent drug dealers. Says Beadel: 'initially when the Jamaicans came down – most of them were from New York – they were more violent or more aggressive than local [African-] Americans from DC, and they did intimidate the you-know-what out of them.'

More to the point, posse 'soldiers' and 'enforcers' physically eliminated anyone who dared to resist their advances. Part of the problem for the indigenous drug dealers was that their horizons were limited to the goal of accumulating money. The rudies, by contrast, were into making money and seizing power. The narco-terrorists basically wanted to set up their own personal 'garrison'-style power bases.

When the gunfire finally ceased, the successful posses had divided up their newly-acquired turf into multi-block areas. The African-Americans who continued to trade there did so because they had been conscripted into the lower layer of the posses or had received the ruling group's blessing. The predominantly Jamaican-inhabited Meridian Hill and 'Malcolm X' Park areas were just two of the many to fall under posse control.

Once in place, the wily posses took painstaking steps to protect their considerable investments. Sophisticated surveillance equipment was installed in buildings housing crack dens and drugs dumps. In the apartments they controlled, the gangsters routinely lifted up the carpeting and cut holes in the floorboards beneath to conceal their drug hoards. No effort was spared. 'I've seen them replaster walls where they'll hide their narcotics,' says Beadel. Another indication of their organisation, power and resources showed up in a separate case where every African-American in a four-storey apartment block was put on to a posse's payroll. Some were employed as look-outs, others as dealers and 'mules'.

Where holes appeared in this new drug landscape, wholly new Washington-based posses sprung up to fill them. Two of the most notable were the Payne and Champagne Posses. However, they were pretty amateur-ish in comparison with their more established stablemates. These groups were opportunistic. Formed by like-minded Jamaicans, they relied almost entirely upon their status as Jamaican nationals, as opposed to allegiances based on politics and longstanding friendships. In short, they lacked the cohesiveness of the posses that had arrived in America a decade earlier.

The Payne faction was taken out of commission after a brief, but fruitful reign of terror. Founded by three

members of the same family, they ran their small organisation from the Hummingbird, a local Jamaican nightspot
and reputed centre of drug dealing. Washington DC
police, including Beadel, put an end to their activities
in 1990. Two of the triumvirate were imprisoned for
thirty-six years each, the other got thirty-eight years.

The Champagne Posse (they got their name from their
members' predilection for going to nightclubs, ordering
crates of champagne and giving away what they could
not drink) have also had their setbacks. Several members received lengthy sentences after one of their 'baby
mothers' informed on the group's activities.

Such women are crucial weapons in the armoury of
law enforcers like Beadel, more so than surveillance
operations or attempts to infiltrate the posses. To Beadel
the reason for this is as old as time itself. 'Men have a
habit of cheating on their women, that's natural history,'
observes the detective. 'But if your woman finds out
you've cheated on her, she'll burn you in a heartbeat. And
those guys like to brag to their women about what they've
done – who they've shot, who they've killed, who they've
robbed, ripped off – and they'll brag. The woman will tell
me everything if they get her mad.' Hence, the end of the
champagne days for the posse's top brass. (Undeterred,
however, a splinter group soon started up under the name
of the Champagne Magnum Posse.)

Copycat posses were not the only new phenomena to
hit Washington's streets. As is customary, once the posses
had settled down they began to blend into the background
and recruit African-Americans to do their bidding. 'Your
local [African-] Americans,' explains Beadel, 'will like
to hang around them . . . because if they can do right by
them they can get a free supply of narcotics or access
to weapons or the women.' In Chocolate City, though,
the hangers-on were given additional responsibilities as
the Jamaican bosses moved up the corporate ladder.

The Rude Boys, says Beadel, educated their indigenous black charges in how to front and run a successful drug operation. 'Now its gotten to the point that the Jamaicans have settled down *per se*,' he continues, 'and the Americans will shoot without reason.'

Understandably, it was the law-abiding community which suffered most when the posses set up shop in the American capital. Finding people willing to relate their experiences is extremely difficult – local residents are understandably fearful about speaking out. 'Everyone in the Jamaican community will know who the [posse] members are,' asserts Officer Beadel, but getting them to speak out about them or their activities is a different matter. At home or abroad, Jamaicans tend to remember the ghetto code: 'See and blind, hear and deaf.'

'Larry' is one who temporarily forgot it, although he insisted the author forget his real name in return. 'The whole of DC has become more violent,' he says. 'This place now, you go [out] sometimes at night and, shit, you have to be careful how you drive round because its pure Jamaicans out there.'

A restaurateur and a Jamaican himself, 'Larry' made his home in the capital in 1970. He remembers distant, happier times: times when business was good; when he felt safe; and enjoyed the life he worked hard to build for himself. Those days, says 'Larry', were prior to the early 1980s when posse members 'started to have parties, and after the parties they [would] try to shoot each other and shoot up the place . . . making problems for business people and neighbours.'

Since the Jamaican drug gangs arrived 'Larry' claims that he and his business have suffered. 'I get hurt three times here trying to get [dealers] away from outside my place.' In the worst of the attacks, he required nineteen stitches in a gash under his right eye. Apparently, a crack dealer who refused to move away from his store front decided to make his point by assaulting 'Larry' with a broken coke bottle. Given what he knows about the posses, though, 'Larry' is the first to admit that he got off lightly.

In spite of his lot, the Jamaican immigrant is not bitter. The same, however, cannot be said of all the people who pursue them. Dave, the ATF agent, is one who openly confesses to having his view of Jamaicans as a whole coloured by the excesses of the few. 'I have to tell you it has!' he admits. 'It shouldn't but it has because the majority of the ones I have come across are filthy, violent people.' All this from a man who admits to living next door to a 'very nice, very pleasant,' industrious Jamaican and her family. 'I'm not saying they're all wrong!' he continues. 'I'm just saying when you say "Jamaican" to me, I think crack, violence, shootings. And that's what's wrong! But that's all I'm seeing, y'know?'

Dave's anti-Jamaicanism is born as much out of the Rude Boys' menacing violence as it is out of utter frustration with the failure of law enforcement to bring them to justice. Forget the vagaries of local and federal law, agents like Dave have their work cut out simply apprehending suspected posse members – even when they have them cornered.

Detective Beadel has compelling grounds to support his controversial view that the rudies are the most erratic, not to mention, violent, bunch of criminals he has ever encountered. 'I've done search warrants in fourth- and seventh-floor apartments, and I've never seen an American that would jump out of a window. But a Jamaican will,' he says. That they are desperate and fearless is beyond question. 'I've seen guys break both legs,' he adds, 'and still try and crawl away with their arms.'

Death-defying stunts like these help to explain why
the rudies are such a formidable foe. Beadel himself is
at a loss to explain it. The only thing he can think of
is that they are so desperate to get away that the risks
involved pale into insignificance. Again, he points to the
fact that their chances of escape are improved by the fact
that, unlike their Jamaican counterparts, American police
officers are not going to shoot them.

Incisive detective work aside, nailing posse members
has often come down to a combination of witnesses and
informers (who are few and far between) and sheer luck.
All three of these imponderables were united in the
case of a successful ATF strike against a Washington-
based rudie.

An enterprising agent, Dave set about solving the problem of identifying habitually nomadic posse affiliates. His
system involved surreptitiously taking photographs of
suspected Jamaican gangsters from his Oldsmobile sedan;
a former partner snapped some 4,000 photographs over a
ten-year period. Dave's photo album is supplemented by
a network of colleagues that extends to places as far afield
as Kansas City, Los Angeles and New York because, he
says, 'in some of these cases Jamaicans show up here, or
ours show up there'.

On one notable occasion his painstaking detective work
ended in a young Rude Boy called Butter winding up in
a sticky situation. Butter's demise began, as so many
others do, with a dispute over a drug deal. In fact, he
believed he had been short-changed by his dealers. Butter
was bitter.

Accordingly, the Dunkirk Posse overseer and three of
his best 'soldiers' paid an unannounced late-night visit to
the home of the man who had supposedly ripped him off.
Butter and his henchmen tortured the four residents (three
women and a man) but failed to get his money back. So, he
executed the women and critically injured the man, and

left. In spite of his extensive injuries, the male shooting victim – who incidentally was not the man who was being sought – remembered the Jamaican ghetto gangster code: 'See and blind, hear and deaf.' He resolutely refused to tell the police anything about the incident. But a young woman, who was hiding in a closet during the attack, did. The information she provided about Butter did not help to advance the local police investigation but Dave, however, was able to identify a character who used that 'tag' in his substantial catalogue.

The ATF agent went on to organise a photographic line-up. 'I had his photo, no one else did,' he recalls with pride and pleasure. 'I took the photo in, gave them ten photos so they could have a legitimate spread. That girl picked out the shooter and the three that were with him, and that boy is now in custody without bond pending his homicide [trial].' Butter was twenty years old at the time of his arrest.

Butter's tender age and savage disposition are not the only astonishing features of this investigation. It is, perhaps, symptomatic of the vicious impunity with which posse *gundeliros* tend to operate; a telling reflection on the confidence they have in their narco-terroristic tactics. Either way, without it, Dave would not have progressed the case. The fact is that Butter *knew* the young woman was hiding in the closet 'and yet he went in there and killed three and not the fourth who could be an eyewitness,' says Dave. 'Why he did it,' he confesses, 'I dont know.'

A number of other successes have been scored against the posses and their members at both local, State and Federal levels but these are insignificant when one considers the overall situation. DC's history of the war against the posses has made for grim reading. As Dave and others will confess, defeating them has been like trying to empty the Atlantic with a tea cup.

Dave's sentiments are echoed by the host of politicians
and public officials who have seen the posses' handiwork.
For years Washington DC has battled gamely against the
Jamaican narco-terrorists, and the drug menace in general.
The fruits of their labours, however, have scarcely made a
dent in the posses' structures.

Operation Caribbean Cruise was the city's first major
push against the posse intruders. The biggest single raid in
DC's police history, it was designed to ensnare hundreds
of posse dealers, and seize their massive caches of drugs
and armaments. To that end, on 22 February 1986, a massive force of DC's 'finest' staged a series of co-ordinated
lightning raids across the inner city. The results, however,
were nothing like those the designers had anticipated. A
measly twenty-seven arrests, the confiscation of a paltry
thirteen firearms and a total of only US$27,000-worth of
narcotics.

Suspicions circulated that the showpiece operation was
a disaster because corrupt police officers had tipped off
many of the Jamaicans under suspicion. Either way, matters were only worsened when several innocent Jamaicans
who were caught up in the raids sued the local government
for alleged police harrassment. From then on, any notions
the DC constabulary harboured about repeating the exercise in the future were completely dashed.

In 1986, the DC force also embarked upon another
adventurous anti-drug campaign. Codenamed Operation
Clean Sweep, it involved a general sweep of the city's
open-air drug bazaars and dealing centres. While not
confined specifically to the posses, top local police
officials clearly anticipated that the sweep would help
the overall fight against them.

Operation Clean Sweep was more successful in some
ways, but equally ineffective in others. The high point
was that over the two and a half years of its commission,
squads of DC police officers made a phenomenal 47,000

arrests; and added almost fifty per cent to the district's swollen prison population. The downside was that the operation did not make the slightest bit of difference to the availability of narcotics on the streets, or the violence that attended them. On the contrary, the violence rose as the drugs markets expanded.

In a slight departure from purely official action, as the drug-violence problem got out of hand, the Nation of Islam felt compelled to step into the breach. In April 1988, at Mayfair Mansions, which had been a respectable housing project until the posses adopted it as a crack-dealing centre in 1986, the black Muslims organised round-the-clock patrols to stamp out the trade. Unarmed except for two-way radios, the religious devotees hassled the project's dealers and intimidated their customers. Remarkably, after a short while both dealers and buyers got the message. Unfortunately, however, besides returning Mayfair Mansions to some semblance of order, the effect of this action was to displace the trade to other vulnerable areas.

By the time of the Nation of Islam's courageous actions, Washington DC had been plunged into a state of widespread panic. Matters finally came to a head in 1988. Prompted by an epidemic of publicly-executed black-on-black slayings, New Hampshire Senator Warren Rudmen was one of the first to pass judgement on the ghastly situation on the other side of the Potomac. 'We can't have people killed and blood running in the streets like some Third World capital run by a despot,' he bitterly complained. Not only had the posses arrived, they had come to the attention of the folks on Capitol Hill.

Responding to outcries like these, Washington Mayor, Marion Barry, leapt into action. In an effort to stamp out (juvenile) narco-terrorism, he imposed an 11 p.m. curfew on the city's under eighteens and legislated a five-year prison sentence for anyone caught in possession of a gun whilst committing a crime. However, Barry's draconian initiatives were doomed to failure; the Mayor had missed the mark completely. And, besides, his embattled police department was in no position to baby-sit the city's youngsters. (The Washington police were propping up the national league table of unsolved murders.)

Meanwhile, in March 1989, President Bush's newly-appointed drugs tsar, William Bennett, came into office making all the right noises. In a highly controversial (some said, foolhardy) move, the President declared that Washington DC was a 'high-intensity drug trafficking area'. As soon as he was sworn in, and before he even had an office with his name-plate on it, Bennett announced that US$100 million of special federal funds would be pumped into the capital's emergency anti-drug effort. Washington DC, the former Reagan Education Secretary decreed, was to be his first 'test area'; a blueprint for tackling the nationwide drug and gun plague.

Bennett's programme sought to convict and imprison 500 of DC's deadliest drug criminals over the space of a year and a half. Its success or failure rested on the expertise of what was called the Metropolitan Area Task Force (MATF), a hundred-strong, multi-agency group of law enforcement experts. Crack personnel were pooled from Customs, the DEA, FBI, INS, Internal Revenue Service, Secret Service and the United States Park Police. In addition, five intelligence analysts were seconded from the Pentagon.

DC's local expertise was conspicuous by its absence. In fact, Bennett made numerous public statements spelling out his disenchantment with local government and police efforts. To that end, he did not condescend to consult with them on his initiative.

However, for all their joint efforts the MATF did nothing to restrict the level of drug availability, violence and murder. In fact, all the indications were that the overall situation got progressively worse. As always, it was business as usual for the posses and their rivals.

The failure of such a prestigious team to eradicate or even dent the capital's drug menace speaks volumes for the scale of the problem. At another level, it puts ATF agent Dave's pessimism and downright anti-Jamaicanism into perspective.

If anything, the mountainous difficulties involved in taking the posses off the streets of DC have only increased with time. Of late, the ominous responsibility of restoring law and order to the American capital (or at least returning it to the more manageable situation that prevailed before the posses rode in) has been hampered by a combination of the guile of the Jamaican criminals, and the relative lack of resources made available to fight them.

Recent local and federal laws have been enacted like those which carry a mandatory jail sentence for drug dealing or carrying a gun within 300 metres of a school. But for every law there is a legal loophole. Or, the vagaries of the laws themselves make it easy for the Rude Boys to escape punishment. 'As far as keeping ahead of law enforcement [is concerned],' argues Dave, 'they've become knowledgeable about sentences, amounts of drugs and so on.

'For instance,' he explains, 'if you're caught with an ounce of marijuana in Virginia you'll probably be sentenced to five years. In DC you can have ninety-nine pounds and they don't charge you with a felony. It's a possession, or possession with intent to distribute marijuana. It's a joke!'

Forrest, his partner, recalls a real-life example. 'We had a Jamaican who hadn't cut his hair since 1972,' he recalls. '[We discovered] eighty-three nickel bags – $5 bags – of marijuana [hidden in it]. Probably a hundred grams or thereabouts – he's looking at a misdemeanour!'

Dave can see no end to the posses' fatal activities. 'It's too lucrative,' he says. 'There's too much money to be made. And even though you've got some stiffer penalties, they're still gonna do it.' The anti-posse experiences of agents like Dave have led him to believe that in order to defeat them law enforcers will have to turn their backs on conventional policing methods. In keeping with Detective Beadel, he believes that they will have to adopt a lateral approach to the never-ending struggle to reclaim the city streets.

It would be more fruitful, says Dave, to confiscate the drug kingpins' status symbols. After all, the motivation for their activities is as much about winning power and respect as it is about getting rich and living the fast life of a gangster. 'Believe it or not taking their toys: taking their cars; taking their jewellery; taking their money, is worse than putting them in jail.' The idea being that the rudie mobsters lose face.

But even in this respect, the posses are once again one step ahead of the law. As soon as the Rude Boys discovered their prestigious possessions were at risk, they made the necessary alterations to their appearances and lifestyles. Instead of buying Suzuki jeeps and BMWs, they rented inconspicuous vehicles. Instead of strutting about town in loud tracksuits and baseball caps, draped in several thousand dollars worth of gold jewellery, like chameleons, they changed their wardrobes to blend in with the urban landscape. Instead of buying houses for cash, they went back to 'living poor' in inner-city apartments. As a result, the rudies are now even more difficult to spot in a crowd.

So what of the future for Washington DC? Will the city ever rid itself of the posse menace? According to 'Larry', the Jamaican-born restuarateur, the answer is a resounding 'no'. 'As far as I see drugs business and this killing,' he mourns, 'I don't see no stopping in it, you hear!' At best, he adds, 'It's only gonna ease down.' Indeed, the way things now look, it seems the American capital has got the posses for keeps.

CHAPTER ELEVEN

Canada: The View from Across the Border

'The hard evidence disputes all suggestions that there is any connection between an increase of crime and the immigrant community. The facts are that everywhere there is an upsurge of criminal activity, much of it connected to drugs and violence.'

P.J. Patterson, Prime Minister of Jamaica
speaking in Ottawa on 14 July 1994

When sprinter Ben Johnson was first across the finishing line in the final of the men's 100 metres at the 1988 Seoul Olympics, the whole of Canada erupted into an explosion of celebration. He had put himself and his country firmly on the international athletics map. By holding off a world-class challenge, the Jamaican-born Canadian hopeful had also reserved himself a special place in the annals of Canadian history, not to mention the hearts of millions of television viewers around the globe. In less than ten seconds (9.79 to be exact) Johnson had become an international superstar. It was too good to be true.

Raised in Canada since his early childhood, Johnson's incredible Gold medal-winning achievement seemed to

vindicate his adopted country's liberal immigration policy. Canada had accepted him, refined his raw talent,
and Johnson had repaid that investment by winning
the ultimate sporting prize; he had come to epitomise
the new, raceless Canada.

This Canadianness was the central theme of the reception to Johnson's heroics at home; his race, ethnicity,
class and general background were all relegated to the
margins. In fact, the first editions of Canada's newspapers out-adjectived each other to lavish praise upon the
country's latest national hero. His unbelievable victory
was plastered in bold, banner headlines across every
conceivable publication: Ben Johnson, Canadian National
Hero. His triumph had given Canada a new lease of life;
the achievements of one man had enabled all Canadians
to hold their heads high.

The fourth and fifth editions of the morning papers,
however, told a drastically different story. The sensational
disclosure that Johnson had failed a random drugs test in
the aftermath of the race obliterated the initial euphoria
over his unprecedented triumph – it really had been too
good to be true. More than that, though, it prompted a
new line in, and style of, reporting. In the event, the
Canadian press tore into Johnson like a pack of starving
hyaenas savaging a defenceless wildebeest. Over the next
few months Johnson, now stripped of his Olympic Gold
medal and 100-metre world record-setting time, was to
gain painful first-hand experience of what it means to fall
from grace.

However, the demonisation of Ben Johnson did not
end with his personal vilification. Rather, the slant of
the reporting of the Ben Johnson scandal uncovered a
sinister side to perceptions of race, ethnicity and nationality in Canada. Moreover, it revealed the overtly racist
underbelly of mainstream white Canadian society. For as
quickly as Ben Johnson had become the all-conquering,

All-Canadian sprint supremo, his duplicity had caused the nation's reporters to strip him of his nationality.

The disgraced sprinter was now described as 'Jamaican-born' or, more commonly, plain 'Jamaican'. Not even P.J. Patterson doubted the rationale behind this callous change of emphasis. 'It was only when he ran into trouble,' remarked the Jamaican Prime Minister, 'that suddenly the Canadian media began to refer to him as a Jamaican.' In the coded form of Canada's journalistic expedience, Johnson had miraculously become the product of another (uncivilised) country where, it followed, a dastardly deception like his was to be expected.

But the Canadian press's distancing of itself from its albeit naturalised citizen did not stop at his media lynching; an entire community was made to pay for Johnson's mistake. In the space of three or four print runs Canada's populous (immigrant) Jamaican – and, by extension indigenous black and Caribbean – communities had become a part of a wider, hidden problem. Purely and simply the 'trouble-maker' had been exposed as one of 'them'.

The image of Canada's Jamaican population has never fully recovered from the battering it took in the years since Johnson's first *faux pas* (he again tested positive for drugs, and received a life ban from athletics, in 1993). Invariably, the backdrop to the stereotyping of the Jamaican community and the counter-claims of official persecution has been formed by the overwhelming national perception of the country's black population being primarily responsible for Canada's violent crime situation.

Over the years, a number of controversies and scandals have seen Canada's immigrant Jamaican and indigenous black communities make the front pages of the dailies for all the wrong reasons. Between 1989 and 1992, for example, the fatal police shootings of nine black men culminated in a violent black backlash, and doomed the aggrieved communities to a volley of bad press.

Indeed, the death of the ninth allegedly knife-wielding victim, shot by an undercover officer in an anti-drug operation, triggered a wave of looting, arson and rioting in Toronto in May 1992. Coming less than two weeks after the apocalyptic Los Angeles riots, the (multi-racial) disturbances served notice that Canada's black population also felt under siege from racist State forces.

Again, all hell was let loose by the fatal, senseless and utterly ruthless shooting of a Canadian police officer in September 1992. The victim was cut down, it seems, because he was issuing a ticket to an errant motorist. Wielding an illegal firearm, the alleged killer shot the policeman in the back of the head. To make matters worse, it later transpired that the murder suspect was a Jamaican former police officer who had been dismissed from the JCF in 1990 for suspected misconduct.

Later, the unprovoked murder of another officer led to calls for a re-evaluation of Canada's immigration policy, especially as it related to 'lawless' Jamaicans.

In April 1993, for example, Art Hanger, a fierce critic of Canada's existing immigration policy, accused Jamaicans of being behind Toronto's rising crime rates. More than 40,000 Jamaicans had legally settled in Canada during the previous decade.

By June of 1994 (a time when influential elements of the Canadian press were openly confessing to national media racism in the reporting of visible minorites) a parliamentarian fired another salvo at the Jamaican community. Prompted by yet another fatal shooting of a Canadian police officer, Liberal Member of Parliament John Bryden called for a public debate on whether Jamaicans were more likely than other minority ethnic groups to commit violent crimes. (A subsequent

Canadian government report revealed that immigrants
were actually *less* likely to commit crime than indigenous
Canadians.)

In August 1994, in the wake of yet another sensationally-
reported black-on-white shooting incident, Canada's immigration authority had to defuse charges that it was
running a vigorously anti-Jamaican policy. The criticism
of Immigration Canada was caused by the revelation that
an unprecedented forty-five Jamaicans had been deported
back to Jamaica between June and July 1994.

There was further controversy in December when it
was disclosed that Immigration Canada had shelved a
pilot project which would have required the compulsory
fingerprinting and photographing of Jamaican entertainers
on arrival at Toronto's Pearson International airport.
Apparently, forty (sixteen per cent) of those who had
entered Canada in 1993 had ended up getting into trouble
with the law – some were even deported.

In truth, over some time there had been several
instances where the lawlessness of Jamaican or Jamaican-
born individuals had led to the whole community being
stigmatised. But it was usually the case that the suspects
involved (especially the latter category) owed much of
their upbringing, education and socialisation to Canadian
institutions and society.

That was certainly the case with the slaying of a
Toronto police officer in June 1994. Even the Canadian
Immigration Minister, Sergio Marchi, said that Clinton
Gayle, the man charged with the murder, was as much a
product of Canada as he was of Jamaica. (Gayle had been
raised in Canada since he was seven years old.) Ironically,
his criminal past prior to the killing had led to an order
being prepared for his deportation to Jamaica. However, it
was stayed on appeal, and he had been allowed to remain
in Canada.

The same was true of one of the two suspects arrested

in connection with the so-called 'Just Desserts' killing in April 1994. Like the police slayings before and after it, the highly publicised incident profoundly shocked Canadian sensibilities, and sent another wave of anti-Jamaicanism reverberating around the country. This tragedy – Canada's first random killing of a civilian – took place in an up-market Toronto café. Georgina Leimonis, the twenty-nine-year-old victim, was enjoying a coffee after a night out at the theatre. In confused circumstances, the only thing that is clear about what happened is that Leimonis died of a gunshot wound to the chest during a tragically botched robbery attempt.

The assailants, Lawrence 'Brownman' Brown and Oneil 'Tiger' Grant, voluntarily turned themselves in in the midst of a huge police manhunt. Brown, a Jamaican in the true sense of the word, was charged with first-degree murder and a dozen robberies in Toronto's West End. His accomplice was charged with manslaughter and the same series of robberies. Grant, a Jamaican-born twenty-three-year-old, had been resident in Canada since the age of twelve, although he had never become a naturalised citizen. A recidivist criminal, like Gayle, his history of convictions had culminated in an order being made for his deportation to Jamaica in December 1992. That, too, had been stayed.

In retrospect, it is difficult to see how the Canadian press – and society as a whole – can justify, or even explain, its stigmatisation of the country's entire Jamaican population. It amounted to racism of the first order.

Acutely aware of this, the question of race has become a deeply sensitive issue in Canada in recent times. In fact, with the politics of political correctness now prevailing, the whole race question has come full circle. The reporting of race and crime is particularly symptomatic of the new enlightenment. Indeed, certain scribes have taken to deleting any mention of a suspect's race, ethnicity or nationality from their reports, even when the victims describe their assailants by racial type.

Even the police now baulk at using race classifications to identify deviants.

As inexcusable as the mainstream perceptions of Canada's Jamaican population are, or have been, there is no escaping the fact that there is no smoke without fire. The problems that Canada and its Jamaican population are experiencing stem from situations created over the past decade, especially by a community that neither wants: the Rude Boys.

During their residence in Canada, the rudies have totally transformed the complexion of the national crime scene. In what is a genuinely placid and law-abiding society, they have single-handedly introduced indiscriminate public displays of gun violence, wholesale crack-dealing and related addiction, and general mayhem. To cap it all, as in the United States – and, as we shall soon discover, Britain – the Rude Boys have inculcated indigenous black, and Jamaican-born, Canadian youth with their nihilistic values; and set them off on the road to violent criminality.

'Some of the commonalities between these groups,' remarks David McCloud, 'are the violence, the use of firearms, the mobility, and the drugs "taxations".' (Drugs taxations being the Canadian term for drug rip-offs.) McCloud is referring to the *modus operandi* of Canada's contingent of criminal Rude Boys. A Toronto police officer, these commonalities have caused considerable policing problems for him and his colleagues over the past ten years or so.

Like other Jamaican descendants, Detective Sergeant McCloud, who hails from St Elizabeth, harks back to a time when the biggest obstacle to policing Toronto's black inner city areas was posed by the small-time ganja dealer. 'The people involved were predominantly dreadlocked,' he recalls. 'They sold ganja on the corner; they lived, ate and spent their money in the community.' In short, the problems they caused could be contained by effective policing.

By contrast, today's organised Jamaican criminal is more sophisticated, he says. He or she is likely to own and operate a legal business (an auto body repair centre, barber's shop or hair salon) to provide a front to launder their illegal profits. To aggravate matters, today's criminal is also likely to be an armed and dangerous gang member.

Canada's first acquaintance with Jamaican criminals came in the mid-1970s. The black-populated pockets of major cities like Toronto, Montreal and Vancouver began to fall under the sway of a hardcore of minor-league drug players. Ignorant of the true source of the menace, the Canadians described the new wave of criminals as Rastafarians.

During the late 1970s and early 1980s Canada became the reluctant host to another influx of Jamaican undesirables. These, however, were far more menacing than the inappropriately termed 'Rastafarian' contingent. A number of the new arrivals fled to the country as unofficial political 'refugees' from Jamaica's homicidal 1980 tribal election war, but their numbers were augmented by a wave of posse fugitives from American justice. By definition, both groups were made up of ruthless murderers and cunning drug dealers. Indeed, a senior Toronto police officer was to complain some time later that his city had become a 'dumping ground' for foreign criminals dealing in drugs and illegal guns.

Jamaican-related crime became a nationally recognised problem in the early 1980s. Between 1982 and 1983, a rash of armed bank robberies perpetrated by

dreadlocked Jamaicans reinforced the notion that the
Rastas were masterminding the black community's violent crime wave. Either way, the visible crime problem
prompted the Canadian police to look deeper into the
relationships between the black community and crime.

In 1984, the Toronto police carried out a study into
similarities between home break-ins, burglaries, robberies
and assorted crimes in the black community. They concluded that there was a definite link between the origins of
the victims and the perpetrators – Jamaica. More startling,
though, the police were forced to accept that these crimes
bore the hallmarks of sophisticated organisation. There
was nothing sporadic, for example, about the pattern of
bank robberies. And a similar level of planning had gone
into the organisation of prostitution, pimping, and the
importation, preparation and distribution of narcotics.

This major discovery led to the formation of the Black
Organised Crime squad (BOC) of which David McCloud
is a key player. Incidentally, the BOC, like the issue
of race in general, has fallen prey to the predators of
Canadian political correctness. While everybody is aware
of the outfit's remit, it is never publicly referred to as
black organised crime. Rather, organised crime is used
as a coverall.

The finely-tuned nature of Jamaican organised crime
was not the only significant police find. In comparing
black organised crime to organised crime and the bikers,
another major Canadian criminal headache, the Toronto
police found that, like their American counterparts, it was
difficult to establish a defined heirarchical structure in the
rudie gangs. While organised criminals and bikers con-
formed to well-stratified cohorts, the Jamaican criminals
were found to be virtually disorganised itinerants.

Sure, ten people might gang together to import, process
and retail drugs; and as individuals those same people
might carry out well-defined tasks such as 'muling' the

product across the border. But, when the mission had been accomplished, it was not uncommon to find male gang members going off to join another crew specialising in bank robberies or women members being recruited into a shoplifting gang.

Naturally, though, the most noticeable divergence between the Rude Boys and their rivals and peers was – and is – their overt violence. Canada is plagued by a number of ethnic and indigenous criminal collectives, but none attract the same kind of public opprobium and police scrutiny as the rudie gangsters. This is not to say that groups like the Italians, Vietnamese, Greeks and 'white trash' do not commit crimes of violence. Violence is as much a feature of the 'mob's' dealings in heroin trafficking and union racketeering as it is in the Vietnameses' prostitution, heroin, international credit-card fraud, and extortion 'businesses'.

Still, one aspect that is common to all of these other groups is that their violence is targeted; they seldom, if ever, harm people from outside of their own ethnic criminal milieu. Not only have we already seen that this is not the case with the Rude Boys, but the level of their violence probably outstrips that of all of their criminal peers put together.

This became particularly evident in the years after about 1986; the era when crack cocaine and the attendant violence that surrounds its use and trade began to make the news. Or, as journalist Philip Mascoll puts it: 'If they quietly sold crack – as whites do – there would not be the same kind of pressure put on them as there is now.'

It was around this time also that the older, meeker, ganja-dealing, so-called Rastafarians were 'displaced' by the posse of Jamaican wanted criminals and 'refugees'; people who had caused serious law enforcement problems in Jamaica and the United States. The pioneer criminal generation had somewhat respected the peace-loving

ethos of Canadian society; they had kept their violence
to a minimum. A country with a minimal homicide
rate, Canada was caught off guard by the violence their
successors unleashed. Now, says Mascoll, 'it's literally a
handful of criminals who make a hell of a problem for
everyone.'

There are currently about six major posses in Toronto
(native Indian for 'meeting-place') and the conurbation
of eight towns that make up the Greater Toronto metropolitan area. The Strikers or Strikas Posse, the largest
single grouping, are joined by the Black Roses, Bulbeye's
and Markham Eglinton crews, the Jungle Massive, and
the Regent Park Posse. There is also speculation about
the presence of a group known as the Hot Steppers. And
the Spanglers Posse, who along with the Shower were a
force to be reckoned with during the mid- to late 1980s,
are also the subject of some gossip regarding their present
involvement in Yardie crime.

The Strikas, originally an American-formed Shower
Posse splinter group, have in the region of fifty active
members and associates. The gang was 'founded'
by a one-time Shower gunman, and staffed by a
gaggle of followers with the same history of pro-
JLP persuasions. However, as happened in the United
States, the irresistible smell of money eventually led to
the disintegration of the posse's political purity. Nowadays, the Strikas welcome experienced PNP 'soldiers'
with open arms.

To all intents and purposes, the Strikas are nothing
more or less than an 'old-school' American posse transplanted to Canada. They also provide a useful model for
Canada's other Jamaican gangs.

Posse members specialise in dealing drugs – crack,
cocaine and ganja. 'My brethren,' remarks Jamaican-born
Philip Mascoll, 'have a hell of a hold on the crack trade;

they control it almost exclusively. That is the drug of Jamaican organised gangsters.'

In general, the two main supply lines for obtaining narcotics are drug rip-offs and importation. The former is the cause of much deadly violence. In October 1990, for instance, the execution-style killing of a Jamaican DJ was attributed to an aggrieved posse. He had apparently 'liberated' two 'kis' of crack that belonged to them. So a group of rudie enforcers snatched him off the street, tortured him and shot him numerous times. His body was dumped in a ditch for all to see.

In terms of the latter source, the most commonly used methods of smuggling narcotics into Canada revolve around recruiting or sending mules to ferry smallish quantities across the border with the United States. All the gangs have established drug connections in cities such as New York. 'The traffic across the border is very heavy,' says Mascoll, a crime reporter on Canada's biggest-selling daily newspaper, the *Toronto Star*. 'They move in and out very quickly. We have people who are wanted here who are caught in New York, and vice versa.'

While making every effort to curtail the level of drug trafficking, Canada's customs authorities have an acute – and some maintain, growing – problem nonetheless. As far back as 1988, customs officials seized nearly C\$400 million-worth of heroin, cocaine and ganja; a twenty per cent rise over the 1987 haul. The difficulties of policing Canada's immense borders are ones that are regularly exploited by Jamaican narcotics couriers. With thousands of visitors from the United States crossing its borders every day, the posses experience few problems in smuggling their wares into Canada. Favoured modes of transportation include rental cars, long-distance coaches and Amtrak, the American national railway operator. However, larger quantities of ganja are often smuggled in on chartered flights.

Gangs like the Strikas Posse are also heavily into bank robberies, business extortion and home invasions. As is common among the posses nowadays, home invasions are carried out for the sole purpose of 'taxing' or ripping off other people's supplies of illegal drugs. There is, however, one unique variation between posses like the Strikas and their American counterparts: the added importance the former attach to gun-running. Apart from the obvious 'business' imperative of being well armed, dealing in firearms is a tremendous earner in Canada because of the country's draconian gun laws. Indeed, firearms purchased in the United States for as little as US$300 can fetch four times as much in Canada. Selling illegal guns is not the only money-spinner. 'The weapons are so popular,' according to an ATF report, 'that apparently some enterprising criminals rent them for $200 a weekend.'

In the early days of the Canadian posse presence, firearms were invariably supplied by the 'parent' posses in New York and Miami. Over the years, however, rudie gangs like the Strikas have turned to their own devices to acquire them. A typical ploy involves the use of 'straw' purchasers to transport the weapons across the United States border into Canada using the same conduits as drug smugglers. Given the volume of traffic, the chances of detection at the US-Canadian frontier are considered slim enough to justify the risks. But they exist nonetheless.

But the posses are nothing if they are not ingenious. In recent times there have been suspicions that the Strikas have turned to another, most unlikely source to obtain illegal weaponry. 'They are thought to be dealing with native Indians on the borders,' explains McCloud, 'who sell them guns, or trade them for drugs.'

If this is true then the Strikas could not have selected a better set of go-betweens. Canada's 300,000-strong, indigenous Indian population is virtually a nation within a nation. Spread out on approximately 2,000 reserves throughout four western provinces and Ontario, the province of which Toronto is the capital city, the American Indians enjoy 'cultural' gun laws which allow them to buy and stockpile wholesale quantities of firearms.

In keeping with the American experience, the original Canadian posses were staffed to a person by supporters of one or other of Jamaica's political giants. However, the onus on making money led to that exclusivity being consigned to posse history. But that has not been the only noteworthy change in posse personnel. Borrowing perhaps from the American example, the rudies have taken to recruiting Jamaican women and African-Canadians, not to mention 'importing' staff from Jamaica.

With regard to the latter, the unofficial backdrop to the controversy over singling out incoming Jamaican entertainers for special treatment was provided by suspicions that visa overstayers were being recruited into Rude Boy gangs. Typically, what would happen is that some wise guy in Toronto would contact a potential recruit from their neighbourhood back 'home', and invite them to perform in Canada. On the strength of the invitation, the Canadian Embassy in Kingston would then issue a three or four day visa. But when the 'performer' arrived, rather than perform, he would go underground.

'We,' says McCloud referring to the BOC, 'recognised they were using this entertainment route to replenish their numbers and mule drugs.' Unfortunately for McCloud *et al*, however, the plan 'became a whole political football' after it was leaked to the press. Hence, its shelving. But McCloud defiantly maintains that the entertainment scam remains a major conduit for recruiting gangsters.

Canadian police and immigration officials are doing all they can in an all-out attempt to exclude Jamaican undesirables. Yet they are virtually powerless to stop the continuing recruitment of Jamaican women and indigenous Canadians into the posses.

The role of women in the posses is multi-faceted. In the traditional setting of endemic Jamaican male chauvinism, women are passive chattel; gangster's molls and 'baby mothers'. Women, like guns, are possessions which men exploit to develop or enhance their 'reps'. Like the gangster who won first prize in a dancehall competition because he boasted twenty-three children by no less than seventeen 'baby mothers'.

According to some, such women get off on this role. With dancehall fashions in mind, Mascoll says they parade around in skimpy, tight-fitting attire to 'catch' a gangster they can call their own. McCloud endorses the view, and adds that women want to be seen with violent rudies; men who can say that they have been involved in shoot-outs with the police and such. As such, certain women take pride in acting as gun baggage when driving around town, or nightclubbing, with *their* man. The idea behind their exploitation being that women are less likely to be searched by male police officers or private security guards.

Generally speaking, women are posse facilitators. Typically, when a posse wants to set up a crack-house, a member will court a single mother on welfare in a public housing development with a view to gaining access to her apartment. (After a couple of weeks it is not uncommon for the whole complex to have been transformed into one big crack-house.)

For all that, though, (Jamaican) women make more substantive, although equally lowly, contributions to posse operations. They mule drugs across the border. They lease vehicles, rent apartments and mobile telephones for male members in their names. Similarly, they act as the owners of various legitimate businesses; enterprises opened by posse members to launder their criminal proceeds.

But it is in the realm of shoplifting that Jamaican women truly hold their own. Jamaican women are big-time, well-organised shoplifters. But even in this business their thoughts invariably turn to their men. That is, apart from stealing to make money, posse women tend to 'liberate' expensive items of clothing such as leather jackets to dress their men up in.

The recruitment of young Canadians into the posses has had far-reaching consequences for both the youth themselves, the welfare of the gangs and the Jamaican community in 'exile'.

Like young people around the (Western) world, African-Canadians are highly susceptible to the lure of materialism. 'He sees what other kids have,' explains Mascoll, 'and he wants it.' The problem, though, is that with the breakdown of the Jamaican family in Canada, there is often no father figure to support a mother's efforts to keep that yearning on the straight and narrow. In short, many young African-Canadians have turned to crime to realise their dreams.

Not surprisingly, Jamaican gangs have become one avenue along which they have trodden to fulfil their ambitions. 'We have a large number of Canadian-born youngsters – Jamaica's biggest loser group – patterning themselves on Jamaican criminals,' explains McCloud. 'These guys are telling black kids that the only way to make it is to be like me,' adds Mascoll more forcefully. 'It's pervasive. And this message has spread beyond poor kids, it's also middle-class kids now.'

And, because of the traditionally violent nature of Jamaican crime, this recourse has hastened the disintegration of the Jamaican community as a whole. 'The image of being a Jamaican is being destroyed,' says Mascoll. As he sees it, the horizons of ambition that once distinguished Jamaicans as industrious achievers have faded into the far distance. Because of the Rude Boy influence, the young are no longer interested in the power of education; they have no interest in becoming doctors or lawyers.

Clearly disturbed by this nascent retrogressiveness, Mascoll complains that 'We have a legion of public housing kids who are growing up believing that it is not on to be a Garvey, a Norman Manley; not to be a leader but to bore a skull with a 9 [mm gun].'

The only winners have been the posses. On the one hand, they have been able to tap into a willing pool of surplus labour. 'The [Rude Boy] criminals are trying to use local born youngsters to do things such as stash drugs, mule, and operate as front people,' explains Detective McCloud.

On the other hand (and this is not unrelated) the beauty of this arrangement is that, once arrested, these youths can be relied upon to do the jail time for their top-ranking employers. Moreover, as Canadian nationals, they are not deportable upon their release from prison. Ergo, they can pick up where they left off.

If anything, Canada's extremely lenient sentencing policy for young criminals actually militates in favour of African-Canadians getting involved in posse gangsterism and crime in general. One disgruntled Toronto police officer went so far as to describe the law as 'a kiss' for juvenile offenders. So, for example, under the Young Offenders Act, a youth convicted of murder can only receive a maximum sentence of five years imprisonment to be served in what the same officer called 'a summer camp'.

Were the excesses of these violent youth confined to posse business, the social and political fallout from their activities would not be so severe. But they are not. In fact, many African-Canadian posse conscripts have set in train a violent crime wave of their own. There is acute concern, for instance, over the numbers of young would-be rudies who have taken to 'counter-jumping'. Basically, this involves juveniles employed as posse runners, enforcers and the like using posse-supplied .45s to hold up Mom and Pop corner shops. In the space of a few short years, then, the influence of the Rude Boy overlords has come full circle.

'Aggression is not always a bad thing,' says Detective McCloud. He cites the controlled aggression displayed by successful salespeople by way of example. The ability to channel that extra rush of adrenaline into constructive outlets, he argues, helps to explain why athletes like the Jamaican world number one 'Sprint Queen', Merlene Ottey – and Jamaicans generally – 'have been successful in all walks of life'.

As a part of his work, McCloud does a lot of lecturing to fellow officers and people involved in the criminal justice system at large. When trying to explain the negative, criminal aggression of some of his fellow Jamaicans, the officer, while never excusing it, always places that aggression in the socio-economic and historical contexts of Jamaican development.

It is the only way he knows to explain the broader reasons why Jamaicans form ostensibly violent gangs, and members of the remainder of Canada's passive, lawful Caribbean populations – the overwhelming black majority – as a rule do not. For although Trinidadians, Barbadians and other English-speaking British Caribbean islanders share a common heritage in most respects, there remain significant differences between them and their Jamaican peers.

The marked differences in origin between the groups is central to McCloud's dialectic. So, he discusses the significance of the modern Jamaican population's origins in the noble warrior tribes of North West Africa to the warrior-like mentality of the typical Rude Boy gangster. (The rest of the Caribbean was populated by slaves from more passive traditions.) Again, he explains how the aggressive nature of those roots help to put the guerrilla warfare of their Maroon progeny into perspective. And he details how factors such as these have made a lasting impression on the sociology and psyche of the Jamaican people.

The message then is that, while the Jamaican pre-disposition towards aggressive behaviour is by no means biologically inherent, the origins and history of the (African-) Jamaican population are a testament to violence. In brief, Jamaicans display a low tolerance threshold to anything or anyone that stands between them and what they want.

This attitude, and the behaviour that goes with it, argues McCloud greatly assists in understanding why countless Jamaicans have prospered in the West. But, of equal importance, it also helps to explain why other black people have had a better chance of making it. Ironically, Philip Mascoll has independently reached much the same conclusions. 'The reason why Barbadians can make it is because of Jamaican aggression,' he reasons. 'There's nowhere a more aggressive person in the world.'

This aggression (or its criminal manifestations at any rate) underpins the reasons why Rude Boy gangsters are so violent. By the same token, the readiness of the rudies to execute outrageous violence puts the sustained Canadian law enforcement drive against them in recent years into bolder perspective. Nowhere was this violence more evident than Toronto in the early 1990s, and nowhere was the assault on the Jamaican gangsters more sustained.

Toronto proper has a population of about 2.8 million people, of whom roughly 150,000 are Jamaicans or of Jamaican descent. Vigilant policing over the last couple of years has taken much of the sting out of the criminal violence caused by the estimated 500 rudies who use the Jamaican communities for cover. But the earlier part of the decade was blighted by a cycle of gruesome, bloody violence. 'Between 1991 and 1993 it was incredible here,' recalls Mascoll. 'The crack dealers were popping each other left, right and centre.'

Those inter-posse conflagrations were triggered by a round of savage turf wars. As the rudies went all-out to establish open-air drug bazaars in the city's deprived public housing schemes, the battle for supremacy left an unprecedented, and disproportionately high, number of (Jamaican) people dead and injured. 'In 1991, we had thirty-two homicides out of seventy-eight involving hand-guns,' recalls Detective McCloud. 'Of those, twenty-one were black, including eighteen Jamaican-on-Jamaican; and half of those were in 'booze cans' [shebeens].'

The gun violence situation deteriorated the following year. 'In 1992, out of less than a hundred murders,' sighs Mascoll, 'twenty-six were black – all Jamaicans – and twenty-five out of the twenty-six [featured] Jamaican killers.' Most of the murders over this period were drug-related. But others fell into a grey area; they showed how the posse mentality was beginning to infect the Jamaican community as a whole.

One such killing took place in the early hours of Sunday 28 April inside the Blues and Cues Club, a Jamaican haunt. The victim was Jamaican-born twenty-seven-year-old Christopher Levy, a Bell Canada employee. Another man, the function's promoter, was injured in the assault. The deadly altercation was allegedly sparked by a dispute over the payment of a cover charge to enter the premises.

The suspected assailant, Leighton Francisco 'Peppy' Anderson, was bailed and promptly fled to Jamaica. The twenty-two-year-old was subsequently tracked down by the Toronto police and extradited to stand trial for murder and attempted murder. And, as if to highlight the thin line that often exists between 'real' crime and 'emotional' crime, Peppy was also ordered to defend himself against another two attempted murder charges. The Rude Boy had shot at two Toronto police officers in August 1991.

Diligent police work of this order has been responsible for the incarceration or deportation of several prominent Yardie faces in recent times. One of the most notable scalps was that of Larkland Dave Garrison also known as Paul Ferguson, and known to one and all as 'Dust'.

In Jamaica, Dust had held the distinction of being Jim Brown's right-hand man in Tivoli Gardens. 'He came to Canada and was involved heavily in taxing,' explains McCloud. 'He was extorting – because of his fearsome reputation in Jamaica – from Jamaican businesspeople and other gang members, money and drugs.'

However, the elder statesman of Jamaican criminality was not undone as a result of his activities in Canada, even though at the time of his arrest he was believed to be the Strikas Posse don in Toronto. Rather, it was his involvement in the bloody wave of shootings in west Kingston in the wake of Jah T's murder in February 1992 that caused his undoing. High on the JCF's Most Wanted list, he was deported after a failed two-year court battle to answer charges in connection with the aforementioned offences.

Another gang whose activities were disrupted by the Canadian penchant for deportations is the Markham Eglinton mob. Like the Jungle Massive and Regent Park cohorts, the Markham Eglinton crew take their name from the Toronto area where they reign supreme. However, internal power struggles caused by sustained police pressure have caused the gang to change their name 'every three months', according to McCloud. Interestingly, one of the names they chose was the Yardie Crew. The reason: two of their ranking members, including Rob 'English' Simpson, were born in Britain.

Willie Hagheart's Toronto chapter of the Black Roses

Crew also boasted a British member. However, Mark Johnson a.k.a. Johnny Marshall was deported to Britain. A mobile bunch, last reports were that he had taken up residence in Jamaica.

Finally, probably the most notorious victim of the Canadian purge was one-time reggae star, Robert 'Rankin' Dread' Blackwood. The epitome of international Rude Boy mobility, his is a story that takes in Jamaica, the United States, Britain and Canada.

Rankin' Dread fled to Canada in June 1989. During his 'sojourn' in Toronto he was arrested and charged with stabbing a girlfriend; he was released on bail and promptly went underground. He also served a twelve-month prison sentence for beating a Toronto police officer about the head with a huge rock. The well-travelled rudie was deported to Jamaica after his attempts to gain refugee status failed; 'I would rather die than stay in Canada,' he was reported as saying. Rankin' Dread's subsequent expulsion in November 1992 on two counts of assault, illegal possession of a firearm, impersonation, and entering Canada on an illegal passport, brought to three the number of countries that had ejected him.

For the time being, a combination of vigorous policing and the resolution of drug turf wars have quelled most of Toronto's posse-related violence. But with avaricious, unpredictable and totally ruthless characters like the rudies around, the situation is in a constant state of flux. In 1993, for example, Dave Sylvester Francis was shot through the heart, and his corpse dumped on a grass knoll near a busy Toronto highway. A Jamaican was charged in connection with the horrid attack on the Jamaican-born teenage victim. And in 1994, two gangs let their guns do the talking in a bitter battle for unchallenged control of the major, unclaimed Jane and Finch municipal housing estate. Only time will tell what the future holds.

*   *   *

In the meantime, the Canadian authorities have developed a range of innovative strategies to combat the posse menace. Indeed, as soon as the Canadians realised that the Jamaican community shunned the criminal parasites who fed off it as much as the rest of society, it began to legislate ahead. One of the systems it put in place was fast track deportation. 'The immigration department has taken a very stiff line of late,' explains Mascoll, 'deporting people on criminal charges a lot quicker.'

It can be argued that this merely displaces the problem. But the prevailing wisdom seems to be that so long as the deportees are not jeopardising the Canadian national interest, it is not their problem.

Canada's drive against possemania has also been greatly assisted by the significant number of law enforcement officers of Caribbean descent in its employ; men and women who can go undercover and liaise more easily with the black population. David McCloud is one of several Jamaican-born policemen in Metro Toronto's 5,200-strong detachment. He specialises in gathering intelligence on the Jamaican gangs. 'In fact,' he says, 'we are referred to as the I Posse by some of these posses.' The 'I' stands for intelligence.

The I Posse have led the field in perfecting anti-posse techniques. For example, his unit came up with something called the Trigger Lock Programme. A firearms interdictment programme, the success of the strategy depends wholly on intelligence gathering. 'Based on our own intelligence,' he explains, 'we target the locations where these armed criminals hang out,' and raid them.

'It's been very successful,' McCloud continues, 'to the point where it has been borrowed and adapted by other forces.' The resulting raids have led to the seizure of arms, the arrests of posses members, and a plethora of deportations. 'We felt it necessary to go that route,' he explains, 'because prior to that the courts saw them as isolated criminals, not related to ongoing criminal organisations . . . Now we're getting more stringent sentencing – and I hope that continues.'

The intelligence network has also borne fruit in other areas, too. The high level of Rude Boy mobility puts everyday policing at a disadvantage. To counteract this, the four forces that make up Greater Toronto's police contingent have begun to pool their intelligence. 'This is crucial,' stresses McCloud. 'When [posse members] move into an area they are unknown. They can operate for years because they're not known.' The shared intelligence strategy aims to put a stop to that.

There is no particular reason to believe that the communities over whom the posses inflict their brand of ruthless terror should be any less afraid of them than those in Kingston or New York. However, Toronto's Jamaican community appears to be willing to fight back. 'People are turning against the dealers,' explains Mascoll, 'they're saying: "we don't want you in our neighbourhoods." A lot of the clubs are coming under fire; gathering places, after hours clubs, and drinking dens.'

They have grown tired of the violence surrounding the drug trade; tired of the drug addiction and the crimes that go with feeding it; tired of seeing their young sons sent to prison or to the grave for involvement in it. A man with first-hand experience of black-on-black crime and violence – he was held up by a gun-toting thirteen-year-old in New York, and got shot in Jamaica – Mascoll has a great deal of sympathy for what the people of these besieged communities are trying to achieve.

Above all, perhaps, the recent community backlash has been accelerated by the price it is being made to pay for it. In short, the community action is a reflection of the hurt it feels as a result of the brutal attack on its reputation. For nowadays in Canada, it seems, black equals Jamaican equals criminal. And, as such, the feeling is that the Canadian authorities believe that they can act with impunity when dealing with black people.

In the summer of 1993, the Jamaican image was again buckling under the weight of yet another unseemly incident. This time, however, the furore was prompted by police action. The controversy involved the alleged illegal public strip-searching of a Jamaican woman for narcotics. On 10 August, thirty-nine-year-old Audrey Smith claims that she was made to stand naked before three Toronto police officers – two men and a woman – on the corner of Jameson Avenue and Queen Street West, a busy downtown area.

Tracey Peters, the female officer, was said to have removed Smith's jumpsuit, bra and panties, before telling her to bend over, to examine between her buttocks with a powerful torch. Peters' colleagues were alleged to have looked on. When the search had been completed – no drugs were found – Smith claims the officers left her to dress herself as motorists and passers-by looked on.

Smith, who has become something of a *cause célèbre* in Canada, filed a C$650,000 lawsuit against the three police officers in May 1994. The officers themselves were charged with disreputable conduct by the Toronto police. Meanwhile, a public inquiry was ordered into the incident in April 1994. After two failed attempts this finally got underway a year later. Smith, who was grilled by a police lawyer, did not testify on the first day because she was refused permission by Air Canada representatives in Kingston to fly to Toronto. Apparently, someone else had been using her name.

Smith's legal proceedings had yet to be heard when this book went to print. But whatever the outcome, it appears that, as long as the Rude Boys and their gangs remain entrenched in Canada, there is little hope in sight in the short term for an improvement in the Jamaican image.

CHAPTER TWELVE

The Rude Boys, Britain and The Yardie Myth

> 'I am very concerned about the way the whole Yardie myth is being promoted by the Metropolitan Police and the way the press is colluding with it.'
>
> Diane Abbott, MP, as quoted in the
> *Daily Telegraph*, 30 September 1988

Diane Abbott was right to be concerned. By the time the black Labour Member of Parliament for Hackney North and Stoke Newington was accusing the police and press of 'conspiring' to concoct a black criminal phenomenon, the so-called Yardies had been making headline news on a regular basis for the best part of a year.

What she probably did not know was that the police had actually picked up the rudie scent as early as the end of 1985. Vice squad officers in London had been deeply suspicious that various known Jamaican pimps were actually part of some kind of organised criminal structure. By 1986, their specific misgivings were buttressed by additional information obtained by the police's Criminal Intelligence Unit.

In 1987, Scotland Yard catalogued an assortment of anecdotes, suspicions and facts about these criminal interlopers in the form of a confidential report. That the Yard was taking rumours about these villains extremely seriously was evident from the list of prominent desks the 'secret' document landed on. Put together by the recently-formed National Drugs Intelligence Unit (NDIU), it was dispatched to the Home Secretary, the heads of Customs and Immigration, and every British police constabulary. Not only that but the Yard assigned an intelligence officer to gather information on the Yardie mobsters' criminal activities on a full-time basis.

The NDIU report assessed that, in the short-term, the Jamaican gangsters (who included Rankin' Dread) were out to control 'West Indian' crime. To that end, it was confirmed that the group had built up power bases in Birmingham, Bristol, Sheffield and Nottingham.

Of far greater concern, however, was the situation in London. With strongholds established all over the capital, including parts of Ms Abbott's north London constituency, it seemed the Brixton area in south east London was the only one holding out against the onslaught of the Jamaican gangsters. (In truth, Brixton was already heavily under the rudies' influence by this stage.)

Having taken the black communities (an event the NDIU saw as inevitable) the report's authors pondered the Jamaican bandits' next move. Would they be content with what they had? Or would they then 'turn their attention to the domination of all criminal activities, irrespective of who controls them?' The confidential briefing stated that the Yardie felons had already made contact with terrorist organisations including the IRA and Angry Brigade; big players in the illegal arms trade.

Summarising the political roots of the gangs in Jamaica, the paper also highlighted the fear that the profits of their drug dealing operations could be going back to support the political struggle in Jamaica. Vestigial remnants of Jamaica's mini-Cold War seemed to dominate the Yard's reasoning on this point. The feeling was that such proceeds were intended to help the People's National Party in the violent overthrow of Edward Seaga's Jamaica Labour Party government. The NDIU was not to know it, but those days were gone; the rudies they had identified were solely interested in accruing personal fortunes and enhancing their individual reputations.

If true, the sum of these shocking revelations raises a fundamental question. Why was the public not informed about the threat immediately? Why did the better part of two years elapse before news of them was 'leaked' to the press? The answer is symptomatic of the troubled politics of British race relations; a history which by this time had put the police, and the State as a whole, on the defensive.

According to a front page report in the *Daily Mail* in December 1987, 'senior officers' had taken a decision to deliberately suppress information about the rudies. The rationale being that (apart from gaping holes in their own knowledge about this nebulous criminal entity) the Yard 'did not want to risk offending black communities'. And as Diane Abbott's response suggests, the police were right to believe the black communities would not be best pleased to learn that some of their villainous counterparts belonged to an 'exclusively West Indian [crime] syndicate'. At best, Scotland Yard's reluctance to divulge information about the rudies any earlier seems to have been an exercise in race relations diplomacy.

Whatever the case, the disturbing contents of the NDIU report demanded that the police alert the public to the impending situation. That is, by 1987 the Rude Boys were thought to pose such a tangible threat to public safety and law and order that the police clearly believed

it would have been a gross dereliction of their duty to
suppress their knowledge of them any longer. To publish
might be to damn Britain's already fragile race relations
to an even more uncertain future; but that chance had to
be taken.

The results were predictable. There was a wave of
mass media hysteria, especially amongst the tabloid
press. 'I was investigating a murder in east London
at the time that that all hit,' recalls Commander John
Grieve, Scotland Yard's head of criminal intelligence,
'and every newspaper said it was a Yardie killing.' Not
so. 'Everybody was homegrown to Stoke Newington –
there wasn't a "Yardie" in sight,' says the commander.
'I don't think anybody had been to Jamaica.'

On the surface, this kind of misinformed reporting was
to be expected – after all these criminals were black.
But that fact – the aspect of the story which gave it
its 'newsworthiness' – was treated in such an appalling
manner that the essence of the revelations were lost in
a fog of damaging black misrepresentation; one that has
caused serious damage to the black image.

So what was so awful about the exposure of the
Yardies? What was so catastrophic to have such a lasting
effect on Britain's black communities? Quite simply, it
was the Yardie phenomenon. Or, more precisely, the way
it was defined.

In the rush to inform the masses about that danger in our
midst, it seems the *cognoscenti* neglected to establish the
facts. Indeed, the first thing to become apparent was that
neither the police nor the media had a clear understanding
of what or whom they were dealing with.

The media was certainly not alone in not knowing the
full picture; the fact was that the British authorities knew
very little about these characters. And nowhere was this
shortfall in understanding more pronounced – or more

destructive – than in the collective christening of the criminals involved as 'Yardies'.

The NDIU report referred to Yardies, and it is almost certain that the media took its lead from that quarter. However, it was not long before the police began to distance themselves from the term.

A good example was heard at the inquest in May 1989 into the death of the ironically named Rohan 'Yardie Ron' Barrington Barnet. When asked by the coroner to explain what a 'Yardie' was, a policeman was quoted in a glossy *Observer* article entitled 'HEIRS TO THE KRAYS' as responding, 'It's a Press word which has been going around.' He continued, 'It could be said that a Yardie is a young Jamaican male, invariably involved in drugs, violence, extortion and robbery.'

'We don't even like referring to them as Jamaican Organised Crime or anything like that,' says Commander Grieve of his unit's all-embracing philosophy. 'We don't see it like that. We see it as drug-related violence of which we've got a significant percentage come from the Caribbean. But we've got some from South America, some from China, some from Thailand.

'And we've got an awful lot come from Hackney and Battersea.' Moreover, he says, 'We don't use the word "Yardie" unless we can possibly help it.' And even then it differs wildly from the way it was defined in the coroner's court.

What is certain is that wherever the Yardie coinage came from, the term has stuck. Unfortunately, though, it has neither been correctly defined nor consistently applied during the period of its usage. And, amongst other things, this oversight has led to a damaging gulf in British understanding about who these Yardies really are, and what they are about.

The Yardies were initially described by David Gardner in the *Daily Mail* in December 1987 as 'a black

Mafia-style organisation'. (The police subsequently made repeated efforts to assure the media that the rudies were not, but to no avail.) However, in the same article the 'Yardies' became a 'cult' with violent 'followers'. The name itself, wrote Gardner, derived from backyard: 'West Indian patois for the Jamaican homeland.' He was close on the latter count, but still some way off the mark.

Terry Kirby, the *Independent*'s accomplished crime reporter, was far more circumspect. 'Its derivation varies according to whom you ask,' he pronounced in an article from January 1988. 'Yard is,' he wrote, 'either Jamaican slang for home, a Kingston slum, or just a colloquialism for a criminal who is black.' Good effort. But Kirby, too, was more wrong than right.

Within a few years, the activities of the so-called Yardies had qualified them for official inclusion in the English language. But with a welter of contradictory definitions to choose from compilers of dictionaries had a major task on their hands in deciding which version to cite. Invariably, they plumped for the wrong one.

Ironically, among the plethora of definitions provided when the Yardies were a new reporting phenomenon only one seems to have approached anything like the authentic meaning of the word. It was furnished by the *Guardian*'s Angella Johnson and Peter Murtagh in February 1988. It stated simply that 'In Britain, the term Yardie originated as a word to describe one's home in Jamaica: the yard around the house.' Thus, 'Yardie' is simply a word a Jamaican resident in Britain uses to describe Jamaica.

Commander Grieve confesses to disliking the word; he rightly thinks it causes confusion. Still, when he has to use it his definition is pretty similar. 'We would say "Yardie" has got very precise connotations for us here,' he explains, 'which is that it relates to somebody that's comparatively recently come from the Backyards.' Not a criminal; just a recent arrival from Jamaica.

This is critically important. For it follows that what a Yardie most definitely is not, is a Jamaican criminal. No more, in fact, than a Sri Lankan is, by definition, a Tamil Tiger guerrilla; or an Irish Catholic is a Republican terrorist; or an Islamic Iranian is a Muslim Fundamentalist; or a white Briton is a football hooligan with Fascist leanings.

The social cost of this wholesale misrepresentation cannot be underestimated. It has irreparably tarnished the otherwise faultless image of the vast majority of Jamaicans, their off-spring, and – by default – every black person in Britain. The term Yardie has effectively done a massive disservice to, even criminalised, the mass of 'nice and decent' black people who work, pay taxes, vote, and generally make positive daily contributions to the health and prosperity of the United Kingdom.

The problem with the term Yardie in its mainstream usage is that it makes no distinction between Britain's coterie of (black and) Jamaican criminals and the black crutches of its society: the home helpers and consultant doctors; Sunday school teachers and university professors; neighbourhood watchers and police inspectors.

It belies the popularity, excellence and dedication of some of Britain's biggest celebrities such as the Jamaican-born trio of athletes Linford Christie, Lennox Lewis and John Barnes.

It contradicts the major accomplishments of black achievers like Patricia Scotland, QC; Trade and General Worker's Union leader, Bill Morris; Labour Party front-bench MP, Paul Boateng; and the multitude of faceless, disciplined and hard-working black parents who raise their children to be honest and decent human beings. In short, the term Yardie tars one and all with the same criminal brush.

For all that, though, as in Jamaica, the United States and

Canada, the criminality of a hardcore of Jamaicans (and, in this instance, their young black British 'converts') has done nothing to enhance the reputation of the silent black majority, either. In fact, their activities have played into the media's hands.

In effect, the Yardie Rude Boys have almost single-handedly fuelled a major crime and drug crisis within the black communities, the like of which has never been known in Britain. Through their nihilistic activities and glamorous lifestyles, the rudies have consigned a large portion of young black Britons to a life of hard drugs, violence, gunplay and general criminality; accelerated the break-up of many (already fragile) black families; and, planted, nurtured and harvested the all-weather seeds of communal destruction, epidemic fear and chronic despair.

The inherent racism and racialism of British society aside, no one group has done more damage to the reputation and well-being of the nation's black communities in recent times than the Rude Boys. They alone, for example, introduced the plague of gun terror and black-on-black murder to the streets of black inner city neighbourhoods. Or, as a nineteen-year-old, black south London male succinctly states it: 'Racism isn't killing black people; black people are killing black people.'

It is a mark of the rudies' advance that that view is a far cry from the one that Britain's black communities have grown accustomed to hearing over the decades. The history of black (as in African-Caribbean) settlement in this country has largely been one of anti-black bigotry and violence; a scenario in which black people have been – and continue to be – blamed for many of the ills that have befallen British society.

Indeed, the demonisation of Britain's black population has become a staple feature of the diet of the Fourth Estate and, by extension, mainstream society. An appreciation of how this mentality has evolved is crucial to an understanding of how the Rude Boy menace is both perceived by society and tackled by law enforcement in Britain.

And, crucially, the corollary helps to explain why the rudies have been able to carve a comfortable niche in the black communities, relatively safe in the knowledge that their 'hosts' are unlikely to help the police with their proverbial enquiries. To that extent, it is the story of the chickens coming home to roost.

The story of the Rude Boys in Britain can be divided into two parts: the pre-crack era up to the late 1980s; and the crack era since then. This chapter will deal in the main with the first phase.

Black people have lived in Britain since the sixteenth century. In the mid-1500s it was fashionable for the aristocracy to 'import' Africans into their households. They came as domestic workers or simply living curios. Either way, the Africans involved were status symbols; expressions of the wealth of their owners.

The majority of the nation's black population arrived in Britain between the mid-1950s and mid-1960s – a handful of Caribbean ex-servicemen arrived on the SS *Empire Windrush* as early as 1948. They came in response to the British Government's call to the Commonwealth for assistance in rebuilding the country's war-shattered industrial infrastructure. Companies like London Transport even set up recruiting offices in the Caribbean, and Conservative Members of Parliament, like the Health Minister, Enoch Powell, played an instrumental role in attracting people to come and work in the National Health Service. The manifest intention was that the new workforce would take on the low-paid work that the indigenous population no longer found attractive.

Journeying to Britain was seen as an attractive proposition for a number of conflicting reasons. On the down side, there was the entrenched social deprivations and economic uncertainties of the immigrants' homelands; with the end of the Second World War a stack of meaningful employment opportunities had dried up. In terms of Jamaicans and other Caribbean dependants, though, there was also the fact that the nearby United States, a favoured location for migrant workers, had stopped non-American immigration to the mainland in 1952.

On the plus side, however, there was the historical colonial-imperial relationship between the Caribbean and the British Isles. Without exception, the people of the Caribbean viewed Britain as the 'Mother Country'; the country to which they owed allegiance. But there was also the irresistible (and progressive) British Government enticement of citizenship for those who took up offers of work, and their families.

This pioneer generation of Caribbean workers (the overwhelming majority of whom were Jamaicans) had been brought up to believe that the streets of the Mother Country were literally paved with gold; Britain was supposed to be the land of untold opportunities for personal betterment. For all that, though, the evidence is that most of the 130,000-odd Jamaicans who had taken up residence by 1958 had no intention of staying. They proposed to earn sufficient money to return home, and start a new life there with their families.

In the end, it was the harsh realities of the 'system' that militated against those ambitions and which resolved most to send for their families and take up permanent residence in Britain. In those days, new settlers tended to look for a home and a job in the areas where their friends and relations had settled, irrespective of their origins. An ubiquitous group, on arrival Jamaicans in London tended to head for Brixton and Camberwell. Meanwhile, a host of 'smallies' (Caribbean small islanders) wended their way to areas like Notting Hill and Shepherds Bush.

For the earliest settlers, life in Britain was incredibly tough. Apart from the country's cold climate, they were forced to contend with the coldness of its people; people whom they had romantically looked upon as white cousins. Home-seekers found that potential landlords were reluctant to accommodate 'Coloureds, Irish and Dogs'. Skilled workers found that their qualifications were redundant in the eyes of British employers; and the unskilled suffered from the 'last in, first out' syndrome when it came to redundancies. Meanwhile, those searching for recreational outlets found that pubs and clubs operated a 'colour bar'. Some mainstream churches even encouraged black worshippers to go elsewhere, or to occupy pews at the back of the church, out of harm's way. It was as if the terms 'race prejudice' and 'racial discrimination' had been coined especially for them.

Just as bad as their actual treatment was the general ignorance of their 'hosts'. Incredibly, when they had first arrived there were people in Britain who genuinely believed that black people had tails and lived in mud huts in the jungle. Countless white mouths flopped open in amazement when their owners discovered that not only could these people talk, but they could speak English.

This tragi-comic ignorance was only to be compounded in later years when the initial novelty of the black presence had worn off. Indeed, by the late-1950s the (black) immigrant population was deemed to be a central part, if not the root cause, of Britain's growing 'race problem'.

The 'gut' prejudice of mainstream society was often as contradictory as it was bizarre. On the one hand, black people were castigated as indolent, welfare 'spongers'. While on the other, they were rebuked by jealous whites when they scraped enough earnings together to buy small terraced houses and cars. Some said they were clannish and anti-social, but there was also widespread concern about miscegenation caused by the sight of black men 'courting' white women. The black population was in a no-win situation.

This lunacy reached the first of several explosive climaxes in the summer of 1958. On the night of 25 August, the rundown St Ann's Well Road area of Nottingham was plunged into ninety minutes of 'race rioting'. At the height of the disturbance 200 black and white people set about each other with an array of impromptu weapons. In the aftermath of the disturbance, there was no mistaking who was being held responsible for fomenting it. Some whites clamoured for a curfew to be placed on the 'coloured' population, although there was no provision in law for such an action.

Local Members of Parliament (one Labour, one Conservative) critically questioned the Government's 'open door' policy towards immigration. 'I have believed for some time that there ought to be something in the nature of a quota . . . on people coming into this country from oversea,' commented Tory MP for Nottingham Central, Lieutenant Colonel J.K. Cordeaux. 'I have been worried about this matter for some time because I feared that something serious like this might occur.'

While all this was going on the press moved in to find out what had actually occurred in Nottingham's 'jungle', as a *Daily News* reporter referred to the area. To a publication, and in line with the mood of the nation, the consensus was that the whole affair had been orchestrated in advance by a hardcore of Jamaican thugs. (Hardly surprising when one considers that not one of them took the time to elicit the reactions of the black communities.) 'I was talking to a Pakistani last night,' confided a young white miner who had been attacked in the affray, 'and he said he could have told me there was going to be trouble with the Jamaicans on Saturday . . . They were looking for trouble.'

'There was blood everywhere,' added a Mrs Byatt. 'The darkies were going for anyone in sight. These assaults were not the work of humans.' She called for a curfew to be imposed on the local 'coloured' population. 'Everyone in this area is of the same mind,' she said.

Ironically, the fears expressed by the mainstream were only confirmed by happenings 130 miles south in London on the same night. For there was a similar disturbance involving 200 people in the heart of Notting Hill in west London.

On 15 September 1958, nine youths aged between seventeen and twenty years were sentenced to four-year prison sentences for their part in the Notting Hill fracas – nine white youths. In fact, the trouble had been precipitated, as one of the men later confessed, by them going out on a 'nigger-hunting' expedition.

It seems that when the police and the media had had time to reflect on the causes of the disturbances in Nottingham and Notting Hill, they found that, in both cases, the unprovoked, racist attacks of a posse of Teddy Boy *agents provocateurs* were to blame. By that time, of course, the seeds of anti-black misrepresentation had already been sewn in the minds of the wider population.

These incidents set the tone for future perceptions of the British race problem. A decade later, the race question was again thrust to the top of Britain's social and political agendas.

One major difference with this installment was that it did not emanate from the streets; it came from Parliament. The driving force behind the controversy was Enoch John Powell, the Conservative Member of Parliament for Wolverhampton Southwest. An outspoken intellectual, some said visionary, he had been leading up to his infamous attack on Britain's immigration policy for some time.

In February 1967, Powell had written an article in

the *Daily Telegraph* denouncing the perils of a decade of seemingly unfettered Commonwealth immigration on the 'native' population. 'Those were the years,' he wrote, 'when a "For Sale" notice going up in a street struck fear and terror into all its inhabitants. I know: for I live within the proverbial stone's throw of streets which "went black".'

Mercifully, the immigration free-for-all that Powell dreaded had been slowed down; the vast majority of new arrivals being dependants of the pioneer generation. But that did not stop the prominent Member of Parliament from playing on white fears about the alien cultures within their midst. On 20 April 1968, the master orator delivered the most famous (and costly) speech of his long political career. On the eve of the second reading of the Race Relations Bill, the by now Opposition defence spokesman prophesied future racial strife.

'As I look ahead I am filled with foreboding,' he declared with one eye focused on the volatile racial politics of the United States. 'Like the Romans, I seem to see the River Tiber foaming with much blood.' The Government's liberal immigration policy was, as he eloquently put it, 'like watching a nation busily engaged in heaping up its own funeral pyre'; the manifest implication being that the Government was building the source of Britain's own destruction.

Dubbed Enoch Powell's 'rivers of blood' speech, it drew heavily on the fears of his 'ordinary', 'decent' constituents; like a defenceless, single white pensioner who had lost her husband and sons in the war. By now, the only remaining white home owner-occupier on her street (the rest having been purchased by 'Negroes') she wrote to Powell expressing her fears about going out. 'Windows are broken,' he said with regard to her complaints. 'She finds excreta pushed through her letter box. When she goes to the shops she is followed by children, charming, wide-grinning piccaninnies. They cannot speak English but one word they know. "Racialist," they chant.'

Rightly condemned as racist, the speech cost Powell his job in the Shadow Cabinet; Opposition leader Ted Heath sacked him the following day. But Powell's sentiments struck a chord with a large portion of the wider population. Four thousand dockers (and others) went on strike in support of him. They carried placards with legends like 'Back Britain not black Britain' emblazoned across them. In addition, the rebel Member of Parliament received approximately 45,000 letters of support; roughly two for every letter of disapproval. Overnight, Enoch Powell became the patron saint of middle Britain on the 'race problem'.

Throughout the 1970s and 1980s (and even in the 1950s and 1960s) Britain's black communities made vociferous complaints about the way their concerns were misreported, trivialised or completely ignored by the media. The belief was that the mass media was working in concert with the Establishment. Judging by the slant of many reports, the black community had ample justification for those suspicions.

Of equal concern during this period were black complaints about their allegedly racist and hostile treatment by the police. These really began to take off from the 1970s onwards; by which time the black population was approaching the two million mark or four per cent of the total population.

The consensus opinion was that the 'racist' police wilfully harrassed, brutalised and 'fitted-up' innocent black people, the youth especially. Invariably, this 'canteen culture' of police racism was seen as the first step along the road to criminalising the pioneer and first-generation British black populations.

A detailed study of these allegations belongs in another work. But suffice it to say the period under review threw up countless instances wherein police forces coughed up tens of thousands of pounds in compensation to wrongfully arrested black citizens, and numerous criminal convictions were quashed on appeal.

Throughout their recent history in Britain, black people have often been viewed as excitable, unpredictable and essentially criminal characters. The knee-jerk response to anything coming out of the black communities has been to equate it with crime. Take, for example, the reception the Rastafari received in the mid-1970s. A new phenomenon (but a black one) these dreadlocked devotees of Emperor Haile Selassie were invariably dismissed as members of some secret, drug-crazed, violent criminal cult. In turn, such stereotypes helped to cement the view that black people are predisposed to commit crimes of violence. As a consequence, Britain's black communities have come in for special types of reporting and policing.

In the 1970s, the 'in-thing' when it came to policing the black criminal 'menace' was the Special Patrol Group (SPG). Formed in 1965, the long since disbanded unit was the closest thing the police had at the time to a paramilitary force. An anti-crime detachment, the SPG was originally intended to act as a reserve force for divisional police squads. But, in a climate in which black was becoming synonymous with crime, it played a leading role in London rounding up black suspects in high crime areas such as Brixton, Peckham, Deptford, Dalston, Harlsden and Notting Hill. Because it fell under the Yard's umbrella as opposed to normal divisional command, the feeling was that its officers were frequently heavy-handed in their dealings with black people, because they would not have to answer for them.

The work of the SPG during the 1970s, and that of the Metropolitan police as a whole, was given a boost by the so-called 'sus' law. Repealed in 1981, the antiquated Vagrancy Act of 1824 (as it was formally known) effectively gave the police carte blanche to stop and search anyone deemed to be a 'suspected person'. The overwhelming evidence is that young black males were disproportionately overrepresented in the 'suspect' category.

By the early 1980s the youthful elements of Britain's urban black communities had reached breaking point. They were disillusioned by an educational system which they believed had failed them. They were disheartened by the paucity of meaningful employment opportunities society had to offer them. They were angry at the discriminatory treatment meted out to them by the police. They had had enough.

These endemic feelings of alienation and oppression culminated in a series of turbulent and destructive inner-city upheavals between 1980 and 1985; conflagrations which were usually preceded by controversial police actions. While these confrontations presented the nation with various opportunities to review its record on race relations, overall the disturbances themselves did little to contextualise the grievances the protesters complained of, and nothing at all to improve their public image.

On the contrary, the initial reaction of the press to the uprisings was to dismiss them as unprovoked outbursts of criminal lawlessness. So, when the St Paul's area of Bristol exploded on 2 April 1980, no mention was made of the long history of antagonistic police-black relationships, or of the police drugs raid on the Black and White café on the Grosvenor Road 'frontline' that ignited it. Similarly, when the young people of Brixton took to the streets in April 1981, the press ignored the equally strained relationship between local black people and the police, and Operation Swamp '81, the aggressive police anti-crime operation that sparked off the trouble.

In March 1983, the black communities were hit by another criminal bombshell. This one related to the involvement of young black people in violent street crime – muggings by another name. For the first time, Scotland Yard had released crime figures broken down into ethnic groups. And, although the statistics in question related to less than four per cent of all crimes committed, the media focused entirely on them. Having previously made mugging coterminous with black crime in the public imagination, the revelation that young blacks were twice as likely as young whites to commit them was like manna from Heaven to the media.

This notion that young black Britons posed a serious criminal danger was aptly reflected in other areas, too. One that caused considerable alarm was the phenomenal numbers being sent to stand trial on serious offences. Between 1984 and 1985, for example, Home Office statistics revealed that in the Metropolitian Police area more than half of seventeen- to twenty-year-old black males were prosecuted for indictable offences. (The corresponding figure for white youths was just under twenty per cent.)

To journalist Ambreen Hameed, this was not a sign that black youths were disproportionately more criminal than whites and Asians; it was proof that they were more likely to be singled out for scrutiny by the police. 'We are no longer talking about a serious miscarriage of justice,' she observed in *New Statesman and Society*, 'but of something more akin to mass persecution.'

The overwhelmingly negative treatment of the nation's black communities by the 'system' continued throughout the decade. A second round of major urban disturbances in the autumn of 1985 gave the press in particular another opportunity to reactivate its anti-black smear campaign. In quick succession, Handsworth in Birmingham, Toxteth in Liverpool, Brixton, and Tottenham in north London, erupted into violence.

The events in Tottenham were the most devastating

to the black cause. In October, the Broadwater Farm upheaval in Tottenham sent the media into an overdrive of vicious reporting after the brutal killing of Police Constable Keith Blakelock.

One might have thought that this procession of cataclysmic disturbances would have suggested to the Government, the police, the mass media, and the public at large that something was seriously amiss with British race relations; that there was at least a modicum of truth to the arguments that were being put forward to explain them. And, in fairness, there was a degree of soul-searching on the part of the attitudes and behaviour of many of the former. But not all. In 1986, for instance, with memories of the 1985 disturbances still fresh in the public's minds, Terry Dicks, then Conservative Member of Parliament for Hayes, clearly felt free enough to rubbish 'West Indians' for being 'bone idle'.

It is into this troubling context that the Rude Boys made their official début in the late 1980s. And, importantly, what success they have enjoyed in Britain has been shored up to a certain degree by the kinds of circumstances and events outlined above; things which began to unfold long before many of them were even born.

True, the Rude Boys have developed an awesome reputation for their ability to strike fear and terror into the lawful, and Britain is no exception. But putting that to one side for a while, there can be no doubt that the British criminal justice system's efforts to rid society of their menace have not been progressed by society's often woeful treatment of its black counterparts. Many a law-abiding black citizen would like nothing better than to see the back of these gangsters – people who are infecting their children and communities with drugs, violence and crime. But too often they are reluctant to help the 'system'; a structure that has caused, and continues to cause, them untold grief.

Alarmist exposés about the Rude Boys began to appear in the second half of the 1980s, but in reality they had been drifting into Britain since the late 1970s and early 1980s. In keeping with their peers who headed for the United States and Canada, the rudies came to Britain to escape the fall-out from the vicious events surrounding the 1980 General Election.

The press had been hauling immigrant Jamaicans over the coals since the 1950s and that tradition continued basically unchanged into the early 1980s. But, unbeknown to the press, some of the Jamaicans they singled out during this latter phase formed the advance party for the later influx of what they would call Yardies. Rankin' Dread, the scourge of Jamaican, American and Canadian law enforcement, was one. In truth, he had arrived in the late 1970s.

At least two statements about Jamaicans from the period seemed to give prior credence to Diane Abbott's later police-press 'conspiracy theory'. One flowed from the mouth of newly-appointed Metropolitan Police Commissioner, Sir Kenneth Newman. 'In the Jamaicans,' he boldly announced in 1982, 'you have people who are constitutionally disorderly . . . it's simply in their make-up. They are constitutionally disposed to be anti-authority.' Newman's neo-Darwinism was greeted with howls of derision by the black communities and anti-racist bodies; calls were made for his immediate resignation. By contrast, the press lapped it up.

And in a report by John Weeks in May 1982, the *Daily Telegraph* went so far as to draw parallels between the lawlessness of these unwelcome Jamaicans and that of their homeland.

The report drew the ire of H.S. Walker, the Jamaican High Commissioner to Britain. He was moved to rebuke a top-ranking police officer featured in the article for what he saw as a totally unjustifiable attack on his counterparts in Britain. '. . . it is rather sad,' he stated in a letter to the editor, 'that a police officer in a position of some responsibility, while claiming not to be racially biased, should make offensive and insulting remarks about people, the vast majority of whom are respectable and law-abiding . . .

'Jamaica welcomes, even invites, constructive criticism,' Walker concluded. 'However, we find unacceptable criticism based on misrepresentation of the character of our society and people whether in Jamaica or abroad.'

The top policeman, however, was not alone in noticing the growing influence of Jamaican criminals on the British mainland. Across London, for instance, young black people had also begun to notice a sea change in the mood of their communities.

Stubby was alerted to the change at the start of the 1980s. Born in Clarendon in Jamaica but raised for the better part of his thirty-two years in England, he observed a harder, no-nonsense edge about the manner of some of the faces that had begun to appear on the streets of south London. 'A different breed of people come inna the area,' he recalls. 'Pure dogheart [wicked] man.'

Paulette, another inhabitant of south London, picked up the same vibe. A self-confessed raver in her teenage years (she is now twenty-nine) she remembers the days when reggae dances were universally happy experiences. So, even if one person 'bunced' (inadvertently bumped into) someone else, the incident was likely to end in smiles and mutual apologies. That situation showed the first signs of change in the early 1980s, she says.

British-born of Jamaican parentage, Paulette's first encounter with the new wave of Jamaicans came in 1982 when she 'bunced' one at a dance in north London. 'I had a run-in with a posse of north London Yardie women;

I thought they were from north London,' she recalls. However, instead of the usual round of smiles and mutual apologies, Paulette and her friends ended up in a scuffle with the irate Jamaican women. 'It's safer nowadays to go to soul clubs,' she says.

It is impossible to know how many Rude Boys poured into Britain during this early period. The fact is that the rudies had by now perfected the technique of entering countries on false passports. It is certainly the case that Rankin' Dread used this method to circumnavigate immigration when he arrived in Britain in 1978.

These illegal aliens were joined by an indeterminate number of young Jamaican dependants who had been legally sent for by their parents. This trend picked up significantly towards the end of the decade. Speculation that the Thatcher government was about to end the absolute right of male Commonwealth immigrants to settle their wives and children in the United Kingdom led to a mad rush on the part of the former to be reunited with the latter. (In the event, the 1988 Immigration Act put an end to the right of Commonwealth dependants over the age of eighteen to join their families in Britain.) Most of the children involved had been left behind to be reared by relatives; few knew their parents well. More than a few were what Jamaicans themselves call 'renk and out of order', unruly.

Even so, it was the illegal category of Jamaican that drew most attention from the black communities. As soon as they had arrived the Rude Boys moved to traditional Jamaican strongholds; places like Brixton where they were sure to feel at home; where they could be absorbed into the law-abiding black mainstream.

An altogether different phenomenon from anything the average African-Caribbean adolescent had ever come across, the rudies caused quite a splash in their adopted communities. In fact, their aggressive dispositions and violent natures helped to give the bad boys status; they became something akin to visiting celebrities. It caused a big problem, says Stubby. Instead of 'running them [chasing them away], the youth bigged them up [flattered them]; they gave them respect.'

With the apparent blessing of the local black underworld, the Rude Boys spent the next few years consolidating their position. Slowly but surely the gangsters made their impression felt in crimes such as organised prostitution, loan-sharking, extortion and illegal gambling. Serious inroads were also made into street-level ganja dealing; one set of dealers giving way to another. The erstwhile small-scale trade in powder cocaine began to take off, too. The rudies found that they could make relatively easy money in Britain.

And it was during this period that a new crime became popular in the black communities: the drug rip-off. Seeing poorly protected drug houses as easy targets (this was years before crack made its British début) quick-witted Rude Boys started using guns to hold them up.

Of all the so-called Yardies to leave an indelible imprint on black crime in Britain, none left a bigger mark than Errol Codling. A man with a penchant for aliases (he had twenty, including Winston Brown and Robert Blackwood) he actually came to fame under the name of Rankin' Dread. In a mixed 'career', by the time he was finally deported to Jamaica in November 1988, Rankin' Dread had been the principle subject of a television documentary and enjoyed a Top Ten pop chart success.

Why Rankin' Dread opted to come to Britain is a mystery. What is clear, though, is that he left Jamaica because the Jamaican police wanted to speak to him in connection with, amongst other things, the shooting of two of their own. However, like all ambitious immigrants, once ensconced in Britain, he was determined to do well for himself.

When he first arrived in the country, Rankin' Dread was something of a fixture at the Four Aces Club in Dalston, east London. And it is there that he got his first big break. Owned by the legendary Sir Coxsone sound system operator Lloyd Coxsone, he made a name for himself as a 'toaster' (the 1970s label for a DJ) by comically extemporising over the system's output. A talented performer, in 1980 Rankin' Dread had a national one-hit-wonder with a number called 'Hey Fatty Boom Boom'; a humorous expression of his physical attraction to 'mampies', 'full-bodied' women. A few small-scale reggae hits followed, but his recording career was effectively over.

Rankin' Dread did not despair. A typical Rude Boy, he put himself about in the pursuit of other money-making concerns. To that end, his became a familiar face around black London: from Stoke Newington and Clapton north of the Thames to Brixton, Clapham and Peckham on the south side. His other interests also led him to faraway places like Nottingham and New York. A clue to those other enterprises comes from the fact that he was deported from the United States in 1983 after receiving a conviction for possession of ganja.

Additional clues surfaced after his return to Britain – again on a false passport. Rankin' Dread was known to be a 'close friend' of Yardie Ron Barnet, the man whose inquest was mentioned earlier. Yardie Ron was the victim of a frightening early morning shoot-out in Harlesden, west London in August 1988. The shooting began as he was about to enter a pre-Notting Hill Carnival blues dance. Somewhere in the region of ten rounds were discharged during the gun battle: Yardie Ron, a twenty-six-year-old, took two in the chest; at least one other knocked out the bedroom window of a nearby house. The only fatality among three shooting victims – he shot the other two – Yardie Ron was bundled into his BMW and rushed to

St Charles Hospital in Notting Hill, where he died soon after. A man the *Daily Star* called 'One of the top Yardies in Britain', Yardie Ron had been a successful drug dealer until his demise. Specialising in cocaine and ganja, his choice of motor gives some indication of how successful he had been.

The police attributed his killing to a feud, presumably over drugs. It is certainly the case that the shoot-out bore all the hallmarks of a Rude Boy vendetta. To begin with there were the highly public circumstances in which it took place; and the utter disregard shown towards potential witnesses. There was also the multiple use of high-powered weapons. Detectives later recovered spent shells from three high-calibre firearms: a .45, a .455, and the obligatory rudie 9mm.

Yet, even though the battle took place outside a crowded dance and woke up the neighbourhood, the police failed to come up with any witnesses. Local residents were understandably fearful about providing statements about people who were happy to settle their disputes using guns in the street. Meanwhile, revellers at the dance needed no reminding of the ghetto code: 'See and blind, hear and deaf.'

One, it has to be said, totally unsubstantiated rumour that spread like wildfire among the ghetto *cognoscenti* had it that Rankin' Dread was behind the 'hit' on Yardie Ron. That said, he was also thought to have been involved in the murder of a Nigerian drug dealer earlier in the year. In fact, Rankin' Dread has been linked to more than thirty murders in the United States, Canada, Britain and Jamaica, where, amongst others, he is alleged to have murdered four policemen. The reputation he has acquired for lethal violence might have been one of the reasons why Scotland Yard placed him on their Most Wanted list.

By the time Rankin' Dread was deported he had been dubbed The Godfather of British Yardie gangs by some of the tabloids. Curiously, his formal involvement in British gangs was never established (by them or anyone else to the best of our knowledge) but Rankin' Dread was known to be involved in a host of criminal activities ranging from prostitution to drug dealing and rip-offs. Before he was deported from Britain, he had also featured as the prime suspect in two rapes and had dabbled in armed robbery. Early in 1988, for example, Rankin' Dread allegedly single-handedly shot up and robbed a dance in a community centre in Nottingham; stripping the bar and its customers of their money and jewellery.

In May 1988, Rankin' Dread's criminality brought him to the nation's attention. He featured in an episode of *The Cook Report*, the Independent Television network's tabloid investigative series. An 'exposé' of the Yardies, Roger Cook (the programme's presenter) singled out Rankin' Dread as the master villain behind a burgeoning and dangerous Jamaican Mafia-like drug and crime organisation. But he failed to make the charges stick.

Cook intercepted him as he was walking down a busy London street with his young daughter in his arms. When the accusations were put to Rankin' Dread, he was as oblivious to them as Cook was to the presence of the young girl. Accused of involvement in drug dealing, murder, and organising Jamaican criminal gangs, the rudie did not even break his stride as he calmly denied the charges put to him. Rankin' Dread was the epitome of cool.

However, by the time *The Cook Report* was broadcast, Rankin' Dread's reign of terror had effectively come to an end. The Metropolitan Police caught up with him when they raided a shebeen in Clapton, east London in April 1988. One of several people arrested, he was charged with possession of ganja and cocaine with intent to supply. However, rather than undertaking the costly and time-consuming task of pursuing him through the courts, the authorities decided to deport him back to Jamaica on the grounds that he had entered the country illegally. Much to the relief of the British police and the communities he plagued, Rankin' Dread was eventually escorted back to the island on 11 November.

On his arrival in Kingston, Rankin' Dread was promptly arrested and charged with the double police shooting dating back to 1978. The Jamaican authorities then made, what in retrospect turned out to be, the major mistake of granting him bail. They were hit with the full force of that error on the day Rankin' Dread was scheduled to appear in court – he failed to show. A massive police hunt subsequently failed to locate him. And it was not until a year later that the rudie surfaced in Toronto. He had flown in to Canada on a British passport in the name of one Michael Dix.

After causing mayhem in Canada Rankin' Dread was once again deported to Jamaica. But like their Jamaican counterparts, the Canadian authorities also made the mistake of granting him bail – with similar results. He absconded. And it was while Rankin' Dread was once again on the run that he offered a chilling footnote to the people of Britain. When a *Sunday Mirror* investigation tracked him down in May 1990, he vowed to return to Britain. Or, as the rather confused report stated it: 'Former Rankin' Dread pop star and Rasta drugs baron Errol Codling . . . brazenly boasts he'll return to "clear his name".'

However prominent he might have been, Rankin' Dread was just one of a hardcore of original Rude Boys trying to make a killing out of crime in Britain around the early to late 1980s. By the second half of the 1980s, the threat the rudies posed was apparent by a string of violent crimes including murder.

Drug-related incidents were thought by the police to be behind the murders of at least six black men between

1986 and 1988; Yardie Ron was the fifth victim. Innocent Egbulefu, the small-time Nigerian drug peddler is widely credited as being the first fatality of Rude Boy violence in Britain. Egbulefu had allegedly made the mistake of passing off a mixture of culinary herbs and tea leaves as ganja and selling it to some rudies. Accordingly, on 1 March 1986, the five rudies he had 'scammed' made an unannounced visit to his high-rise flat in Islington, north London. Shortly after gaining access the aggrieved Jamaicans threw him out of a window. On impact, eight floors and ninety feet below, Egbulefu was still clutching the remote control unit for his television set.

Defenestration is not unknown to the rudies, but a more common means of killing is by the gun. Shortly before his execution, Michael St George Williams had been involved in a heated argument (supposedly over the spoils of a £100,000 jewellery heist) inside the Bronx Club in Stoke Newington. A Porsche-driving, market-stall holder, he was found dead behind the wheel of his luxury motor in May 1987. He had been blasted in the chest with a shotgun.

Two Jamaican men were convicted of his murder in January 1988. Leroy 'Fitz' Hughes, a reggae guitarist, was sentenced to life imprisonment. Meanwhile, the trigger-man, one-eyed Norman 'Bicycle' Campbell, a paranoid psychotic who had not long been released from Park Lane security hospital in Liverpool, was ordered to be detained at Her Majesty's pleasure in a maximum security hospital.

Killings of this sort were highly unusual in the annals of British crime. So, too, was some of the raw violence associated with Rude Boy criminals. Take, for example, the circumstances surrounding an armed post office raid in London in December 1988.

Having been tipped off about the planned robbery of an East Acton post office, the Metropolitan Police undertook a lengthy surveillance operation on the half-dozen gang members involved and when the robbers emerged after pulling off the job, six armed police officers were lying in wait.

In bygone times, when the gun-toting police challenged 'blaggers' in circumstances such as these, the latter would usually drop their guns, raise their hands in the air, and repeat the oft-cited legend, 'it's a fair cop'. Not so these rudies. They opened fire on the police. Three of the robbers and two male detectives were wounded in the ensuing shoot-out, none fatally. In all around thirty shots were exchanged, some of which came from the two Colt .45s and a 9mm Luger recovered by the police after the incident. 'All three had been fired and were cocked and ready to fire again,' a Scotland Yard spokesperson told the press.

By early 1988, the Rude Boys seemingly unlimited capacity to create havoc led to the formation of a dedicated police squad to focus on them. However, that the unit was set up at all owed a great deal to the behind-the-scenes intelligence-gathering work and agitation of a coterie of concerned Metropolitan Police officers. The mastermind behind the formation of that informal network was a young policeman named John Brennan.

A former professional footballer, Detective Sergeant Brennan has since risen to become one of the world's leading authority on the rudies. His police-related investigations into Rude Boy criminality have taken him to Jamaica and the United States, while his academic work has resulted in his gaining a Masters degree on the subject. He is, however, more than just the rudie oracle. DS Brennan's police work has turned him into something of a celebrity, even amongst the Jamaican gangsters. Easily distinguishable by his height, athletic build and shock of short, blond hair, rudies the world over have bestowed upon Brennan his own street tag: 'Blondie.'

It is all a far cry from Blondie's earliest experiences with the rudies in the mid-1980s, when he was a just another Police Constable based in Stoke Newington. Even then, his introduction to the Rude Boys was not really the product of face-to-face dealings with them – he had never even heard of a Yardie at that stage. Rather, Blondie's involvement in, and subsequent 'obsession' with, the rudie phenomenon came as a direct consequence of the intractable difficulties he and his colleagues were encountering in trying to solve what turned out to be rudie crimes. In short, they were getting no assistance from within the local black communities.

Blondie was highly perplexed by the black communities' omertà or code of silence. That black people were afraid to speak out was manifestly obvious. Yet the reasons for that fear were less clear. The situation might have been more understandable had Blondie and company been able to put their finger on a major-league villain who had put the word out for the community to keep quiet. But there was no evidence that such a character existed; these villains were simply unlike any he had ever come across.

Eventually, Blondie's concern led him to start phoning up police stations around London in an effort to find out if other Metropolitan officers were experiencing similar problems. He even placed an advert in a force newspaper. From the various responses, it turned out that the Jamaican criminal headache was not unique to Stoke Newington.

On discovering that he was not alone, Blondie organised a series of informal get-togethers with a handful of similarly troubled peers. Convened after work over a pint in a south London pub, the assembly pooled information on various Jamaican 'faces' whom they believed were the source of many a local policing problem. Officers in other parts of the metropolis spoke of similar problems involving gangsters who went by the same street names; villains like Tuffy, a rudie who will feature in the following chapter.

Of equal concern to the group, however, was the fact that a disturbing trend was emerging; one which they, as local officers, could not deal with effectively. In fact, they could offer each other nothing more than informal assistance and moral support. Moreover, if the problem was to be seriously addressed, moves had to be made by the Yard's top brass. The question, though, was, given the unsavoury political implications of focusing on exclusively black crime, would their bosses be prepared to stick their necks out?

Thanks largely to the agitation of senior officers like Detective Chief Superintendent Roy Ramm, the answer was 'yes'. In February 1988, Scotland Yard set up SO 1(8) or the Yardie Squad as it became known. Under the overall stewardship of Commander Roy Penrose, the squad's day-to-day business was co-ordinated by DCS Ramm. Its remit was to concentrate on gathering intelligence about, and carrying out surveillance on, the Jamaican gangs' activities in north-east and south-east London. Realising the transient nature of the rudies' operations, however, the squad was also charged with the responsibilty of liaising 'with relevant constabulary forces throughout the country and abroad'. The Yardie Squad was clearly a bold undertaking.

In announcing the 16-member detachment of both Yard and divisional officers, Deputy Assistant Commissioner Simon Crenshaw spoke of the unit's intention to 'operate against this cancerous growth'. 'The patient,' he added, 'is the black community' up and down the country. That this 'cancerous growth' of no more than a couple of dozen rudies had already made serious inroads into the black communities was evident from more than their geographical web of influence. It was also to be gleaned in the copycat effect that stemmed from their vicious *modus operandi*. That is, seeing the effectiveness of the ruthless Rude Boys' terror tactics, hundreds of indigenous black criminals had jumped on to the bandwagon; they now enhanced their reputations by calling themselves Yardies.

Codenamed Operation Lucy, the Yardie Squad assumed a novel approach to the matter in hand. It slowly evolved from being a purely intelligence-gathering unit to a semi-operational hit squad. Finding that the gangs were not structured along conventional lines (a Rude Boy could be a don, a street dealer and an enforcer on any given day or all at the same time) they realised a concerted attack on the leadership stratum was meaningless. To compensate, the rudie hunters decided to target anyone who fell into the general bracket of Jamaican criminal.

Squad members homed in on the gangsters' support systems; the 'baby mothers' who did cheque book fraud to raise money which might go towards financing the purchase of guns to carry out bank jobs, or drugs to sell on the street. The subtext to this operation was very much to stop the rudies from making any further inroads; to stop them before they grew too big.

Operation Lucy managed an impressive strike record. Through a combination of hi-tech surveillance techniques and the use of informants, the team managed to arrest several hundred suspects, a fair percentage of whom were subsequently deported as illegal aliens. It was also responsible for identifying a nationwide drug distribution set-up, and building up a database of some 200 suspected criminals.

One of the deportees to fall foul of the unit was Rankin' Dread. In fact, he was one of twenty suspects arrested in

the Yardie Squad's first showpiece offensive against the
rudies. The Jamaican 'Godfather' was ensnared at 5.38
a.m. on 14 April 1988 in a lightning raid on a shebeen
at 19a Clapton Way, Clapton, east London; a derelict
property owned by Hackney Council, and described by
a Yard spokesman as a 'focal point for . . . serious
and organised black crime, particularly trafficking in
cocaine'. The property had been under surveillance for
several weeks, and the raid well-rehearsed in advance.

The thirty-two-strong raiding party, which included
local police, came prepared for trouble. Indeed, the
blitzkrieg was spearheaded by members of the Yard's
PT18, the recently-formed, unarmed equivalent of PT17,
the tactical firearms squad. Kitted out in black body
armour, shin guards and helmets, and carrying shields,
the anti-riot 'gladiators' disorientated the sixty or seventy
occupants with 'dragon lights', ultra bright torches, and
instructed them to lay face down on the ground.

Apart from the arrests made, the police recovered several weapons including a machete, and what DCS Ramm
described as 'the largest lock knife I have ever seen'.
Small quantities of ganja and cocaine were also seized.
No guns or crack were discovered. Nevertheless, Ramm
was happy with the operation. However, the Yardie
Squad chief qualified his enthusiasm by stating that
the police had not yet 'conquered the Yardie problem'.
Little did he know then that Operation Lucy's days were
numbered.

In fact, in 1989, much to the annoyance of the operation's membership, the Yardie Squad was disbanded.
After eighteen months, its specialist functions were
deemed to be inappropriate and obsolete. To what
extent, if any, this view was shaped by the politically
sensitive nature of the operation is unclear. But it was
certainly the case that attention moved away from the
specifics of the rudies to another new menace: crack

cocaine. And, with that uppermost in their minds, the mandarins at Scotland Yard replaced Operation Lucy with the grandly named Crack Intelligence Co-ordinating Unit (CICU).

CHAPTER THIRTEEN

Impressions on a Criminal Landscape

'In May last year, as President Bush launched a
£750million offensive against violent crime tied to
drug abuse, Britain was warned about the crime
wave's most chilling aspect. Crack . . . which had
cut a swathe of misery through America . . . was
on its way here . . . Suddenly, at bushfire speed, the
word crack entered the British vocabulary . . . [But]
Crack . . . has not caught on in Britain. There is a
very important lesson to be learned in all this: that the
wider conclusion that anything America suffers today
Britain must endure tomorrow just doesn't add up.'

Mihir Bose, *Daily Mail*, 13 August 1990

In his article 'Nightmare that never happened', Mihir
Bose berated leading government politicians who, after
heeding warnings from America, had clambered aboard
what he called the country's 'great crack bandwagon'.
Bose's message was clear: no matter how honourable
their intentions had been, the nation's political leaders
had over-reacted.

'What everyone seemed to miss,' he contended, 'was
the crucial difference in lifestyles and values in both
countries'; Britain was simply not like the United States.

Moreover, 'The notion that we are merely an island offshoot of America is damaging,' he added, not least to race relations.

Implicitly borrowing from British society's long-standing 'island fortress' mentality, Bose produced 'evidence' to support his thesis that Britain was, well, unique. Yes 'we' had problems, but he concluded, 'it is time we put more energy into solving the problems that really exist in our own backyard.'

However, within months of Bose's strident dismissal of the high-level fuss whipped up over the long predicted, but apparently non-materialising, violent crack explosion, compelling evidence was surfacing to dismiss his view that it had been a well-meaning hoax. For instance, the *Voice*, Britain's biggest-selling black newspaper, produced a welter of drugs workers, black community leaders and police officers, all of whom strongly asserted that crack was making serious inroads into the black communities.

'Things are deteriorating rapidly,' observed Viv Reid, the black co-ordinator of an East End anti-drugs project. 'Two years ago police warned of crack taking a hold in Britain, as in America.' Now, two years on, he and fellow drugs counsellors were 'starting to see the effects'.

Generally speaking, those 'effects' were not simply confined to increasing numbers of narcotics abusers presenting themselves at establishment's like Reid's for help with overcoming their drug problems. They were also making an impact on the rising incidence of crime and violence. 'We are seeing an escalation of drug-related crimes and wanton violence,' said Lee Jasper, a resident of Brixton and chair of the National Black Caucus, 'as well as wars between different posses out to control the market.'

For all their concern, Reid and Jasper's observations

merely highlighted a situation that had been acknowledged in the black communitiy for some considerable
time. Indeed, as much as a year earlier the *Voice* had
produced disturbing evidence of the progress cocaine and
crack had been making into the black heartlands of the
capital.

Since then the *Voice* had 'uncovered even more worrying cases,' it said. Cases like that of an eight-year-old
boy who was both addicted to, and dealing in, cocaine. Or
the gang of young people who carried out a daily string
of street robberies to finance £3,000-a-time drug binges.

Revelations about the onslaught of crack did not
improve with time. In April 1992, for example, an
Association of Chief Police Officers (ACPO) drug conference was warned of the narcotic's easy availability. 'If
you want crack,' said Detective Inspector Frank Sole, the
head of Scotland Yard's Crack Intelligence Co-ordinating
Unit, 'you can go to Brixton and many other places where
you can buy it, morning, noon and night, every day of
the year'.

Worse still, he told the ACPO delegates of children as
young as twelve dealing crack on the streets of London;
of a tide of increasing gun seizures, violence and murder
surrounding the trade; of the manifest popularity of the
drug amongst women reflected in the number of arrests
and sightings entering crack-houses; and, of witnesses
being too frightened to give evidence against those deeply
involved in the mayhem it spawned.

By November 1992, the police were telling the British
public that crack had spread out from the inner cities into
the suburbs. Not only was it available to, and being abused
by, middle-class (white) people, but finding money to buy
it was generating a serious crime wave in suburbia.

And while the Home Office did its best to defuse fears
that crack use had reached epidemic proportions, the
findings of a confidential report it commissioned painted

a different picture. A seven-city survey, taking in places as diverse as London, Newcastle, Bristol and Peterborough, found that more and more people were experimenting with crack, and that the narcotic was becoming easier to get hold of.

Even normally reserved members of the broadsheet press were beginning to panic. 'The police and Government strategy on drugs is in disarray,' warned David Rose and Barry Hugill in the *Observer*, 'as evidence grows that the use of crack cocaine has become a national epidemic, responsible for a wave of violent crime.'

By July 1994, the situation was showing signs of becoming critical; it seemed more than ever that crack was winning the war against sanity. The *Sunday Times* ran a front page piece which, amongst other things, estimated that three-quarters of Liverpool's prostitutes used crack. Worse still, the report spoke of a terrible new phenomenon that had been turning up around the country during the previous twelve months. 'More than 160 "crack babies" have been born addicted to purified cocaine over the last year as the street drug sweeps Britain's inner cities,' it claimed.

And, if further evidence of the drugs' widespread popularity were called for, a fitting example came in November of the same year. That crack had become the people's drug was proven by the humiliation of a forty-year-old, middle-class white actress. Kate Gielgud-Killick, the great-niece of legendary British actor, Sir John Gielgud, was caught *in flagrante delicto* by undercover police as she bought crack from a street dealer on All Saint's Road, Notting Hill's open-air drug bazaar.

Gielgud-Killick, allegedly scarred for life by a dealer who supplied the Marquess of Blandford, was later arrested. In April 1995, she testified against the dealer. In court it transpired that only days before their transaction was video-taped, the dealer had been released on £10,000 magistrate's bail, against the police's wishes, after being arrested with £1,300 worth of crack.

Crack's rising popularity is confirmed by Detective Sergeant Keiran O'Connor. 'I can't say that it's not growing,' admits the specialist at SO11, the Metropolitan Police's crack intelligence-gathering unit. 'Basically, what I've been told,' he explains with regard to statistics from drug dependency agencies is that 'you'll find that crack addicts are growing.'

In a round about way, Mihir Bose's article had been inspired by an apocalyptic warning given three years previously of an impending British crack plague. That prediction had been made by Robert Stutman, chief of the Drug Enforcement Agency's New York division.

A veteran 'commander' in America's perennial War on Drugs, Stutman had visited Britain to address the 1989 ACPO conference. His confidential, frank and self-effacing speech created something of a stir, to put it mildly. Almost shocking in its bluntness and honesty, Bob Stutman's address was certainly not suitable for the faint-hearted. Indeed, because of its prophetic, not to mention mobilising, nature, it deserves to be quoted at length.

Drawing heavily upon America's disastrous experience of crack cocaine, Stutman admitted he and his anti-drug colleagues had 'screwed up'; he implored his British counterparts to learn from their mistakes; to guard against the 'it can't happen here' mentality.

In nothing short of a rabble-rousing delivery, Stutman outlined the universal popularity and far-reaching spread of the narcotic in the United States. 'Crack is an equal opportunity drug,' he declared. 'It affects blacks, whites, Hispanics. It affects rich, poor and in between; it has left the ghetto and moved into suburban America. It has taken over and changed our society.'

The essence of that 'change' could be gleaned from

the profile of the crack user, any user. 'You don't need a person with a predisposition towards violence,' he maintained. 'It gives you a feeling of omnipotence, I am the strongest son-of-a-bitch in the world, nobody can touch me; and at the same time it gives you a sense of paranoia, of why are you picking on me.'

The DEA man went on to say that of all the people who had tried crack on three occasions, three in every four had become addicted to it. Naturally, the American authorities had tackled this menace head on. But, asked Stutman, 'Did all the arrests and the seizures make any difference? The answer is, absolutely not.' The cost of law enforcements' inability to cancel out the crack menace? America now had a situation reminiscent of the daily body counts in Vietnam; only now cities like his were counting dead American police officers instead of soldiers.

Yes, but what did any of this have to do with Britain? With American cities now saturated with crack, said Stutman, its traffickers were being forced to move on to new pastures. In short, Britain was increasingly being seen as a lush, ungrazed field. It was only a matter of time before the country would be swamped with crack cocaine.

And with that in mind, Stutman made a startling prediction. 'If you don't attack this potential problem, and it's more than potential in Western Europe,' he said, 'I will guarantee you that three years from today you will look back on the good old days of 1989 as pleasant.'

Stutman, the doom-laden soothsayer, certainly struck a chord with the government, police and media; hence, the 'you all got it wrong, nah, nah, nah nah, nah' tone of Mihir Bose's article. But did they? The truth is that Stutman's sole mistake was to forecast a universal crack plague for 1992.

Crack had certainly made a catastrophic entry into many black and working-class communities by then.

And it had become a staple feature of many middle-class lives, too; many a blue chip City firm, for example, had had to secretly employ private drug counsellors to wean their young prodigies off the narcotic. But, by 1992, no doubt partly because of the preventative action taken after Stutman gave his warning, crack had not caused anything like the human devastation in Britain that it had in the United States.

That was certainly the Metropolitan police's view as of April 1995. 'Stutman came over, y'know, like Mr Doomsday – the end of the world's coming. No way have we got to the proportions it has in America, no way!' explains DS O'Connor.

Maybe not. But O'Connor is candid about the implications the drug's growing popularity is having on the Metropolitan Police's efforts to stamp it out. The veteran drugs cop is currently one of ten officers who deal with SO11's 'intelligence of drugs and violence'. However, he predicts, the unit's numbers 'will probably increase by the end of the year. Obviously the problem's expanded. The intelligence is expanding. So we need more people to deal with that.'

It is, of course, easy to be glib in retrospect but the fact remains that even before Mihir Bose wrote his article a stream of evidence had surfaced starkly indicating what lay in store for Britain.

One major indicator was the rising quantity of cocaine seizures by Customs officers. The amount confiscated had fallen between 1987 (363 kilos) and 1988 (280 kilos), but the real picture was itself shrouded by another sign, a massive single seizure of 208 kilos in 1987. Discounting that, the trafficking trend would have shown an eighty per cent increase through the year. 1988 was also the second consecutive year that cocaine hauls had outstripped heroin.

A few months later, fears about the imminent arrival of crack were being expressed by Home Office officials and government ministers. In May 1989, Graham Angel, head of the Home Office's criminal policy department, told a Common's Select Committee that, while it had not made the predicted inroads into Britain, 'We are right to signal an anxiety about crack, as our contacts in the United States have shown.' Customs had already seized 250 kilos of cocaine, close to the total for the previous year, by this time.

The following month, in anticipation of the inevitable crack onslaught, government ministers signalled their intention to head it off at the pass, so to speak. (In reality, crack, or rock as users were calling it, was already ensconced in a number of depressed urban communities.) Tim Eggar, a Foreign Office minister, called the narcotic 'by far the greatest threat that faces the UK. It is worse in its implications than the threat posed by any known disease,' he added.

By the autumn, crack had officially turned up outside London in cities as far afield as Wolverhampton in the West Midlands, Liverpool and Cardiff. Meanwhile, Avon and Somerset police had made their first crack find at the Glastonbury festival.

On the police front, the Yard created the Crack Intelligence Co-ordinating Unit, which controversially superseded the wholly anti-Rude Boy-orientated Operation Lucy team. A joint Police-Customs venture, the intelligence-gathering outfit was sooned joined by immigration officials.

But undoubtedly the most chilling indication that crack had made its début with a vengeance was provided by a man nicknamed 'Rambo'. Real name Brian Tomlinson, he was jailed for seventeen years in June 1989 (a year before Bose's piece) for a series of burglaries and brutal attacks on women in north London.

A self-confessed 'crackhead', Rambo preyed on wealthy (white) women. In one frightening attack, he threatened to cut off a victim's finger unless she handed over her wedding ring. In another, he sat on a woman's stomach, and threatened to kill her if she refused to hand over £20,000 worth of cash and jewellery. A company director's wife, she was eight months pregnant when he attacked her; the ruthless assault caused the victim to go into labour.

A former altar boy, Rambo had a long record of violent crime – he even raped a woman who had helped to feed his crack habit. In sentencing him for various offences (including firearms and, unusually, possession of opium) trial judge James Curtis described the Jamaican as a 'slave to crack'. He further noted that 'under the influence of cocaine he would behave like the devil himself'. But the most revealing comment about the prevailing situation came from the man the *Daily Express* had dubbed the 'drug-crazed black Mafia "Yardie"' himself. When he was arrested, Rambo allegedly admitted to police: 'I eat and sleep cocaine – it has become a way of life. My mind is controlled by the Yardies who send me cocaine. They own me.'

Today, local newspapers are filled with the crimes and violent crimes of those who have succumbed to a trade that has become a virtual Rude Boy monopoly in the black communities. Like vampires, crack and the violence it spawns are sucking the lifeblood out of legions of people from all walks of life; it does not recognise age, gender, race or socio-economic status. Its trade and abuse are helping to fuel an urban, suburban and rural crime wave. In fact, crack has proved to be so dangerous that the very mention of it sends conservative British police chiefs rushing to soap-boxes to call for the routine issue of firearms to better protect their charges.

As accomplished a journalist as he undoubtedly is,

Mr Bose would do well to think twice about being so dismissive of the crack threat today.

It is somewhere between two and three o'clock in the morning. In the small kitchen of a top floor flat in a terraced house near Brockwell Park, just down the road from Brixton, two young black men wax lyrical about the condition of their brothers and sisters. Passing a professional microphone (plugged into a massive, twin cassette ghettoblaster) between them, the two would-be DJs extemporise their 'reality' and 'culture' lyrics over an hypnotic, digital reggae rhythm. As one cassette tape supplies the backing, the other simultaneously lays it down with their vocals. They DJ strictly for fun; but they are polished and articulate, nonetheless. If nothing else, they have a lot to say. But then again the subject they have chosen offers a lot to talk about.

The kitchen 'venue' shows the tell-tale signs of a long vigil at the 'mic' during this boys' night-in. Under the stark glow of a bare, heavy-duty light bulb, a half dozen empty, dented Special Brew cans stand to attention at various 'posts' on the chipped, formica-topped kitchen table. They could be guarding the large metal ashtray – misappropriated from a nearby pub – itself almost hidden beneath a mountain of ash, cigarette ends and unburned paper, cigarette box cardboard, screwed up slivers of Rizla, and spliff butts. A solitary, half-smoked spliff rests precariously atop the heap, a pathetic trail of greyish blue smoke indicating it has all but given up its struggle for air.

During a review of their material, Stubby, the thirty-year-old host, and his guest, 'Little Joe,' expand on the general subject matter. A powerfully-built but heavyset, dark-complexioned emigré Jamaican, to look at him Stubby fits the bill perfectly as the Yardman's Yardman; he is the stuff white media-induced nightmares are made of. From his low-cut, 'flat-top' hair-style with obligatory patterns sculpted into the back and sides, passing his blood-red Marina string vest, down to his 'regulation' baggy 'shot-up' jeans cuffed at the bottom to show off his beige, desert boot-style suede boots. Stubby would not warrant a second glance in Rema, Tivoli Gardens or Jones Town.

Still, Stubby's appearance belies a pronounced concern about the change that has descended on his own backyard. The stranglehold crack has on many of his peers is a major worry. 'Poor man ain't got money,' he observes, 'but poor man will find money to buy crack.' Indeed, as he rightly points out, crackheads will rob, steal, whore or 'sell dem batty' to get it; anything.

A seasoned 'street man', the tentacles of crack have even reached into his life – and he is not a user. Stubby pines the friendships he has lost to the narcotic and its related gangsterism. 'It's a drug that keeps its own company,' he says in words that contradict his marginal British education. 'If you no [don't] smoke it, they don't move with you anymore, or you with them.' But worse, 'It's got to the point where there is paranoia on the streets, because no one knows who's using it.'

Stubby even admits to knowing or having known black 'baby mothers' who have turned themselves into crackwhores or otherwise gone out on the beat to secure money to smoke crack. He talks of a male user who introduced his partner to it, got her hooked, and sent her out on the streets to raise money to finance both their addictions. And of an old friend who, in a fit of pique, punched his mother in the eye because she turned down his demands for cash to buy crack. The memory fills him with a sorrow he cannot disguise.

'The majority of violence is over that,' says Little Joe. He should know; he committed enough while hostage to its unsavoury effects. 'I even robbed friends: begged a one pound or stabbed them,' he admits. 'It's funny now,' he grins, 'but it's an evil thing. You've got to feel it to know it!'

Those days are indeed a thing of the past for Little Joe. A glowing symbol of the ability to beat rock addiction, he is currently wrapped up in the formative stages of achieving his ambition of becoming a lawyer. 'I used to pipe it hard [smoke a lot of crack], and I was aggressive,' he admits. 'I used to pipe it in darkness – no TV, no music. On the street you're para [paranoid] – who's he looking at; you're ready to do him. Now, I don't worry.'

Little Joe is twenty-one. A rural Jamaican by birth, he has lived in London for less than a decade. But during that relatively short space of time he has been to hell and back. Immune to the effects of racism at 'home', he went through a painful period of adjusting to it in Britain; one which a caring family environment in a comfortable home could never fully compensate for. Extremely intelligent and articulate, he nonetheless took little away from his experience of secondary education.

Inevitably, Little Joe fell into the wrong crowd. Petty crime, drug abuse and two short terms inside young offender institutions followed. And, until his miraculous conversion, he admits he was destined to end up as just another young black recidivist 'crim'.

Because of his 'near death' experiences with crack, Little Joe is prone to preach with all the zeal of a born-again Christian. Naturally, it frightens him to think that there are legions of young black British people out there still paying homage to rock cocaine. According to his analysis, the blame for this has to be shared between the 'system', the 'devotees' and their communities.

But the bottom line, the principal reason so many of his peers are involved in crack, whether as traders or customers, he says, is opportunity – or lack thereof. 'You put fifteen rats in a cage and heat it,' he explains, 'and they'll step on each other to get out – by any means necessary. People want to be someone.' And crack has the power to make them feel like someone.

Little Joe has an unlikely soulmate in Bob Lawrence, the Chief Constable of South Wales police. In September 1989, Lawrence prophetically asked an international conference: 'How do you deter young people who are underqualified, who have underachieved in other areas, from what is to them a God-sent opportunity?' The crack dealers would destroy individuals and communities, he warned, 'But at the end of the day, all they will see is a golden opportunity to make lots of money.' And so it has been.

It is impossible to quantify the numbers of black people actively involved with crack; but the vast majority of black people in British prisons languish there because of convictions for drug-related offences. This awful state of affairs begs the question of how, when people like Robert Stutman went to great personal lengths to spell out the dangers that lay on the horizon, did it come to this?

The short answer is that the Rude Boys masterminded and orchestrated the whole sordid affair. They simply tailored the *modus operandi*, which had served them so well internationally, to meet the specifics of the British environment.

As always, the rudie drug traffickers entered Britain on bogus passports. Even when they were caught, and subsequently expelled as illegal aliens, established posse members returned time and again with different identities and passports. So, Jamaican Stephen Fray was deported in February 1992 after being released from a four-year sentence for crack dealing. He was back by April, and deported again in September.

Still, Fray had a lot of catching up to do if he hoped to match the records of some of his peers. For example,

Neville 'Scorcher' Grant, an Original Rude Boy and long-time illegal 'resident' in Britain, was deported three times in the 1980s alone. Meanwhile, by 1993 other rudies have been known to have been expelled from Britain nine times.

With a ready supply of dirt-cheap, stolen British passports on the market in Kingston, it seems there really is no stopping those rudies who choose to do business in Britain. This trend is especially worrying as Britain, and London in particular, has been earmarked as a lucrative arena in which to trade crack.

Matters are not helped by a loophole in immigration law which remains an open invitation for illegal aliens to enter the country. The rule provides for people refused entry into Britain to secure temporary admission, with the proviso that they stay at a notified address, and keep in regular contact with the police. But where the Shower, Spanglers, Gulleymen, Jungle, Spanish Town and other rudie posse members who enter the country are concerned; they simply go to ground.

Ironically, by the late 1980s the immigration authorities had wised up to the syndrome of Jamaican criminals breaching British frontiers. Indeed, in what appears to have been a totally unauthorised counter-offensive, low-ranking immigration officials developed Operation Yardies, an attempt to keep the rudie criminals out. If it worked it only had marginal success. For by early 1991, a confidential Home Office immigration department study complained that a dozen Shower Posse members were penetrating border controls with the utmost of ease.

Two years later, the National Criminal Intelligence Service (NCIS) was warning of the possibility of an influx of Rude Boys. Concern stemmed from Jamaican Prime Minister P.J. Patterson's post-1993 election victory promise to get tough on lawless gang members in Jamaica; a promise which opened up the possibility that such criminals would subsequently congregate in countries like Britain. Commenting on the overall problem a few months earlier, a tabloid newspaper claimed that previously deported rudies were even ringing up police officers to taunt them with news of their return.

'We are aware that there are people coming over here,' says DS O'Connor, 'but actually to monitor that, it would be impossible, basically.' These people fall into basic two categories, he explains: visa overstayers; and felons who travel on bogus passports.

Many of both are caught and returned, but keeping them out is another matter. 'The turnaround I've been told is about thirty-six hours,' O'Connor explains. 'You can actually be deported, go back to whatever country, and then get back here within thirty-six hours under a new identity.'

The easing of European border restrictions has only made this easier, no matter what the ethnicity of the illegal entrants; apparently Turkish criminals abuse this freedom to make 'business' trips to countries like France, Germany and Holland. However, says O'Connor, 'If you're talking about Jamaicans, you're talking about people that will fly from Jamaica to Britain to America to Canada in the same way that I would catch a train to south London, north London – it's as easy as that.'

Naturally, once they had breached Britain's defences, the rudies gravitated towards the populous black communities. Typically, they made a number of women friends all over the place; some were, or were to become, 'baby mothers'. With an array of domestic bases to turn to, and a bewildering assortment of aliases to choose from, at any given time, the Rude Boys proved a handful for law enforcement – when the latter were aware of the former's presence.

Once ensconsed in the black communities of Britain's inner cities, the Rude Boys joined forces with like-minded

Jamaicans to peddle hard drugs. A small group would come together, commit enough crimes (armed robbery was a favourite) to raise the money it needed to buy a 'ki' or two of cocaine, buy it, 'bake' it up into crack, sell it, and watch the profits flood in. Then, as soon as the last rock had been sold, the gangsters would go their separate ways.

O'Connor expands on the present situation. 'Jamaicans coming over here don't come over in gangs, as such. You have your posses – I believe they're called – over in Jamaica . . . whether it's a political posse or they're just posses going under the mantle of a political group.

'Now from there, they may come over as a posse and work about here, and then head back again, or whatever, just make their money. But you never see them in great gangs over here, the actual Jamaicans themselves.'

To sell the crack the gangs adapted existing rudie ganja distribution networks to traffic in cocaine and crack, a trend first detected by the Yardie Squad. Between 1987 and 1989 their grim determination to push the cocaine cousins led to a sharp fall in the narcotics' market prices. A gram of cocaine became obtainable at a mere £40; the select drug's 'champagne' days were over. Even so, as the 1980s came to a close, cocaine was wholesaling at around £20,000–£24,000 a kilo in London, up to four times the asking price in New York. Even before it was converted into crack, which initially changed hands for anywhere up to £40 for a rock weighing about a fifth of a gram, there were profits to be made a plenty.

'It's a commodity isn't it, really?' says Sergeant O'Connor. 'Crack actually is very, very good if you wanna make money. I mean, from very little drugs you can make vast amounts of money. And blacks, whites, whoever wants to sell it – and they're selling it – it's just to make money.'

What the Rude Boys needed to reel in those profits,

though, was a solid infrastructure to operate in. No problem. By the late 1980s, violent rudies were targeting and invading residences in deprived council estates and crumbling tower blocks. The poor and vulnerable were exploited, enticed or intimidated into transforming their homes into fortified crack-houses. Failing that, unoccupied residences were squatted. Either way, the rudies tried to keep one step ahead of law enforcement by constantly alternating their crack bases.

Not only did this public housing ploy furnish them with a ready supply of outlets and 'customers', but, with policing of these areas concentrated on containment measures, it provided them with relatively secure indoor market-places.

At the same time, on the 'frontlines' of the black communities, hash and ganja (the traditional black narcotics of choice) began to fall into conspicuously short supply. Loosely speaking, there had been an element of fierce competition between the old vanguard of ganja dealers with their average weeds and the new with their top-quality varieties, for some years. But now many of the new-style dealers began to shun the 'herb' altogether. A new breed of dealer had emerged; one which could not care less about the customary black intolerance towards hard 'white people's' drugs. With their sights set firmly on making 'sensible' money, they moved on to the streets with rock and powder cocaine. Pretty soon, heroin was being offered for sale as an antidote to the helter-skelter crash following cocaine abuse.

Acquiring drugs was easy enough. With valuable experience of the drug business in Jamaica and the United States, the rudies came with filofaxes full of drug contacts; setting up a buy was never more than a phone call or two away. In all honesty, the Jamaican drug gangsters could quite easily have bought their supplies from the well-established, big white British

crime families – still the real power players behind
British organised crime.

But this latter scenario would have involved the use
of expensive middlemen; a reduction in profits. Besides
which, an abiding aspect of the Rude Boy *modus
operandi* is the shipment of piecemeal quantities of
cocaine. Anyway, attracting 'mules' to ferry a kilo or
two of cocaine for them was never going to be a major
headache to organise. Few could resist the offer of an
all-expenses-paid 'holiday' to Jamaica or the United
States, and a £1,000 or so on top. Topping the list
of favoured 'mules' were big-bodied black women, and
prostitutes of any description.

'There is a significant black problem, but it's one of
a whole series of significant problems. It's sufficient
for us to put resources into it, but it isn't the only one,
and it isn't the most important,' stresses Commander
Grieve.

Within that, however, the Metropolitan Police's intelligence chief, who leads the crusade against drugs and
violence in London, identifies a particular trafficking
headache. 'And not,' he adds, 'at the highest level of
dealing. What we call "smuggler ants" – a kilo here, a
kilo there. Most we've ever seen is about five or six kilos
in one hit . . .

'And we routinely deal with 600-kilo jobs' from South
America. Indeed, Customs' seizures of cocaine rose a
staggering 224 per cent in 1994. Meanwhile, in spite
of the fact that the vast majority of 'mules' are white,
half the visitors Customs searched in 1993 were black.
Today's cocaine trafficker is also increasingly exploiting
the British postal service.

Increasingly throughout the 1990s, however, there has
been an important sea change in the methods used to
acquire drugs. The old practice of a gang of potential
crack peddlers getting together to make a 'raise' (whether

through armed robbery, fraud or anything else) to raise the money to buy a kilo or two of cocaine has become old hat.

Nowadays, again in concert with recent trends in Jamaica, Canada and the United States, British cities have become the venues for violent rip-offs of cocaine and crack between rival rudie dealers and others. In February 1994, already concerned about the upsurge in gun crimes amongst the Rude Boys, an NCIS organised crime briefing expressed fears about the concomitant creation of 'a mini arms race' as a result of this phenomenon.

However the Rude Boys came by their drugs, it was only a matter of time before they (and their black British pretenders) had won a stranglehold on the national crack market. So, from a situation where crack was unheard of in Britain in 1987, and Customs officers made only three rock seizures in 1988, the drug had mushroomed to account for sixty per cent of all cocaine confiscations in 1992. Seven in ten of those seizures were in London, but crack could be found in almost three-quarters of the forty-three police constabularies in England and Wales. The rudies and their willing apprentices were behind the bulk of the trade.

It follows that numerous rudies were getting fat off the crack trade. 'Crack is the fast-track to making money,' says Paulette. She draws a distinction between occasional users and the 'paracats'. 'They're the ones the dealers live for,' she says, 'the paracats [crackheads] . . . who just can't stop tek it.' They take it twenty-four hours-a-day.' More than that says Paulette, who 'juggles' a little weed to make ends meet, 'With people like that around a rock seller can be out [on the streets] for a couple of hours a day and make thousands.' Indeed, a paracat will spend £200 or more on crack at a time.

'It's all about . . . designer threads, [mobile] phones,

big drive, running syndicate,' offers Stubby, another self-confessed part-time 'weed man'. 'It's a hard life if you can survive, but it's a good life.' The wisdom in Stubby's words is plain to see around his south London 'manor'. For several years now, it has become familiar to see young (unemployed) black men (and, to a lesser extent, women) 'posing' in the latest model Golf GTi convertibles, Suzuki jeeps, three, five, six and seven series Beamers (BMWs) and, for the most successful traders, Mercedes sports cars. One change, though, is that many have now taken to hiring such vehicles. That way they can hold on to the symbols of material success that bolster their 'reps', without the fear of having them confiscated by the authorities.

There have been other alterations, too. The bleepers which the dealers used to carry to alert them to customer enquiries have been replaced by mobile phones; the trade is so competitive nowadays that only those who respond immediately can hope to close a deal; some drug entrepreneurs have even started their own dial-a-crack services. And, for the most part, the thousands of pounds worth of gold jewellery that used to festoon necks, fingers and wrists, has been left at home for safe keeping; such gratuitous displays of wealth have become too conspicuous both to the police and opportunistic street robbers. At the end of the day, though, cocaine/crack dealers are very much the ghetto's kings and queens.

With Britain's illicit drug industry valued at between £3billion–£5billion-a-year, the profits available to the most successful of these types are astronomical. For those prepared to put in the hours, £1,000–£2,000 a day or even £10,000–£20,000 a week, is attainable. In a notable example, a Jamaican jailed in 1991 for ten years for crack dealing was found to have salted away over a million pounds in cash and property. (Rumour has it that even now he is sitting on a small fortune in investments and property abroad; patiently awaiting to be reunited with them on his release.)

Until his arrest and conviction, Wendell 'Skully' Daniels was a regular sight in Brixton's illegal gambling houses. He regularly gambled thousands of pounds at the tables, although to look at him one might have wondered why he did not use his money to buy some decent clothes. A canny drug baron, Skully's understated appearance was deliberate; he wanted to live to enjoy the profits of his trade which included houses and businesses in the United States, United Kingdom and Jamaica.

Skully's nemesis came when he was stopped by two uniformed policemen while driving along Railton Road, once Brixton's 'frontline'. During the 'random' stop, the officers conducted a thorough search of his boot. It was then that they allegedly happened upon what appeared to be a large, light-coloured slate. Rumour has it that the beat officers were on the verge of letting him go, when they decided the strange object warranted further examination. It turned out to be a solid, one kilo block of crack. The search also netted a 'ki' of cocaine and a pound of ganja. The second biggest police drugs seizure of 1991, the combined haul was valued at £180,000.

However, for all the breathtaking profits made by the few, the typical crack dealer leads a much more modest existence. Those, and there are many of them, who sample their mechandise, often find it difficult just to make a profit on their investment. Add to that the unrelenting competition for good pitches and customers, and all the elements are in place for an explosive situation. As the crack trade has evolved in Britain's black communities, from Bristol to Nottingham, Manchester to London, Birmingham to Leeds, extreme violence has become an integral feature of it.

* * *

'There are people fighting turf wars over the sale of crack,' warned Sir Paul Condon, the Metropolitan Police Commissioner, in October 1993. 'They are armed, desperate criminals who are prepared to shoot indiscriminately.' Sir Paul's comments about these 'ruthless criminals' came a day after the third of three fatal shooting incidents in London within the space of twenty-four hours.

One of those 'indiscriminate' fatalities was Police Constable Patrick Dunne, a popular community beat bobbie murdered on duty in Clapham, south London. However, while there was never any doubt that his two assailants were black, it was supremely ironic that no formal link was ever identified between them, the rudies and the local crack trade. The universal media assumption that the killers were Yardies stemmed mainly from the fact that the unfortunate teacher-turned-policeman was gunned down by black men in the crack badlands of south London.

Commander Grieve disagrees. 'The newspapers all said "Yardie shooting of Patrick Dunne",' he scoffs. 'I have not seen a single, solitary scrap of evidence that says it has got anybody that fits any definition of "Yardie" I know.' Moreover, even though charges are still to be preferred, he adds, 'I would say it's much more likely the people who shot Patrick Dunne were home-grown.'

That said, if certain newspaper accounts of PC Dunne's slaying are accurate, his murderers fitted the profile of ruthless Rude Boy enforcers. The bicycle-riding constable's death – he had been investigating a domestic incident in Cato Road – came just moments after the reckless execution of a mid-level drug dealer. A Ghanaian, William Danso died in a hail of seventeen bullets; he was struck by five of them. Apparently, Danso had been chased around the room where he was killed. When PC

Dunne went to investigate, he was shot in the chest with a single 9mm round from a distance of some ten metres. Various reports claimed his killers laughed, and let off a gun salute, as they fled the scene. The point is that, by the time Patrick Dunne was killed, gun violence (like crack) had become synonymous with the rudies in various parts of London. And Clapham was one.

Commissioner Condon's alarming observation came a few months after he had predicted that Britain's 130,000 police could be 'packing' firearms within ten years; a disturbing reflection, he said, of the hard facts about increasing terrorism and gun-related crimes. In terms of the latter category, in the metropolis the total nearly doubled between 1983 and 1992. Such offences also suffered a fifty per cent increase nationally during the four years to the end of 1991.

Still, the Commissioner had not yet exhausted his opinions on the controversial subject of arming the police. In March 1994, a sensational double shooting incident once again forced Britain's most senior police officer to presage the strong likelihood of his charges bearing arms. 'I have always said the arming of the Met will be event-driven,' he said after the ruthless but non-fatal shooting of another two of his men in Brixton. 'This shooting takes us closer to being armed. I see it becoming more and more probable,' he said.

In this particular case, the shooter was caught, convicted and sentenced to twenty-five years imprisonment in February 1995. Jamaican-born Leroy Smith, already on the run after staging an armed escape from police custody, had fled to the United States after the shootings. Ironically, he was arrested there in connection with another shooting incident allegedly relating to a British student who had turned down his demands for her to mule drugs for him, and was deported back to Britain. Unrepentant, he allegedly told his girlfriend

that he was sorry that he hadn't got the officers 'good
and proper'.

By the time of Smith's attack, however, the issue of
arming the police had become a national political hot
potato. In May 1994, an opinion poll commissioned
by the Police Federation (PF), the body that looks
after the interests of rank-and-file officers, found that
large proportions of its membership favoured the wider
issuing of arms to the police. The Police Federation
representatives were particularly keen to see this happen
in 'dangerous' high crime areas like Moss Side and
Brixton. Against this disturbing background there was
even talk of low-ranking officers refusing to patrol such
places without better personal protection; one of many
signs of a growing crisis of confidence in the practice
of British policing at the time.

In the same month, possibly as a result of those
murmurs of discontent, Sir Paul announced his decision
to send more armed officers out on patrol in London.
And, for the first time since the Metropolitan Police drew
up firearms regulations in 1884, certain officers were
to be permitted to openly carry guns in side holsters.
At the same time, a decision was to be made as to
whether regional crime squad officers in the south-east of
England should be allowed to carry machine-guns during
certain types of operation. The logic being that many of
the organised criminals they were up against possessed
increasingly powerful semi-automatic weapons; weapons
which seriously outmatched the police's standard issue
revolvers.

Speculation about arming the police transcended London
and the south of England. In July 1994, the ACPO
chairman reiterated Sir Paul's sentiments. 'If the situation
on the inner-city streets gets wilder we can anticipate
that as a matter of routine officers will face armed
criminals,' said Jim Sharples, the Chief Constable of

Merseyside, 'then as a matter of routine we will have to arm them.'

In reality, British police forces had been stealthily arming their charges for years. The days when criminal delinquents and hoodlums said 'it's a fair cop' when the likes of Dixon of Dock Green 'felt their collars' are a distant memory. As the murder of PC Dunne aptly demonstrates, some of today's villains would more than likely shoot the ficticious copper before they went 'quietly' with him.

Throughout the 1990s criminals have increasingly demonstrated their unerring determination to play for keeps. Firearms offences against Metropolitan police officers rose almost 600 per cent in 1993 alone. In the halcyon days when Officer Dixon pounded the beat, even hardened criminals like the Kray twins would have run a mile before they levelled their weapons at an unarmed officer of the law; they might have been vicious, but they still had moral standards. And etiquette demanded that one did no harm to people who played no part in the gangster world.

Not anymore. Today, the tacit gentlemen's agreement that existed between the criminal underworld and the forces of law and order has been unilaterally torn up, discarded and forgotten. Now, even the meekest of Britain's desperate criminals make Graham Greene's Pinky, the protagonist of *Brighton Rock*, look like a sissy, and the fabled East End twins, like precocious children. And as long as this remains so, the day when the nation's police will routinely carry weapons to protect themselves is something of a foregone conclusion.

However, widespread calls for the routine arming of the 'thin blue line' have largely come about since the emergence of a frightening new criminal and his attendant gun culture. Indeed, if there has been one catalyst for this heated gun debate, it has been the violent excesses perpetrated by the crack-dealing rudies (and their black British 'devotees') during their brief occupation of the British isles. Propelled by the high-octane desire to deal crack, these gangsters have been shooting it out for the right to control the best street pitches and run-down housing estates for years.

This gunplay started in earnest during the late 1980s, and has regressed steadily throughout the 1990s. Rudie-inspired turf wars over the sale of rock cocaine had reached serious proportions, especially for those who lived within shooting range of them, long before the nation's top peace-keepers began to express serious alarm.

That said, it was no coincidence that the Metropolitan Police Chief was prompted to raise the issue of Rude Boy gun violence during his first newspaper interview after taking up the job. 'The level of violence is such,' he told the *Independent on Sunday* in the summer of 1993, 'that they do not mind shooting each other just to save selling [crack] that day.' Yet, the situation he spoke of had been so bad for so long that had he been in the job in 1990, his observations would no doubt have been much the same.

'They are just as much conceptual turf wars, as they are geographical turf wars,' explains Grieve of the present situation. Conceptual turf wars? 'That's about this is our area of criminality, you keep out of it. I don't mean a few streets. I mean "we're dealing in crack, you aren't!" "We're dealing in stolen jewellery, you're not!" And out of that you then get the robberies of one dealer upon another.'

Of course, Rude Boy violence, which is not confined to London, has reared its ugly head in a number of ways and areas. Apart from territorial disputes, it has been triggered by drug rip-offs, police drugs raids, and rep-building, minor disputes. It has thrown up cases of savage torture, and involved serious injury to innocent bystanders.

Perhaps one of the most worrying aspects of this syndrome is that most of the everyday madness goes unreported to the police. The victims are either too frightened or too deeply involved to make reports. Ergo, they either forget about them or, more commonly, resolve to even the score against the perpetrators. Similarly, all but the most serious of gunshot and knife wounds are treated by the victims themselves; the rudies steer as far clear of the 'system' as possible.

Outside London, there have been numerous instances of crack-related rudie violence, shootings and murders. The black communities of Birmingham, Bristol, Nottingham and Manchester have borne the brunt of the drug-related mayhem. Still, cities with smaller black populations have not escaped the maniacal violence, either.

Shortly before Christmas 1993, two men were shot and injured as the result of an altercation in the Chapeltown district of Leeds, an area noted for drug-dealing. One of the victims was shot in the back, but the duo's ordeal did not end there. In fact, as the two men hurriedly drove towards Leed's famous St James's Hospital, their attackers decanted into another two cars and pursued them. Finally, on arrival at the hospital's forecourt, four miles away, the other man was shot in the head.

Chapeltown has had its ups and downs as far as gun violence is concerned. But the Moss Side precinct of Manchester has developed a particularly damaging reputation for drug-related gangland violence. So much so, that the tabloids have dubbed the enclave 'Britain's Bronx', and the city itself, 'Madchester'. Much of that violence, which includes several brutal murders, has been triggered by indigenous black drug gangs. However, even though these outfits number Jamaican-born,

British-socialised members, local police have not dis-
counted the influence and involvement of genuine rudie
criminals.

For example, in 1993, the head of the city's drug
squad pointed to the fact that local gangsters modelled
themselves on the nihilistic principles of posse gangsters.
Speaking at ACPO's thirteenth annual drugs conference
in May, Superintendent Peter Brennan (no relation to
DS John 'Blondie' Brennan) spelled out his fears in
no uncertain terms. 'We have good reason to believe,'
he said, 'that there are strong ties between some of our
gang members in Moss Side, and Jamaican criminals
in Kingston and London.' The frenzied nature of Moss
Side's violence gives a clear indication of how those links
have manifested themselves.

But the worst of the chaos has unfolded in London,
south of the river in particular. Today, gunshots are
heard to 'bark' on a regular, if not daily, basis on the
streets of inner London; places where the spectre of gun
violence has become a sad fact of life for the blameless
residents who occupy them. In fact, the list of affected
London towns is so long that it reads something like a
phone directory: Balham, Battersea, Brixton, Camberwell,
Catford, Clapham, Croydon, Dalston, Deptford, Hackney, Harlesden, Kennington, Lewisham, Notting Hill,
Peckham, Shepherd's Bush, Stockwell, Stoke Newington,
Streatham, Tooting, Vauxhall, and Wembley.

North of the Thames, there has been a catalogue
of drug-related violence covering a broad spectrum,
including scores of recorded shooting incidents. In March
1991, for example, a police officer was killed during a
massive drugs raid on the Stonebridge Estate, a sprawling
concrete wilderness in Harlesden to the north west of the
capital. Codenamed Operation Howitzer, the raid netted
£500,000-worth of crack – at that time the biggest single
seizure of the narcotic in British history. Two firearms

were also discovered. But the otherwise successful operation was tainted by the shooting dead of a policeman.

In terms of utter ruthlessness, the killing of Cassandra Higgins ranks high on the list. A Jamaican visa overstayer, she was certainly no angel. Still, her demise was shocking by any standards. The nineteen-year-old was stripped naked by five Rude Boys in an eighteenth-floor crack-house on the Cathall Road Estate in Leytonstone, east London. Then, to the horror of those who looked on, she was thrown out of the window 160 feet to the ground. Higgins's death, in September 1993, was thought to have been the result of a rudie drug deal double-cross on her part. The brutal murder was witnessed by several people, but true to form the lips of those assembled were welded shut by the force of the posse code: 'See and blind, hear and deaf'; in fact, not one person was willing to go to court to testify against the killers.

There was also the case of Leroy 'Scarface' Lesley, a top-notch Rude Boy who replicated American posse don Delroy 'Uzi' Edward's approach to settling social disputes. His moment of madness came in November 1993, in front of 200 witnesses, and a video crew, at a farewell party in Stoke Newington.

Scarface got embroiled in a heated argument with a fellow reveller at the bar of the Roots Pool Hall, his eventual murder victim apparently 'dissed' (disrespected) him. The confrontation looked to be over when Scarface stormed away. However, the gangster, an illegal immigrant who had 'previous' for firearms, drugs and violent offences, returned soon after with a gun (he had been using his girlfriend as gun baggage) whereupon André Blackman, the murder victim, was clinically shot. Scarface then turned his 'machine' on to Blackman's best friend before shooting, chasing and pistol-whipping him. The third victim was shot by accident. A beauty consultant, she was hit after the killing when Scarface let off a gun salute into the air. A notable scalp in the war against the rudies, he was jailed for life at the Old Bailey in August 1993.

Across the river in south London, the problem with gun violence has turned it into something of a Wild South. Nowadays, shooting incidents (the black-on-black variety, especially) have become so mundane as to scarcely merit more than a nib (news in brief) mention in the local press. By contrast, in the early 1990s, the rising tide of such incidents prompted the Metropolitan Police to set up a dedicated squad to tackle this largely rudie-inspired phenomenon.

The bold initiative – bold because, by virtue of its remit, it focused exclusively on black criminals – came in the form of Operation Dalehouse. Barracked in a nondescript warehouse-type structure in Thornton Heath, south London, the operation was set up in August 1991 following an orgy of crack-related violence across a wide area centred around Brixton. Its inception came after a rash of thirty (recorded) crack-related shooting incidents in the space of just six months to April that year. However, the catalyst for its formation was provided by a savage armed 'blag' on a south London jewellers, which featured an attempted murder.

That the prevailing situation was perceived to have got out of control was reflected in the strength of the Dalehouse team. In a climate of scarce resources and all-round belt-tightening, an incredible thirty-six officers were detailed to the squad. Headed by Detective Superintendent John Jones, a sagacious veteran investigator straight out of the Inspector Morse mould, Operation Dalehouse was clearly seen as a police priority.

The team, which included Blondie Brennan, carried out a wide range of duties. Raids and searches on the homes of suspected rudies were a staple feature. A high priority was also placed on carrying out sophisticated high-tech surveillance of criminal suspects believed to belong to the estimated twenty posses in the area. Meanwhile, intelligence-gathering became a pro-active element with Blondie and others charged with the responsibility of cultivating and setting up a network of black informants.

Dalehouse was nothing if not successful. A model of its kind, during the span of Dalehouse's operations the incidence of reported crack shootings fell to about a sixth of the norm. The squad made close to 270 arrests, and secured a number of high-profile convictions. The biggest single success coming at the expense of members of the Spanish Town Posse, which had secured a firm foothold in its quest for crack-dealing supremacy. In all, Dalehouse arrested and charged four suspects with murder, and another twenty-one for attempted or conspiring to murder. There were also three arrests for armed robbery. In addition, scores of rudies were deported as a result of the team's vigilance, three-quarters of whom had entered Britain on bogus passports. Officers also seized around thirty illegal firearms, including machine-guns, and confiscated £1million-worth of rock.

Cynics argued that Dalehouse merely displaced the rudie crack-gun violence problem to areas like Stoke Newington. This observation was justified to an extent, but at the end of the day those criticisms were short-lived. For, after fifteen months, much to the chagrin of those involved, Operation Dalehouse was disbanded in November 1992, a victim of its own success.

With the rudie situation in south London once again 'under manners', senior officers quickly found new details for the squad's membership. Although, that said, some, including Blondie, were transferred to the South-East Regional Crime Squad which, along with a few independent, local police initiatives, assumed the responsibility of combating the Rude Boy menace.

The product of what many officers privately regarded

as folly was plain to see in the months and years following the scrapping of Dalehouse. In short, with the enforced moratorium on south London drug gang violence brought to an abrupt end, it was a signal for the Rude Boys *et al* to resume normal service. This was graphically reflected in the return to arms. Around eight crack-related murders were recorded in the vicinity of Brixton alone up to the spring of 1994. Meanwhile, PC Patrick Dunne was gunned down in the blighted area in October 1993.

With the obvious exception of PC Dunne, the most notable of these homicide statistics was one Christopher Alexander 'Tuffy' Bourne. Tuffy's killing made national headlines. This was partly because it came less than a day after another black drug dealer had been 'blown away', just two miles away. But equally newsworthy was the gangland-style of the execution.

The symbolism of Tuffy's life and death did a lot more than highlighting the chronic problem of crack-related rudie violence in south London. In many ways, his rise and fall crystallised the global irresistibility of the violent Rude Boy crack culture, and the manifest everyday difficulties faced by the world's law enforcers in their struggles to nullify it.

Like Scarface Lesley, Tuffy was an illegal alien with plenty of 'form'. A product of Tivoli Gardens, his criminal career spanned the Atlantic Ocean. It began in Kingston where he was a much-respected, ranking Shower Posse gangster. The rudie was just nineteen when he was jailed for life in 1978 for a double murder. However, as luck would have it, his sentence was subsequently reduced, and he was paroled in 1985.

A loving father to nine children in London, Tuffy was no stranger to Britain's immigration and criminal justice systems. During his residency in Britain, the thirty-four-year-old was convicted and imprisoned for fraud and drug offences. His criminality, combined with his illegal entry, caused him to be deported on two occasions.

The first expulsion came in September 1989, after a spell at Her Majesty's Pleasure on a drug conviction. Oblivious, he was back in Britain on a false passport by November. Tuffy was actually apprehended by immigration officers, but soon escaped from detention. He was not caught again until January 1991, when he was arrested again; this time for circulating bogus banknotes. A year later, the rudie was returned to Jamaica.

Tuffy apparently made several attempts to sneak back into Britain before he finally succeeded on 5 February 1993 – even then he had to jump a barrier at Birmingham International Airport, and make a run for it. News of the fugitive gangster's return led to his name being placed on the South-East Regional Crime Squad's Most Wanted list. In fact, the squad (now including the ubiquitous Blondie) had had him under surveillance him for some time, and was close to picking him up when he met his violent death.

With his fearsome reputation for 'badness', Tuffy had become a master of the art of the gun-negotiated drug rip-off; he made some big cash, too. And it was this practice that led to his death. The beginning of the end of Tuffy's short life started at around 9.30 p.m. inside 54, Vassell Road, a Lambeth Council-owned property just off Coldharbour Lane in Brixton.

A known 'crack den', the word is that the rudie went there with the express intention of 'taxing' its 'proprietors'. Unfortunately for him, his gambit had been anticipated in advance; his killers had, as they say in ghetto Kingston, 'planned fi him'. A verbal fight broke out, one which inevitably climaxed in a shoot-out. Tuffy was struck four times, by shots fired at close-range by at least three gunmen. Several more shots peppered the wall behind him. Incredibly strong, he staggered out of the premises before collapsing on the paved area outside

the complex. When the police arrived they recovered a
.45 Webley, believed to be his.

Tuffy died later in King's College Hospital on Denmark
Hill, less than a mile away. If anyone could have saved his
life, it would have been the medical staff there. Indeed, no
other British hospital outside Northern Ireland has more
experience of treating gunshot wounds than King's.

Tuffy is not the only one to have slipped through the
net. Informed sources claim that the hospital's mortuary is
home to at least six Rude Boy victims of the south London
crack war; murdered men whose corpses cannot be disposed of because nobody knows their true identities.

'There's nothing like that,' argues Commander Grieve.
'What there is is – not just at King's College, but across a
range of hospitals – there are shootings where people are
dead that we've never got to the bottom of . . . Yes, there are
unsolved murders but they're all in the public domain.'

A measure of the respect Tuffy had and the internation-
alism of the rudie culture was proven by the fact that his
slaying sent reverberations across the oceans and seas to
Kingston, Jamaica. News of the episode in Brixton sent
enraged Shower gangsters in Tivoli Gardens reaching for
their 'forty-fives' and 'nines'. Amid irresistible rumours
that a band of Brixton-based Spanglers gun hawks were
culpable, violent revenge attacks were launched on the
posse's Matthew's Lane stronghold. As a result, several
more deaths and injuries were absorbed into Jamaica's
gargantuan list of 'war' casualties.

Back in England, there were further signs that Tuffy
had been well-regarded. During his time in England, he
had earned the respect of many youths for carrying on the
Jamaican ghetto tradition of sharing his wealth; this made
him a highly popular figure in the gangster world.

Indeed, after his sentence was handed down for the
murder of Tuffy, Raymond 'Emma' Grant, the only one
of four co-defendants to be convicted, verbally insisted

that he had been 'fitted up' by prosecution witnesses. In fact, in a remarkable – unprecedented even – turn of events, more than fifty witnesses stepped forward to testify against the defendants.

The evidence against Emma, one of two Jamaicans, clearly impressed the judge of his ruthlessness. Judge Lawrence Verney, the Recorder of London, sentenced the twenty-eight-year-old rudie to life imprisonment, with a recommendation that he serve at least twenty years.

As horrific as it has been, the nonchalant propensity of the rudies – original and would-be – to 'rinse' their guns on each other on the streets of Britain is only the most visible aspect of their reign of terror. That said, predictably, such indiscriminate displays of gunmanship have registered in a tally of innocent victims.

To date, the most notable victim was Katrina Bernhard. She was caught in the crossfire of a shoot-out on Railton Road in Brixton. The attack happened moments after she left a wine bar where she had been enjoying a special under-sixteens night-out with her parents. Thirteen-year-old Katrina was shot in the arm.

Katrina's injuries were accidental. But other people, innocent and not so innocent, have become victims of the rudies' well-practised penchant for torture.

One completely innocent Jamaican woman sustained horrific injuries after falling foul of her nephew's treachery. They had travelled together from Jamaica on vacation. However, unbeknown to her, the woman's nephew had 'muled' a consignment of drugs for a rudie in London. However, no sooner had the courier landed, than he went 'missing'.

Undeterred, Eldon Brown, the would-be recipient, kidnapped the 'mule's' young aunt, and took her to a flat. For the next three days she was subjected to a sadistic campaign of torturous 'interrogation'. She was laid out on the floor like a sheet and ironed all over her body; 'fastened' to a settee by having metal coat hangers shoved through the skin in her arms; stabbed; subjected to oral sex at gunpoint; and, whenever she passed out, 'revived' with scalding water poured over her. In the end, the torture victim only escaped by risking her own life, jettisoning herself through a window. Twenty-five-year-old Brown was convicted of torture, kidnap and sexual assault on 11 December 1992, and sentenced at the Old Bailey to ten years imprisonment.

Another notable female victim of torture was not so blameless. The twenty-year-old Nigerian, had smuggled in a consignment of heroin for a rudie drugs outfit. Later on the same day in 1991, she was visited at her high-rise London flat by four rudies from a rival gang; they had come to rip-off the 'smack'. However, the 'mule' steadfastly refused to tell the interlopers where she had stashed the haul. To loosen her tongue, they too gave her an 'ironing' on her stomach, shoulder, breasts and face, and used the hot water technique to prevent her from passing out on them. In the end, the courier gave in, and told the gangsters what they wanted to know, but not before she had received third degree burns.

The police were alerted to the situation after alarmed neighbours rang them to report hearing screaming. However, in spite of her nightmarish ordeal, the young woman refused to make a police statement; it seems even Nigerians know the posse code. And, after her burns were treated in hospital, she discharged herself and disappeared without trace.

Tossing drug dealers from tower block windows, torching the homes of (suspected) informers, terrifying potential prosecution witnesses, torturing loyal 'mules', these are just some of the practices which help to account for the rudies' quick-fire success in insinuating themselves so thoroughly on to the British organised crime scene. As ever, though, the key that most easily unlocked the door was fashioned in the shape of a gun.

More than that, the rudies' worship of powerful fire-arms has actually fuelled the creation of a ferocious all-embracing British gun culture. Since the rudies started 'slinging' guns with gay abandon, firearms have very much become the new currency for a growing body of the youthful British criminal fraternity – black and white. Hence, repeated police warnings about the future inevitability of a routinely armed police force.

Even though guns have long been a part of the British crime scene, the wholesale introduction of gun law emanated from the Rude Boys. Veterans of indiscriminate, everyday gun-toting in Jamaica and the United States, they single-handedly removed the longstanding British taboo on casually brandishing 'shooters' in the commission of crime.

The likes of Commander Grieve are reluctant 'to be seen to be pointing the finger at the Jamaicans', not least because of the good working relations SO11 has with the Jamaican Government and police. 'Y'know,' he says, 'I knock that diplomatically off balance, I lose a great deal.'

However, he admits that the Metropolitan Police has a significant problem with 'groupings of criminals' who 'have a culture of armed intervention in all kinds of activities. Not just in robbing one set of dealers, not just protecting what they do, but carrying guns for a whole series of other cultural reasons.

'So we get shots fired at all kinds of social occasions. We get shots fired in the ceiling at dances. We get shots fired in the ceiling at parties. We get guns waved about over disputes about women, cars, jewellery, music, door-keeping – all those kind of things.'

The general rush to arms has been bolstered by a number of unwelcome developments. The most sinister among these has been the increasing availablity of illegal weaponry.

Illegal guns are entering the expanding underground weapons market from numerous sources. De-activated weapons, those which have had their barrels blocked and firing pins removed, have been turning up on the streets after being re-activated. They can be bought from a variety of outlets: specialist weapons magazines, army surplus stores and crooked, licensed gun dealers, among them. Costing about one-tenth of the price of the genuine article, criminals have found that it pays to have them put back into working order.

In terms of ready-to-fire weapons, certain disreputable gun shop owners are also suspected by the police of selling their products directly to criminals. Another source is domestic burglaries, especially for older weapons and shotguns. Then there are illicit sales made by an unlikely source: discharged British soldiers; especially those who did tours of duty in Northern Ireland or fought in the Gulf and Falklands wars. And, staying on the military theme, since the disintegration of the former Soviet empire in Eastern Europe, a multitude of deadly weapons have been smuggled into Britain. This, in turn, has been abetted by the post-1992 opening up of Britain's trade barriers with its European Union partners.

The rudies have exploited these various supply lines to pick up weapons like .38s and .45s for as little as £200 each – with ammunition. State-of-the-art weapons come at a much higher asking price. An Uzi, for example, changes hands for about £1,000, a day's pay for a successful rock seller. However, there is also compelling evidence to suggest that the rudies have been utilising existing contacts in the United States, and even Jamaica, to supplement their domestic supplies.

Consequently, for those in the know, laying one's

hands on a firearm has never been easier. With an estimated three million unregistered firearms circulating
in Britain – no one knows the exact figure – British
law enforcement has experienced major problems in
keeping illegal weapons out of the hands of would-be
gun criminals.

Without doubt one of the biggest headaches for the
police has been keeping these deadly arsenals away from
the Rude Boys. For, like make-up to a cover girl, guns
have become a necessary rudie accessory. The greatest
demand has come from crack-dealing gangsters. Forget
about hiring or dusting off a sawn-off shotgun, the sort of
thing that old-time (white) 'blaggers' used to do. Anyone
with serious aspirations of getting into, or protecting
their niche in, today's crack business has to walk with
'steel'; their own 'steel'; it is their only (real) protection
against the competition. And besides, many of the players
involved with rock hail from Jim Brown Country, from
environments where a gun is always on hand; where the
gun is the chief negotiator in disputes; where shooting to
kill wins status and respect. So for these sorts carrying a
gun is cultural.

As always, the rudie preference has been for high-
powered semi-automatic weapons. While the police
most commonly seize low-grade and obsolete guns
from Jamaican criminals, there have been a number of
confiscations of powerful weapons, too. In May 1993, for
instance, a rudie crack dealer in south London was arrested
in possession of a Czechoslovakian sub-machine-gun. In
November of the same year, two rudies were jailed for
eighteen years for attempted murder – they had forced
two rivals to jump from a third-floor balcony, and threw
a third over after brandishing a Tokarev automatic pistol.
And, a few months earlier, the South-East Regional Crime
Squad recovered seventeen firearms, including three Uzis,
during a series of raids, many of which were on rudie

households. The raids actually came less than a day after a police sergeant had been shot in the head with an Uzi.

With that kind of nihilistic behaviour abroad, it is understandable that this new breed of gangster shows no compunction about popping off shots at unarmed beat officers, or shooting innocent passers-by who inadvertantly get in their way during fire-fights with rivals. Incidents such as these are merely occupational hazards in a highly competitive market-place, a setting in which gun 'diplomacy' is the most effective method of staying alive.

Yet, if the rudies' rabid, drug-fuelled gun culture has generated national alarm, it has not caused more soul-searching anywhere than within the afflicted black communities. The panic has centred on the hypnotic effect the rudie criminal culture – violence, guns and crack in particular – has had on African-Caribbean and British-West African youth.

The latter, mainly Nigerian faction, became actively involved in the early 1990s, and have been growing in strength ever since. 'The Africans are firming up,' says Stubby. 'They're bringing in nuff H (heroin) and C (cocaine).' They have also proved to be a fruitful source for rudie drug 'taxations', leading to a pervasive lack of trust to develop between the general populations.

According to Little Joe, in many ways this youthful slide into criminality is to be expected. 'The youth are taking over,' warns the reformed crackhead, during one of many ganja-inspired, early morning soliloquys. 'They're bred on a diet of one-parent families. Their fathers are dead, in jail or "missing"; their role models become rude street boys. By the age of twelve their mother's can't tell [them] nothing. You see some trainers, you go and get it. Society says "spare the rod", and the kid turns out spoilt. He gets kicked out in the third year – no education, no wealth – but all around he sees the white man's status. He can't get a job, but wants it. Inevitably, he turns to crime. Why? Because the system of society makes you do it!'

In the same way that the religious Rastafari provided thousands of young black people with role models in the mid-1970s, the materialistic Rude Boys have become the idols of too many in the 1980s and 1990s. In short, studying 'badness' has superseded practising goodness as the choice of this particular generation.

Seeing the kind of glamorous lifestyle that awaits successful crack dealers – designer wear, sexy women, fast cars, cash and the status that goes with them – alienated young black Britons have tried to claw their way into the industry. But in order to get on board and stay in the hunt, they have had to 'tool' up.

Even the police have accepted this imperative. 'The traditional English criminal, whether black or white, had not been used to carrying guns around,' Detective Superintendent John Jones explained to journalist Malcolm Macalister Hall. Commenting on the violent situation in south London in a *Times* feature from March 1992, the Operation Dalehouse supremo continued, 'What is happening now is that these Yardie characters are more or less forcing the black English criminals to do the same. Otherwise, they're going to get shot.'

'They get this thing about the Jamaica style of the guns,' says DS O'Connor. 'Y'know, they live by the gun, they die by the gun. And I've been told that if they live to thirty-five, they think themselves lucky. Now I can tell you that in the last two to three months, I've had people involved with crack and firearms,' he says, 'and nothing to do with Jamaica, either.'

'They might have got it from Ronnie Kray for all I know, or the Chicago gangster – which they did,' insists Commander Grieve. He points to US law enforcements' past dealings with the mob by way of qualification. 'When the FBI bugged them – and this is all documented –

they heard them watching the Godfather films. And they started changing their names, and doing things in accordance with what they saw Marlon Brando doing,' he says.

Harking back to the mid-1980s, though, the commander confesses to the 'cultural' influences the presence of certain Jamaicans had on the host community of the capital's criminals. 'There was a number of our home-grown people,' he recalls, 'who lived and worked and committed crime here in London who'd never been closer to Jamaica than Jamaica Road SE1.'

Moreover, these people, 'saw a style of dress, a style of haircut, a style of behaviour, and they went round saying that they . . . were "Yardies" . . . which they weren't – they were from here!'

This trend was reflected equally in bogus reported sightings of so-called Yardies, which emanated from the police themselves. Says O'Connor of these reports, 'And when you actually look into it, you find out it's Joe Bloggs from down the road, whose taken up a name . . . to get a bit of street credibility, and that's it.'

People at street level see it slightly differently. 'More British blacks are "packing" [carrying guns] now because they know they're up against the Yardies. That's how the Yardies have made them carry on,' reiterates Paulette. 'It's like having a handbag now, it's that casual.' 'Man out there on the rampage,' adds Stubby, another who is deeply concerned by the black British trend towards 'tooling' up.

The good news – if one can call it that – is that the demand for guns amongst black adolescents seems to have levelled off. Nowadays, those making enquiries about weapons are what are called 'gaps', people who have never owned one. The bad news, however, is that an alarming number of these gaps are young black women.

However, there are already more than enough guns and gangsters in circulation to service the perennial crack war. In a disturbing trend, these fierce encounters have been waged between and among rival Rude Boys, African-Caribbean and British-West African drug mobsters.

A twenty-two-year-old black man shot dead outside a club in Peckham in June 1994 was thought to have been the victim of a drugs feud. He was felled by two men armed with a double-barrelled shotgun as he sat in his car. In October, another young black man was gunned down outside a pub in Camberwell, south London. The nineteen-year-old, who had earlier been acquitted of a double shooting, was thought to have been killed in a gangland revenge attack.

One of the biggest problems with the escalating pattern of black-on-black shootings and killings is that so many fall into the grey area of conjecture. In fact, the ongoing situation is sometimes so confused that one is very often left wondering what exactly sparked particular incidents. For, as is the Rude Boy wont, guns are fired as much in the pursuit of drug-related business as they are in personal anger.

In October 1991, Mark Burnett was gunned down as he watched Capleton, a top Jamaican DJ, perform to a 2,000-strong crowd at the Podium nightclub in Vauxhall, south London. Nobody knows, or was prepared to say, why. In February 1992, Clinton 'Mr Palmer the Mic Ninja' Eddie was shot dead outside his home in Wandsworth, south London. A well-respected DJ, a man who was not 'mix-up' in the gangster world, he had only recently cut what turned out to be one of his last tunes, 'Too Much Gun'. Nobody knows for sure why he was killed, but rumour has it that he had asked some dealers to peddle their drugs elsewhere.

The only certainty in all of this is that the Rudie-inspired gun culture has led to a deadly situation developing on the streets of black Britain. Nowhere is this gun mania more severe than in the capital, where the black murder rate has rocketed over the past several years. Black people make up less than seven per cent of London's population, but are majorly overrepresented in the city's murder statistics. In 1988, the tally stood at twelve per cent. By 1992 it had spiralled to twenty-four per cent, making black people more than three times more likely to be murdered than white people – even more so at the end of a gun. And, with black teenagers as young as thirteen routinely packing guns, there are no indications that the situation is going to improve in the foreseeable future. 'It's like people ain't got no respect for the law,' says Stubby.

The police have had a chequered history of fighting the Rude Boy menace in London. 'We are policing the capital on a stop-go basis,' argued Sergeant Mike Bennett in the wake of the fatal shooting of PC Dunne in October 1993. The chairman of the Metropolitan Police Federation continued: 'Overnight we go from combating crack to battling burglaries . . . We have got to go back to being a law enforcement agency.'

A controversial figure, Bennett got himself into hot water in March of the following year with an off-the-cuff remark about black criminals. He told a television interviewer that 'Some members of the black community pose the greatest threat to law and order.' He later qualified his observation by stating that he was referring to the 'Yardies', but not before he had become the subject of an internal police disciplinary enquiry over allegedly racist remarks.

'I know Mike very well,' says Commander Grieve in an effort to defuse the internal controversy. 'You have to see him for what he is, which is the Federation rep, representing his members and their fears. They love continuity, don't they?'

That said, Bennett's observations won him the backing of a large proportion of his frustrated peers and superiors. And, with regard to his analysis of the Metropolitan Police's 'stop-go' policing in particular, it has to be said that he had a point. The truth is that the Met has chopped and changed to the point where confusion reigns over the nature of their approach to the rudie problem.

In the beginning there was the highly successful Operation Lucy which targeted suspected rudies. However, this initiative was deemed to be politically incorrect – racist even – because of the specificity of its focus, and it was disbanded.

Detective Sergeant O'Connor comes at it from an altogether different perspective. 'Operation Lucy was an area-based problem,' he explains. 'It started off as a murder inquiry and went on to bigger things, and [the general problem] became too big for them really.'

Lucy's crucial intelligence-gathering network was smashed in the process of it giving way to the Crack Intelligence Co-ordinating Unit in October 1989. CICU had nineteen officers drawn from the police, Customs and immigration services, but no overall head, leading to charges that it was unco-ordinated.

CICU proper only lasted about nine months. Although, when the joint operatives parted company in August 1990, amid a wave of media jibes that the authorities had over-reacted to the crack threat, a small residual police complement soldiered on under CICU's banner. However, these specialist officers were eventually redeployed to more general duties in the spring of 1993. This decision also led to criticism of Scotland Yard's anti-crack crime strategy, even though many disgruntled officers argued that by focusing on crack, instead of crack dealers, the unit was doing little to tackle the root cause of the problem: the Rude Boys.

At the same time as CICU was going through the motions, the startlingly successful south London-orientated Operation Dalehouse came on stream. Then it was dropped in November 1992.

Finally, in June 1993, responsibility for tackling the rudie crack menace was devolved to local police operations and the Yard's more central SO11, the Yard's crack undercover surveillance team. Under the capable leadership of Commander John Grieve, a former head of the drug squad, a dozen undercover police and immigration officers have been assigned the task of countering the crack menace. However, in what can only be regarded as a complete volte-face, the spotlight has once again been thrown on to the rudies. The message now seems to be 'forget about political correctness, it's time to take out the rudies'.

Half of the crack squad of undercover operatives, which includes former CICU members, have been sent out into the field to gather intelligence and cultivate informants. They also work closely with divisional drug squads. All of the information received is stored in a powerful central computer, making it easier for the police to keep tabs on the mobsters.

Throughout the 1990s local police operations have enjoyed various levels of success in combating the (rudie) crack-dealing problem. In February 1992, for instance, Operation Welwyn took forty-six suspected crack (and heroin) dealers off the streets around central London's King's Cross and Euston train stations. A famous red-light district, local prostitutes had complained that the intimidatory activities of Rude Boy and other dealers had been driving their punters away.

In May 1993, Operation Tean dislodged nineteen, predominantly rudie, dealers from the area around Stoke

Newington High Street. In the course of an eight-month-long surveillance operation, undercover officers had purchased up to £5,000-worth of rock from the hordes of street dealers.

Operation Injake made eight arrests in a high profile raid on 90 Landor Road, Clapham in July of the same year. The operation, which involved armed police on stand-by, was targeted at what a police spokesperson described later as 'almost the epicentre of drug-dealing in the capital'. Fittingly, the premises were bricked up after the raid. However, while a small quantity of ganja was recovered, no crack was found.

Finally, in May 1994, a raid on Brixton's notorious Atlantic pub resulted in another nine arrests. These included the pub's proprietor, charged with allowing his premises to be used for dealing drugs, and a woman dealer. The pub, which stands on the corner of Railton Road, was closed down. It has never re-opened.

However, the Metropolitan Police's first line of attack now stems from SO11. 'I make no denial we changed our response,' says a bullish Grieve. 'We changed our response in line with the philosophy of the force. We moved away from highly centralised squads, and we pushed things out down into the communities. That's part of a response to another bit of the policing problem. You can't deal with different bits of it in isolation.

'Even our most virulent critics have admitted that the solution we're running at the moment is the best they've seen anywhere in the world,' he says. 'I mean, people have come and copied the solution that we've adopted here.'

Having the world's best 'solution' is one thing, arresting and convicting the culprits, another. And over the years the police have suffered considerable pain in putting the rudies behind bars. Apart from the fundamental problems of identifying and keeping tracks on these mobile characters, the police have been burdened by an almost epidemic reluctance on the part of potential black witnesses to provide the evidence they need to secure convictions.

This quandary can be explained in part by the traditional suspicion many black people have about the police's motives, attitudes and practices. But, putting those suspicions to one side, there is also a major problem caused by straightforward fear; potential witnesses realise that it is not always healthy to cross the rudies.

The intimidation of would-be witnesses is a rudie specialty. Over the years hundreds of important investigations and cases, including murder, have had to be dropped at the eleventh hour because those lined up to testify have either retracted their statements, changed their minds in court about their testimony, or simply failed to show up to give it on the appointed day. Indeed, potential witnesses have been beaten up, shot at, had their homes burned down, and threatened with extermination. And, in at least one case, a public-spirited citizen, a man who was courageous – or foolhardy – enough to make a police statement, was seriously injured when he had an electric drill shoved through his cheeks. Savagery like this tends to remind criminals like the Nigerian 'mule' and do-gooders alike that it is safer to 'See and blind, hear and deaf'.

The problem with violence against potential witnesses is so acute that some law enforcers have been calling for the introduction of revolutionary measures to better protect them. Detective Superintendent John Jones, the now retired head of Operation Dalehouse, is one. 'We cannot get convictions without getting witnesses and we can't get witnesses because they are too frightened to come forward,' he told the *Big Issue*, a magazine for the homeless, in July 1994. 'These criminals have allegiances and if one of them is locked up for a shooting, his friends on the outside often threaten or kill the people who gave evidence to convict him,' he explained.

The Jones solution? A law enforcement user-friendly witness protection programme à la Netherlands. His controversial proposal, which came in the wake of forty-five crack-related murders and attempted murders nationwide in just fifteen months, smacks of desperation on the part of the beleaguered police. Yet, if the police are to have a realistic chance of making lasting inroads against these slippery characters, some kind of revolution in their approach to banging them up will have to take place.

SO11 believes they have one. 'We've now got the technology . . . the videoing of particular crack-houses, using undercover officers, and things like that. So we're tackling it from a different perspective, and we're finding more success,' explains O'Connor.

'In relation to crack and the violence it's very difficult to get witnesses,' he continues. 'That's why we need to turn to our technical equipment, and use this to actually catch the criminal in the act; rather than relying on the words of witnesses – because witnesses can walk.'

In the meantime, Britain's law-abiding black majority continues to suffer from the stigma of their totally unwanted association with the Rude Boys. Indeed, complaints abound over the failure of newspapers and television programmes to draw the correct distinctions between the hardcore of Jamaican (black British and African) gangsters and the wider black community.

Witness a flowery report in the *Daily Star* in October 1993. 'They strut along the buckled pavements of our inner cities like arrogant black fighting cocks in their £1,000 Armani suits . . . It's the same story in cities all over Britain where West Indian gangs have cornered the drugs market with sheer violence and a dreadful willingness to kill.'

Reporting of this kind has led to a sustained backlash by
people keen to enhance the Jamaican image. Responding
to an article in London's *Evening Standard*, the Jamaican
High Commissioner to Britain complained bitterly about
its alleged stereotyping of her fellow Jamaicans. Ellen
Bogle took particular issue with an observation made
by Detective Superintendent John Jones in which he
described the rudies as 'the role models for British
blacks'. 'This is a racist slur of the most unpleasant
kind,' she complained in a letter to the Editor in November
1991, 'which is completely untrue.' Many would dispute
the level to which it was true or false.

Ms Bogle's successor, Derick Heaven, has had to resort
to similar tactics. Within two months of taking over as
High Commissioner in April 1994, he was driven to
put the situation into perspective. He, however, was
slightly more forthcoming than his predecessor. 'The
few Jamaicans that are involved in this activity represent
an extremely small percentage and this does not take into
account the significant contibution to the development of
this country Jamaicans have made,' the *Weekly Journal*
reported him as saying. 'This disturbs me,' he continued,
'because it is unfair and negative. We feel almost under
siege over these people – some of whom, I might add,
are Englishmen.'

The gauntlet was taken up by Jamaica's Deputy
Prime Minister, Seymour Mullings, in July. During
a stopover in Birmingham during an official British
tour, he met with Ron Hadfield, the Chief Constable
of West Midlands police force, who appraised him of
heavy Jamaican involvement in the city's drug crimes.
Mullings response was to attempt to put that information
into perspective. 'There are a small number of our people
who become very wayward from time to time and they
have given Jamaica a very bad name abroad,' he said,
somewhat euphemistically.

But Jamaican government officials are not alone in attempting to qualify the situation as regards rudie involvement in British crime. They have found an influential kindred spirit in Commander John Grieve. While admitting that certain black criminals are 'great self-publicists' who 'dress and behave and act in a very flamboyant style' likely to make them 'grist for the publicity mill', he sees another side to the story.

'I'd have a look at some of the culture of some of the newspapers that write some of these articles about it,' he advises. 'I mean, I would say that some of it reeks of xenophobia – I might say, racism – but I don't want to get locked into a battle with them over it, but I would say xenophobia.'

Still, looking to the future, the question arises as to the reception Britain's Jamaican and black communities can expect. With crack more readily available than ever and gunplay more in evidence, one can only hope that they are not subjected to an official witch hunt.

That is exactly what happened to the 323 passengers who arrived in Britain aboard a charter flight from Jamaica in 1993. A staggering 190 passengers, who had each paid £249 to spend Christmas with relatives, were detained – some overnight – by immigration officials in a trawl for rudies. At least twenty passengers were immediately returned to Jamaica.

But the saga did not end there. Six months later the *Mail on Sunday* alleged that 256 Jamaican passengers who had flown in during the Christmas season had disappeared without trace. The allegation was totally false. In fact, the report acknowledged that the deadline on their stays had not even expired at the time the newspaper went to press with the front page story.

'Britain has always been a generous and tolerant country,' a leader-writer wrote on the effects that this sort of behaviour had on Britain's 'glorious' stance

towards harmonious race relations. However, 'without
firm immigration controls,' it continued, 'good race relations, and especially the many hard-working, law-abiding
families of legal immigrants, will be among the inevitable
casualties.'

The problem is that the rudies and their mimics have
already ensured that these people get short shrift. And,
unless and until they and their indigenous black 'devotees'
are taken out of circulation, that will doubtless remain
the case.

In the meantime, one is left to ponder the British (and
global) future of the rudie criminal pestilence, and the
violent crack craze that it spearheaded. The omens seem
to be mixed.

On the one hand, Jamaican, American, Canadian and
British law enforcement agencies have all made mighty
strides over the past few years in their battle to cancel
out the rudie threat. That success has been bolstered
by increasing international cooperation, and innovative
anti-crime measures. In Britain, for example, the use
of ever sophisticated forms of surveillance, informants
and undercover officers has been highly instrumental in
helping the police to get scores of street crack dealers
banged up.

On another level – and this seems to be highly indicative of the (tacit) strategy adopted by their counterparts
in the United States and Canada – cash-strapped British
law enforcers appear also to have opted for a policy of
displacement when dealing with the Rude Boys. That is,
to deport them for illegal entry or overstaying in the
absence of substantive criminal charges; to keep them
on the move. In brief, to turn them into somebody else's
problem. However, when dealing with an ubiquitous
bunch like the rudies, even the police privately admit
the shortcomings in this approach. The fact is that such

deportees have been known to return to Britain within two days.

This leads us to the other side of the coin, the issue of the rudies' legacy of ruthless violence and crack. There can be no doubting the fact that, while considerable, the Rude Boys' British excesses have been blown out of all proportion. The British mass media – for whatever reasons – has decided to make them the country's Number One criminal bogey. However, this provides absolutely no grounds for rejoicing. The fact is that with the black murder rate in the capital doubling within the space of a few years, Britain's predominantly law-abiding black communities are suffering a serious problem with imported and homegrown violent crime. Moreover, that problem – at least the ways in which it manifests itself – is still reducible to the influence of a hardcore of rudie gunslingers.

Like an infectious virus, the rudies' predeliction towards letting their guns do the talking – as practised to great effect in Jamaica, the US and Canada – has contaminated a great many indigenous (black) criminals in whose communities they have settled. Experienced, ruthless and fearless gunmen, they were the trend-setters for (black) Britain's current nightmare of violent and gun-toting crime. They 'legitimised' the mundane carrying of illegal firearms; they introduced the concept of drive-by shootings, public execution-style slayings and what Grieve notes as 'a culture of armed intervention'; they made it 'acceptable' to shoot at unarmed police officers and innocent passers-by. In short, they created the gun culture which indigenous black and white criminals now practice in Britain and abroad.

'There has been a growth in drugs-related violence,' Commander Grieve concedes rather ominously, 'and it's not limited to British-born blacks, British-born Caribbean-origin blacks, or African blacks. It's right across the

board, including some very violent white geezers out
there who go round killing people.' In this context even
the commander would agree that the rudie dilemma is
merely the tip of the iceberg nowadays.

What the Yard's intelligence supremo would most
certainly disagree with, however, is the notion that
homegrown criminals took their lead from the rudies.
Interestingly enough, though, DS O'Connor, one of his
team, appears to see the situation in exactly that light.
A veteran of street drug operations, he says that some
of the non-rudie 'pond life' he comes into contact with
are 'modelling themselves on what is perceived to be
a "Yardie" element . . . You see young British blacks
dressing in the same way as they see people in Jamaica
dressing, and that's the line they go along.'

'It what's come out in book's like Victor Headley's,'
he adds, alluding to *Yardie*, the first of a trilogy of
best-selling black novels about the adventures of a rudie
mule who 'liberates' a consignment of cocaine, and sets
himself up in gangland London on the proceeds. 'It's
what's come out in the media that they do model
themselves [upon],' he continues. 'The music that comes
over here – I mean, you've heard the lyrics of some of
their music. And they get into it!'

And then there is crack, and the violence its trade
and abuse foster; none show any signs of going away.
Far from it. The overall problem is getting bleaker by
the day.

One need only scan the (albeit exceptional) case
of Duane Daniels to appreciate the problems British
society as a whole faces. The nineteen-year-old son of a
convicted armed robber, Daniels led a ruthless 15-strong
Clapham gang known as Posse 28. In December 1993,
shortly before he was sentenced to ten years imprisonment, he set a judicial record by asking for close to 1,000
offences to be taken into consideration at the Old Bailey.

Apparently, many of the street robberies, car break-ins and burglaries Daniels committed were to finance his self-confessed £300-a-day drink and drug habit. Indeed, he admitted to smoking anything up to twenty rocks of crack a day; a drugs test later established that the only narcotic he had not taken was heroin.

The menace of crack is certainly not going to evaporate in a hurry. Recent indications are of the narcotic becoming ever more popular – even discerning Sloane Rangers and City-types have developed a taste for it. 'I feel the majority are taking it,' says Paulette of the view from south London, 'and the minority aren't.' And on that note, as with all illegal commodities, where there is a demand people will step in to service it. 'Yes,' acknowledges O'Connor, 'crack is in abundance because of the finances that can be made from it.' As recently as March 1995 three would-be distributors were convicted at Southwark Crown Court of conspiracy to supply the drug in possibly the most revealing case of its kind to date.

The convictions of Mariame Keita, Andre N'Guessan and Charles Oppon were instructive for at least two reasons. They provided clear-cut evidence that certain Africans are now heavily involved in the crack business, and showed how quickly the demand has grown in a short space of time. In fact, the convictions followed a South East Regional Crime Squad raid on Keita's Park Lane apartment in June 1994 – itself the result of a year long surveillance operation – during which they discovered a massive 5.5 kilos of ready-to-sell crack cocaine. The haul was valued at £1.1million on the street – making it the world's biggest ever; indeed, Mariame's husband, allegedly the operation's 'Mr Big', who was not caught, is believed to be the world's leading crack dealer. (One wonders what Mihir Bose would have to say about that.) Finally, as for the profits accruing from the gang's crack dealings, some of which went into starting legitimate businesses in Ghana, the police estimated them to be in the region of £5million.

To all intents and purposes then, crack and the people who abuse and trade it are here to stay. While the rudies have been incorrectly singled out for blame, there is still no denying the pivotal role they have played in making the situation what it is today. Remember, the US authorities pointed the finger at the Rude Boys for spreading the cocaine derivative along the east coast. Consider also that roughly 5,500 people have lost their lives at the hands of the rudies in the US alone. And think of the unprecedented violent crime wave that followed their colonisation of cities like Toronto.

All in all then crack, the rudies and their 'converts' spell ongoing trouble for the countries in which they settle. What exactly has to be done to eradicate their menace could no doubt fill the pages of another volume. In the meantime, it seems fitting to leave the final words on the British situation to 'Little Joe', the crackhead-turned-law student. 'The government need to do something more,' he argues, with one eye on the paucity of opportunities open to young men like him. 'I don't vote, but Major wouldn't get my vote. How can he lead me when he hasn't lived my life that he's making me live; violent life?'

However, for all his politicking – he devoutly believes the government is behind the trade – Little Joe acknowledges the fact that any solutions to the problem need to start at home, within the affected communities. 'The youth need some form of leadership,' he says, 'someone to look after them; show them the right and proper way.' Failing that, he argues, the only way out from the scourge of rudies, bad boys, drugs, guns and violence is 'our own segregated country, where we can find ourselves and our true God'. He makes no apology for such an uncompromising solution. As far as Little Joe is concerned, desperate circumstances require ruthless solutions.

Index

Abbott, Diane, 363, 365, 382

ACID, see Special Anti-Crime Task Force

Agee, Philip, 82–3

AIDS, 188

Air Jamaica, 109, 110–11

Albert, Richard, 182, 183, 184–5, 186, 188, 191–2, 198–200

Allen, Sharon 129

Americas Watch Committee (AWC), 204–5, 207

Amnesty International 205

Anderson, Errol, 112

Anderson, Leighton Francisco ('Peppy'), 357–8

Angel, Graham, 404

Angola, 72

Anti-Crime Investigative Detachment see Special Anti-Crime Task Force

Arawaks, 148–9

Armed Career Criminal Act, USA, (1984), 309

ATF, see Bureau of Alcohol, Tobacco and Firearms

Austin, Leonard, 206

AWC, see Americas Watch Committee

Ballantine, Desmond John, see Ninja Man

bank robberies, 345–6, 350

Banton, Buju, 145, 193, 285

Barnes, John, 146, 218, 369

Barnet, Rohan Barrington ('Yardie Ron'), 367, 386–7, 390

Barrett, Carlton ('Carly'), 193

Barrett, Valerie, 209

Barry, Marion, Jr., 313–14, 333–4

bauxite 36–7, 58, 71, 83, 85, 87, 93

Beadel, Sergeant 'Beetlejuice', 313, 322–3, 324, 325, 326, 327–8, 329–30

Bennett, Louise, 145
Bennett, Mike, 440–1
Bennett, William 334–5
Berbeck, Trevor, 145
Bernhard, Katrina, 431
Big Issue, 444–5
Big John, 193
Black Roses Crew, 139,
    302, 358–9
'Black Tony', 304, 305–6
Blackman, André, 425
Blackwood, Robert, *see*
    Rankin' Dread
Blake, 'Black Tony',
    304, 305–6
Blake, Vivian, 264, 273,
    304, 305, 306
Blake, Winston ('Burry
    Boy'), 12, 74
Blakelock, Keith, 381
'Blondie', *see* Brennan, John
Blue Mafia, 44
Boateng, Paul, 369
Bogle, Ellen, 446
Bogle, Paul, 163–5
Bose, Mihir, 397–8,
    402, 405–6
Bourne, Christopher
    Alexander, *see* 'Tuffy'
Bowen, Calvin, 211
Brakespeare, Cindy, 2
Brennan, John ('Blondie'),
    391–3, 426, 427, 429
Brennan, Peter, 424
Bristol, 423
    riots, 379
Brixton, 364, 372, 378, 384,
    399, 417, 419, 428
    Atlantic pub, 443

Operation Dalehouse, 426
riots, 379, 380
shootings, 429, 431
Britain
    crack problem, 397–418,
        422–9, 435, 437,
        439, 441–3, 445, 447,
        448–52
    immigration, 371–7,
        410–12
    myth of 'Yardies'
        365–71, 418
    policing, 364, 365, 366,
        391, 393–6, 399, 401,
        403, 404, 414, 418–24,
        426, 433, 440–2, 443
    race relations, 371–82, 447
    Rude Boys in, 363–6,
        370–1, 381–96, 409–18,
        422–53
    see also London
Brown, Eldon, 431–2
Brown, Jim (formerly Lester
    Lloyd Coke), 8–12, 21,
    134, 138, 140, 263, 264,
    305, 306, 358
    as Shower Posse don,
        9–10, 12–17, 229
    arrest and death in
        jail 17–21
    funeral 1–8
Brown, Lawrence
    ('Brownman'), 343
Brown, Winston, *see*
    Rankin' Dread
Bryden, John, 341
Buccaneer programme, *see*
    Operation Buccaneer
buccaneers, 154–6

Bureau of Alcohol, Tobacco and Firearms (ATF), USA, 263–4, 265, 279, 286, 303, 305, 350
analyst 'Anne' quoted, 248, 259, 261, 286, 300–1, 312
Washington agents, 318, 320, 324–5, 329, 330–1, 335–6
see also Dougherty, Cornelius J.
Burgess, Beverly, 2, 20
Burke, Paul, 112
Burnett, Mark, 439
Burning Spear, 190
Burns, Kenneth, 278
Bush, George, 105, 334, 397
Bustamente, (William) Alexander, 27, 32–3, 34, 45, 102, 167–8
Butter, 330–1

Campbell, Norman ('Bicycle'), 390
Canada, 312, 338–62, 389
cannabis, *see* ganja
Capone, Al, 267
Carby, Everald ('Run Joe'), 209, 212–13
Cargill, Morris, 141
Castro, Fidel, 55, 70, 71, 72, 76, 77–8, 85
Central Intelligence Agency, *see* CIA
Champagne Posse, 326, 327
Charles, Pearnel, 79, 80–1, 95, 111
Christie, Linford, 146, 369

Christmas Rebellion, 160–1
CIA, 52, 57, 70, 80, 82–3, 88, 93, 95–6
Cliff, Jimmy, 61
cocaine
in Britain, 385, 395, 399, 403, 404, 412, 414, 436
in Canada, 349
in Jamaica, 99–100, 115–25, 127–8, 130–3, 141–2, 180, 181, 234, 236–7, 282, 296
see also crack
Codling, Errol, *see* Rankin' Dread
Coke, B.B., 9
Coke, Christopher Mark, 209, 210
Coke, Lester Lloyd, *see* Brown, Jim
Coke, Mark Anthony ('Jah T'), 2–3, 220
Coke, Michael ('Dudus'), 140
Collins, Audrey Anna, 209
Columbians, 123–4, 268–9, 301, 302
Columbus, Christopher, 148–9
Comprehensive Crime Control Act, USA, (1984), 309
Condon, Paul, 418, 419, 420, 422
Connor, Cecil ('Modeller'), 305
Continuing Criminal Enterprise Act (CCE), USA, 309, 310

Cook, Roger, 388
Copeland, Donald, 202
Cordeaux, J.K., 374
Coromantes, 151, 158
Coxsone, Lloyd, 386
crack
  in Britain, 397–418,
    422–9, 435, 437,
    439, 441–3, 445, 447,
    448–52
  in Canada, 347, 348–9,
    352
  in Jamaica, 100, 115,
    118–22, 124, 125–7,
    128–30
  in USA, 266, 274, 279–80,
    285–8, 296, 301–3,
    318–21, 324–6
Crack Intelligence Co-
  ordinating Unit (CICU),
  UK, 396, 399, 404, 441–2
Crenshaw, Simon, 393–4
Cuba, 52, 55–7, 70–2, 76–8,
  85, 88, 89–90, 98, 105
Cubans, Mariel, 266,
  268, 269
Cudjoe (Maroon leader),
  152, 153
Curtis, James, 405
Cutty Ranks, 191

Daily Gleaner, 6, 16, 23, 96,
  106, 109, 115, 141, 170,
  173, 201
  on Cuba, 90
  Dawn Ritch in, 6–7,
    139, 141
  Father R. Ho Lung in,
    169, 197
  on police corruption, 203
  Sunday Gleaner, 24,
    212–13
  see also Weekly Gleaner
Daily Mail, 365, 367–8, 397
  Mail on Sunday, 447
Daily News, 95, 374
Daily Star, 387, 445
Daily Telegraph, 363,
  376, 382
dancehalls, 171, 175, 189,
  190, 194, 352
Dangerous Drugs Act,
  Jamaica, 131–2
Daniels, Duane, 450–1
Daniels, Wendell ('Skully'),
  417
Danso, William, 418–19
DEA, see Drug Enforcement
  Agency
death penalty, 67
Dicks, Terry, 381
Dirtsman, 193
Dodd, Coxsone, 189, 224
Dominicans, 301–2, 311
dons, 4, 99–101, 107–8, 120,
  121–2, 124, 138–42
Dougherty, Cornelius J.
  ('Con'), 257, 259, 260,
  264, 269, 270, 272, 273,
  274–5, 278–9, 290, 310
Douglas, Stafford, 127–8
Dreckett, Samuel, 4
Drug Awareness Week, 115,
  124, 131
Drug Enforcement Agency,
  (DEA), USA, 108,
  203, 401
Drug Offences (Forfeiture

of Proceeds) Act, Jamaica,
    (1993), 132
drugs, *see* cocaine; crack;
    ganja; heroin
Dunkirk Posse, 265,
    294, 330
Dunne, Patrick, 418,
    419, 428
'Dust', *see* Garrison,
    Larkland Dave

Early Bird, 225
Eddie, Clinton, *see* 'Mr
    Palmer the Mic Ninja'
Edward, Delroy ('Uzi'),
    275, 290
Edwards, André, 282
Egbulefu, Innocent, 390
Eggar, Tim, 404
elections, Jamaican, 32–3
    1944, 33
    1962, 27
    1967, 47, 51
    1972, 58–9
    1976, 84–5
    1980, 57, 97–8, 102,
        248, 382
    1983, 133
    1989, 99, 105, 134
Estrada, Ulises, 90
Ethiopian Zion Coptic
    Church, 88
Evening Standard, 446
Ewing, Patrick, 145
Eyre, Edward John, 162–5
EZCC, 88

Ferguson, Paul, *see*,
    Garrison, Larkland Dave

Financial Times, 68
Florida, 278, 310
Fluxy, 193
Forbes, Francis, 201
Ford, Gerald, 72
Four Aces Club, London,
    386
Francis, Dave Sylvester, 359
Fray, Stephen, 409
Fredericks, Bill, 273, 286,
    287, 302, 304–7, 309,
    311–12
Fulwood, James, 278, 310

ganja
    in Britain, 385, 413, 443
    in Canada, 345, 347, 349
    in Jamaica, 48–51, 57, 58,
        68, 86–88, 108–15, 180
    in USA, 252–4, 257,
        258, 259–60, 296, 305,
        317, 335–6
Gardener, Keith ('Trinity'),
    97, 129, 206–8
Gardner, David, 367–8
Garrison, Larkland Dave
    ('Dust'), 358
Garrison Gang, 12, 74
garrisons, 25
Garvey, Marcus Mosiah, 31,
    146, 166
Gayle, Clinton, 342
General Council for Human
    Rights Watch, 205
General Echo, 193
Gielgud-Killick, Kate, 400–1
go-go clubs, 181–2
Gold Street Massacre, 94
Golding, Bruce, 2, 22

Gordon, George William, 163–5
Grange, Olivia ('Babsy'), 2, 9
Grant, Neville ('Scorcher'), 410
Grant, Oneil ('Tiger'), 343
Grant, Raymond ('Emma'), 430–1
Green, E. George, 204
Green Bay Massacre, 90–1
Grieve, John, 414, 422, 430, 433, 437–8, 440–1, 442, 443, 447, 449–50
on misuse of 'Yardie' term, 366, 367, 368, 418
Guardian, 368
Gulleyman Posse, 280, 307–8
Gun Control Act, USA, (1984), 309
Gun Court Act, Jamaica, (1974), 64, 65–7
guns, 195–200, 235–6, 270–3, 433–6
traffic, 87, 88, 89–90, 235–6, 263–4, 350–1
Guthrie, John, 153

Hadfield, Ron, 446
Hagheart, Willie, 139, 302, 358–9
Hameed, Ambreen, 380
Hanger, Art, 341
Harder They Come, The (film), 61
Harlem Renaissance, 31
Headley, Victor *Yardie*, 450
Heaven, Derick, 446

Henry, Lenny, 146
Henry, Mike, 2
heroin, 117, 296, 349, 413, 432, 436
Higgins, Cassandra, 425
higglering, 180
Hines, Harold, 209
Holding, Michael ('Whispering Death'), 145
Ho Lung, Richard, 169, 196–7
Home Office, UK, 399–400, 404
Honegan, Lloyd, 145
House of Leo, 189, 194
Hughes, Leroy ('Fitz'), 390
Hugill, Barry, 400
Hussing, Early ('Kong'), 304, 305, 306
hustling, 180–1, 185

IMF, *see* International Monetary Fund
Immigration Act, UK, (1988), 384
Independent, 1, 368, 422
Indians, Canadian, 350–1
International Monetary Fund, 86, 93, 104, 105
convention in Kingston, 75–6
Isaacs, Wills O., 45

'Jah T', *see* Coke, Mark Anthony
Jamaica
agriculture, 36, 58, 60, 85
colonial history, 148–68
crime, 61–3, 107,

136–42, 210, 232–4

drug culture, 99–101, 107–8, 115–18, 138–42, 180, 181, 202–3

economy, 36–7, 58–9, 60, 71, 83, 85, 86, 87, 93, 102–5, 106–8

education, 178, 179, 184–5

health service, 233

Independence Day (1962), 26–7

legislation, 64–7

population, 60

poverty, 37–8, 58–61, 179–80, 182–6

prostitution, 181–2, 186, 188

social violence, 169–76, 186–7, 194–200

tourism, 85, 93, 109, 117, 236, 237

universal suffrage, 29–32, 168

see also Kingston; unemployment

Jamaica Constabulary Force (JCF), 44, 137, 140, 198–9, 200–8, 209–16, 243–4, 248–9
ACID/SACTF 128–9, 205, 207, 208, 210–13
'Never Never Division', 214

Jamaica Council for Human Rights, 205

Jamaica Herald, 115, 213

Jamaica Labour Party (JLP)
anti-Cuba, 76–7
formation, 32–3
implicated in anti-government activities, 75–6, 79–82, 93, 112
and Jim Brown, 7, 8, 13, 15, 20
and patronage, 28, 34–5, 40–1
and political violence, 51, 74, 79–80, 81
and Tivoli Gardens, 11, 13
and West Kingston Wars, 43–5
see also Bustamente, (William) Alexander; Seaga, Edward

Jamaica Observer, 23–4

Jamaica United Front, 95

Jasper, Lee, 398

JCF, see Jamaica Constabulary Force

JLP, see Jamaica Labour Party

Johnson, Angella, 368

Johnson, Ben, 147, 338–40

Johnson, H. Charles, 95

Johnson, Mark, 359

Johnson, Michael, 282

Johnson, Tony, 24, 115, 123, 200

Jones, John, 426, 437, 444–5, 446

Jose Marti School, 77

Jungle Posse, 227–8, 264, 265

Kansas City, 307

Keita, Mariame, 451

Kennedy, John F., 70, 71
Ketelhodt, Baron Von, 164
King's College Hospital, 430
Kingston, 37, 60–1
  anti-American feeling, 285
  Back-o-Wall, 41, 45, 223,
    224, 225
  drugs problem, 118–21
  endemic violence,
    63–4, 124, 137–40,
    173–6, 197
  Hannah Town murders,
    208–9, 212
  Heywood Street Market,
    217–18
  Jones Town, 176–82, 187
  Luke Lane, 218–19,
    231, 239
  Matthews ('Matches')
    Lane, 220, 226, 228,
    230, 231, 238
  Rema, 228
  Riverton City, 182–6, 187,
    188, 199
  Sutton Street, 128–30
  Tivoli Gardens, 5, 9, 11,
    13–14, 41, 74, 220, 229
  West Kingston Wars, 42–7
Kingston and St Andrew
  Corporation (KSAC), 43
Kinsman, N. Richard, 96
Kirby, Terry, 368
Kirlew, Levy, 129–30
Kissinger, Henry, 72
Knee, Bigga, 217,
  218, 221–3, 224–31,
  232–43, 244–7
Knight, K.D., 130–1, 132,
  202, 213–14

Lamberti, Al, 276
Landis, Fred, 95
laundering, money, 297–8
Lawrence, Bob, 409
Leeds, 423
Leimonis, Georgina, 343
Lesley, Leroy ('Scarface'),
  425–6
Levy, Christopher, 357
Lewis, Lennox, 146, 369
'Little Joe', 406, 407–9,
  436–7, 452–3
London, 363, 364, 371,
  372–3, 375, 378, 379, 410,
  420, 438, 440
  Broadwater Farm
    riot, 380–1
  cocaine/crack, 412,
    415–6, 417
  Metropolitan Police, 391,
    401, 403, 414, 426, 433,
    440–1, 443
  PC Dunne's murder, 418,
    419, 428
  violence, 424–32,
    435, 439
  see also Brixton; 'Little
    Joe'; 'Stubby'
'Long Arm', 196–7
Los Angeles, 294, 315

McCauley, Diana, 170,
  174, 187
McCloud, David, 344–5,
  346, 350, 351, 352, 354,
  355–6, 357, 358, 360–1
McCullum, Mike, 145
McGann, Roy, 97
McKenzie, Desmond, 3–4

MacMillan, Trevor, 126, 140, 195, 200, 214–15
Mafia, 268
Mais, Roger, 145
Manchester, 423–4
Manley, Edna, 145
Manley, Michael Norman ('Joshua'), 59–60, 99–100, 145–6
   1976 state of emergency and election win, 52–6, 76, 79–85
   1980 election loss, 97–8
   1983 election boycott, 133
   1989 election win, 105
   anti-crime measures 64–9
   assassination attempt, 94
   and Cuba, 55, 71, 72, 76–7
   destabilisation campaign against, 88–90, 95
   economic policies, 85–6, 105
   and Green Bay Massacre, 90–1
   peace measures, 92, 97, 134
   retirement, 105
   and W. Blake's funeral, 12, 74–5
Manley, Norman Washington ('Moses'), 27–8, 32–3, 45, 143, 167–8
Maragh, Winston, see Super Cat
Marchi, Sergio, 342
marijuana, see ganja

Markham Eglinton Crew, 358
Marley, Bob, 2, 39, 84–5, 92–3, 145, 177, 190
Marley, Rita, 85
Marley, Ziggy, 145
Maroons, 150–4, 165, 356
Marshall, Bucky, see Thompson, Aston
Marshall, Johnny, see Johnson, Mark
Mascoll, Philip, 347, 348–9, 352, 353–4, 356, 357, 360, 361
Massop, Claudius ('Claudie'), 12–13, 91–3
Matalon, Eli, 64, 68
Melgarejo, Fernando, 149
Menez, Juan, 205
Metropolitan Police, 391, 401, 403, 414, 426, 433, 440–1, 443
   SO11, 401, 403, 433, 442, 443
   see also Grieve, John; O'Connor, Keiran
Miami, 250, 255, 262, 270, 276, 296, 297
Military Intelligence Unit, 90
Minott, Echo, 191, 195
'Mr Palmer the Mic Ninja', 439
Mitchell, 'Baya', 12–13
Mitchell, Lamar, 209
'modelling', 188–9
Moonex Affair, 89–90
Morant Bay Rebellion, 163–5
Morgan, Henry, 154–6

Morgan, Natty, 198, 199–200
Morris, Bill, 369
Morris, Mervyn, 145
Morrison, Devon ('Trevor'), 208, 209
Morrison, Richard ('Storyteller'), 17, 18–19, 304, 310
Mullings, Seymour, 446
Munn, Keble, 76
Murder Incorporated, 267–8
Murtagh, Peter, 368
Myrie, Mark, see Banton, Buju

Nanny (Maroon leader), 152, 153
Nation of Islam, 321, 333
National Council on Drug Abuse (NCDA), Jamaica, 117, 118
National Criminal Intelligence Service (NCIS), UK, 410, 415
National Drugs Intelligence Unit (NDIU), UK, 364, 365, 367
National Patriotic Movement (NPM), Jamaica, 93
Neish, Robert, 95, 96
New York, 250, 255, 262, 296, 297
  Crown Heights, 250–1, 280, 308
  murders, 275–6, 278–9, 282–4, 300
  posse murder statistics, 267, 270

Newman, Kenneth, 382
News Independent Caribbean Agency (NICA), 5
Newsweek, 1, 19
N'Guessan, Andre, 451
Ninja Man, 191, 193
Nitty Gritty, 193
Non-Aligned Movement (NAM), 55
Notting Hill, 375, 386–7
Nottingham, 374–5, 378

Observer, 367, 400
O'Connor, Keiran, 401, 403, 411, 412, 437, 438, 441, 445, 450, 451
O'Mard, Christopher, 131
Operation Ardent, 208
Operation Buccaneer, 69, 112, 113, 115
Operation Caribbean Cruise, 332
Operation Clean Sweeps, 332–3
Operation Dalehouse, 426–7, 442
Operation Howitzer, 424–5
Operation Injake, 443
Operation Lucy, 394–6, 441
Operation Rum Punch, 303–4
Operation Tean, 442–3
Operation Welwyn, 442
Operation Yardies, 410
Oppon, Charles, 451
Ottey, Merlene, 145, 355

Pan Head, 193
Park Gang, 226

Parsboosingh, Karl, 145
Patterson, PJ, 105–7, 131,
 134, 135, 210, 215, 284,
 338, 340, 410
'Paulette', 383–4, 415–16,
 438, 451
Payne Posse, 326–7
PCP (Angel Dust), 317, 318
Penrose, Roy, 393
People's National Party
 (PNP), 9, 43, 45, 73,
 140, 176
 failure of policies, 60
 formation, 32–3, 168
 and Garrison Gang,
  11–12, 74
 left tendencies, 54–6, 60,
  71
 and Spanglers, 225, 226,
  231, 232
 see also Manley, Michael
  Norman
Peralto, Ryan, 2
Peters, Tracey, 362
petrol prices, 58, 86, 93, 133
Phillips, Peter, 131
Phoenix Gang, 44
PNP, see People's National
 Party
Police Federation, UK, 420
political patronage, 24–6,
 28–9, 35, 40–2, 136
political tribalism, 23–6,
 32–6, 57, 78–9, 83–5, 86,
 93–4, 96–8
 declines but continues,
  133–6
 drug culture takes
  over, 100–1

posses, 57–8, 98, 101,
 113, 120
 in Canada, 338–62
 drugs trade in Jamaica,
  107–8, 114–17, 122–4
 exodus to USA, 248–53,
  261–5
 US contact with Jamaica,
  235, 237
 US decline, 299–312
 US measures to combat,
  302–12, 331–7
 US organisation, 254–60,
  285–99, 323–8
 US profits/laundering,
  296–8
 US recruiting, 289–92,
  298
 US violence, 252–3,
  265–84, 316–20, 328–31
 in Washington, 270, 296,
  313–37
 see also Rude Boys; and
  individual posses
Powell, Colin, 146
Powell, Enoch John,
 371, 375–7
protection rackets, 235

Quarrie, Don, 145

Racketeer Influenced and
 Corrupt Organisation Act
 (RICO), USA, 309–10
'Rambo', 404–5
Ramm, Roy, 393, 395
Rankin' Dread, 359, 364,
 382, 384, 385–9, 394–5
Ranks, Shabba, 145, 192–3

Rastafari, 49, 59, 88, 146, 190, 378, 437
Reagan, Ronald, 103–4, 108–9
reggae, 59, 145, 171, 189–95, 223–4
　Newark concert, 275
　One Love Peace Concert, 92
Reid, Duke, 189, 223–4
Reid, Vic, 145
Reid, Viv, 398
Rema Posse, 264
Renkers Posse, 275, 290
rent boys, 180–1
Ritch, Dawn, 5–7, 139, 141
Riverton City Posse, 264
Rodriguez, Fernando, 79
Rose, David, 400
Rose, Herb, 79
Roughest And The Toughest Gang, 51
Rowe, Lawrence, 145
Rude Boys, 10, 35, 38–40, 50–1, 57, 147–8, 171, 174–6, 201, 216
　1965 West Kingston Wars, 42–7
　1970s violence, 62–4, 75–6, 90, 172
　1979 truce, 91–3
　1980 violence, 94, 97, 98
　and drugs, 68, 120, 122–4, 132–3, 141–2
　in UK, 363–6, 370–1, 381–96, 409–18, 422–53
　see also political tribalism; posses
Rudmen, Warren, 333

SACTF, see Special Anti-Crime Task Force
Salkey, Andrew, 145
Sandokhan, 198–9, 200
Sangster, Donald 45
Scotland, Patricia, 369
Scotland Yard, 364, 365, 366, 393–6, 442
　CICU, 396, 399, 404, 441–2
Seaga, Edward ('Mr Eddie'), 87, 124, 224, 234–5, 365
　and 1980 election, 97, 98, 102
　and 1983 election, 133
　anti-Cuba, 52, 54–6
　anti-ganja measures, 108–14, 116
　assassination attempt, 83
　background/character 101–2, 103
　economic strategy, 102–5
　evicts Back-o-Wall squatters, 41
　and gangs, 10, 11, 35, 43, 44, 45–6
　and J. Brown's funeral, 2, 3, 4–7
　linked with coup attempt, 95–6
　loses 1989 election, 99, 105
　as opposition leader, 73–4, 80, 85, 93–4
　peace measures, 92, 134, 139–41
　and policing, 208, 248
　suspected CIA links, 73, 95

Segree, Clifton, 23
sex
  and ghetto culture, 187–8
Sharpe, Sam ('Daddy'), 160
Sharples, Jim, 420–1
Shearer, Hugh, 83, 203–4
shoplifting, 353
Shower Posse, 112, 139,
  220–1, 226, 228, 229, 232,
  237, 244–5
  branches abroad 17–18
  and gang truce, 91
  and Jim Brown,
    9–10, 12–13
  in UK, 410, 428, 430
  in USA, 263–5, 273, 295,
    300, 303, 304, 305, 306–7
Sibbles, Dudley
  Gunman, 189–90
Simpson, Rob ('English'),
  358
ska, 38–9, 189
slaves, African, 150, 151–61
  rebellions, 159–61
  see also Maroons
Smith, Audrey, 362
Smith, Leroy, 419–20
Smith, Ruperto Hart, 90
Smith, Wayne, *see*
  Sandokhan
Sole, Frank, 399
Spanglers Posse, 91, 139,
  218–47
  possible presence in
    Canada, 348
  Rema Spanglers, 228–9
  in USA, 264, 265,
    283, 295
Spanish Town Posse, 427

Spaulding, Anthony, 177
Spaulding, Winston, 204
Special Anti-Crime Task
  Force (formerly ACID),
  128–9, 205, 207, 208,
  210–13
Special Patrol Group
  (SPG), 378
Spencer, Earl, 231–2
Spencer-Churchill, Sarah, 89
Star, 174, 201, 211
states of emergency, 46,
  53–7, 79–80, 83
Stone, Carl, 106, 117, 135,
  138, 169, 171–2
Stone Love, 194, 195
Strikers (Strikas) Posse, 300,
  348, 350, 358
strikes, 105, 107, 166–7, 168
Stubby, 383, 385, 406–7,
  416, 436, 438, 440
Stutman, Robert, 401–3
Sufferers, 29–31, 58–9, 145,
  166–7, 183, 201
sugar, 157, 161–2, 166
Sunday Gleaner, 24, 212–13
Sunday Mirror, 389
Sunday Times, 400
Super Cat, 191, 192, 198
Suppression of Crime
  (Special Provisions)
  Act, Jamaica (1974),
  64–5, 66, 76
Surridge, Thomas, 66

Tacky (slave leader), 159
Tate & Lyle, 166
Tavares-Finson, Tom, 2,
  19, 210

Taylor, Marjorie, 140
terrorist organisations, 364
Thomas, Desmond, 202
Thompson, Aston ('Bucky Marshall'), 91–3
Thompson, Dudley, 45, 90, 91
Times, 400, 437
Tingle, Anthony, 137
Tivoli Gang, 10–12, 225, 226
Tomlinson, Brian, *see* 'Rambo'
Tongue, Sharon, 290
Toronto, 341, 342, 343, 344–5, 346, 348–51, 356–62
torture, 283, 431–2
Tosh, Peter, 92, 145, 193
trade unions, 32–3, 105, 167, 168
Trigger Lock Programme, Canada, 360
Tucker, Gerald, 122, 130
'Tuffy', 393, 428–30

unemployment, 37, 38, 39, 58, 60, 85, 104, 185, 196, 233
1938 workers' riots, 31, 48, 165
United Kingdom, *see* Britain
United States of America immigration controls, 372
and Jamaican drug traffic, 49–50, 68–9, 87, 88, 108–18
and Jamaica's friendship with Cuba, 56–7, 70–3

measures to combat posses, 302–12, 331–7
see also under posses
Universal Negro Improvement Association (UNIA), 31, 146
universal suffrage, 29–32, 168

Vassell, Eric, 280, 307–9
Verney, Lawrence, 431
Voice, 398, 399

Wailers, The, 145, 193
Simmer Down, 39
see also Marley, Bob
Walker, H.S., 382–3
Walsh, Courtney, 145
Washington DC, 270, 296, 313–37
Waterhouse Posse, 264
Weekly Gleaner, 99, 169, 207–8, 243
Weekly Journal, 446
Weeks, John, 382
West Kingston Wars, 42–7
Wild West, 267
Williams, Joan, 23–4
Williams, Lloyd, 5, 143–4
on cocaine/crack trade, 119, 120, 122, 124, 125, 126
on decline of tribalism, 136
on drug gangs, 139, 141–2, 221
on Jim Brown, 12–13, 14, 21
on police, 200, 203

on US posses, 251, 252,
    291, 297, 323
Williams, Michael St
    George, 390
Williams, O.T., 182
Williams, Quenston, 202
witness protection
    programmes
    Jamaica, 209, 210
    UK, 444–5
Wolff, Louis, 96
women, role of, 289–90,
    351–3, 438
World Bank, 104
    convention in Kingston,
    75–6
Wray and Nephew, 182

XNews, 119, 120

Yardie Crew, *see* Markham
    Eglinton Crew
'Yardie Ron', *see* Barnet,
    Rohan Barrington
Yardies
    misuse of term, 366–9,
    418
    *for British Rude
    Boys' activities see
    under* Britain
Yellowman, 190
Young, Andrew, 95
Young Offenders Act,
    Canada, 354